Understanding Religious Ethics

For D. M. Y., P. J. G., and W. A. S.,
magistri sapientissimi

"*Monsieur, puis-je vous demander une dernière leçon?*" *demanda Monsieur Marais en s'animant tout à coup.*
"*Monsieur, puis-je tenter une première leçon?*" *rétorqua Monsieur de Sainte Colombe avec une voix sourde.*

Pascal Quignard, *Tous les matins du monde*

Understanding Religious Ethics

CHARLES MATHEWES

A John Wiley & Sons, Ltd., Publication

This edition first published 2010
© 2010 Charles Mathewes

Blackwell Publishing was acquired by John Wiley & Sons in February 2007. Blackwell's publishing program
has been merged with Wiley's global Scientific, Technical, and Medical business to form Wiley-Blackwell.

Registered Office
John Wiley & Sons Ltd, The Atrium, Southern Gate, Chichester, West Sussex, PO19 8SQ, United Kingdom

Editorial Offices
350 Main Street, Malden, MA 02148-5020, USA
9600 Garsington Road, Oxford, OX4 2DQ, UK
The Atrium, Southern Gate, Chichester, West Sussex, PO19 8SQ, UK

For details of our global editorial offices, for customer services, and for information about how to apply
for permission to reuse the copyright material in this book please see our website at www.wiley.com/
wiley-blackwell.

The right of Charles Mathewes to be identified as the author of this work has been asserted in accordance
with the UK Copyright, Designs and Patents Act 1988.

Library of Congress Cataloging-in-Publication Data

Mathewes, Charles T., 1969–
    Understanding religious ethics / Charles Mathewes.
        p. cm.
    Includes bibliographical references (p.) and index.
    ISBN 978-1-4051-3351-7 (hardcover: alk. paper)—ISBN 978-1-4051-3352-4 (pbk.: alk. paper)
    1. Religious ethics.   2. Abrahamic religions.   I. Title.
    BJ1188.M39 2010
    205—dc22   2009047989

A catalogue record for this book is available from the British Library.

Set in 10.5/13pt Minion by Toppan Best-set Premedia Limited

Printed in the UK

Contents

Acknowledgments

All books are impossible, but some are more impossible than others. I suppose the surprise I feel at how hard this book has been to compose is probably better attributed to my expectation that it would be easy. But my delusion was enabled – and then my perseverance through numerous layers of my own stupidity was endured – by many fine students, colleagues, and friends. Insofar as this book teaches anything useful, it is overwhelmingly due to their help, not my own skills.

At Blackwell, and then at Wiley-Blackwell, my editor, Rebecca Harkin, has exhibited superhuman patience at my many delays that have deferred completion of this book. She and others at Wiley-Blackwell – Bridget Jennings, Brigitte Lee Messenger, and Lucy Boon – deserve high praise and awe at their care and management of balky authors.

Here at the University of Virginia, I have taught RELG 230, "Religious Ethics and Moral Problems," once a year for over ten years. That makes somewhere around 3,000 students who have heard me lecture on themes included in this book. I won't name them all, don't worry; but collectively they accepted my stumbling, halting lectures and typically returned real energy and excitement. From many of them I have learned essential things, both about what I am trying to say and how I am trying to say it. In that time I have also had the good fortune to work with excellent teaching assistants, many of whom contributed ideas, questions, or challenges that have gone into this book. I think especially of Sarah Azaransky, Ann Duncan, Karen Guth, Jon Malesic, Michelle Meyer, Gordon Steffey, and Chad Wayner, but I know there are many, many others. Also, colleagues here at UVA and far away helped in many ways as well; I think especially of Eugene Rogers, Paul Jones, Jamie Ferreira, Larry Bouchard, Tal Brewer, John Milbank, Martien Halvorson-Taylor, Elizabeth Shanks Alexander, Anna Gade, Kathy Tanner, Stanley Hauerwas, James Calvin Davis, Jon Schofer, Aaron Stalnaker, and Eric Gregory. Though I could go on almost *ad infinitum*, three people at UVA do deserve special thanks, however. Amy Graeser did a remarkable job with the index of this book, and Mark Storslee served as copyeditor and proofreader extraordinaire. Finally, this class was James Childress's before it was mine. He created it, he taught it, and when I arrived, he handed it over to me. I did not know it would be so important to me, not just as a teacher but as a scholar; and I am inestimably grateful to him for the gift of the class, and owe him credit for the book.

As ever, my daughter Isabelle was a joyous delight throughout the making of this book, and the birth of my son Henry and his first year of life was a wonderful distraction from (and goad for) its completion. My wife Jennifer Geddes was with me from the first time I taught comparative religious ethics, and she has endured, again and again, my many complaints, anxieties, and wrathful anathemas about my students and myself, as well as my occasional moments of happiness, through the ten times I have taught this course. From the beginning she said that I was too hard on them and myself, and she was normally right, about the students.

I wrote this book as a teacher for my students; but it is also by a student for his teachers. Among my life's many great blessings there are few more foundational for who I am than the succession of remarkable teachers who have taught me through my life. In naming three of them, I do not mean to exclude the rest, but to have these three serve as especially vivid synecdoches for all. Professor Yeager, Mr. Griffiths, and Mr. Schweiker: though all three of them are now my friends, they will always be my teachers, and these are the names by which I will think of them to my dying day. To each of them I owe more than my thanks, I owe them, in important ways, my mind, and without them, this book would not be worse, or different; it simply would not be.

Introduction

Conviction and Argument

What's home
but arguments you can't escape?
  (Dave Smith, "Isle of Wight")

Who wants to live a good life? If we think about goodness in a sufficiently wide sense, as a matter not simply of being morally righteous, but of living a rich and flourishing life, it is hard to imagine anyone not wanting that – anyone not obviously crazy, anyway. Everyone in their right mind would want that, wouldn't they?

But how does one live such a good life? Well, there sometimes seem as many answers to this question as there are people in the world. (And given our ability to hold multiple conflicting views in our mind at the same time, perhaps there are more answers than people.) If the urgency of the question makes it one that we all care about deeply, the diversity of answers may well make us despair of finding the right answer to how we should live.

But despair is always only an avoidance strategy. And once we have recovered and returned to our conundrum, the same perplexities remain. What can help us then? This book tries to offer some resources. It introduces the major forms of ethical reasoning of the three "Abrahamic" religions – Judaism, Christianity, and Islam – by looking at those traditions comparatively, across a series of important issues that they all, in different ways, confront.

These traditions are obviously enormously important for our world today. Christians comprise roughly a third of the world's population – 2.1 billion believers, in 2006 – while Muslims constitute roughly a fifth – 1.3 billion. No other religion comes close in numbers of faithful. Judaism is a small faith, with only 15 million or so members alive today; but its influence – both direct and, through its Abrahamic progeny, indirect – on all aspects of our world is enormous. To talk about these three traditions of religious faith and moral enquiry is to talk about a substantial portion of the world – both historically and today.

How are we to introduce these traditions? How are we to begin to understand what they are about? This book suggests that one way of getting at them is to ask a simple question: what do they understand a flourishing moral life to look like, and what do they say about some of the most pressing challenges to that life? That is to say, this book introduces the traditions of moral and religious reflection through asking each a simple question: *How do these traditions of thought deliberate and decide about issues that they deem significant?*

That last phrase is important. The key word in it is *they*: "issues that *they* deem significant." What matters, what is most important, is not necessarily what you or I, were we to assess an issue, would initially call "ethically relevant." These traditions are vision-forming realities, providing particular viewpoints on reality as experienced by their adherents, and concepts with which to describe that view. There is no naïve, innocent "mere description" upon which we can fall back, when the viewpoints diverge. The way they see the world is crucially complicated, and at times irreducibly peculiar. We must get clear on the nature of the problem that they see – for, as we will see time and time again, their understanding of it is not always identical with the understanding that we bring to the issue. Never think that everyone faces the same difficulty, in the same way, that you do; there are few ways to go more quickly wrong about the world than that one.

Other phrases in our central question are no less significant. Consider the nature of the activities this book studies, and which it collects under the remarkably loose catch-all of "deliberate and decide." Quite a lot goes into that phrase. After all, the moral life is not always a matter of direct and immediate logical reflection. Much of the time morality is habitual, not deliberative at all: we rarely reflect on the propriety of politeness, or the impropriety of simply pushing our way past people on our way into a building, or the wrongness of slipping packs of gum into our pockets while we wait in the check-out line of a supermarket. And anyway, who would want us to deliberate about those things? Indeed, there are arguably some situations where thinking may be more wrong than right: we admire the person more who rushes over to save someone from a burning car "without a thought," as we say, than one who struggles to overcome their fear of dying before doing it. A parent who does not instinctively protect their child by sacrificing themselves is someone for whom we may feel scorn – or perhaps pity. As the philosopher Bernard Williams once put it, in a situation where immediate action is required it is possible to have "one thought too many."

Yet it is not quite right to say we are asking about how participants in our several traditions deliberate and decide about what is to be done. After all, none of us are very good at such deliberations. None of us think very well in any dimension of our lives; for evidence of this, just ask anyone for directions. We're lousy representatives of whatever traditions are willing to claim us as their own; why should we expect anyone else to fit more smoothly into their traditions than we do into ours?

Truth be told, we are not actually undertaking any directly empirical studies of members of these traditions; we are looking at the abstract idea of the traditions themselves, at what and how the traditions *represent* their deliberations and decisions. We will not directly concern ourselves with describing how members of the traditions actually go about thoughtfully making their way through the world with its moral and spiritual challenges; all we want to do is come to see perspicuously the stories the traditions tell, both to themselves and to others, about how their adherents should be and behave.

I think you will end up agreeing with me that this is task enough for one book. Just consider the range of issues that rightfully fall under even so restricted a goal as this; even to pretend to fulfill this task, we should discuss moral issues such as friendship, marriage, homosexuality, lying, forgiveness and its limits, the death penalty, the environment, warfare, and the meaning of work, career, and vocation. We should investigate the resources available to address these problems in the Abrahamic faiths, however we identify those resources (on which more in a minute). And we must pay particular attention to what the faiths say about these issues, how these faiths explain and/or defend their conclusions, and how the theological or philosophical convictions of those faiths shape their moral judgments.

I think that is enough, don't you? More than we are used to finding in an introductory book, anyway. Most of the time, introductory textbooks in a topic of academic study are fairly rudimentary – which means, for specialists in a topic, ridiculously rudimentary. Were you to take a physics class, you would not expect to be introduced to the most fundamental issues vexing those working at the frontiers of the field. But that is not the case in a field like religious ethics. Here you will run across the issues and the concerns that remain the most vexing and pressing for specialists who have dedicated decades of their lives to thinking about these matters. Here you will encounter debates in Islam about the proper relation between the sword verses and the peace verses; discussions in Christianity about the propriety or impropriety of homosexual acts and whether marriage is a category that can accommodate same-sex unions; debates in Judaism about the propriety of the death penalty for convicted murderers. Here you will encounter Plato's famous "Euthyphro problem;" different understandings of the moral and religious rectitude of God's demand that Abraham sacrifice Isaac (or, in Islam, that he sacrifice Ishmael); debates about whether Christians are better advised to see their ethics as emerging from a "natural law" available to all people or in the distinct particulars of Jesus's life and teachings properly apprehended and understood by Christians alone; Jewish debates about the religious propriety of gossip and deception, Islamic discussions about the nature of evil as seen through the figure of Iblis, or Satan, in the Qur'an; debates within and between all these traditions about the character and extent and even possibility of forgiveness; and much more.

This book does not offer you summary digested views. It tries to give you a sense of the arguments animating the traditions, as their most serious and profound exponents have understood them. Beware: in this pool there is no shallow end; every part is deep.

Structure and Definitions

That said, we will not actively try to make this harder than necessary. The book is structured in such a way as to move from some more proximate, more close-to-home issues – "personal" issues, issues of moral concern in our everyday lives (for example, the ethics of lying and truth-telling in speech) – to larger, more intimidatingly vast issues of "social" ethical import (for example, how to think about the ethics of war), and finally some truly vast issues on a galactic scale (for example, the nature of good and evil). And within each of these units, the topics will try to move from the relatively more easy to the more difficult as well. We are trying to make things as manageable as possible.

As part of that task, it will help to get clear on some important words we'll use throughout the book. Consider the terms *ethics* and *morality*. Roughly, they both mean ways of deliberating about the right way to live or behave, either as regards particular acts or as regards overall courses of life. Some people will try to tell you that there's a real and important difference between these two terms. Don't believe them. The distinction between "ethics" and "morality" is like the distinction between "religion" and "spirituality." "Ethics" comes from *ethos*, the Greek word for "way of life," which in Latin is *mores*, from which we get – you guessed it! – "morality." People can claim that there's a useful distinction between the two terms, but in fact their co-presence in our language is more an etymological happenstance than a sign that there are two distinct things there already, before we begin talking.

Therefore, I do not distinguish much between ethics and morality. There is no principled distinction between them. Simply put, these different terms come from Greek (*ethos*) and Latin (*mores*) roots. Some philosophers – in the nineteenth century, G. W. F. Hegel, in the twentieth, Bernard Williams – like to make a big hullabaloo over the differences they stipulated between them. And over time they have come to have faint connotations of more or less deliberateness and self-awareness, with ethics being considered more self-reflective, morality as less so, morality concerned with rules and laws, ethics concerned with virtues. But the truth is, in terms of their everyday use in English today, the distinction between them can't bear very much weight. When I talk about either "ethics" or "morality" here, I do not mean that to suggest any disrespect for the term I am not using.

That said, I do note two distinct senses of the term *ethics*. First, it can refer to one's lived life as a whole; second, it can refer to certain difficult situations or cases that can arise in your life. We will approach these matters largely through specific topics of ethical concern that arise most palpably in specific situations regarding more or less concrete issues – what we can call "doing ethics from below." But we will eventually use these topics to ask questions about the whole shape of life that the various answers to these particular concrete problems imply. So we're interested in studying the moral issues not only in their intrinsic interest and urgency, but also as routes into understanding several profound and abiding traditions of moral reflection.

We will look at a variety of such traditions – Jewish, Christian, and Islamic – and work also with various secular approaches. We will want to be very clear about the distinct nature of the moral problem at issue for each tradition. In each case, we should ask: what exactly is problematic about this problem for this tradition? Why do they care, and what precise aspects of the issue do they care about? We'll find in doing so that the moral issues are handled very differently by the traditions because of theological and metaphysical commitments that may seem at first to be some distance away from their explicit ethical reflections. (For example, Christianity is marked very deeply by its emphasis on grace, forgiveness, and love, in a way that makes its position interestingly different from a tradition such as Judaism, which is centered more profoundly upon obligation, covenant, and law.) But at the same time, there are moments in all these traditions where the moral implications of theological or metaphysical convictions seem to be ignored or downplayed, because of some sense in the traditions that those convictions are palpably at odds with the most immediate judgment of the just or good thing to do or to be. (So, again for example, Christians seem convinced also of the idea that some things *may* be unforgiveable, or at least remain unforgiven – and so they develop a concept of Hell; while Jews seem confident that there are times that one must go beyond what is required and do more than is appropriate – and so they develop moral practices of supererogation, of going above and beyond what is sufficient.) But these are not simply differences between traditions; even within the traditions we will see various positions emphasizing different parts of their tradition as they see certain beliefs as more relevant than others. (For example, within Christianity, the Roman Catholic tradition has emphasized the importance of human nature as essentially – which is different from basically – good, while the Protestant tradition has often offered a more dour view of human beings as essentially marked by sin.)

None of these traditions stands alone, and so none of them can be studied in total isolation from one another. All three of these religious traditions have developed in conversation with one another, and all of them continue to be in conversation with each other, and the more secular worldviews that have recently developed. All are profound and deep, and our purpose is to deepen our grasp upon the profoundest roots of these traditions.

But we will see also that the traditions are alive and authentically themselves, not only in their settled views and convictions, but also in how these settled matters do not settle everything, but in fact leave some things even more unsettled than before. (For example, all three traditions understand the obligation of the community to protect the vulnerable, the poor and the weak, out of a conviction that human beings deserve profound respect. But does this commitment to care involve the use of violence on those who are perceived to threaten the vulnerable? If so, does that disrespect the persons on whom the state uses violence – say, in war or capital punishment?) So in a way we'll be moving forwards and backwards all at once – forwards, in terms of looking at particular ethical issues; and backwards, in terms of understanding the reasoning behind religious traditions' approaches to those issues, reasoning often rooted in the traditions' metaphysical and theological convictions.

The Goals of this Book

This book means to give equal attention to the what, how, and why of these traditions. It means to study, first, these traditions' particular judgments on specific issues – that is, *what* they recommend to their adherents – and how they describe those recommendations to their adherents and others. Second, it will analyze the styles and modes of reasoning by which they reach those judgments – that is, *how* they justify their recommendations. Finally, third, it will also look, somewhat more indirectly, at *why* they decide as they decide – that is, how these judgments and forms of reasoning reveal some of the faiths' deepest theological and metaphysical convictions (and deepest debates or open questions) about God, the human, and the nature of creation, among other things – that is, *why* they come to these views. In these ways this book aims to explore the basic contours of three traditions' ethical programs, which are important both in themselves and for how they shape our common life. As will become clear, each of these goals is more complicated than it may first appear.

Audiences

A book like this might be read by different readers for different reasons. I imagine most of its readers fall into one of four camps. First, teachers and students (college and high-school) looking for a general introduction to the moral traditions of these faiths may find this a convenient entry into a rich comparison of Judaism, Christianity, and Islam. Second, those interested centrally in their own particular faiths may find it interesting both to look at their own traditions in conversation with others, and to discover how comparisons with other religious traditions highlight surprising or heretofore under-appreciated aspects of their own faith; while those interested, from within their faith, in the faiths of others may find this a relatively straightforward way to begin to engage those other traditions. Third, those who are interested in interreligious dialogue will find in the book concrete topics for interfaith discussion as well as helpful comparisons of the distinct ways in which these faiths individually understand and deliberate about moral issues. Fourth and finally, people who are not members of any of these traditions, but are interested in these matters out of "ethical" interests or from a general inquisitiveness into different systems of belief and behavior, may not only find the discussions of ethical issues interesting in themselves, but may also discover that the book provides insights into traditions of moral and religious reflection and behavior which continue to influence every person's life today.

Speaking personally, I am interested in it for all these reasons. But I have a special place in my heart for the fourth group – those who want more deeply to understand these traditions of reflection, irrespective of their own personal beliefs. After all, as the Roman Catholic thinker David Burrell puts it, these religious traditions all offer "palpable histories of holiness."[1] They are reservoirs of millennia of wisdom about the perduring challenges of the human condition, reservoirs which we may find various ways to draw on in order better to live our lives. Furthermore, the main imaginative energies shaping our world today – ordering our lives and informing our conflicts – are more often than not fundamentally religious. The great secular ideologies of the twentieth century – nationalism, communism, even to some extent liberal capitalism – have fewer and fewer true believers.

To be honest, however, this book is not useful in any technical sense. It will not teach you any skills that will make you more marketable to employers, at least not obviously. And no one will care how much you know about the topics of this book – not really care, anyway. Its value lies wholly in its *impracticality*. It is not relevant to some career path; it is "useful" for your life. "Relevance" is not the only "relevant" thing to take into account. You're at a job 40, 50, 60 hours a week; but you're a human being all the time, 24/7, and your whole life you will think about what kind of a person you are, and what sorts of decisions you will make. And even in your career you will find yourself time and again confronted with questions that this book addresses. If you are a student reading this you may find that, as you age, you love to return to your alma mater for alumni gatherings. You will find it a nostalgia trip, to be sure; but you may also come to discover and treasure the opportunities you get then to talk about "big questions" with fellow alumni and faculty, and be exposed, once again, to the "great books" – books that raise those questions. This book is largely about those books, the thinkers who composed them, and the communities from which those thinkers emerged.

Intelligent judgmentalism

But most basically, beneath all of these benefits – beneath all the information it conveys – the book offers something else. More precisely, it urges something else on you, and tries to model it. It is a wager, the wager that issues of this existential grip, metaphysical and conceptual profundity, historical and social complexity, are amenable to dispute, debate, and deliberation. It assumes that humans can reflect on and within these worldviews, and that our minds are devices, however imperfect, for such reflection. The book wants to encourage more than simply a spectatorial appreciation of moral complexity. We must get beyond acknowledging differences of opinion and re-learn how to think about right and wrong, how to judge. That is to say, it professes, and attempts to exemplify, a pattern of intelligent judgmentalism.

"Judgmentalism" is a bad word today. Most people seem to have decided, at least tacitly, that judging one another is wrong and to be avoided. Of course, in forming such a thought they have made a judgment, the judgment that judgment of others is bad; and they apply that judgment, usually unconsciously, willy-nilly across all realms of human affairs.

Why are we afraid to make judgments? That is a question lurking behind every page of this book. Now, there is a fairly honorable philosophical tradition that promotes such skepticism. From this perspective the really Big Questions cannot be properly answered, either because they are grandiose mis-formulations of every-day complaints, or because their answers are simply beyond the scope of human knowing. We are better off not bothering with such abstruse metaphysical issues, and more wisely led to attend to how we deal with one another in the everyday of our relations. The ancient Greek skeptic Sextus Empiricus, the sixteenth-century French thinker Michel de Montaigne, the eighteenth-century Scottish philosopher David Hume – they and others, some of religious faith, some of none, have made this argument. The founder of the university I teach at, the University of Virginia, made it most succinctly. In his *Notes on the State of Virginia*, Thomas Jefferson famously said, "It does me no injury for my neighbor to say there are twenty gods, or no god. It neither picks my pocket nor breaks my leg." This is a philosophically respectable approach to take to our situation.

Unfortunately, many today have significantly less coherent reasons for rejecting moral judgment as morally bad. There are lots of reasons local to our particular historical moment. After all, we live amid a dizzying plurality of ways of living. Students today – whatever their religious faiths – will regularly live with people who are Christian, Jewish, Muslim, Hindu, atheist, and agnostic (and of any of those categories there are a myriad of variants). In such a setting, we are wary of presuming that we know enough about another's views to judge them. We wisely appreciate that people experience the world in very different ways. And so we decide that the safest course, for social harmony, is simply to refuse to judge anyone for what they do. So we come to believe we must not do so, and we seek to extirpate all judgmentalism from our mind.

This is a regrettable position, for it assumes that there is some way to avoid judging. But there is not. Human thought is necessarily normative, because humans are normative – that is, because we cannot help but judge. We make sense of ourselves, and others around us, by following rules, more or less, and that means we are always thinking about right and wrong. We are even thinking about right and wrong when we are in the business of stepping outside the clearly appropriate – for knowing right and wrong involves knowing how to follow the rule and how to bend it, by knowing enough to distinguish "bending" a rule from "breaking" it. This is not a contingent fact about us that we should deplore and fix; it is rather a fact about our behavior as the kinds of creatures we are. And it is seen most potently in the powerful cultural moral proscription today – a moral commandment, in fact – that the first and greatest sin is to judge another person.

That we judge that judging is wrong does not mean that we in fact escape the act of judgment. (The fact that we *judge* judging to be wrong – and communicate that judgment to others who violate it – shows that.) It is rather that we never face up to the fact of our condition as necessarily exercising moral judgment, as creatures who orient themselves in the world through such judgment. The problem is that all our tolerance is really little more than a laissez-faire indifference rather than a genuine apprehension and appreciation of one another's differences. And hence we never think, in direct and thoughtful ways, about how to orient ourselves morally in the world. So when the time comes for us to make such judgments, we often find ourselves less well prepared to make them than we need to be. And that is regrettable.

To do better, we need examples of intelligent judgmentalism. And that's what the traditions are: well-worked out means of living more or less coherent lives in a deeply puzzling and challenging world. They show us how to be thoughtful in our judgments, so that we can internalize these skills and learn to apply them for ourselves.

Furthermore, they give us models of *thinking like* others, by showing us the basic categories and convictions out of which some other people have tried to organize their thinking and their lives. Understanding that is the direct goal of this book's introduction of the moral vernaculars of these traditions: for these traditions do not offer rigorously reasoned programs of moral decision-making, but rather vernaculars in which moral matters can be made visible and vivid, so that we may reflect on them from multiple angles. Each of these vernaculars will make some aspects of the problem, some facets of the situation, more prominent than others, and these vernaculars will differ in what they make so prominent – so that two thinkers from these traditions will often look at the same topic and see very different moral problems. But that is not to be bemoaned, it is an achievement to be proud of: increased competency in the traditions' languages will not lead to resolution of all problems, but rather to the increased specificity and precision of the disagreements.

So that's what we'll do. But before we get started, we must spend a little time on some fairly technical matters about how to choose what counts as "properly" Jewish, or Christian, or Muslim; so those of you not inherently interested in these matters may want to skip the next few pages.

Methodological Matters

Still here? Great. You've obviously realized I was lying a little bit just above, when I suggested this was boring. In fact, these "technical" puzzles of apparently merely methodological interest are actually quite gripping – I mean, who can decide what is properly Christian or not? What sort of criteria can we use for that? Who said I get to choose what is "authentically" Muslim, or Jewish or Christian?

Authenticity?

Well, there is no straightforward answer to that question. In a way, I want to avoid it, by relying on voices from within those traditions themselves. I will try generally (but not exclusively) to depict those faiths as they are represented by various, often conflicting, classical and modern authorities and thinkers. This doesn't really avoid the problem entirely, as I have to choose among many different thinkers when I do this. The only selection criterion I will use here is that the figures should not stand too far outside the "center" of their traditions. How do I determine what is the center? Well, I don't, not really; I do not try to pinpoint a center, but rather recognize a wide zone of more-or-less common convictions, beliefs, and arguments (the last is important) that a significant majority of the historical manifestations of the tradition would recognize as their own. Precision is less important here than conceptual capaciousness, because I want to err on the side of generosity of inclusion. Why do I want to do that? Because I am not looking to determine some "orthodox" vision of these three traditions – as we will see, the desire for orthodoxy first and foremost is a quite distinctively *Christian* desire – but rather to see the traditions not in some clear and distinct doctrinal formulae, but as large-scale ways of living life.

There is an important point at issue here. These traditions are not so much composed of a collection of settled conclusions, but are instead sets of live and enlivening arguments, arguments that are still ongoing. We can think of them as what the English philosopher Michael Oakeshott called "languages of self-disclosure." Such a language "does not impose upon an agent demands that he shall think certain thoughts, entertain certain sentiments, or make certain substantive utterances. It comes to him as various invitations to understand, to choose, and to respond. ... It is an instrument to be played upon, not a tune to be played."[2] When we look at these traditions, we are not trying most fundamentally to get a perfect representation of some configuration of convictions, but rather get a sense of *how* they argue, *what* they argue about and with whom, and *why* they argue how, about what, and with whom they do.

Incommensurability?

Besides this concern, others will be dubious of any such comparison because they think that it is impossible to make such comparisons useful or illuminating, simply because the standards of judgment in these traditions are so fundamentally different. Who are we to judge among them? What can we do but confirm our own prejudices in doing this? (I note that this actually strikes to the heart of liberal education – but I won't go into that here.) In some fundamental ways, these views suggest, these discourses are *incommensurable* – unable to be reconciled, brought to agreement or synthesis, or even compared in terms that they would all recognize as reasonable terms of comparison. They're just too different. What, that is, can we really learn from bringing them together like this?

Part of the job is the job of all comparisons: in short, to make the strange familiar, and the familiar strange. When we undertake such comparisons, we enter into a weird and liminal zone – a frontier region of uncertainty and suspension. But it is a productive experience. By juxtaposing things that we do not normally compare, we discover things that would otherwise go unnoticed. The positions enrich one another, not least by provoking each other. And besides, none of the religious traditions lack resources to understand that experience of suspension, nor must they all condemn it as wholly anathema. These traditions know what it is to encounter the stranger, and even to learn from her or him; they will approve of these encounters, even if we may find them strange and alarming.

Accuracy?

There is yet one more set of concerns, these ones even more powerful. These concerns all are ways of expressing a salutary appreciation of the real and rich complexity of the traditions, and the profound difficulty of finding useful ways of comparing such different traditions. People impressed by such concerns argue for a more fine-grained, close to the ground, understanding of the contours and contextual character of traditions' moral formulations. First of all, such worriers charge, aren't we confusing breadth of scope with depth of understanding? Aren't we, that is, skipping over the surface of deep and profound issues, and deep and profound traditions, in a rapid tour that leaves everything the same blurry shape? Secondly, how can we know that we are not simply imposing procrustean categories – that is, categories that simply don't fit – on these traditions? And thirdly, aren't we doing the same thing within any tradition itself – that is, aren't we simply arbitrarily imposing an illusory stability on what some tradition says? Judaism is a three-thousand year old religious tradition; who should speak for it? Contemporary Jews (and if so, which ones?)? The "greatest minds" of the tradition – but who are they and how do we decide who they are? You see the problem.

My conviction is that religious traditions are *not* infinitely plastic. There are boundaries beyond which those who claim to be in the traditions are actually becoming something else. Sure there are contestable zones, where some will say the innovator is out, and others will say they're still in. But such cases offer their own kind of illumination too, as both sides reveal, in the arguments they use for their debating, what they take to be central to the tradition and what is more marginal.

Moreover, abstraction is not necessarily our enemy, so long as we recognize it as abstraction. We must not assume that the concepts we use are in fact perfect representations of the realities that we try to describe by their use; nor should we despair, because we must use such imperfect concepts, that the task of conceptual understanding is itself a futile endeavor. So long as we know that we are undertaking a pragmatic task of getting a better understanding of matters that would remain thoroughly obscure to us if we did nothing, we cannot be faulted if our findings remain sketchy and, from the perspective of the expert, vague. There is a famous saying in ethics, that "we must not make the best the enemy of the good," meaning that a person's dissatisfaction with anything less than perfection can blind them to the value of things that are only partly successful, partly accomplished. We can agree, and suggest to these critics that they misunderstand our ambitions in this book. The best should not be made the enemy of the adequate.

Arguments You Can't Escape

This book may well vex your expectations. You'll want to find clear answers. You'll want solid solutions. You'll want closure. But there won't be. You'll find debates; you'll encounter imponderables, decisions for which we lack sufficient evidence, on either side, to make them in confidence. And these things will insinuate themselves in your mind. They may unsettle your own views. Why won't I make this book simpler? Why don't I want to make this as digestible as possible? Why won't it be tidy, or easy?

It's not because I don't care – rather, I care, but in the *opposite* direction: I care that this book try to approach the level of moral sophistication these traditions reflect – the sophistication that people use every day, in our ordinary living.

And to do that, it has to be hard, because what each of us do, every day, in thinking about our lives, is incredibly complex – more complex than any of us can grasp. No computer can ponder the simple question "what ought I to do in this situation?" No computer ever will; if it does, we will no longer call it a computer, we'll call it a person.

In one sense, humans are deeper than what they take to be their settled convictions seem to tell them they are. There is a deep complexity to what we are doing all the time. You use arguments all the time, without thinking about it. But beginning to think about it can have an effect on us similar to that produced by thinking too much about how to ride on a bicycle – that is, you may fall off.

But I think that, unlike riding a bicycle, we're not all already morally competent, let alone experts – we're all still only beginning to understand what our moral convictions ought to lead us to do. So we'll think about those moments you fall off the moral bike – the ruptures in your normal life, the moments when you stop and wonder – what ought I to do? I'm in a situation of moral ambiguity here – and different people have different suggestions about what to do. In short, theory has broken out: what am I going to do now?

The crux of the book, then, is argument – I want to expose you to arguments, like radioactive isotopes, in the hopes of you catching something of their force. I want you to become more fully what you already are. I want to help you become owners of and participants in the arguments that already, at a less conscious level, constitute you, make you who you are in your being. You think of yourself in certain terms – a person, a student, a daughter or son, a citizen, a believer – and these ways of thinking about yourself give you a certain series of vocabularies to think about yourself. What I want to do here is help you to more actively (that is, more thoughtfully) inhabit those roles – to extend your understanding both horizontally, across the full scope of moral resources that you've inherited, and vertically, to deepen your understanding of what these moral beliefs mean.

But what are the ingredients of argument? First of all, real argument is not sheer disagreement. Disagreement is simple contradiction, and that is boring. Argument, genuine argument, is anything but that. It is threatening, imperiling, thrilling, and sometimes even useful. Nor is it simply differences that make an argument. You need some common thing to differ over, something to disagree about. Argument is reasoned debate, not just for the sake of more debate, but for the sake of getting things right. After all, it is your life that is at issue here. (Often, the argument is not a matter of two sides having different information, but a matter of interpreting things differently – understanding the force of claims differently, or weighing different facts differently.)

Arguments of this sort – real arguments – are rarely resolved. In fact, you'll find that the traditions we're studying are not alive so much in their settled convictions, but rather in their unsettled and unsettling arguments, the arguments they are having with themselves. Traditions, that is, are essentially ongoing arguments, in much the same way that families are defined by ongoing debates.

This complexity means that people beginning from similar or identical premises will often differ about where to go with their claims. Often, two friends or spouses will differ dramatically. (Often, the fiercest fights we have are with those with whom we feel we have no need to fight – the ferocity here is fed by our outrage that there could be any disagreement on the matter at hand.) Major religious traditions – traditions that people have tried to inhabit, faithfully, for centuries – are no different. They're not just answers; they provide the questions as well. The assumptions don't settle all the disputes – they open up other questions, enable new difficulties to come into view. So the traditions not only differ between themselves about these matters, for any number of reasons (especially their theological and metaphysical commitments); they also differ within themselves.

This truth is not just useful for understanding those traditions most alien to us. It may well be just as illuminating to those most familiar. All too often we confuse familiarity with understanding, and distance with incomprehension. What is closest to us; what lies ready for use beside our chair; the one who walks at our side; the home we've always known; the family we've belonged to, and who have belonged to us – all these things are so close to us, so handy, that we do not often wonder at them, at the mystery of their bare being, let alone ponder what it is like to be them. But familiarity and comprehension are not the same thing.

In doing this, you'll find that the foundational conventions you rely on are themselves the products of arguments; in fact, that they are moments in an argument that continues to this day. That shouldn't surprise us, even though it does. As the poet Dave Smith has said, "what's home / but arguments you can't escape?" Home is not a place of settled safety but the place where you live – and we live by changing, not by staying the same. You should realize something of the profound complexity of the issues facing you in your moral life, *and* the deep sophistication of your own thought as you think about those issues, *and* the enormous diversity and richness of the resources available in the religious traditions we study to help you think about these issues.

However, this destabilization is not a paralyzing skepticism, but an ennabling humility, that allows us to go forward in fear and trembling, with a deeper appreciation of what you always already know.

"Tradition" and the "liberal arts"

You'll find the traditions are like this as well – more ongoing arguments and deep questions than settled convictions. So this book will *not* teach you some things as well. It will not teach you what is the right Jewish, or Christian, or Muslim way to think about various topics. Nor will it teach you what Jews or Christians or Muslims have always believed about various topics. I will use phrases like "for Jews," or "for Muslims," but in fact this is always simply a short-hand to introduce some general way of approaching a matter. As you will see again and again, I am not making any claim that my account is the only right way to understand these traditions; I am merely proposing it as one useful way of beginning to understand their views.

This will still make many of these traditions' faithful quite nervous. They want to say that there is a right way – namely, their own. And of course ultimately they may well be right. We must forthrightly recognize a tension this sets up between our project and many of the traditional projects of the religious traditions we aim to study here. This tension exists because the program of "liberal education" stands in interesting and palpable conflict with the agenda of these traditions. The traditions are emphatic in their single-minded normativity – this is right, all else is wrong, all should be seen from this perspective. This can sound like a contrast between the close-minded "them" and the open-minded "us," but that contrast is a bit too tidy (not least for manifesting a remarkable close-mindedness itself).

It is ignorant and cowardly of us to say that this tension is simply the traditions' fault, that it exists because the traditions are premodern, or unenlightened, or primitive; it is equally the fault of "liberal education" itself. For that education has a worldview of its own, a worldview that conflicts in some basic ways with these traditions' own. This tradition, of liberal education, is more optimistic about the individual's capacity to comprehend, more hopeful about the powers of individuals so educated to come together to shape their societies for the better, and more confident that the intelligence developed in such an education can serve the public good and make a better world and better individuals. That we may resonate with this worldview in ways that make it hard for us to see it as contestable is no reason for us to ignore the fact that it quite clearly *is* contestable. But it is; and these other traditions do, in fact, tacitly contest it quite radically.

Possibly some will dislike liberal education being so fundamentally, so radically challenged in this way. But that's too bad, for the challenge is good. In fact, a large part of the value of this engagement lies in the radical character of each side's critique of the other, the way that neither side can accommodate the other's self-representation, or even more the other's representation of them – each side's picture of the other. To struggle with how another sees you – to learn how you appear to them – is one of the most valuable aspects of such a project. And after all, "liberal education" is purportedly ideologically committed to this sort of radical critique, and so should welcome it; this book is premised on the hope that it will. Traditional religions, on the other hand, also must find resources, from within their heritage or from without it, for understanding and responding to the condition of radical contestability in which all of us today find ourselves.

In a way this book is a wager, a wager that we can in fact try to do what it sets out to do. If we can't – if a book like this is impossible – it says something important about matters larger than just this book. It says something about the prospects for human learning and understanding in the twenty-first century, and indeed something about the prospects of liberal education – and perhaps the worldviews that have informed it – in the future. And the somethings that it says are not happy somethings. So we should give it our best effort.

All this can sound like a wildly Romantic vision of free-thinking individuals bravely striking out on their own, the past be damned. But I'm not encouraging you to sound your barbaric yawp across the rooftops of our multi-religious world. This is not about expressivism or liberation. It is about self-knowledge, about learning more fully the arguments that make you up, that compose *you*. This book won't make you morally "better." No book can do that, on its own. But there is a way that, in reading this book, I hope you become a better person – better in the sense of a richer, more thoughtful "owner" of the arguments you can't escape.

The question of modernity

A book like this – a comparative project of all three Abrahamic faiths – is only possible in the conditions of liberal modernity. This is not meant to be a self-congratulatory statement; it is meant to get at three important truths.

First, it is simply an expression of fact. This book is not, then, a *historia errarum*, a history of the errors believed by other cultures or other times, nor is it a record of the curious and unintelligible customs of other benighted peoples. It is an effort to represent fairly and frankly a series of quite significantly diverse models of life within a single frame of vision. But attempting such a project is distinctly modern. In no earlier era, nor in a culture not fundamentally informed by liberal habits of mind and behavior, could such a comparative undertaking be attempted – an undertaking which tries strenuously not to misrepresent the objects of comparison by accepting uncritically the categorical schema of one of the traditions as true and then cramming the others into it. This is not to say that this book succeeds at this task, but rather that such an ideal is the author's aim – and also, and no less significantly, it is an aim that you the reader can understand, is likely to approve of, and would almost certainly assume to be the *right* one.

Second, even as we tacitly approve such an aim, our very commitment to understand others on their own terms should make us aware of why such a project would seem alien and anathema to many representatives of those traditions. It would be alien because the idea that one's own tradition cannot adequately represent another's views at least tacitly suggests that one's own tradition is in some deep way inadequate – and if that is so, why continue to affirm it? So premoderns would raise the question about the possibility of being Jewish, Christian, or Muslim, and participating in this project; or they would accuse the participants of being *only superficially* Jews, Christians, or Muslims, and more profoundly something else – members of the tradition of "Enlightenment liberalism," perhaps.

Third, this approach raises questions about modernity's opportunities and dangers. These opportunities and dangers seem to me to be both inextricably intertwined and inescapable for us. They are inextricably intertwined, for it is the sheer fact of real pluralism that dislodges us from our traditional habits of parochial self-satisfaction, and starts us down the road of questioning and skepticism, a questioning and skepticism that can lead to tolerance and appreciation of the manifold goods of our world, as well as a more profound and enormously enriched appreciation of our own traditions. But it can also lead to a shallow and superficial attitude of glibness about reality and our lives. And these opportunities and dangers are inescapable, because there is nowhere to go in our world where we could avoid these realities. I mean this geographically and in terms of our values and commitments. In my town of Charlottesville, we have manifold kinds of Christians, Reform, Conservative, and Orthodox Jews, Hindus, Buddhists (from China and Tibet, as well as California), Muslims from all across the *dar-al-Islam* – and I live in a small town in central Virginia. Migration and global mass communication ensure that the diversity of human religious and existential commitment is brought unavoidably before our eyes, wherever we are. Furthermore, there is no way of living that shuts us off from these matters; as scholars have been arguing for several decades, fundamentalism, of whatever religious version, is itself a modern solution to a modern problem. Even the Amish who turn their backs on this world still live with the knowledge that there is a world to which their backs are turned. For all these reasons, the challenges of modernity are inescapable for all the traditions in this book. So this too is a challenge that this book must, and will, address.

Conclusion

None of this will be easy. Indeed, in some ways, being moral is increasingly difficult today. We are increasingly seduced by two pressures that do damage to our understanding of moral agency. One is a kind of pharmacological fatalism, the other is a kind of consumerist nihilism. Let me explain what I mean.

Today, we are confronted by a kind of *pharmacological fatalism* – the belief that we are determined by our genes, our chemical make-up, and what drugs we take to improve ourselves. Recent advances in medicine and psychiatry have led many people to reject accounts of moral responsibility in favor of biological determinism, in which what you do (and thereby who you are) is out of your control – you're a compulsive liar, or a sex addict, or a workaholic, or you had a terrible childhood, or you're prone to violent mood swings – but in no way are you responsible for these maladies or for their effect on other people (like, say, if you physically assault someone for no reason when you're drunk). We should be careful here – I'm not saying that people who take medications to keep themselves stable are not helped, nor am I saying that there are no such real problems. What I'm saying is that other people, people who aren't actually sick at all, have begun to use these excuses to excuse themselves. (It's worth noting, on this, that these excuses are never used when we do good things, but only when we do bad. When was the last time you saw anyone say "but I'm a compulsively kind person, I can't help it" or "I was raised in a just family and that's why I'm a just person"?) These temptations, then, press on our understanding of *bad* agency, when we are wicked or weak.

On the other hand, we also feel the seductions of a certain picture of *consumerist nihilism* – the other kind of temptation – that presses on our understanding of good agency. This is the belief that, in selecting goods for ourselves, we best understand the moral life as a project of becoming a certain kind of person on the model of consumerist shopping – we pick a kind of moral self off the rack, so to speak, with no really relevant guidelines for selecting one kind of moral self over another. I don't mean this to be a direct attack on the sort of "live and let live" relativism we find a lot today (not a *direct* attack, mind you); rather, I mean to highlight, and I aim to make you doubt the idea that, what you want to do with your life is a matter wholly of personal *whim*, which is uninformed by anything deeper than your own personal choice on the matter.

None of us are actually so totally bereft of moral resources as this picture wants to paint us. In thinking about our lives, and in thinking about our actions as they make our lives, we have not too little information to guide us but too much – we are saturated with moral beliefs that can help (or hinder) our moral decisions and moral formation. Perhaps what we need is a way of organizing our moral worlds.

That's what we want to do here – to do a partial inventory of the resources we have available in our world, fairly close at hand, in thinking about the shape of proper human life. This book will help you, I hope, to use that enormous inheritance to think articulately about your life and decisions. In all likelihood it will not make you better. But it will, I hope, make you more thoughtful about what is right and wrong, and bad and good.

Part I
Preliminaries

1

God and Morality

God said to Abraham, "Kill me a son."
(Bob Dylan, "Highway 61 Revisited")

Introduction: Principles, Theory, and Morality

What is the relationship between God and morality? Are humans who believe in God (and which one?) more likely to be moral, righteous, flourishing people? Or are they more prone to be immoral – intolerant, inflexible, absolutist, arrogant, and parochial? Both of these views have been enunciated from time to time. Both in fact have strong constituencies today. Many intellectuals see religion, especially monotheism, as destructive. Most Americans, however, see it as pretty much the only way to be moral; poll after poll says that most people in the US distrust atheists, far more than other groups, and they distrust them because they find it hard to believe they are moral. Clearly, this is a live question in our world. It is especially pointed for a book like this one. How do its two most basic components – religion and ethics, God and goodness – fit together?

Ironically, representative thinkers of these traditions challenge the common assumption that morality and belief are two sides of the same coin. Indeed assertions of the opposite are quite frequent. "Principles are what people have instead of God": so contemporary Christian novelist Frederick Buechner has put it in his delightful *Wishful Thinking: A Theological ABC*.[1] And that is a claim that Jews and Muslims can make as much as can Christians. It is an overstatement, of course; all such claims are. But it gets at an interesting truth, the truth that these religious traditions stand in a quite uneasy and ambivalent relationship with the moral systems which are often described as deriving from them, and which are often said to be ungrounded or irrational absent faith in these traditions' God.

This chapter looks at the nature of the relationship between God and morality. What happens when moral reflection occurs, when theory breaks out? And how is moral deliberation related to the religious convictions of the Abrahamic faiths? Are morality and Abrahamic religions wholly separate? Are they complementary? Are they conflictual? Here I will argue that they are some mix of both. At times these faiths reinforce morality, and at times morality reinforces these faiths; but at other times the two terms stand in deep and profound tension. That tension must be investigated, in order to understand the distinctive character of both Abrahamic religious faith and moral conviction, in their distinctness and in their similarities. That is what this chapter does, first by offering a very schematic picture of what moral theory is, then by discussing the ways that the Abrahamic faiths relate to moral conviction, and finally by suggesting one useful model for thinking about the fraught relationship between morality and these religious traditions, a model that will stand in the background for the rest of this book – H. Richard Niebuhr's model of "the responsible self."

In this chapter we will begin by talking about deliberation, but you'll see how quickly we end up talking about moral being and character.

A Very Sketchy Sketch of Ethical Theory

To begin with, it will help to have a sketch of the scope of what we mean by moral theory. What is it to *be moral*? What is it to *act morally*? Together, these two questions constitute the object of basic moral reflection. Consider, for a moment, how you think about morality, about doing good. Typically, if you are considering this in the moment of an ethical decision, your thinking has two components. First of all, you are asking what is the right thing to do in this situation. What path, among the paths available to me, is the one that I should travel? But beyond this immediate question, a deeper one looms, just over the horizon: what does this choice say about me? What does my decision here reveal about who I am and what I care about? What does it reveal about the what, or the whom, to which I understand myself to be accountable? In general, what picture of the world do I, in light of this situation, now see myself to assume? Many possible courses of action are ruled out by us from the beginning; when we are asked about why we never considered these, we typically give some variation of the answer "I cannot imagine living with myself if I had done that." That phrase is quite interesting, actually; it suggests that not every conceivable option is a *live* option for us – one that is viable for us to take, given who we are. Our understanding of ourselves, and our commitment to a certain set of people, will often mean that certain routes of acting are never really considered; if we were to take them, we would become – or have been revealed to be – fundamentally different people than who we thought we were.

This anatomization of a typical moral situation can go in many directions. Suffice it to say here that we see how, in thinking about moral situations, we are not simply engaging in a kind of "Monday-morning quarterbacking," or second-guessing a referee's call, or a coach's strategy, or an athlete's performances, in a particular instance. No, in thinking about moral acting, even in the most basic way, we find we are led on to ask questions about moral thinking, or ethical deliberation, and moral being, or character and integrity. And that is as it should be. In asking "how does ethical deliberation work?" we're not asking *why* – not about asking the so-called "meta-ethical" question of "why be moral?" – but rather about *how* – the mechanics of morality.

In thinking about this *how*, we are actually asking two sets of questions. First, we are asking, what do you do when you think about morality? How should you think morally? Furthermore, how should we think morally if we are religious? In a way, these sorts of questions are about the formal logic of the process of moral deliberation. Second, we are asking, what resources can we find that might help us answer the first question? What sort of role should our religious commitments play in our moral reflection and deliberation? These sorts of questions are about the material data, or given, through which and with which we think morally. And both are important.

When we begin to try to articulate a theory about how to think about moral life, we can begin from one of several starting points. Roughly speaking, we might begin by thinking about morality in terms of goals, rules, or character. Typically, we divide ethical theories up, in the contemporary academy, as beginning with one of these three. The first group of approaches we consider *consequentialist* theories, theories which begin from reflection on the consequences of actions, either considered as individual actions with distinct sets of consequences, or as types of actions with typical sorts of consequences; utilitarianism is a classic example of this sort of moral theory. The second group we consider *deontological* theories, that is, theories concerned with the sort of absolute laws or rules that the agent must obey – in other words, what their obligations (in Greek, *deon*) are in some setting; Kantian theories, organizing moral life around a universalization principle (akin to the Golden Rule), are classic examples of this approach, but this group also includes divine command ethics, and those committed to some understanding of the natural law. The third group is often called *virtue* theories (and is sometimes, to my mind improperly, classified as a type of consequentialism); such theories focus on the kind of character that our actions, repeated serially over the course of a lifetime, are prone to habituate in us; like paths in a forest, worn down by generations of humans and animals following in one another's footsteps, repetition of actions over time grooves into us the habits that make those actions a kind of "second nature" for us. Famously, Aristotle's theory of the human as developing a range of virtues, "excellences" or capabilities over their lifespan (and especially in their first fifteen or twenty years), is an example of this.

Now, any of these theories can accommodate aspects of the others. Obviously, consequences matter to all sorts of people; and the idea of rules as rules "no matter what" is a powerful idea for any moral thinker; and all people recognize the power of habit in shaping people's moral fortitude, and can acknowledge the importance of education in making moral people. Yet for all that, the three approaches do differ in interesting ways, as we will see throughout this book.

So now we have a sense of the scope and depth of moral reflection, and a very rough sketch of the sorts of ways thinkers have tried to theorize moral being, character, action, and deliberation. Simple enough, yes? But now things get more complicated; for next we will begin to see how God enters into morality.

Divine Commands and Moral Obligations

Reflection on morality in the Abrahamic traditions begins with the Decalogue, the Ten Commandments. The Decalogue sketches the basic framework for all three religious traditions this book explores – Judaism, Christianity, and even, in a different way, Islam (which has a semi-parallel to the Decalogue in the Qur'an (17:22–40)). The rest of the traditions are almost all just commentary on the Decalogue – that is, attempts to extend and apply the commandments enunciated there to the full range of human experience.

Some insights are apparent simply in the fact that the Decalogue is handed down from God. The bare act of *giving* the law itself already suggests that this view looks on what we might call "moral rationalism" – the idea that rational reflection might be sufficient to understanding and fully inhabiting the moral life – as inadequate; for God has decided humanity needs to be *informed* of its rights and duties. (For the Abrahamic traditions, this is true about the law given to Israel at Sinai, of course, but also of the so-called "Noahide Covenant," given to all humanity by God after the Flood.) Furthermore, this "giving" suggests that a relationship is at the basis of ethics – a relationship between two living agents.

So there is some tension between the "positive law" of Judaism's Torah and what thinkers in all three traditions have argued is a "natural law," a moral order inscribed in the fabric of the cosmos, or written on the human heart, and at least partially discernible to the sensitive observer. Such a "natural law" is more immediately available in some forms of Christianity (especially Roman Catholicism) and, at times, in Islam. But all three traditions negotiate between fidelity to the positive law, such as the Decalogue, and some construal of natural law.

The Decalogue has two parts, or "tablets." The first tablet offers a series of identity-conferring characteristics; who God is, who "we" are, what we owe to God and to our elders. But this identity is anything but morally neutral. In fact the moral charge is, if anything, more potent in the first tablet than the second. This is established in the first commandment: "I am the Lord your God, who brought you out of the Land of Egypt." If we put ourselves in the position of those to whom this commandment is addressed, it is not merely information we are given here. Here, God's identity is tied to our own, and vice versa; were we to forget ourselves as those who have been redeemed, we would forget God as the redeemer. And the opposite is true as well: it is the first historical mark of this God's identity that this God is a saving God. Because of this, we owe our lives to this God. And this God is a jealous God, who will remember and punish if we do not worship.

Of course, there is a deep connection here between properly religious piety and the obligation properly to honor and attend to those human elders who preceded us, and initiated us into human community. (This is why the fifth commandment, the one which concludes the first tablet, is to "Honor your Father and Mother.") But in the end, even that piety towards our parents must be referred back to God, to whom we (and our elders) owe our lives, our freedom, our histories, "the land that the Lord your God is Giving you" – everything. My identity and my relationship with this God are inextricably intertwined. There is no me without this God, and the crucial fact about this God is that this God, and this God alone, has *redeemed us*: that is what the first tablet declares.

The second tablet provides community-constituting rules; how do we act regarding those around us (our "neighbors"), given the identity of God, self, and community that the first tablet has established. These rules are meant to organize society in successful ways, and as such are not of deep theological interest on first blush.

But take a closer look. There is a problem with the Decalogue as it stands, especially in the second tablet. These commandments are almost all negative; they are forms of proscriptions, of "thou shalt *nots*." Do not murder, commit adultery, steal, bear false witness, or covet your neighbor's goods (including his wife – patriarchy is very much in place here). What about what we *should* do? Here, it says very little. This is a problem, as the tradition recognizes; for the next three chapters – 21, 22, and 23 – are concerned with explaining and fleshing out what the code entails for living, and for "tough cases," situations where rules seem ambiguous or conflict with one another.

The basic problem with understanding how to use such a list of "thou shalt nots" is precisely in learning how to apply them – how we are to employ the commands of God in governing the everyday details of our lives. This is not just a problem with the Ten Commandments – it's a problem no matter what the moral source or authority you use.

We have a hint in the Decalogue itself, in its prohibition of "graven images." This prohibition is clearly linked to an appreciation of some sort of a radical difference between God as Creator and God's creation, between the author of the cosmos and any of the artefacts that exist within it. Nothing can "represent" God in this cosmos, because anything that is thought to do so invariably distorts God by highlighting some features of creation as more revelatory of God than others. For our immediate purposes, however, the crucial fact is that whatever this analogy is, it is fairly distant because of the Divine's superiority.

Part of this is just the Divine's radical transcendence of creation. But another part of the difficulty comes from something positive about the Divine that these traditions, perhaps paradoxically, affirm. And that is, that this God is a living God – a God who is ever new, a God who can surprise you. This makes humanity's temporal existence crucial. It allows us a real history, not just as a matter of ever-repeating cycles of time, but in terms of genuine newness.

And yet the commandment offers a deeper lesson still. After all, the temptation to make images of God reveals that humans recognize not just a chasm, but some sort of positive relationship between God and humanity as well – enough to feel the temptation – and to think that we can be related in some positive way to the ultimate source of our being. We will see in later chapters that all three accounts explore the roots of this temptation through suggesting some sort of positive analogy between the human creation and the Divine person. Indeed, while Islam resists too literal a construal of the idea of the image of God in humanity, it compensates for this by amplifying what the law says; the Qur'anic texts do not simply prohibit, but include the prescription to do the right. From its first formulation, then, Islam sees the fulfillment of morality not just in forbidding wrong, but also in commanding the right.

In general, though, the connection is clear, seemingly straightforward, and positive: morality is real because God stands behind it, and God stands behind it because in some way God's will, and perhaps God's own being, is manifest in the moral behavior that God commands. God endorses morality, and morality deepens its adherents' relationship with God. Pretty simple.

The Natural and the Supernatural

However, there is a problem here, a problem that becomes visible soon after anyone formulates this theory in this way. For God and morality seem often to be at best obscurely related, and there are times when they seem opposed to each other. Sometimes it seems that God's will about what to do is inscrutable, and sometimes God's will and the moral law seem frankly to conflict. Classically, these problems have been represented in two stories – one about a son's dealings with his father, the other about a father's dealings with his son. We will look at each of these worries in turn.

Euthyphro's dilemma

The best place to begin with the first worry is in fact right near the beginning of the tradition of Western philosophy itself, in a small gem of a philosophical dialogue written by Plato, entitled the *Euthyphro*. The story of the dialogue is simple. Just outside the law courts in Athens, waiting to go inside, Socrates meets the upperclass Euthyphro – a man renowned for his religious wisdom – and they converse. (Importantly, Socrates is there as a preliminary for his own trial for "impiety" and "corrupting the young," a trial that will lead to his death.) It turns out that Euthyphro is there to prosecute his own father, who let one of his workers die. Socrates is astonished that a son would be so confident of his moral standing to prosecute his own father, and seeks the sources of Euthyphro's confidence, by admiring his piety. As the conversation goes on, it becomes clear that much relies on Euthyphro's conviction, ultimately revealed, that piety is whatever the gods approve of. But that answer just provokes Socrates's almost naïve question, which has haunted philosophers ever since: "But Euthyphro, is the pious loved by the gods because it is pious? Or is it pious because it is loved by the gods?"[2]

The question Socrates is asking here is one of the relationship between God and the moral order. Is one prior to the other, and if so, which? Socrates's views, let alone Plato's, are hard to pin down. (Plato set this dialogue at the beginning of Socrates's trial for impiety for a reason.) But their views don't matter to our purposes; what matters is that the dialogue grips us with a challenge we feel. This challenge grips us because it captures a crucial moment in our own thinking about these matters. After an initial unquestioning acceptance of the coherence between piety and righteousness, we eventually begin, in our lives, to ask questions regarding where they may come into conflict. And the Euthyphro dilemma is useful there, so long as it is only the first, not the last, word on things. (It wasn't even that for Plato.)[3]

A great deal of philosophy consequent to the *Euthyphro* was an attempt to respond to the challenges formulated in it. One very powerful response, articulated most influentially by Aristotle, was quite radical. On its account, being moral is understood as the *natural* thing to do, in some complicated sense of "natural."

There are two aspects of Aristotle's proposal that we must appreciate. First of all, it suggests that morality is deeper than our conscious willed decisions, more a matter of habits and attitudes than actions (this is why much of ancient moral thought was largely about virtues and character). Most reflection is not preactive, but reactive; most of our deliberation takes place after the fact, or in response to confronting a challenge that is put before us – not one that we have chosen of our own free will. One danger of imagining moral deliberation with a too-simple model of self-starting reflection is simply that that is not the way most of us live. Thinking is, in this way, a kind of a response to suffering, to actions upon us.

Second, because morality is deeper in us, in this way, and not so amenable to conscious control, it is part of our natural constitution as part of nature, not something that in itself distinguishes us from other parts of nature. This makes this approach, by and large, part of a larger outlook typically called *naturalism* – the idea that human behavior can be understood, ideally, entirely in terms of how humans participate in natural processes that other creatures participate in as well. This view is popular with a wide range of philosophers, from Aristotle in fourth-century BCE Athens to David Hume in eighteenth-century Edinburgh, and many in our own day.

Naturalism has as its goal the smooth fit of humans into the world. On naturalism's understanding, humans are just one more part of a larger organic cosmos, and ideally should not disrupt the flow of nature. The ideal here is thus a natural immediacy of response on the part of agents in any number of settings. Much of our life is sub-reflective in this way. Indeed, much of life is actually *non*-reflective, for often we simply act in a way pretty much indistinguishable from automata. Examples of this are not hard to find: you drive a car mostly automatically; you are polite in general without deliberation (thus the famous line, "a gentleman is someone who is only rude on purpose"); and the ideal ethical actor is morally good in an almost reflexive way. So understood, naturalism is a powerful moral vision of the world and humanity's place genuinely *in* it.

Abraham's test

However, in the Abrahamic traditions, the human in part transcends their immediate "natural" surroundings, and is not fully determined by them. The human *stands before God* in some way distinct from the rest of nature. Hence, were humans to fit smoothly into the functioning of the world, they would be no better than beasts. Instead, they are called by God to account for themselves, and perhaps creation, in a unique way.

This commitment illuminates these traditions' common concern with idolatry. God is a living God, changing and confronting you with living demands, and thus the first sin is acting as if God is dead, frozen, an ossified statue. The God of Abraham cannot be reduced to a seamless set of axioms or rules, a moral algorithm that will smoothly produce the right answer for its devotees every time. A moral system like that has a hard time recognizing the mystery, the complexity, and perhaps the tragedy, of human existence – the obscure ways that good and evil collide in us to create a mystery that no human thought, it sometimes seems, can penetrate.

In all this, what this God suggests is not only that God transcends nature, but that humans do as well. *We are more than nature*, in some way. (Christianity more strongly affirms this than do Judaism or Islam, but they have it too, simply as part of the logic of having God be distinct from, and governor of, a partly corrupted creation.)

But there is a danger here – it means that there is always lurking a latent tension, and at times an explicit conflict, between God's commands and what seems "natural" to us to do. For after all, this God is a jealous God, a God of singularity, exclusivity, possibly violent intolerance. There may well be moments when God may demand something that is fundamentally unnatural. This God created the cosmos, after all; therefore, these traditions attest, this God needn't be held accountable to its maxims and its norms.

An example of this tension is not hard to find. We talk about these three traditions as "The Children of Abraham." But we forget that all the traditions say Abraham almost killed his child on orders from God. Since it is safe to say that no sane father would want naturally to kill his own child, it is clear that the tradition was alert to this tension between the natural and the supernatural from a very early stage. Indeed, the scriptural sources suggest what is actually a more profound analysis of the tension we have identified here than many philosophers or theologians do. So I want to look at those texts next.

Here is the story, commonly called the Akedah (the "Binding"), as recorded in Genesis, chapter 22, verses 1–19:

And it came to pass after these things, that God did tempt Abraham, and said to him, "Abraham!" and he said, "Behold, here I am." And he said, "Take your son, your only son, Isaac, whom you love, and go to the land of Moriah; and offer him there for a burnt offering upon one of the mountains of which I will tell you."

And Abraham rose up early in the morning, and saddled his ass, and took two of his servants with him, and Isaac his son, and cut the wood for the burnt offering, and rose up, and went unto the place of which God had told him.

Then on the third day Abraham lifted up his eyes, and saw the place far off.

And Abraham said to his servants, "Stay here with the ass; and I and the boy will go up ahead and worship, and come again to you." And Abraham took the wood of the burnt offering, and laid it upon Isaac his son; and he took the fire in his hand, and a knife, and they both went together.

And Isaac spoke to Abraham his father, and said, "My father;" and he said, "Here I am, my son." And he said, "Behold the fire and the wood: but where is the lamb for a burnt offering?" And Abraham said, "My son, God will provide a lamb for a burnt offering;" so they both went together.

And they came to the place of which God had told him; and Abraham built an altar there, and laid the wood in order, and bound Isaac his son, and laid him on the altar upon the wood. And Abraham stretched forth his hand, and took the knife to slay his son.

And the angel of the Lord called to him from heaven, and said, "Abraham, Abraham!" and he said, "Here I am." And he said, "Do not lay your hand upon the boy, nor do any thing to him: now I know that you fear God, for you have not withheld your son, your only son from me."

And Abraham lifted up his eyes, and looked, and behold, behind him a ram was caught in a thicket by his horns: and Abraham went and took the ram, and offered him up for a burnt offering in the place of his son.

And Abraham called the name of that place "The Lord Will Provide:" and to this day it is said, on the mount of the Lord it shall be provided.

And the angel of the Lord called to Abraham out of heaven a second time, and said, "I swear by myself, says the Lord, that because you have done this thing, and have not withheld your son, your only son, I will bless you, and make your seed as many as the stars of the sky, and the sand on the seashore; and your seed will possess the cities of their enemies; and through your seed shall all the nations of the earth be blessed: for you have obeyed my voice."

So Abraham returned to his servants, and they rose up and went together to Beer-sheba; and Abraham stayed at Beer-sheba.

Consider some of the details of this story. God asks Abraham to sacrifice Isaac, which meant effectively to leave behind his family, just as God had first asked him to leave behind his family in Chaldea – just as God asked Abram to leave behind his name, and his identity, and become Abraham. Indeed, because God had established the covenant with Abraham through Isaac, and not Ishmael, the call to sacrifice Isaac meant that Abraham was being asked to sacrifice his very name – "Abraham" was glossed as meaning "father of many nations." To sacrifice Isaac is to sacrifice himself.

There are many noteworthy things about this passage. Here I will note only a few. First of all, the language used is significant. Note in particular the use of the word, *hinneni*. Roughly translatable as "here I am," the word communicates more than just one's location. It identifies the speaker as one who is attentive to the inquisitor, one who is available to them, who will be responsible to them. In short, it recognizes a relationship of obligation of moral concern and solicitude for another. In this passage, it is spoken three times, each time by Abraham, once directly to God, once to God's messenger, when they call to him; so Abraham is clearly putting himself at God's disposition, as an instrument of God's will. Yet this is not simply obeisance to a tyrannical deity; Abraham has already challenged God, on ethical terms, as regards God's plan to annihilate Sodom and Gommorrah (in Genesis 18). Indeed, there Abraham expressed his confidence in God's justice – "shall not the judge of all the earth do right?" (Genesis 18:25) – in the same episode in which he learns that God will grant him a son, whom he will name Isaac. Here, in contrast, Abraham simply hears and follows: *hinneni*.

Interestingly, however, Abraham also offers this same reply to a human – his son, Isaac – thus suggesting that Abraham recognizes a similar kind of moral accountability to Isaac alongside the accountability that he offers to God. What is more, in his use of the word *hinneni* in both settings, there is no evidence that one is prior to the other. Each has a legitimate claim on him, Abraham seems to be saying; and in the equivalent answers he provides to them, even after he has heard the demand of one to sacrifice the other up unto him, he seems to refuse to recognize any moral differentiation between them.

The language of *hinneni* appears throughout the Hebrew Bible and Old Testament as a language of fidelity, attention, and availability. (It is shadowed in the New Testament with the Koine Greek term *idou*, typically translated "behold!") The prophet Samuel receives his call from God three times, but only responds to God the third time, upon being directed by Eli on how to do so: namely, to reply to the call with *hinneni* (1 Samuel 3:9–10). And on the other side, it is precisely Adam and Eve's refusal to reply to God's call in the Garden, after they had eaten of the fruit of the tree of the knowledge of good and evil, that prompts God to ask them if they have disobeyed the divine command.

Now consider also the Qur'anic passage in this regard. Here is the story in the Qur'an:

> Among his followers was Abraham.
> He came to his Lord with his whole heart.
> He said to his father and his people, "What are you worshipping?
> "How can you choose false gods, instead of the true God?
> "What is your opinion of the Lord of the universe?"
> Then he looked up to the stars.
> He said, "I am sick,"
> So [his people] turned away from him and left.
> He turned to their gods, and said,
> "Do you not eat? Why do you not speak?"
> He then destroyed them.
> His people came at him in a great rage.

He said, "How can you worship what you carve
"When God has created you, and everything you make?"
They said, "Build a blazing fire and throw him into it."
They schemed against him, but We humiliated them.
He said, "I will go to my Lord; He will guide me."
"My Lord, grant me a righteous son,"
so We gave him good news, that he would have a patient son.
When the boy was old enough to work with his father, Abraham said, "My son, I see
   sacrificing you in a dream. What do you think?" He said, "Father, do as you are
   commanded and, God willing, you will find me patient."
When they had both submitted to God, and he had laid his son down on the side of
his face,
We called out to him: "Abraham."
"You have fulfilled the dream." This is how We reward the righteous.
That was an exacting test indeed.
We ransomed his son with a momentous sacrifice.
And We let him be praised by succeeding generations.
Peace be upon Abraham.
This is how We reward the righteous.
Truly he is one of our faithful servants. (Qur'an 37:83–109)

This also tells the story of the sacrifice, though the details are equally revealing in
their own right. Here the story is traditionally understood as the story of Abraham
and Ishmael, not Abraham and Isaac. And here the story is explicitly associated with
Abraham's hostility to his family's business of idol-making, and his smashing of the
idols. This association is presumably not accidental: children are, after all, almost
inevitably their parents' idols. The text recognizes an ineliminable tension between
fidelity to God and fidelity to the world in a slightly different way than in Genesis;
here the requested sacrifice flows naturally from the smashing of the idols. Of
course, in the Qur'an both Abraham *and* Ishamel were overtly willing to undertake
the sacrifice, whereas in the Genesis telling, Isaac seems ignorant of it beforehand.
Yet the essentials of both stories are the same: the father, the parent, is asked to
sacrifice the thing he most loves in the world, and he shows himself willing to do
so. What the world gives, and what God demands, can come tragically, disastrously
apart.

Now, none of these faiths are willing to say that their God is Baal, actually
demanding that we throw our children into the fire. They all directly refuse this
blood-logic. But none of them blanch from the full reality of what they suggest may
be required by a life fully faithful to the God they serve. Judaism makes it a recur-
rent theme, one that returns at different moments in the tradition as a perpetual
temptation for humans to mistrust God. For Christianity, in contrast, the tension
reaches its climax and its resolution in the death on the cross and resurrection from
the grave of Jesus Christ. In Islam, it becomes more visibly a test, but also a warning.
As we will see later, it is the purity of Iblis's monotheistic devotion to God that
causes the angel to refuse God's commandment that all the angels bow down to

Adam, a refusal that constitutes the core of Iblis's rebellion against God and the angel's transformation into *ash-Shaytan*, Satan.

In each tradition, however, it is a powerful and vivid story. It challenges our attempts at moral deliberation, especially when we conceive of moral action in naturalistic terms, as tending towards automaticity. God's commands create an inner space in the human, a space that can be the stage for a tension between God and morality. Perhaps indeed there is an ineliminable tension between the absoluteness of morality, and our own capacity to comprehend and in some sense control that absoluteness. Perhaps, that is, the absolute exists in our lives only with a penumbra of judgment surrounding it, judgment of our own inevitable failure to obey it fully in our lives.

After this episode, Abraham and Isaac are never recorded as speaking to one another again – and neither are Abraham and Sarah. Indeed, Abraham's life moves rapidly towards its end. First he secures a wife for Isaac, in the story of his servant and Rachel at the well; then Sarah, his wife, dies, and he secures a burial place for her on Hittite land. Then Abraham himself dies. The division between Isaac and Ishmael is apparently resolved, at least provisionally, when they bury Abraham in the cave of Machpelah near Mamre, in the field of Ephron son of Zohar the Hittite (Genesis 25:9).

Each of the traditions gives the story a central liturgical place. The Akedah is the fixed reading for Rosh Hashanah, the Jewish New Year, and the ram's horn sounded in that service is associated with the ram caught in the thicket; furthermore, the Akedah is also part of the daily morning service. Christians read the story just before Easter, or at the Easter Vigil, and clearly it is meant to foreshadow the sacrifice of Jesus – God's only son – in the crucifixion. In Islam, Abraham is not simply a nomad, but a pilgrim, like Moses, but the pilgrimage is to a barren land, the location of the Kaabah, the House of the Great Covenant, which is built by Abraham and Ishmael after the event of the near-sacrifice. Even today, pilgrims on the hajj in Mecca chant "*labbayk*," "here I am" – echoing *hinneni*.

So the traditions do not solve the tension captured in these stories, but rather try in their own ways to make it palpable and unavoidable. In doing this, they suggest that any ethic that does not accommodate both the "horizontal" claims of natural morality and the "vertical" claims of God on us is inadequate. Any ethic that cannot understand Ahbraham's answer of *hinneni* to both God and Isaac will not capture the moral richness of this situation. Is there a viable moral alternative that offers us some advance on our earlier models? In short, we need a model of the self that can accommodate Abraham, and Abraham's *hinneni*. Where can we find it?

The Responsible Self

Perhaps the best such account is that offered by the twentieth-century Christian ethicist H. Richard Niebuhr (1894–1962), who wrote a small book entitled *The*

Responsible Self. Niebuhr was dissatisfied with then-existing accounts of how to understand the human moral adventure, in no small part because they ill-suited those who were struggling to live out their lives in covenant fidelity to a living God. As an alternative, he offered the idea of the "responsible self," which he thought more fully suited humans' experience of moral life under God.

The image of "responsibility," for him, illuminates aspects of our life as agents in ways that other, older forms of thought about morality do not. So to understand why this is a valuable symbol, we must understand what it is supplementing.

Niebuhr thought that there were typically two models of the moral life. He called these the models of "man the maker" and "man the citizen," and on his understanding, they each ask different fundamental questions and imply different pictures of morality. The first – which Niebuhr named "man the maker" or "man the fashioner" – asks the question, what is my goal, ideal, or *telos*? What, that is, is *the good*? This model builds upon one particular insight about the human: "What is man like in all his actions?… he is like an artificer who constructs things according to an idea and for the sake of an end."[4] We use such practical ends-and-means reasoning all the time, in all aspects of our lives. For example, you might be disappointed with your short temper, and so you train yourself to be more patient with those with whom you disagree; over time this can work to change your character – if not dramatically, at least significantly. This is clearly an important dimension of the moral life.

But the validity of this model is significantly limited. After all, we do not always find ourselves in situations where means-end reasoning is helpful for our moral reflections. For example, sometimes you must choose among obligations or commitments, and rank them; most college students, I would wager, rank loyalty to friends over observance of the protocols of academic integrity, so that they would not betray a friend who they caught cheating on a test. (Though perhaps there are different senses of "loyalty to friends" that could operate here.) We wake up in the middle of things. We're swarmed by laws, rules, dictates of etiquette. We come to self-awareness in the midst of right and wrong, of commandments and rules, and we must take account of them, we must rank them. Of the many allegiances you have, which ones are most important?

So another image is often used in critical contrast to the man-the-maker image; and this is what Niebuhr calls "man the citizen." This figure asks, most fundamentally, what is the law by which I should live my life? The question here is not about the goal I seek, but rather what is the *right* framework within which I might pursue any goal? It is by asking this question that humans come to see themselves as embedded within communities, as members of communities. It is by asking this question that we come to see others as other "selves," worthy of our moral consideration.

These two models of the moral life each capture something important about the moral life. But both formulate their insights in ways that make it impossible to accommodate the insights of the other. They are, that is, incommensurable, unreconcilable with one another. They identify different aspects of our moral experience and each stubbornly argues that their aspect is the central one. And neither can therefore recognize the genuine moral significance of the other aspect. As each insists on building a picture of the moral life around their own partial (in several senses) apprehension of morality, the inevitable conflict between the two symbols suggests neither is wholly adequate to our needs. We must have another, more encompassing picture that can accommodate the importance of both insights.

So, as a way to offer a superior account, Niebuhr proposes a third picture, which he calls "man the answerer," or the responsible self. This picture begins from "the image of man-the-answerer, man engaged in dialogue, man acting in response to action upon him."[5] Here the moral life is understood as a conversation, a dialogue between various partners, and this model assumes the human asks a different fundamental question from either of the others: what is going on, and how should I best respond to it? What, that is, is the *fitting* thing to do here? In using this symbol, we will come to understand human actions, particularly but not exclusively those actions that are especially morally charged, as in a certain way *responses*, answers, to actions of others upon us.

This helps us see some things the other concepts left obscure. For example, it makes sense of human suffering in a certain way. "It is not simply what has happened to them that has defined them; their responses to what has happened to them have been of even greater importance, and these responses have been shaped by their interpretations of what they suffered."[6] We are never simply victims; if in no other way, our agency is manifest in how we receive and respond to the hurts and blessings inflicted upon us by the world.

This account is useful for many reasons, but for us most especially it is useful because it carefully identifies and anatomizes four distinct dimensions of the moral life, all of which are crucially in play for ethics in the three Abrahamic traditions. We can think about these dimensions as ways of mapping our moral experience in terms of the past, the present, and the future, and in terms of our lives in community.

First, as we said above, action is a response to action upon us, which is prior to our action; we are not allowed to set the terms of the game under which our moral life is played; we come into the game with it already underway, and we simply must act within it as it comes to us – we're not allowed to start it all over again.

Second, these "responsible" actions are responses to actions that themselves are interpreted by us. This is important because our interpretation of a situation always in part determines how we respond to it; sometimes, in fact, the interpretation is the decisive factor. For example, we would expect different responses to someone sneaking up and dumping a cooler full of ice water on one's back from a football coach whose team had just won the Super Bowl than from a professor delivering a lecture to a bunch of drowsy undergraduates. And all of us have felt the sting of someone else's casual remark to us, when that casual remark touches an old but still sensitive wound we have long harbored (how many times do we find ourselves responding frostily to someone's innocent remark, when we are in fact responding

to a history of personal injuries of which they themselves are completely ignorant?).
How we understand the context into which we are acting matters for how we act
in response. Furthermore, this interpretive background, which at least partially
determines how we act in response, is itself not entirely within our conscious
control. That is why practical jokes can go awry; in our example, the now-drenched
professor can respond in good humor to the soaking, or feel outraged and enraged
and turn on the jokers, or feel so humiliated that she must flee the lecture hall
entirely. Any of these responses is possible, and none of them will be simply and
sheerly self-consciously chosen by the professor; unconscious motives will always
play a part.

Third, each action is a response that looks to the future and expects to be held
accountable for itself. Indeed, responsible action anticipates such future
accountability; that is, the actor takes under consideration the fact that they will be
asked to account for what they did, how they did it and why they did it. If the
professor is able to resist the urge to lash out or flee, it may be because she
understands that their actions have a future-oriented aspect to which she should
attend.

In all these ways, Niebuhr says,

> an agent's action is like a statement in a dialogue. Such a statement not only seeks to
> meet, as it were, or to fit into, the previous statement to which it is an answer, but is
> made in anticipation of reply. It looks forward as well as backward; it anticipates….
> It is made as part of a total conversation that leads forward and is to have meaning
> as a whole.[7]

Actions are not only about the past and present, about what has been done and is
being done to us; they are also significantly about the future, and express our beliefs
about what sort of future we should like to inhabit. We respond in our actions in
the full knowledge that we will later be held accountable for how we respond now.
Responsibility lies in the agent who stays with her action, who accepts the consequences and is willing to weave the action into a larger life story. The twentieth-
century literary critic Kenneth Burke (1897–1993) vividly describes this idea in the
following story:

> Imagine that you enter a parlor. You come late. When you arrive, others have long
> preceded you, and they are engaged in a heated discussion, a discussion too heated
> for them to pause and tell you exactly what it is about. In fact, the discussion had
> already begun long before any of them got there, so that no one present is qualified
> to retrace for you all the steps that had gone before. You listen for a while, until you
> decide that you have caught the tenor of the argument; then you put in your oar.
> Someone answers; you answer him; another comes to your defense; another aligns
> himself against you, to either the embarrassment or gratification of your opponent,
> depending upon the quality of your ally's assistance. However, the discussion is inter-
> minable. The hour grows late, you must depart. And you do depart, with the discus-
> sion still vigorously in progress.[8]

Burke's image quite crisply puts in our mind the nature of our moral action as action that takes place, essentially in time, with some things earlier than it that it is responding to, and other things yet to come that will respond to it. Our actions are not merely superficially temporal; their particular historicity is part of what makes them the particular things they are.

But the historical and temporal dimensions of our moral agency – the way they extend across time – are not the only register in which we must think about our moral lives as responsible, according to Niebuhr. For those lives also take place in community, in some community or particular set of communities, among whom we number ourselves and from whom we in large part take our identity. Those social settings decisively shape the nature of our actions and our agency. Because of this, the responsible self is not only responding *in time*, but also responding to a particular understanding of its audience or audiences; and every audience has expectations that must be taken into account in order for your action to be intelligible to it. This is the fourth dimension of responsible action: an action is a response that is for a certain community and hence reveals some social solidarity, some fundamental attachment to a community of people – however imaginary, however far away in space and time from the person acting in the here and now; in this way there is always a whole "cloud of witnesses" surrounding your action and contributing to its distinct meaning.

In sum, for Niebuhr, "The idea or pattern of responsibility, then, may summarily and abstractly be defined as the idea of an agent's action as

1   response to an action upon him,
2   in accordance with his interpretation of the latter action, and
3   with his expectation of response to his response; and
4   all of this is in a continuing community of agents."[9]

In a way, all of these dimensions are visible in Abraham's single, simple word *hinneni*. In using that word, he recognizes (1) that another has made a claim on him, (2) a claim that he construes as a legitimate claim, and he anticipates (3) that his own response – "here I am" – will lead the claimant to ask something of him that he should be disposed to provide, in order (4) to keep the relationship between them alive and moving forward.

It is all packed not only into the *hinneni* Abraham speaks to Isaac, but also into the *hinneni* he speaks to God. For as I said earlier, Niebuhr does not simply think that this account is useful for understanding our moral lives simply as human moral agents in sheerly human moral communities. He thinks it also offers a picture of the life of the moral agent before God. As he says, it "offers us … a key – not *the* key – to the understanding of that biblical ethos which represents the historic norm of the Christian life."[10] The responsible self, that is, is not just a useful picture of the ethical self; it is a useful picture of the *theological-ethical* self.

Niebuhr suggests this is so for two reasons. First of all, the responsible self focuses moral attention on the agent as free and accountable in a lively way. Like the craftsman model, the freedom of human agency is acknowledged and respected on this account. But like the lawgiver model, that free agency is put in a complicated relationship with powers and dynamics that both bear down on the person and sustain and empower her as well. Given that human actors who are religious understand themselves (or should understand themselves) to exist in the worshipful service of a creative and sovereign God, a model of responsibility accommodates their experience more fully. The image of responsibility, that is, captures something of the tense dialectic between freedom and constraint that religious agents experience at the core of their moral lives, and that is captured in Abraham's free response of *hinneni* to God and to Isaac.

Secondly, this account implies a vision of the source and structure of the moral order that is more in tune with what he thinks "the biblical ethos" entails. That is to say, the picture of the human as a responsible self creates far more space for a genuinely *living God* to be a functional part of this account of morality than either of the other accounts. For after all, the crucial character of God in the biblical ethos is dramatic. God is not fundamentally identified as a lawgiver or as the supreme good, but rather the crucial agent in the historical drama – the primary actor, the first cause, the dramatist. This picture of the self in relation to God better captures the quality of vitality and surprising freedom that marks all of God's action.

Niebuhr's account is not meant to be exclusively Christian, and at a minimum it succeeds, I think, in being amenable to the other Abrahamic traditions, at least in how it sketches the crucial dimensions of how adherents to any of these three traditions must think of themselves as standing before God. It is a general account, needing much specification, but in emphasizing the way that these traditions see human agency as a response more than an initiatory action, it captures something very important that we must keep in mind in coming chapters.

Conclusion

So things are far more complicated than we might at first assume. Far from simply and straightforwardly reinforcing one another, these traditions' depiction of the relation between God and human morality is alert to the tensions and possible contradictions between them. This is, perhaps, a far darker and more troubled picture than one hopes for, or at least expects. But while it is less comforting, it has the advantage of being true: more accurately representative of the experience of humans over several millennia of attempts to live in faithful relation to this God. Now it is time to turn to the various ways in which the traditions have tried to depict what that "faithful relation" looks like.

2

Jewish Ethics

This chapter, and the two following, are attempts to offer preliminary sketches of the three traditions we'll be studying, using a very broad brush. What are they supposed to teach you? They're very dangerous chapters. They seem to promise real and satisfactory knowledge of the traditions. But in their very abstractness, they promise far more than they can actually deliver. It is too easy to see the traditions' views as systematic, harmonious, and lucid; and it is especially too easy to see them that way when they are treated at some distance from particular issues and from particular attempts to inhabit the tradition and address those issues. Tolstoy famously said that all happy families are alike. This is true of abstract traditions, as well – they all look as shiny and new as used cars on a dealer's lot. It's only when you take them out for a test drive that you begin to get a sense of how they really work.

For these first three chapters on the traditions in general, then, readers should beware. The point of these chapters is not most basically to convey little gobbets of information; they are rather meant to get you to think about these traditions as they discuss the good life and how we ought to think about "moral problems."

The point of these chapters is related to two goals of the book, one pragmatic and the other idealistic. Pragmatically, the book simply wants to unpack these arguments – their basic structures, their key terms, their assumptions about the nature of God, the world, and the human being that they build upon in working out their solutions. But the book's real hope is not simply to increase your stock of information about how people reason. The real hope is that this understanding can help you imaginatively to enter these traditions, to think like an insider. This is why, after a really astonishingly quick and excessively abstract trip through these traditions, most of the book explores attempts to do "ethics from below," so to speak – ethics as it is found in difficult situations that may have some reality in your lives. The point of this is to show you that you're already doing ethics in your ordinary moral discourse, and that you can develop those skills ever more fully – not only so that you speak your own most "native" ethical language, if it happens to be one of the three discussed here, but also so that you attempt to learn something more of one of the other two as well.

With that caveat, we turn now to Jewish ethics.

Election

In the traditional self-understanding of Judaism, the Jews are a race of angels. I don't mean that all individual Jews are good or sweetness and light; that would be a condescending anti-Semitism that is almost as bad as a vicious one. Nor do I mean that Jews are disembodied spirits with wings. Although historically the Jews' emphasis on particularity and fulfilling the concrete obligations of the law have been depicted as supporting Christian anti-Semitism regarding Jewish literalism, such distortions ought not allow us to ignore the fact that Judaism puts a deep importance on incarnation and embodiment and concrete particularity.

When I say that Jews are a race of angels, I mean angels in the original, literal sense of *angeloi*, the Ancient Greek word for "messengers." Jews are, on Judaism's religious self-understanding, *messengers*. They are God's chosen people, the elect, and they are not elected simply to some heavenly salvation (as election means for many Christians). Rather, here election means that the Jews are God's people on earth, representatives of God through whom God "speaks" to the whole world. They tell all others who they are and what to do, so that those others are "placed" by the message with which the Jewish people have been entrusted. As Isaiah puts it, they are to be "a light unto the nations" (Isaiah 49:6, 51:4). They are ambassadors of God, God's messengers.

Their message is twofold: they tell all people who they are – they "place" all of humanity, give them their context and meaning. Secondly, they provide them with a restatement of the basic ethical code that all of humanity is to live by. This is sometimes called the "Noahide Covenant," the covenant God makes with Noah and his descendants after the Flood. On their own self-understanding, the Jewish people are not simply communicating with their words, but in their deeds. They are properly speaking *icons*, symbols of God's will for the world. That is what I mean by calling them angels – something specific, and to our ears somewhat idiosyncratic.

The same is true with my use of the word "race." I do not mean to give the category of race any kind of theological legitimacy. It is first of all a very modern category – before the sixteenth or seventeenth century, the category of "race" in the sense of a strictly biologically determinate inheritance did not exist – and also it is a deeply complicated and fraught category. That is to say, all this talk about identity and the simple identification of some people as "the Jews" is far too simple. Politically, it is obviously dangerous to talk about "the Jews" and name them as a "race" at all. After all, it is precisely such racist categories that underlay the muderous eliminationist anti-Semitism of Nazism, and may continue to play a role in various forms of "ethnic cleansing" even today. Yet Judaism can seem a fundamentally ethnic identity, a "natural" fact, an inescapable ascription. It can seem that

Judaism is the most historically antique and still persisting instance of what we call "identity politics."

But in fact things are much more complicated than this. It is not even religiously licensed to talk about "the Jews" as if they constituted a natural category of human beings. For in a deep sense, no one is "naturally" Jewish. What could this mean? It would mean that God recognized the Jews as already Jewish before Abraham was chosen. But Abraham himself was chosen by God, not for his nature but because he was who God chose. The contemporary American Jewish thinker Daniel Boyarin puts it well: "the biblical story is not one of autochthony [self-origination] but one of always already coming from somewhere else."[1] To be a Jew is to be given a gift from outside oneself, that one has not merited.

The tradition recognizes this in interesting ways. Traditionally, converts in Judaism have their last name changed to "ben Avraham" or "bas Avraham" – son or daughter of Abraham. This not only signifies that the convert has now joined the line of Abraham; it also signifies that Abraham, the original Jew, was also the original convert. As Boyarin puts it, "there is a sense in which Israel was born in exile," and this is as true metaphysically as it is geographically.[2] Whether one is a convert to Judaism or born into it, then, you are given your identity through Abraham, as a gift; who you are, that is to say, is not your own.

Just as the People Israel have a complicated relationship with their own identity, so too have they historically had a complicated picture of the status of the rest of humanity. The "election" of the People Israel does not mean "election" in the contemporary common religious sense (which is implicitly a *Christian* common sense) – an election that is a salvation for one group, from a perdition to which the rest of humanity is condemned. Israel is not in some simple way *saved* by this election. Indeed, in a very important (and for contemporary Jewish thinkers, problematic) way Israel is marked out for special suffering, as a wayward world will respond to God's call to humanity – embodied in the Jews – with hostility and violence. Nor, in Israel's election, is the rest of the world condemned. The election is election into a certain role in the drama of the world's salvation; it is an election *of* one people *for* all the nations.

Because of this, Judaism, unlike both Christianity and Islam, divides the world up into many different moral communities, not simply those who are saved (by being in the "right" community, which is invariably "ours") and those who are not (by being outside that "right" community). Judaism has a fundamentally pluralist mindset about the human race's moral life. Certainly, that plurality is due in part to human moral failure, a shadow cast by humanity's overweening pride, as seen emblematically in Genesis's story of the attempt to build the Tower of Babel. So in some way this plurality is a bad thing. Yet it is not itself a sign that all communities outside that of the Jews are damned.

Indeed, Judaism recognizes a universal code – comprised in the seven Noahide laws, which compose the Noahide Covenant. This covenant forbids idolatry, murder, blasphemy, adultery, theft, and eating flesh from a live animal, and prescribes (most broadly) having "just laws." The Talmud affirms that those who live by this covenant – whom it calls "the righteous among all nations" – will have a share in the world to come.[3] The Jews' particular religious story exists in distinction from this more universal and all-encompassing story of humanity's judgment, as good or bad, by God. In many ways, in fact, Judaism's obligations make the life of a Jew harder, not easier, before God; for not only must they fulfill God's expectations for all humans as set out in the Noahide Covenant, they must also keep faith with the special obligations incumbent upon them rooted in the covenant revealed at Sinai.

The election of the People Israel is election into a particularly demanding relation with God, a relation defined by the covenant God makes with them.

Covenant

The idea of the covenant is crucial here. A "covenant" is an agreement between two parties, detailing the obligations pertaining to each party. It is often compared with a contract, though typically a covenant is understood to be more comprehensive, more powerfully binding, and more difficult to annul than a contract. It implies both a relationship, with its connotations of openness, ambiguity, and growth, and a legal contract, with its connotations of fixity, clarity, and closure. Furthermore, a covenant is typically between two parties of unequal power. In terms of Jewish thought, the covenant that God makes with the people Israel is especially powerful, because it does, in part, create the people Israel in the making of the covenant itself. They become God's chosen people by consenting to live in covenant.

Many Jewish thinkers explicitly affirm that, in some sense, all the Jews who ever were or will be stood at Sinai and made the covenant. As the Passover Haggadah states:

> In every generation one must look upon himself as if he personally had come out of Egypt, as the Bible says: "And you shall explain to your child on that day, 'It is because of what the Lord did for *me* when *I* went free from Egypt'" (Ex. 13:8). For it was not alone our forefathers whom the Holy One, praised be He, redeemed, but He redeemed us together with them, as it is said: "He freed *us* from there to bring us to, and give us, the land that He promised on oath to our forefathers."

And the tradition recognizes its import from the beginning: the highest and in some ways most basic virtue is arguably *emunah*, faith or fidelity to the covenant. Yet the mark of Jewish allegiance is not an inner act of belief, as it is in most of Christianity; the crucial criterion is keeping the commandments that compose the covenant.[4] The covenant, then, is an identity-conferring relationship. When Israel accepts the covenant, it becomes Israel; outside of the covenant, Israel is merely an assemblage of people wandering around the desert. The covenant *names* Israel.

The naming of Israel names God as well. God has become the deliverer, the redeemer, the savior. Where Israel was too weak to save itself, now God has rescued them. This pattern – of weakness or helplessness on humanity's part, and of an extra-ordinary redemptive power on God's part – echoes through the other traditions as well. When the People Israel looked back on the stories of their rescue from Egypt, and understood that event to be foundational to their faith and their community, they did not know how profoundly their realization would affect future generations, and future "branches" of the tree of Abraham.

What they did know, though, was that it was at Sinai, following the rescue from Egypt, that the relation between them and God was decisively realized. It was there that God gave them an identity, and there that God's own identity as the redeemer was revealed. On their own self-understanding, they are that community who on Mount Sinai received the Law, or Torah, who by accepting and living by the Law, keep faithful to the covenant that God made with them. And much of both of those identities was revealed in the object of revelation on Sinai, the tablets of the Law.

Law

What, then, is the Law? The law – *halakah* in Ancient Hebrew – refers most broadly to the Torah, or "the teaching," which is understood to compose both the "written" and "oral" Torah. The written Torah is composed of the "five books of Moses": Genesis, Exodus, Leviticus, Numbers, and Deuteronomy. The oral Torah is composed of the Mishnah (a philosophical law code), Tosefta (another law code), the two Talmuds (the Babylonian Talmud and the Jersualem or Palestinian Talmud), and the Midrash, or commentaries on scripture. The oral Torah is meant to illuminate and elucidate the written Torah, but it itself is hardly an unambiguous set of texts, and has produced manifold interpretive approaches over the centuries.

More literally, the *halakah* is composed of the *mitzvoth*, the commandments, that are found in the written Torah; these number 613. Each of the 613 *mitzvah* that comprise the *halakah* in the narrow sense implies several different obligations as well: 365 proscribe certain things (e.g., "thou shalt not murder"); 248 prescribe other things (e.g., "thou shalt honor your father and mother"); the rabbis thought this was so that there was one prescription given for every day of the year, and one proscription given for each organ in the human body (the rabbis thought there were 248 organs). Though they seem very precise and particular, in fact the *mitzvoth* are meant to inform the whole shape of the righteous person's life – not simply his or her outward conduct, but also their inward being, in order ultimately to enable them to relate rightly to God.

In this way, the Law is not simply an ethical and cultic code, though that code is the medium whereby it is expressed. It is not simply a matter of "thou shalts" and "thou shalt nots." That would be external, even superficial. The Law is not that. The Law saturates life; it is an ethic, as we will see, of "pots and pans," of the deeply mundane as well as the highest human aspirations. Ultimately, the mundaneity is all about a quite high goal – the absolute dignity of all of humanity. The contemporary rabbinics scholar Elizabeth Shanks Alexander suggests that the best description of following the Law is what is found in Psalm 26:11: "to walk with God" and to walk *like* God, as God walks. To follow the Law is to *know God*, which is to *know God's will*, since who God is, is properly known by what God wants (in this, as in so much else, God is unlike us, who don't know what we want, and never want anything fully). And to know God's will is to participate in God's plan for the world, which is a plan governed by law. Thus the Law makes it possible to live in holiness, or *kedushah*. This is why the law has more than merely an aroma of sanctity around it. Indeed, the rabbis defined a heretic as one who claimed that neither justice nor a judge exists – someone, that is, who denies the reality of law.[5]

As so comprehensive, the Law is the vehicle for a flourishing human life. The Law is about life and death – the Law is given so that the people Israel might live by it – and, the rabbis added, "and not die by it." It may be the case that, as I said earlier, Judaism recognizes the ethical equality of all peoples and the capacity of all to live lives pleasing to God; but it is part of God's covenant with the Jews that *this* way of life, as somewhat closer to God than the rest of humanity, is especially pleasing to God. Moses ben Maimon, better known as Maimonides (1135–1204), thought the Law perfected the whole person, body and soul. It does this because it gives those who follow it a privileged way into intimacy with God. Even those elements of the Law which seem (to people today, anyway) most clearly and sheerly identity-establishing for the Jewish community – say, the liturgical commemoration of Passover, or the dietary dictates – mean in part to provoke in the observant contemplation of God's great mercy to humanity, and so to more deeply cultivate a pleasant and joy-producing disposition of gratitude in the believer. Though it comes from "outside" the created order, as God's revelation the Law is not antithetical to that order. Indeed, it enriches and completes that order, from beyond it. Historically, Jews believed that, by living in the Law, they performed a cosmic role in assisting God's will for creation – thereby helping to complete the work of creation itself.

Because of what one may call its supranatural origin, and because it works on its adherents to perfect them over time, obedience to the Law is never finally and fully accomplished. To obey the Law is not something that can be done out of a dry and sterile literalism; obedience must be done, it can *only* be done, out of love for God. And to "receive the Law" is what the Jews do throughout their life. They are always receiving it. It is something that has been given to them already, but it is not yet given to them in its fullness. To be a Jew, on this understanding, is to be caught in a powerful tension between "already" and "not yet," to be waiting, and to be taught to be waiting, for the completion of your very being.

The classically recognized central site for all these debates is the Talmud, wherein the life of the Jewish people is textually exemplified. Scholars normally call "Rabbinic Judaism" the period of Jewish history from the second century CE to the sixth century CE, when the Talmud was in the process of being "fixed." The Talmud has two parts – the Mishnah, or text, and the Gemara, or commentary. There are two *gemara* on the same *mishnah*, namely, the Jerusalem or Palestinian composed in Palestine, and the Babylonian, composed in Babylon; the Babylonian is longer. Often, the name "Talmud" identifies the *gemara*, and so you will sometimes see a text as the "Babylonian Talmud," when the *mishnah* is the same in the Palestinian one. In modernity the status of the Talmud has become more a live topic of debate than it was at any time before. And yet directly through study, and indirectly through its formative influence, in style and content, on the Jewish intellectual traditions, the Talmud remains the central site for Jewish ethical and religious reflection.

What's interesting, from our point of view, about the Talmud is that, as a site of raging legal debate, it enables a debate that offers no final decision on its claims. The Talmud is a classic example of what the Russian literary theorist Mikhail Bakhtin (1895–1975) named *heteroglossia*, a text with a jumble of multiple different voices and types of speech. The Talmud is a jumble of voices which defy hierarchi-calization and organization – even legibility – to any but the trained eye; and the graphic anarchy of the page is mirrored in the experience of encountering the text when one realizes that it is in some sense bottomless, with no definitive authority to whom all others defer.

Yet the Talmud and the Jewish tradition of legal commentary that it embodies is far from a chaotic structure. One can perhaps best understand it by suggesting that it manifests a deep tension within the tradition, a tension between the over-whelming energy of God's revelation, given to humanity, and the need for that energy to be channeled and organized so that humanity might live, and not be consumed, by it. For all its seeming disjointedness and multiplicity, the Talmud is very much a textual manifestation of the People Israel wrestling with God and God's commands. It renders the euphoria of revelation slightly less intoxicating, slightly more sober; it tries to rationalize and stabilize the powerful religious force of faith in a monotheistic living god. This is what the tradition means when it says that "the task of prophecy was taken from the prophets and given to wise men."[6] Even God, the tradition says, studies Torah: God spends a quarter of each working day (three hours) studying Torah, and a further quarter teaching the Torah to schoolchildren.[7]

The Law's open-endedness has profound implications for Jewish eschatology, the tradition's vision of the end times, the ultimate destiny of humanity and the fulfillment for which all of creation was longing from the beginning. As the source of the Law is God, so the goal of the Law itself is messianic – the "Day of the Lord" will come when the Torah given at Sinai is engraved on the human heart, so that all will know the Torah innately. When the Messiah comes, only then will Jews be able properly to engage in full practice of Torah, which will perfect the entire world to serve God together (Zephaniah 3:9). When God's will is done by the People Israel, then the whole world will see how the destiny of Israel is the destiny of all; the destiny of Israel, and the human's ultimate flourishing, is found in studious conversation with God. All dimensions of the Law will be able to be practiced, and thus humanity will be able to fully complete God's commands to them – pleasing both God and humanity (Jeremiah 31:33).

Yet this eschatology is not simply a matter of waiting around for the Messiah. The tradition repeatedly complicates its straightforward proclamations of the

Messiah's arrival with certain moral behaviors that the Jews can do to "hasten" the messianic coming. Indeed, at some times, the tradition suggests, the conditions for the messianic age rely primarily on the behavior of the Jews themselves. As the Talmud reports:

> R. Joshua b. Levi met Elijah standing by the entrance of R. Simeon b. Yohai's tomb. He asked him: 'Have I a portion in the world to come?' He replied, 'if this Master desires it.' R. Joshua b. Levi said, 'I saw two, but heard the voice of a third.' He then asked him, 'When will the Messiah come?' – 'Go and ask him himself,' was his reply. 'Where is he sitting?' – 'At the entrance.' 'And by what sign may I recognize him?' – 'He is sitting among the poor lepers: all of them untie [them] all at once, and rebandage them together, whereas he unties and rebandages each separately, [before treating the next], thinking, should I be wanted, [it being time for my appearance as the Messiah] I must not be delayed [through having to bandage a number of sores].' So he went to him and greeted him, saying, 'Peace upon you, Master and Teacher.' 'Peace upon you, O son of Levi,' he replied. 'When will you come, Master?' asked he. 'Today', was his answer. On his returning to Elijah, the latter enquired, 'What did he say to you?' – 'Peace upon you, O son of Levi,' he answered. Thereupon he [Elijah] observed, 'He thereby assured you and your father of [a portion in] the world to come.' 'He lied to me,' he [R. Joshua] rejoined, 'for he said that he would come today; but he has not.' He [Elijah] answered him, 'This is what he said to you: Today, if you will hear his voice.'[8]

"Today, if you will hear his voice." The Law, that is, perfects life, but it cannot be understood to end or finish it. If anything, receiving the Law makes its adherents ever-hungrier for more life yet to come – for the full ability to delight in God's will and walk in God's ways that will be the great blessing of all humankind upon the Messiah's coming. The Law is both the promise of the eschaton, the end of time, and – if we would but hear the Messiah's voice, which is the voice of the Law – the eschaton itself.

Law and Ethics

All of this raises an interesting question: what, in the Jewish tradition, is exactly the relationship between the discourse on Law and what we might call "religious ethics"? Are they the same, does one encompass but go beyond the other, are they incompatible – what? The relationship between Law and ethics in traditional Judaism – more specifically, whether there is any sort of extra-legal space for ethics – is a matter of serious debate. Much of the debate seems to hang on the anachronistic use of categories such as "ethics," which are arguably absent from much premodern philosophical and religious reflection, and often vaguely used even today.

Clearly, normative questions are at the heart of a great deal of Jewish thought. But much of the energy of the tradition seems taken up with minutiae that seem far afield from what most people today would call ethics. If we think of ethics as the study of the right shape of human life, and the proper nature of the morally charged human action, why is it important to be concerned with meal customs, or with the moral status of menstruating women, or with the amount of work your farm animals can do on certain days of the week? And yet all of these, and many more, are topics taken up in Jewish Law.

If this is so, what exactly is the role of theory and reflection, of philosophy, in Jewish moral life? This is a very deep and fraught issue. Jewish thinkers have, from the earliest ages, argued about the place of Greek philosophical reflection in the tradition. Philo (20 BCE–50 CE) was a significant Jewish thinker who argued for the interpenetration of Greek philosophical tradition and Jewish religious tradition. In the middle ages this debate was focused around two stark positions. On the one hand, Judah Halivni (1086–1145) argued that the God of Abraham and Israel, and the God of the philosophers, have nothing to do with each other. On the other, Maimonides (mentioned earlier) argued that Greek philosophy and the Torah are ultimately coherent, and in fact complement each other in this life. In the modern world the debate is taken up by major thinkers such as Hermann Cohen (1842–1918), in his Kantian interpretation of the Jewish tradition as "ethical monotheism," and Franz Rosenzweig (1886–1929), who argued that thinking *within* Judaism was merely "ornamental," and not fundamental to the faith.

As one might well expect, there is no settled answer to this question, but rather a series of voices offering ever-more thoroughly articulated incompatible views. What is interesting, however, is that the purported concreteness of Judaism is paired with one of the most abstract and universal ethical notions ever elaborated – namely, the idea that each human is made "in the image of God." In Judaism the most mundane is joined to the most metaphysical, with the consequence of this being a blurring of the law/ethics divide, which underscores the need to get beyond the mere "minimal" duty, to genuinely living out the covenant.

This is seen in the idea in Jewish ethics that there is a tacit obligation to act *lifnim mishurat hadin* – beyond the line of the law, beyond the bare minimum. That is to say, the rabbis recognize a "morality of aspiration," but law can be aspriational as well – aiming to be moral.[9] Even as the law is a baseline, it always reaches beyond itself, toward a higher sense of righteousness.

Given all this, it is well worth our while to study the tradition from the bottom up – to begin with what occupies the tradition, to see it in action – before we can get to our more grandiose themes. That is what we will do next.

A focus on the mundane

In terms of the material points, Jewish ethics is marked by a profound focus on the everyday, the mundane. The contemporary American-Jewish thinker Menachem Marc Kellner has gone so far as to say that it is "a religion of pots and pans in the eyes of those who derogate its concern with actions," one that "contains minutely detailed teachings regulating that behavior."[10] In this it is less like Christianity and more like Islam, at least as the latter has developed into an overall cultural system. Both attend to matters which seem, from the perspective of those of us from a Christian heritage (whether we are Christian believers or not), fundamentally matters of unimportance for one's spiritual life.

Why is there such an emphasis on the mundane in this tradition? Obviously the reasons are manifold, but here is one moral point: perhaps it entails a savvier recognition of the limits of human achievement. There is an emphasis on justice, on sufficiency, on mere decency, as enough of an aim. Do not try to shoot too high in your expectations of yourselves or one another; it is enough to respect your neighbor. Do not ask to be caught up in a soul-ravishing love of God at all times; it is sufficient to remember certain rules of decorum, and a certain etiquette of behavior. Faith need not be extraordinary; indeed, faith can flourish best, the tradition says, when it is woven into the everyday patterns of our everyday life. So here is one take at an answer to the question of the relation between law and ethics: ethics is rooted in law – and ethics is not a matter of hearing the divine command or a radical conversion of the heart, but the simple and difficult practice of listening and obedience.

If that is one moral reason, here is one theological reason: in this tradition, the minutiae of behavior shine out in transfiguration because of God's election of the people, and their life, as revelatory of God's will. All action thus has *iconic* import – import as revealing something, if it is proper, of God's purposes for the world, and thus of God's will towards the world. This gives action a powerful, effectively unsurpassable quality as revealing God's will. Action has moral dignity because it is *theophanic* – revealing of God and God's purposes.

From the mundane to the image and likeness of God

So the connection between the minutiae of the ethical code and the absoluteness of the moral demand is both deep and strong, and is anchored in the perception that God has ordained such meticulous attention to behavior as revelatory of God's purposes for humanity as a whole. But how is this relationship effected? What is the relationship between the mundane character of much of what Jewish ethics discusses, and the profound sanctity that it ascribes to those mundane actions? More specifically, how does Jewish thought relate respect for neighbor to awe before God? The Jewish tradition is well known as instigating the idea that humanity was made in God's "image" (ancient Hebrew, *tselem*) and "likeness" (*demuth*). The primordial scriptural text here – Genesis 1:26 – is straightforward: God says, "Let us make man in our image, after our likeness." This idea – that the human bears in some distinctive way the stamp of God's being, that humans are, in some sense, an "echo" of God – is decisive for the later traditions of Christianity and Islam as well. But how exactly does the tradition understand and articulate this relationship?

Here is one interpretation of the relationship. One might say that Jewish faith, and also Christianity and Islam following it, has at its core a sense of the radical sovereignty of God – the way that God stands absolutely outside of the created order, existing both "before" and "beyond" it, and, as Creator, as the source of the creation itself. The apprehension of this radical sovereignty, and its representation in ritual, in worship, and in the moral life of the community, serves as the experiential foundation of faith. (By "foundation" I mean not necessarily the beginning, but the most fundamental apprehension of God in this tradition.) The tradition naturally finds its moral obligations to be rooted in this apprehension as well. In some way, then, the religious awe that is at the core of the faith – the awe at the God who moved over the deep before creation came into being – is, it is argued, in some distant way the same awe that we should feel before each human. To say that humanity bears the image of God is to say something to the effect that humanity bears an unqualified and absolute moral value precisely insofar as it participates in God's value. In this way to disrespect humans is to suggest that God does not bear this absolute value; conversely, to respect others is to worship God. Thus, right behavior towards others is not simply a good thing because God commands it; it is a good thing because in some fundamental way you reveal your relationship to God, to the source of all being, in your treatment of your fellow humans. Ironically, then, a tradition that emphasized the radical otherness of God – the way that this God was not conditioned by the cosmos, but was the cause of the cosmos – was the one that first formulated the idea that humans, just by the bare fact of their humanity, bear some absolutely fundamental analogy with the divine, an analogy which invests them with a certain kind of absolute value that they would otherwise not possess.

There is a problem here, however, in the tension between what we might call the objective demand for justice and fairness, and the inescapable fact that our actual valuing of other humans is clearly shaped by, if not determined by, the particularities of our subjective valuing of them. We simply love some people more than others, and treat them differently. We have "special attachments" to some people that we do not have to others. So we care more about our family and friends than we do about strangers we pass on the street. How can we confront this problem of basic interpersonal inequality?

The tradition recognizes this difficulty and grasps it at its most difficult point. Fairly early on, in Leviticus, we get this famous insistence: "Do not hate your brother in your heart. Rebuke your neighbor frankly so you will not share in his guilt. Do not seek revenge or bear a grudge against one of your people, but love your neighbor as yourself. I am the Lord" (Leviticus 19:17–18).

The legal demand for equality can be related to the ethical and psychological reality of inequality by recognizing from the beginning that each person has the same, which is to say infinite, value in God's eyes. The best way to realize this, the tradition seems to say, is to understand that you are to value others just as much as you value yourself.

In making us grasp the value of others only by equating it with how we value ourselves, it raises a question: does it mean how we *should* value ourselves, or how we *in fact do* value ourselves? By doing this, the tradition makes us recognize the distance between how we normally perceive ourselves and others. More concretely, it makes us recognize how inegalitarian we are, and sets us the moral task of reducing that inequality, at least somewhat, over the course of our lives.

But the danger here now becomes that we will reimagine ethics as the task of expanding our selfishness and self-centeredness to include others in our narcissism. That is far from the point. So, in order to escape the sheer subjectivism of this starting point, we must come to see other people, in their otherness, as worthy of respect. For the truth is our self-love is not itself a morally righteous kind of love; it is selfish and grasping. What looked at first like the gold standard of ethical treatment turns out, upon closer inspection, to be itself ethically inadequate.

Yet the tradition recognizes that, in themselves and on their own, other people do not easily provoke such respect in us. The tradition's response to this fact is significant. Instead of most fundamentally scolding us, and insisting that they *should* provoke such respect in us and then growing angry with our flawed moral sensibilities when they do not, the tradition makes another claim: the ontological source of their honor comes from their peculiar relationship with God. Their honor, that is, is derivative from God's honor, and our capacity to respect them, it seems, stands in some sort of organic relationship with our pious reverence before God. When we honor them rightly, that is, we are also honoring the God who made them and graced them with the divine image. This encourages humility on our part and, when joined to our ability to love particular people, offers the motivational basis for a moral psychology that demands that all be treated with a certain radical respect.

This idea of the human as "created in the image of God" and somehow bearing God's image in the realm of creation – not unlike how the Jews as a people are God's messengers on earth – is one of the most powerful of religious insights in any of these traditions, and indeed one of the most important things that Judaism bequeathed to Christianity and Islam. The central idea here is remarkably daring: humanity, in some unique way, is valuable, above and beyond other things in God's creation, because it bears some special similarity to God. This has powerful, directly ethical effects. As the *Tractate Sanhedrin* says, "the first person [Adam] was created alone, in order to teach you that whoever causes the death of any person, scripture regards him as if he destroyed a whole world; while one who sustains the life of any person, is regarded as one who maintains an entire world."[11]

But this affirmation also has serious ontological, cosmological, and theological implications. For many thinkers today see this assertion of a link between the human and God as one of the most powerful forces indirectly motivating our disastrous contempt for non-human creation. Ecologically minded thinkers find this vision calamitous in that it encourages us, they think, to degrade the import of non-human creation even to the point of not caring about it at all. We will see in later chapters that this concern is a real and vexing one for many today.

Whatever its ecological implications, however, its ethical implications for interhuman relations cannot be gainsaid. To affirm that humans are created in the image and likeness of God is to affirm that in facing another human you are facing a creature whose value to the universe, and for God, is significantly proportionate to God's value – that, however distant, there is some positive relation between God's worth and this creature's. This does not denigrate God, however, or subject God to an earthly metric; it elevates the human. In confronting a person, you confront someone of intrinsically immeasurable worth; and however you choose to value them for the quirks of their personality, or the charm of their voice, you must honor and respect what they are in themselves.

Yet you encounter a person when you encounter yourself just as much as when you encounter another; and Judaism, particularly because of its sustained engagement with Christian and post-Christian rhetorics of radical self-emptying love, is profoundly worried about an excessive, even narcissistic, fixation on self-abnegation in ethics. This does not mean that Judaism does not see humility as crucial; certainly, Judaism counsels humility in its faithful. Humility is important as a check on pride, the temptation humans have to violate one another's integrity and so to dishonor them. But humility is different from self-humiliation, and rabbinic ethics is against the latter as strongly as it is for the former, and for fundamentally the same reason: one must always respect the basic integrity of individuals as bearing the image of God, and that commandment extends over the self as much as it does to others. One has duties to others, but one also has duties to oneself, and the duties to oneself can in fact trump the duties to others. There is no in-principle demand to subordinate the self, in the name of self-denial, to the service of one's fellows.

Conclusion: The Challenge of Modernity

As we will see with all three of these traditions, Judaism has struggled to discern how to retain a grip on its adherents in the modern age. Modernity as a social, cultural, and intellectual revolution has put challenges to these traditions that they have confronted more or less well – and that they continue to confront today. Before ending this chapter, we should say something about those challenges and how they complicate a simple appropriation of premodern resources for modern Jews.

The challenges we could enumerate here are manifold. Let me focus on four. First, Judaism faces a series of challenges to its understanding and practice of authority. On the one hand, traditional Jewish authority has been challenged by the modern world's undermining, in many people's eyes, of the conviction that the history of the Bible tells the literal truth about the world; that is to say, the authority of the Bible, and of the traditions associated with it, looks far more shaky today than it did four hundred years ago. On the other hand, just as traditional sources of authority have been undercut, rival understandings of what constitutes an authoritative source have appeared; most obviously the Enlightenment philosophical idea that humans ought to think for themselves, and exercise autonomy and independence in their moral and religious deliberations, is a powerful goad and motivation for individuals to begin to resist traditional recommendations to accept what the tradition has taught without question.

Major Jewish thinkers have engaged with both of these challenges. Figures such as Baruch Spinoza and Franz Rosenzweig struggled in their work with the meaning of tradition and authority. On the autonomy of the individual, thinkers like Moses Mendelssohn on the one hand, and Hermann Cohen and Meir Soloveitchick and Martin Buber on the other, all struggled with the meaning of, in Soloveitchick's phrase, "the lonely man of faith's" fidelity to the covenant. These debates profoundly – if at times, invisibly – shape the character of the explicitly ethical debates we will study in coming chapters, so that questions of the proper nature of authority, and the relative weight to give different sources of authority, will repeatedly appear as central issues in surprising ways.

Second, modern Judaism faces a series of challenges to its received cultural and social norms. For almost the entirety of the past two millennia Jews lived largely as outsiders in the societies they inhabited, forced to live in ghettos and suffering grievous persecution. The evil and inhumanity of this reality is, for readers of this book, I hope, relatively well known. But modernity saw the collapse of many of these prejudices, and the rich integration of Jews into many majority Christian (or post-Christian) societies. This integration has been obviously for the good. But it has led to one problem: the marginalization of Jewish communities had been one way for those communities to ensure their coherence and continuity into the next generation. Integration has created a situation where questions of Jewish identity are profoundly in play in a way and with a centrality that they have not possessed for a very long time, if ever. Questions of what is "authentically" Jewish or "truly" Jewish (and for some assimilationists, "too" Jewish) create a range of challenges that contemporary Jews, even those living in the self-confessedly Jewish State of Israel, must confront. Again, these issues, we will see, shadow the debates of Jewish thinkers on moral behavior, and especially "authentic" Jewish behavior, in many complicated ways.

Third, along with the integration of the Jews in modernity, a certain pattern of social relations, best understood as "patriarchy," has also come under siege. As is the case with all three traditions, Judaism has been an intensively male-centered religion. The reasons for this certainly have something to do with the social settings in which each tradition found itself; but it is folly to deny that each has, in its own way, lived in a symbiotic relation with a male-centered social order – reinforcing its strictures on women's second-class membership far more than some of those traditions' representative intellectuals ever challenged those strictures. With the emergence of a modern social and economic order, however, the patriarchal social structures that had been so long in place were unable to be sustained anymore. The new challenges of social equality and non-differentiation have served as a powerful goad to rethink the shape and nature of the obligations of the Jewish people as regards the Law.

Fourth, and in a way distinct to Jewish thought, there is a properly theological crisis brought on by the Holocaust, or what Jews typically call the Shoah, the Hebrew word for "calamity." ("Holocaust" is a Greek word that means "burnt offering," and most Jews do not think of the Shoah as an "offering" to God, but as a crime against God as much as against the People Israel, and the human race in general.) It is hard to overemphasize the impact of the Holocaust on Jewish thought, though it has taken several generations, so far, to be felt. It is hard to explain fully the felt shape of the reality of the Shoah to Jewish thinkers. There had developed, over the millennia, a certain kind of Jewish "theodicy" – a vision of why God allowed evil to befall creation, and in particular why God allowed the Jews to suffer as much as they did, repeatedly. (Murderous pogroms and riots against Jews by Christians (and others) are recorded as beginning no later than the third century CE.) But the event of the Shoah is so vast as to negate comparisons with any previous brutality against the Jews; it raised profound questions about the meaning of God's purposes for Israel, questions that last pressed upon the whole People Israel with anything like this intensity only with the destruction of the Temple in Jerusalem by the Romans in 70 CE. The effect of this in Jewish life and thought has already been felt, of course, but like that earlier calamity, the changes may take several centuries to sort themselves out.

We could go on forever, or at least for several entire books, on any one of these challenges – as indeed we could go on as well for any of the topics discussed earlier in this chapter. But this will have to do for a orienting introduction to the dimensions and dynamics of this tradition. Pretty much every claim put forward in this chapter will be challenged, nuanced, and contradicted in coming pages. For now, however, we will turn to the other traditions to try to get an initial grip on them in a similar, all-too superficial way.

3

Christian Ethics

I am biased. I come to this book with my own values, and see things from a particular perspective. This does not invalidate my claims. After all, non-perspectival accounts of things such as religion are simply impossible, and in fact I think my perspective is the right one. (That's no surprise, of course; anyone who holds a view seriously, and who is not insane, thinks it is the right one.)

But my perspective on things may seem, from time to time, odd to you. And I warn you, for this chapter in particular, my view of "Christianity" is indelibly shaped by my being a Christian of the general Protestant variety. So non-Protestant Christians, Roman Catholics and Eastern Orthodox, may find my views odd or confused. And Protestants will probably disagree as well. I hope you all feel free to contest what I say. The point here is simply to get us to think in a new and potentially richer way about these religious traditions. Use what I say in that light.

Ironically, my proximity to the material where Christianity is concerned offers its own challenges to objectivity. Normally, we think that proximity to a subject, familiarity with it, makes our knowledge of it more firm, more solid. But in the case of religions, I think you'll agree, proximity seems to render someone's claims more questionable, not less. Being an "insider" means, it seems, that you're more likely to present a sunny, or at least a slanted, picture of your tradition. So there are different challenges to objectivity, and we must be alert to all of them.

I judge that most readers of this book live in majority Christian cultures (or at least "culturally Christian" cultures), and so will of necessity be familiar with some of the rudiments of the Christian religion – its calendar (especially the holidays of Easter and Christmas), its institutions, its basic story. Because of this, my aim in this chapter, unlike the chapters on Judaism and Islam, is not to offer a detailed outline of Christian faith. In a manner that is not true for those other traditions, when it comes to Christianity, people in our society are more likely to miss the forest for the trees, and ignore the big themes because they know some collection of minutiae. So here I will assume that most people reading this book will be roughly familiar with some of the practices and beliefs of Christians, and I will try to say something directly about what those practices and beliefs *mean*.

In the service of that aim, I offer three propositions about Christianity and ethics, which will inform my exposition and which I think decisively shape Christian ethical reflection historically and today:

1   Christianity is a religion for losers.
2   Christians are not called on to be just; they are called on to love.
3   "Ethics is sin" – that is, ethical deliberation is deeply problematic.

Let me say something about each of these in turn.

Christianity is a Religion for Losers

Christianity is a religion of human failure and defeat, human weakness and frailty – about losers. The central message of Christianity is that Christ – the Messiah, the savior – redeems humans, because they are helpless to do it themselves. That's bad enough. But what's worse is that Christ succeeds by failing: by dying. And one iconic (quite literally) image for Christianity is of Christ portrayed as dying, betrayed and abandoned, on a cross. Yes, of course, Christ is resurrected – but we cannot rush to salvation, the tradition says, without going through death; we cannot win until we have lost. The gospel narratives recount a story of people failing and betraying Jesus, and being saved despite themselves. In fact, the most important thing about Christians seems often to be that they die – they die to themselves, they die to the world, they die to death, and are reborn.

This may sound shocking and abhorrent, even impious. But why does it seem that way? Nowhere have I said this is reason to mock Christianity, or Christians, or Christ. Indeed, it seems to me that a religion built around defeat in this way has a great deal of support from reality. Most of us *are* losers. You do the math – most lives end sad, defeated, despairing. The odds aren't good. Failure, on any measure, seems more common than success. Yet when we say this, it sounds shocking or outrageous. But why? Why is that so hard to say? Why so difficult to admit?

Crucifixion and resurrection will inevitably trouble our received moral assumptions. But from the tradition's perspective, that's fine and dandy; for those assumptions should be troubled; we need to see how deeply deceptive they are, the tradition says, in order for us to break out of the profound lies that we inhabit. Christianity suggests that our resistance to thinking about our predicament is itself important – significant of the profundity of the human predicament, the calamity humanity has inflicted upon itself, and of the deep terror we feel at admitting it to ourselves. For if we must admit that our troubles are far greater than we could ever hope to solve, how are we to be redeemed?

All this is to say, Christianity insists that the most dramatic truth about the human condition, considered on its own, is the *failure* of human agency to achieve anything like what it sets out to accomplish. Humans lose agential priority in this account; we are simply not the most important actors in the cosmos. Because humans are saved by another, we do not do the most important work in our world. On this account, as in Judaism and Islam, the central actor is God – in creation, in sustaining that creation, in the work accomplished in the salvation effected by Christ, and finally in eschatology and apocalypse. Even before the Fall, humans were not primarily actors but receivers of action – not most fundamentally creators but creatures, created by God and loved by God. Humans do not accomplish things on this view; humans are *accomplished*. All of Christian ethics takes place in the light of this complicated insistence that humans are, in the German Reformer Martin Luther's phrase, "more acted upon than acting." And the fundamental Christian moral task is suitably captured in terms of *waiting* for God's action, not aiming first and foremost to build the kingdom of God on earth.

Because this tradition depicts the human in far more dire straits than is elsewhere the case, it depicts the human problematic not most basically as a question of achieving goodness, but of escaping evil – as in need of dramatic rescue. In contrast to Judaism, which emphasizes the naturally weak and fallible character of human beings, and perhaps Islam, which underscores the ability of humans to overcome their weaknesses, Christianity emphasizes *sin*, and a certain picture of sin at that – sin as slavery, sin as servitude. Humans are not simply flimsy, folly-filled creatures, we are often *malicious* and egotistical, and our follies are rooted in a primal flaw that we cannot escape in this life. And because of this condition, humans should aim to be, not first and foremost virtuous, but saved.

This insistence on failure runs against the grain of human understanding and expectation, and thus entails a second major claim of Christianity: namely, that there is a rather dramatic gap between what the Christian God expects of people and what intelligent people have understood to be the contours of a truly flourishing life. Christian ethics is more exercised by the difference between these two visions than is either Judaism or Islam. It does not so quickly assume that "the good" is easily or naturally known. It assumes that we are in profound need of illumination and outside guidance on this matter. Christianity assumes that humans do not actually know what's good for them, or that their knowledge of what's good for them is profoundly obscured. This is another way in which Christianity is a religion for losers. It is a religion for people who do not trust their own impressions of the way things are.

The implications of this account for Christian ethics are quite profound. Christians have to "realize" their sinfulness, to come to grasp it, for it is only thereby, the tradition affirms, that humans can receive grace. But does this realization occur "before" you are saved, or can one only see the depths to which one had fallen from the heights of salvation itself? What, that is, is the relationship between being accepted or rejected, between being judged and being forgiven? Some Christian thinkers say that you recognize your sinfulness first and then accept grace (the twentieth-century American Protestant theologian Reinhold Niebuhr once said that sin is the only empirically confirmable doctrine that Christians have). Others affirm that the experience of acknowledging one's sin may be the primary act of the Christian believer, but they argue that that acknowledgment's priority is not onto-logical but merely temporal – that the capacity to recognize one's sins is itself a gift of grace (the twentieth-century Swiss Protestant theologian Karl Barth once said that only Christians sin). Both sides agree, however, that proper apprehension of one's fallen state is a sign of the enormous gap between the way things normally happen in our world and the way God wants them to happen. And for humans to begin to function as they are meant to function, they must undergo a radical trans-formation, away from their habituated patterns and into a new kind of life – a radical alteration in one's being, captured in Greek by the word *metanoia*. They must become what the Apostle Paul called "a New Creation" (2 Corinthians 5:17).

How does this change happen? Questions about the precise nature of this trans-formation inevitably run up against the paradoxical nature of the language that Christianity has often used to describe this transformation. What look like intelli-gible phrases become obscure and impenetrable when one begins to try seriously to understand them. How can "the old" become "the new"? How is one "born again"? If in this life we are in death, how are we to be resurrected?

The extremity of the language is not simply meant to be poetic, but to capture something of the radicality of the proposal. The changes in the individual, from sinner to justified, are not simply a matter of a change in one's opinions. The change in vision required here is brought about by a change in the person's desire-structure – what it is they think is valuable, what it is they intuitively want – and a concomi-tant change in their will – what it is they try to do. This radicality is required, again, because of the depth of the calamity afflicting the human. There is no depth or level from which humans can act to repair themselves, no inner oasis of purity from which we can begin the necessary renovations. We must be saved; we will not save ourselves. This is what St. Paul means when he says, in his letter to the Philippians, "work out your own salvation with fear and trembling; for it is God who works in you, enabling you both to will and to work, for his good pleasure" (Philippians 2:12–13).

All this is to say that the status of "the world" in Christianity is far more fraught and unstable than in Judaism or Islam. Christianity from its earliest days imbibed a leaven of apocalypticism that made it always uneasy about the standards and adequacy of the world, both for good and for ill. Theoretically speaking, there are actually two categories of "the world" in Christian thought – the world as the created order that God intended it to be, and the world as the *fallen* world that humanity inhabits today, East of Eden. But by and large, when Christians start talking about "the world" today, they typically do not mean the first, good, sense of the term. Christians will typically get nervous quickly if others suggest that their faith fits well in the world.

In part because of this complicated understanding of the necessity of the world's rescue, and the priority of God's action before the world's significances, this tradi-tion has spent a good bit more time than Judaism or Islam have on the character of the rescuer. Speculation about God is rampant in this tradition, and much of the tradition is occupied with debates about the nature of this God – for this God's identity is simultaneously more important and more obscure than it is in the other traditions. In Judaism God has satisfactorily articulated what God expects in the covenant with Israel, and inquiry focuses on the meaning of the covenant. In Islam God's intentions are perfectly and fully expressed in the Qur'an, and so inquiry has focused on the meaning of that text. Only in Christianity is God's will positively obscured by the story, especially given its many surprises; and yet it is in Christianity where the will that guides that story is quite literally life-saving.

Because of this, for Christians, sacred doctrine is revealed theology about God, while for Jews and Muslims, sacred doctrine is the legal interpretation of the Divine Law – the interpretation of Talmud for Jews, the practice of *fiqh* for Muslims. The latter sense of sacred doctrine is less amenable to interpretation in strictly philosophical terms. This is one reason why Christians are more prone than Jews or Muslims to use philosophical sources that do not originate in Christian thought-forms, even though Christians have a much more troubled picture of the relationship between how the world presently is, and how it was meant to be and will ultimately be again, at the end of time.

This is especially important because Christianity has come to believe that the act of believing certain things about this God is intrinsic to, or efficacious of, salvation. Of the three Abrahamic faiths, only in Christianity can the faithful be reasonably called "believers" first and foremost.

Beliefs about this God are legion, but they tend to focus on three claims about God: (1) this God is the Creator, from whom all things derive their existence and to whom all owe gratitude for that existence; (2) this God is the sustainer, from whom all good things come, by whom all things flourish, and to whom all owe gratitude for their ongoing existence and delight in the world; and (3) this God is the redeemer, who will in the end secure the healing of the elect, and allow them to enter into the full flourishing of their lives as God intends them to do. We should say something about each of these claims:

- *This God is the creator, from whom all things derive their existence and to whom all owe gratitude for that existence.* As creator, God stands "behind" Creation and so nature has a noumenal power and possibly a theophanic (God-revealing) capacity.
- *This God is the sustainer, from whom all good things come, by whom all things flourish, and to whom all owe gratitude for their ongoing existence and delight in the world.* As sustainer, this God underpins all human efforts at righteousness, and is the sustaining moral energy of all our efforts to be good.
- And *this God is the redeemer, who will in the end secure the healing of the elect, and allow them to enter into the full flourishing of their lives as God intends them to do.* So God's aims for humans are God's own, and often beyond humanity's understanding, and so the Christian moral life stands in some sort of suspension before an eschatological "last judgment" that renders the meaning and significance of all of our actions somewhat provisional before that last judgment.

As we shall see, these three claims all, in complicated ways, inflect the explicitly ethical claims that Christians make in surprising ways.

The claim that "Christianity is a religion for losers" is thus helpful in several ways, in getting us to understand some of the more complicated dynamics of the Christian tradition. But it is also useful because it frankly identifies a theme, or a motif, in Christianity that has provoked some of the tradition's harshest critics. And that is this: Christianity can sound *too* good to be true. It can sound like the projected wishes of those who have never gotten what they wanted in their lives. It can seem like a beautiful hothouse flower, blossoming out of a manure of resentment. This is how profound critics of Christianity, like Friedrich Nietzsche, thought of it. Nietzsche thought that Christianity was really simply an expression of "slave morality," the systematized longings of the world's oppressed for a world in which they are not enslaved. And Nietzsche thought that this fact – Christianity's very powerful attractiveness – was actually one of the most powerful pieces of evidence against Christianity's plausibility. *Of course*, he argued, this religion is powerful just because it offers such beautiful consolation for the harshness of the world. But given that our experience of the world is such that such consolations must always be deferred to an indefinite future, is not the happiness of this story more than a little suspicious? This worry is good to keep in mind, as Christianity's idealism sometimes will appear to be *too* idealistic – all-too-easily taken in far too idealistic directions.

Christians Are Not Called on to be Just; They Are Called on to Love

The second claim about Christianity follows, in a roundabout way, from the first. Justice is not immediately a matter of primary concern for Christians; its role always seems subsidiary to love. This is not to say that Christians cannot be concerned about justice, but rather that justice typically seems to them somehow secondary, derivative, perhaps deficient. The tradition demands that Christians hold themselves to a higher standard.

This insistence on the primacy of love relates to the character of the God affirmed above. For on this vision the primary fact about creatures, and especially humans, is that they are desired and loved by God. As the Christian theologian David Ford says:

> People are desired by God. At [Christianity's] heart is trust in being overwhelmingly desired by a God who loves them. They are created by God, blessed by God, addressed by God, chosen and called by God, forgiven by God, taught by God, and given God's Son and Spirit. In other words, any activity of theirs is rooted in a radical passivity. How this passivity relates to human activity is perhaps the most basic issue of all in Christian ethics.[1]

To understand love, then, is to grasp something of a key to how Christians are supposed to understand their being. Love is not just an emotional coloring to their world, on this account; the Christian faith claims that it is an ontological fact about reality. As the Apostle John wrote, "whoever does not love does not know God, because God is love" (1 John 4:8).

Love is a weird thing, simultaneously passive and active. Indeed, in a way it is more fundamentally passive than active. If we think of love as something wider than sexually erotic attraction, we see that experiences of "falling in love" – with friends, books, professions, preoccupations – are far more common in our lives than a narrow fixation on romance will lead us to believe. We never choose love, pick it from a menu of equally viable, equally distant options; we discover that we are already in love, already mixed up with the other, our fates intertwined. Only then, after we discover we are in love, does our voluntary agency play a role; for then we must decide what to do about our newly recognized condition.

This passivity is not just experienced in love. It is found in experiences of being chosen, being forgiven, being called. Christians experience themselves, or are disciplined by their faith into experiencing themselves, as fundamentally recipients of God's action upon them. Out of God's primary love to humanity, then, Christians are called upon to love God back and to love what God loves, and in the way God loves it – to participate in God's love. Christian ethical practices are then forms of obedience that often move towards participation, and can in some religious communities culminate in *deification*, in becoming God-like.

What does this love mean for the behavior of human beings today, in this world? Consider two passages from the New Testament, passages that have deeply informed the development of Christian ethics. The first is from Paul's letter to the Philippians, about what exactly God calls Christians to do in imitation of Christ:

> If then there is any encouragement in Christ, any consolation from love, any fellowship in the Spirit, any compassion and sympathy, make my joy complete, that you be of the same mind, having the same love, being in full accord, and of one mind. Do nothing through faction or conceit, but in humility regard others as better than yourselves. Let each of you not look to your own interests, but to the interests of others. Let the same mind be in you, that was in Christ Jesus: who, though he was in the form of God, did not regard equality with God a thing to be grasped, but emptied himself, taking the form of a slave, being born in human likeness. And being found in human form, he humbled himself, becoming obedient to the point of death – yes, even death on a cross. (Philippians 2:1–8)

Here, the paradigmatically good act is to "empty" oneself, to humble oneself, to become a servant of others. This "emptying" (in the New Testament's Greek, *kenosis*) suggests a radicality of commitment that recapitulates, perhaps even goes beyond, Abraham's near-sacrifice of Isaac. It requires a deeply mobile self, a self that is remarkably sensitive to what others lack, and what they need, and that is able to move to help them immediately, heedless of what it costs. Indeed, in several of the gospels Jesus is reported to command his followers to love their enemies (Luke 6:27–29; Matthew 5:38–44). Such a love requires a self that is not too committed to itself, or – again, as with Abraham – that has any attachments in the world that would cause it to hesitate before helping the other.

To most Christians today, this will seem pretty extreme; does this really mean what it suggests? Many early Christians seem to have thought so; as the next passage from the Gospel of Luke attests, they saw insuperable difficulties in following Jesus if you have deep attachments to other people:

> Now large crowds were traveling with him; and he turned and said to them, "Whoever comes to me and does not hate father and mother, wife and children, brothers and sisters, yes, and even life itself, cannot be my disciple. Whoever does not carry the cross and follow me cannot be my disciple. For which of you, intending to build a tower, does not first sit down and estimate the cost, to see whether he has enough to complete it? Otherwise, when he has laid a foundation and is not able to finish, all who see it will begin to ridicule him, saying, 'This fellow began to build and was not able to finish.' Or what king, going out to wage war against another king, will not sit down first and consider whether he is able with ten thousand to oppose the one who comes against him with twenty thousand? If he cannot, then, while the other is still far away, he sends a delegation and asks for the terms of peace. So therefore, none of you can become my disciple if you do not give up all your possessions." (Luke 14:25–33)

What kind of a religion is it that demands that you love your enemies and hate your family? The African theologian Augustine of Hippo (354–430) once asked his congregation that in a sermon; it is a good question for Christians in any age.

"God is love." If God is so defined by radical excess, then it is no wonder that Christians are so haunted by calls to endless acts of self-sacrificial extremity; all that stands in the way of that vision being perfectly realized is the stubborn recalcitrance of human nature to return always to the familiar sights and smells of home. There is thus an absolutism and stringency to the demands put on human beings, and throughout history this absolutism has eventuated in a repeated dynamic of Christians developing a conviction that the world as they find it is inescapably hostile to their calling, so that they must flee from the world, as in monasticism, or transform the world, as in the various waves of reform that have suffused Christian history.

Christianity's focus on love makes it harder for Christians than some others to accept an "ethic of reciprocity." Justice – reciprocity – is a matter of a zero-sum game; there is something of a whiff of selfishness about demands for justice, on many Christian accounts. The Christian worldview does not suggest that there is just enough to go around. It says instead that the world is marked by *excess* at every stage – excess of goodness in creation, excess of sin and rebellion in the Fall, excess of gratuitous mercy in the Son's mission in creation. Jesus's teachings reflect this by *radicalizing* morality: we should not do things for some future reward, but as a reflexive response to the way things are, an outflowing of love.

Whether or not this was Jesus's intent, the troubling of the language of justice has from an early stage, and repeatedly, been a mark of Christian moral-theological rhetoric. (It is not the case that justice dropped out of discussion in Christian thought, obviously; but Christian efforts to work straightforwardly for justice are always shadowed by a theological hesitation about the this-worldly earnestness of the effort.) The language of "justice" is complicated in Christian thought, because it combines what we might see as this-worldly justice and what we might see as other-worldly righteousness of the holy. St. Paul combines the ancient Hebrew terms *mishpat* (judgment) and *tsedeqah* (righteousness or justice) in his use of the Greek term *dikaiosune*, or equity, treating it as "righteousness" pure and simple, with Christ as the "just man," which can be known because of Christ's love for humanity. Thus, in being "just" we are to love; as Romans 13:8 says, "Owe no one anything but love; for he that loves his neighbor, has fulfilled the law." Justice should have no independent weight on this interpretation. While this is a bit extreme, Christians have come close to saying it – or indeed have said it – many times in the past, do so in the present, and in all likelihood will continue to do so in the future.

One does not have to think hard, as a modern person, before a whole host of questions present themselves about this understanding of the relationship between justice and love. Certainly, many questions of fairness arise here as concerns about whether the Christian faith's expectations are, properly speaking, superhuman.

More than that, thinkers within and without the Christian faith have often asked questions about the easy sentimentality of claims like this. Is it really possible, they ask, to imagine a workable ethics for the world we inhabit that is indifferent to justice? Is it realistic to imagine that all you *really* need is love? Real questions on this front remain. There are many situations in which the call to sacrifice yourself is easily employed by the strong over against the weak; and in fact women especially have been taught a form of Christian behavior which seems to hinder their capacity for self-assertion, even in the face of manifest and massive injustice. The emphasis on love can sound dangerously blind to its own hypocrisy. Can you live in the world on the basis of love alone?

"Ethics is Sin"

Like Judaism (and as we will soon see, like Islam as well), Christianity suspects individual attempts to figure things out. To reason ethically seems to be an attempt to try to figure out what to do – which is often an attempt to try to figure out what you can get away with doing, without being blamed for doing it. Because of this, ethical deliberation in Christianity, when it occurs, typically tries to understand itself as a matter of obedience, not independent decision. Christians are supposed to *wait* until they have discerned what God is calling on them to do. Recall H. Richard Niebuhr's *"responsible* self": an emphasis on receptivity and a suspicion of seizing primacy in action is embedded deeply in the Christian mindset.

Nonetheless, Christians are called to do things, and this action requires deliberation on their part. The main task of Christians is twofold, and can be understood as embodying two different forms of responding to God's redemption of humanity.

The first is forming the church, and acting within it to proclaim the gospel to the world; the other is coming to see oneself in a new light. In both of these actions, Christians typically are taught to see their own agency as fundamentally secondary.

On the one hand, Christian responsibility takes shape as a loving and grateful response to God's gracious action in Christ for the salvation of humanity. This happens in the church; indeed, in a way, it happens *as* the church. In the community of believers that is the church, the three great moments of the Christian narrative are enacted: judgment, repentance and forgiveness, and sanctification. "The church" is that body of believers who first and foremost hear the Word of God declared against the vanities of worldly sin; that is, they hear and receive the judgment of God condemning them. But they also and simultaneously hear in that word of judgment the New Word that God also speaks, the word that says that God has also already forgiven them for their trespasses. This provokes that repentance and renewal of life which ultimately, through God's gracious providence, leads to the community's sanctification – that is, its becoming altogether holy and approvable in God's sight. Because this action is so radical a transformation, it is never accomplished short of the Last Judgment; indeed, in this life it is at best barely begun. It is through experiencing themselves as undergoing this twofold activity throughout their lives that Christians are drawn ever more fully into the life of the church.

The Christian church is in its own way the central institutional manifestation of the apocalypticism latent in Christianity. The idea of "church," or *ecclesia*, is pretty unique. Structurally it exists in tight association with the Christian understanding of "the world," not as created but as fallen. Even though the Christian idea of the church evolved out of the Jewish idea of the "People Israel," Judaism has no such concept as church, understood as something more than a geographically local body of believers who practice their faith together. Islam has no such concept either; it has the *umma*, the worldwide community of the faithful, but there is no opposition between it and the world; the opposition there is between those who have submitted to God's law and those who are still in rebellion against it. The Christian church is a different kind of sociopolitical reality – a community with overtly political expectations, but with no presumption of supplanting or rivaling the current political order in the present historical era.

The value of the category of "church" lies in its enabling, or encouraging, what sociologists call "structural differentiation." By this they mean that the category of "church" specifies a particular social structure with its own purpose and inner logic, alongside other social structures, such as explicitly political or commercial ones. For all its many alliances with political power, Christianity always bears within itself this notion of the body of believers as called out from other social bodies for a particular kind of activity – call it worship – that can only properly occur in, and as, the church. This differentiation renders it conceptually possible for the church to exist alongside other "worldly" institutions. The danger is that it inevitably marks those other institutions out as somehow stained with the problematic quality of being sinful, fallen, irredeemably "worldly." So it creates a structural pluralism in the world only at the cost of implying that that world is, again, calamitously misguided.

All this raises questions about how Christians are to behave in and towards the world. Here, over the centuries, Christians took over two categories from its background in Second-Temple Judaism: the categories of stewardship and covenant. Christians took "covenant" to signify the idea that God has called all people to join the church and to begin to serve God in grateful response to God's forgiving and redeeming action upon them. This is a development of earlier Jewish thought, wherein the Christian understanding of the covenant is formally identical with the received understanding, even as Christians proclaim the covenant has been extended to include all of humanity and not just the People Israel. The Christian affirmation of the covenant means that as a secondary task, Christians are to assume the responsibilities of stewardship, of caring for God's creation, in light of their central task to enter more fully into communion with God in the church.

This points to the second form of Christian responsibility: Christians are called upon not just to respond lovingly and gratefully to God's action, but to come to see themselves as sinners, "with a past." To see oneself as a sinner who has been redeemed is to alter one's understanding of the story of one's life. What once was important is now less so, or is important for other reasons than it was before. What looked like a great career, or satisfying academic success, now looks like an enormous exercise in selfishness and distraction from the really important things in life – faith and family, say – and an exercise that has harmed others in a fairly pathetic quest for material gain or the anxious desire to seek the approval of one's superiors. What looked unimportant is now very important; a series of failed relationships, once chalked up to "growing up," now reveals a deep and disturbing pattern of narcissism or humiliating self-abnegation in order to validate a self-image in which one wants desperately to believe. Most importantly for Christians, however, one can only see oneself in these ways *after* one has gained some critical distance on these vicious patterns of behavior, by gaining some new gracious status or deeper knowledge of the course of one's life. One need not experience a dramatic episode of "conversion," a singular event in one's life which divides that life into a before and after; people can be Christian without ever in their adult lives being "born again." The important thing is a growing vision of one's life that comes into focus as a complicated and deepening dialectic of sin and grace, of failure and redemption, where one's successes are ascribable at least in part to divine help; but for one's own failings, one has only oneself to thank.

This account troubles free-standing intellectual deliberation. After all, this account of Christian responsibility seems inevitably to raise serious questions about the adequacy of the individual's mind to understand even what is closest to them – namely, their own life stories – and to render them especially sensitive to seeing their own action as possibly prideful and therefore sinful. Karl Barth famously (famously among theologians, anyway) said "only Christians sin," and insofar as one understands that to mean that the self-conscious category of sin is a distinctively Christian one, it may well be so. To learn to be a Christian is to take upon oneself a certain understanding of agency that renders agency quite suspect, unless it is seen as the manifestation of God's action in and through humanity – which renders human action fairly invulnerable to criticism.

The sort of concern that such a view provokes is not surprising. It seems deeply vulnerable to charges of authoritarianism, and of being diagnosed as caused by a fear of being responsible for one's own thinking, the ultimate mark of a botched maturity. By teaching believers to understand themselves as first and foremost part of a church, these critics charge, Christianity undermines any viable individualism; and by teaching believers to see themselves in their own individuality, as fundamentally sinners, the "good news" of the Christian gospel snuffs out whatever embers of freedom and individuality survived the earlier ecclesiological deluge.

While Christians may not agree with these charges, it is worth hearing them, if only for the believers in order better to appreciate the perils that some of their most acute critics have identified in their faith.

Conclusion

Such is the structure of Christian ethics. It is a way of living with powerful moral and spiritual energies, but which also contains buried within it powerful moral and spiritual ambivalences and ambiguities about the ultimate value of these energies and their ultimate purpose in the world. The basic structure of the question here asked is simple: are Christians called straightforwardly or in some way directly to transform the world into the kingdom of God, or rather to endure the world, until Christ's second coming, or is there some other third way?

We will see these tensions emerge again and again in the chapters to come. For now, we can leave this tradition and turn to our third and final one – Islam.

4

Islamic Ethics

Did we not give him eyes,
a tongue, lips,
and point out to him the two clear paths?
(Qur'an 90:8–10)

Especially in the case of Islam, where so much is not known or easily misconstrued, we must beware what Kevin Reinhart calls the "conceptual drowsiness" of many received typologies.[1] As a book title by Vartan Gregorian puts it, more than either Christianity or Judaism, Islam is "a mosaic, not a monolith." There is a great danger of thinking of Islam as a totalizing system of doctrines; in fact it was historically quite adjustable to cultural contexts. It is deeply diverse, because the core of the tradition is fundamentally quite spare.[2]

Along with the very idea of Islam itself, another category is likely to put our intelligence to sleep when we apply it to Islam: namely, the category of religion itself. I want to argue that Islam is in an important sense *not* a religion – if we understand "religion" in the typical Western, and even more parochially American, sense of *creed* or *denomination*, one aspect or component of a larger social system, an aspect fitting neatly into the whole and not troubling it. Our use of the word "religion" signifies something that knows its place. It's typically something we imagine as a matter of "internal" spirituality, something someone does in their privacy, with their individual existence. It is interior. It is personal. It fits tidily into the slots that the world offers it, and doesn't disrupt the ordinary flow of the everyday.

Well, for good or ill (probably both), that is not how Islam works. Islam is not a *part* of the world, it is a "way of life" – in Arabic, *din*. (In the Islamic Republic of Iran, Islam is actually described as an *ideology*, a language for understanding and shaping life.) More concretely, it is a project for making the world holy, making us and the world *pure*. Because of this, Islam is a *necessarily* incomplete – until the eschaton – project of world- and self-transformation – it aims directly to transform that larger social system.

Because of this, it will be good to get some basics down about Islam before detailing its explicitly ethical dimension. We will do that next.

Fundamental Concepts

The word *islam* itself means to submit, to surrender to the divine will. A *Muslim* is "one who submits." The founder of the faith is the Prophet Muhammad, who lived from 570–632 CE. Islam is understood to have begun as a distinct self-conscious religion with the flight of Muhammad and his followers from Mecca to Medina – the *hejira* – in 622. Since then the Muslim calendar has been tracking the lunar years following that date; the year 2008 was 1430 AH ("After Hejira") and the year 2010 was largely in 1431 AH ("After Hejira") and it runs from December 18, 2009 to December 6, 2010.

Islam emerged in a deeply cosmopolitan culture of trading cities, amid various other religions, including tribal polytheism, Judaism, and various forms of Christianity. It was cosmopolitan not least because the Quraysh tribe, Muhammad's own tribe, attacked him and his followers – so destroying the basis for the understanding of society that Muhammad had inherited from his family. The *umma* was the response – a transnational, trans-ethnic, in principle polyglot community of all the faithful, irrespective of the marks of tribe, people, nation, or race. Islam provided order and stability to a vast and cosmopolitan world, between the Atlantic and the Oxus river in Central Asia. Early on, in fact, the religion became especially concentrated in cities, and it shares many of the urbanities we associate with city dwellers; indeed, in much of Islam, to move to a city has always been a meritorious act.

From the beginning, then, its cosmopolitan character required that Islam confront its relationship with other religions, and especially Judaism and Christianity. It came to understand itself to be a development and reform of those other traditions, finding its place in the narrative of the family of Abraham through his first son Ishmael and his mother Hagar. Muhammad understood his mission to be extending the call of Israel and Jesus to the whole world, and reforming it, dedicating the believing community to total commitment to the one God (which is where the term *Allah* comes from – it is a derivation of *al-ilah*, which simply means "*the* god").[3] Islam understands itself to be most simply the final refinement of these traditions, their consummation and correction regarding God's expectations for humanity, definitively detailed in the Qur'an; to which we turn next.

Sources of Authority in Islamic Reasoning

There are two large sources of authority in Islamic reasoning. First is the Qur'an, "the recitation" the sacred text of Islam. For the faithful believer (*mu'min*), it is the literal word of God. But one should be careful here; the Qur'an is not the "Muslim Bible." Yes, it is roughly as long as the Christian New Testament, and similarly divided into sections (chapters, or *suras* – 114 of them, composed of verses, called *ayat*, which is also, as we shall see, translated as "sign"). But the similarities can mislead, much as the Christian New Testament is not the "Christian Bible" as opposed to the "Jewish Bible" of the Hebrew scriptures. First of all, Islam respects the sacred books of both the Jewish and Christian traditions, and incorporates significant segments of the narratives of both the Hebrew Bible and the Christian New Testament into its teachings. Secondly, the Qur'an is not quite the same thing as a Bible. Literally, it means "the recitation," and it is the revelation accorded Muhammad, transmitted to him by the archangel Gibreel. (It was written down only in bits and pieces during his life, and then compiled and "fixed" textually only after Muhammad's death, and canonized in written form by Uthman, 3rd caliph (644–52).)

The vast majority of Muslims across the centuries have believed the Qur'an to be the perfect record of what the archangel Gibreel recited to Muhammad, as God told him to recite. The Qur'an is composed entirely of exceptionally powerful lyric poetry. Consider the story of how Muhammad first received the Qur'an. He was on a sort of private religious retreat, in a cave outside Mecca, and awoke from sleep to find someone holding him down, pressing a cloth over his face. "Recite!" (*ikra*) a voice said; "I cannot recite!" Muhammad replied, for he was illiterate. Two more times the voice ordered Muhammad to recite, and when for the third time he said he could not, the voice replied:

> Recite! in the name of your Lord, who created,
> created man from a blood clot;
> Recite! and your Lord, Most Bountiful One
> who teaches by the pen,
> teaches man what he did not know.
>
> (96:1–5)

This became the first five verses of the 96th *sura*) of the Qur'an. Thus did Muhammad's reception of the Qur'an commence.

In a way, the Qur'an is sacramental, itself a material means of holiness, a way of participating in God – in some sense more akin to the Christian Eucharist (the ritual of Communion, or the Lord's Supper) than to the Christian Bible. The Qur'an is the word of God for Muslims, but in this case it is somewhat akin to how Jesus is the word of God for Christians.

Many people think that the Qur'an is a rigorously legal text, but in fact it is literally an assemblage of poetic verses that shape the soul and inform the mind as much as guide the will of the believer. Of the 6,346 verses in the Qur'an, around 500 "have the form of law," directly commanding or forbidding believers to do something. Indeed, in the entire Qur'an there are only about 200 verses directly commanding believers to pray, and three times that number commanding believers to reflect, to ponder, and to analyze God's magnificence in nature, plants, stars, and the solar system.

There are recognizably "Meccan" and "Medinan" styles in the Qur'an, by which I mean that the *suras* divide up into groups for stylistic and content-related reasons. The Meccan *suras* are the earlier ones, first recited when Muhammad and his community lived in Mecca; they talk about God's majesty, unity, afterlife, resurrection; the Medinan *suras* are later, from the community's sojourn in Medina; they are more concerned with legislative and social issues, and other things. Because the Meccan *suras* are generally shorter, while the Medinan *suras* are generally longer, in the Qur'an as it was eventually compiled the Medinan *suras* are mostly placed earlier than the Meccan *suras* are.

The second source of authority in Islam is the called the *Sunnah* ("trodden path"), the example the Prophet set in his life; this is typically mediated through gathered collections of sayings or stories of the Prophet, conveyed in narratives which are evaluated for their trustworthiness, which comprise the *ahadith* (singular, *hadith*), meant to complement and unfold the Qur'an. Muhammad functions as a paradigm for believers, and the acts of his life and the words of his sayings remain normative in a powerful way for the faithful. The Prophet is a "beautiful model" (or "pattern of conduct") (Q. 33:21) for all humanity, and his nickname – al-Amin, "the trustworthy" – is meant to communicate that he is the paradigm of proper behavior. The Prophet mediates the divine – either mediating the divine's message, when he became the recorder of Gibreel's recitation of God's verses, or mediating the divine presence through his exemplification of God's will. (If it is the presence that is mediated, the emphasis is more on mercy; if the message, the emphasis is more on duty.) There are many thousands of *ahadith*, collected over the centuries following Muhammad's death. No uniform and determinate "canon" of *ahadith* exists (though some collections are more central than others), which increases the plurality and complexity of Islamic practice.

Together, the Qur'an and the *Sunnah* form the source material out of which Shari'ah, Islamic law, is composed; and Shari'ah will be our main guide in explicitly ethical matters in this book. Shari'ah is a complicated term. Typically, it is translated as "Islamic law," but in fact it simply means "the way," the way to water – *fiqh* is not simply what we would call "jurisprudential competence" but more like tact, or insight. The intellectual discipline of interpreting the Qur'an is not properly speaking *theology*, but rather *usul-al-fiqh*, the "science of understanding sources." It is not speculation, but interpretation.

So even though Islamic law looks like an essentially legal system, it is so only if we do not think of that as opposed to an ethical system. It encompasses what many non-Muslims would consider to fall under the latter category. It includes exegesis of the Qur'an, analysis of the *Sunnah*, determination of whatever consensus exists among the scholars (*ijma'*) of the tradition, and can extend to argument by analogy (*qiyas*) from earlier cases. Like Jewish law, then, Islamic law is a comprehensive way of trying to live thoughtfully and faithfully under Allah's sovereignty in the world.

The Five Pillars of Islam

As in Judaism, the crucial criterion for Islam is praxis, not interior belief. Indeed, some scholars have suggested that there are three fundamental dimensions of Islamic practice. First is *islam* itself, the act of submission, differentiated into the "five pillars" of Islam; second is *iman* or belief in God, the prophets, angels, the holy books, the day of judgment, and God's foreknowledge; third is *ihsan*, or spiritual virtue, a capacity of the soul to see God face-to-face – to create a deep intimacy with God – for whose cultivation you are supposed to pray. The first of these dimensions is "external" or material; the second is cognitive and mental; the third is affective and dispositional, about the heart.[4] This praxis shapes a whole way of life, along multiple dimensions: inner and outer, space and time, the individual and the community. To see what I mean, I want to turn to what can be considered the skeletal form of any even moderately pious Muslim life – namely, the praxis of Islam, famously known as the "five pillars" of the Islamic faith.

Shahada

First is the profession of faith, the *shahada*. This is a simple statement, spoken before witnessess: "I bear witness that there is no God but God, and Muhammad is the messenger of God." The corollary of this statement of belief in God is the recognition of one's accountability before God: there will be a "Day of Judgment," of accounting or reckoning, the *Yawm-al-hisab*.

The components of this statement warrant explication. First, the affirmation is not a neutral descriptive claim; it has existentially committing characteristics. While it is fundamentally a verbal profession, it is not simply a verbal act; the phrase "I bear witness" means more than "I affirm that …" In fact, in classical Arabic *shahada* means "to witness," to see with one's own eyes, and it has legal connotations. To "bear witness" in this way is not simply to affirm something, but to be willing to give testimony for it. To bear witness is a public act; one has a new place before others, when one is ready to give such testimony. It is the first step towards making one's life entirely a vessel of testimony to one's faith, the first step towards martyrdom, which comes from the same root (*shahada*) as "witness."

Furthermore, the content of the affirmation is far more profound than it may at first appear. To say that "there is no God but God, and Muhammad is the messenger of God" is to underscore the powerful purity of the Islamic vision of God. For Muhammad, knowledge of God was about the purity of one's vision of the most pure God, and much of early Islamic thought on God was negative, a critique of various kinds of idolatry and what Muslims saw as the metaphysical confusion of the Creator with the creation. The Qur'an repeatedly expresses hostility to idolators and what it depicts as the misbegotten attempts of Christians to complicate, or even undermine, God's unity and identity in the doctrines of Christology and Trinity. Ironically, the clarity of this theological vision of God meant that central Islamic intellectual energies went into areas other than theological speculation, for there was very little genuine insight to be gained.

Again, this affirmation of the unity of God is meant to be existentially transforming. Conscious belief in God *integrates* life in multiple dimensions – psychologically, morally, sociopolitically. You become psychologically integral, in a particular way, by being committed to this most radical other; you become moral because you understand the obligations put upon you; and you become a member of the *umma*, the community of the *dar-al-islam*, the "house of peace." (Though we should note that the division of the world into the *dar-al-islam* and the *dar-al-harb*, or "house of war," is a post-Quranic development, accomplished by the distinguished Muslim juristic thinker Muhammad b. Idris al-Shafi'i (d. 820 CE).)

The *shahada* is the foundational act of Islam. Without the explicit and self-conscious acceptance of the role of witness, and without the explicit affirmation of the unique sovereignty of God, nothing else matters. But once this is in place, more follows.

Salat

The second pillar is daily prayer, or *salat* – a ritual prayer time that occurs roughly at dawn, midday, afternoon, sunset, and night, and facing towards Mecca, as best as can be determined. There is also midday worship on Fridays and the religious holidays of end of Ramadan (*Eid al-Fitr*) and completion of pilgrimage to Mecca. Before you begin to pray you wash yourself thoroughly. The connection between prayer and cleanliness is not a superficial one, as is shown by a *hadith* about Mohammed. He asked his companions, "If there was a river flowing by your house and you bathed in it five times a day, would you ever be dirty?" They said, "No." Muhammad said, "That's what prayer is."[5] Another *hadith* records the Prophet as saying that "ritual prayer is the ascension of the believer," meaning that the ritual movements of *salat* can be seen as reenacting Muhammad's ascension to God. Regular prayer trains the individual in certain ways and constantly calls them back to relation with God; it also recognizes the import of community, as it is a communal exercise as well.

We should not downplay the importance of such rituals, nor imagine that rituals are something somehow premodern or antique. Our age is just as ritually obsessed as every other civilization in human history; we simply do not recognize it. Our days, and our lives, are lived out in an automatic panoply of rituals that are the more powerful the less visible they are to us. Three meals a day? The weekend? Go to a gym at 6 a.m.; do you think each person there individually and spontaneously decided to wake up early and run on a treadmill? The German philosopher G. W. F. Hegel once said that "the morning paper is the modern man's morning prayer," and insofar as we today have other, more fungible sources of information, we have not lost our reliance on ritual.[6] The regular prayer of *salat* orients the believer in a way different than the way many in our world are oriented.

Zakat

The third obligation is *zakat*, or the practice of almsgiving. Muslims must donate a regular proportion of their goods to others less fortunate than they are. *Zakat* is etymologically related to "to thrive" or "to be pure" – the idea is that almsgiving is as much about purifying yourself, loosening your attachment to material treasures and pleasures, as it is about being nice to people with less than you. Also, by attending to another's needs, you are being forced *outside of yourself*, as it were, forced genuinely to see them. So the practice of *zakat* loosens the bonds that tie humans to worldly possessions and wealth, and calls our attention away from goods to focus on people, thereby realigning our values and vision in two different ways.

Ramadan

The fourth obligation is the annual fast of Ramadan: the holy month during which Qur'an was revealed to Muhammad. Faithful Muslims are expected, barring legitimate medical reasons (and for infants and nursing mothers), to fast from dawn to dusk. This fast is not simply an abstention from eating, drinking, and smoking, but from all things that lead to sensual pleasure. It is a joyous and holy time, a time when one remembers the real pleasures of life and scrapes away the dead layers of merely fleshly pleasure.

Because the fast is determined in terms of the Islamic lunar year which has 355 days, the month of Ramadan moves steadily backwards every earth year by ten or eleven days. It travels through all four seasons in a cycle of 33 years. This means that the fast is experienced in different ways. In winter it may be a matter of not being able to have a warm cup of coffee or tea; in summer, a cool drink of ice water. Depending on how far north or south one is, the fast may last only six or seven hours a day in the depths of winter, or it may stretch over eighteen or even twenty hours, near the summer solstice. In this way Ramadan is not fixed to any one natural season, but slowly, over the course of years, teaches the faithful about the full range of ways that nature tempts them towards a too-easy commerce with the material world.

The point of this practice is to alter one's pattern of living – to break out of the usual patterns, reset one's mind, reorient one to God. As was the case with *salat*, the point here is to use temporal structures to remind oneself of supratemporal aims.

Hajj

Fifth and finally, there is the hajj, the pilgrimage to Mecca. All Muslims are enjoined to attempt this pilgrimage, at least once in their lives. It is obligatory provided you have the financial means. Before the twentieth century, this was a task that could take years, coming and going; a *mu'min* living on the Philippine island of Mindanao, for example, or in Timbuktu, on the southern edge of the Sahara, had pilgrimages of thousands of miles across open ocean with pirates, or vast deserts full of hostile nomads. Today, roughly two million Muslims make the hajj every year.

What is the point of the hajj? Most basically, it is a collective commemoration of the sacrifice story of Abraham, which is taken to be representative of the struggle for true faithfulness that is the centerpiece of the Muslim's life. It is meant to be a focus of asceticism, and to emphasize the pilgrimage character of the moral struggle, and of the Muslim's life as a whole.[7] Pragmatically, the hajj generates a powerful sense of cohesion across the whole scope of Islam by generating a powerful imagined *umma*.

For those who undertake it, the power of this experience can be overwhelming. In his autobiography, Malcolm X reports that his experience of the hajj transformed his understanding to so great a degree that he took a new name after it, and moved decisively away from his hostility towards collaborating with white Americans. He saw too many people, of all races, on the hajj, he believed, to reject the idea of cross-racial harmony as impossible:

> There were tens of thousands of pilgrims, from all over the world … all participating in the same ritual, displaying a spirit of unity and brotherhood that my experiences in America had led me to believe never could exist between white and non-white … what I have seen, and experienced, has forced me to rearrange much of my thought-patterns previously held, and to toss aside some of my previous conclusions.[8]

It is in ways like this that the hajj is central in creating and recreating the *umma*, and thereby reinforcing Islam's basic message of the unity of God and the community of believers.

Arguably the central geographic goal of the hajj is the *ka'ba*, which means "cube," a square building in Mecca, measuring approximately 30–40 feet each side, around which the faithful walk seven times, in a counter-clockwise direction. Up to Muhammad's time it was a shrine to many gods, filled with their idols, and from the beginnings of his revelations, Muhammad wanted the *ka'ba* purged of the idols and dedicated to worship of the one true God. (It seems to have been conflict about this, among other things, that precipitated the final break with his tribe, the Quraysh, who were the guardians of the idols and the shrine.) Muhammad finally gained control of the *ka'ba* in 630, and destroyed all the idols. But the *ka'ba* is actually simply an empty cube – whose emptiness alludes again to the fact that God is *not here*, that God transcends even these most basic fundaments of reality as we perceive it – namely, the dimensions of spatiality themselves.

The hajj is a pilgrimage full of what may look like ironic paradoxes. It is understood as a return of sorts, even if the faithful have not been there before. (The idea of return is a form of conversion – in Latin, to turn around (*convertere*) or transform; the return of the hajj is a kind of deeper journey than geographic, it is a way down into the self, and upwards towards God.) A faithful Muslim prays five times a day towards Mecca, and so they know where it is relative to their daily life. The hajj takes them where their body has been aimed, and then returns them to their everyday lives, with everything the same, yet everything transformed. It serves as a once-in-a-lifetime reminder that every human on earth is always a pilgrim, journeying toward a day of judgment at the end of time. Also, circumambulating the *ka'ba* is not simply going around in a circle; you are finding your place in the cosmic order. Indeed, the hajj provides a rationale for the *umma*, reminding the faithful of the *umma*'s deep historical roots and distinctive purpose – gathering people from the four corners of the globe – as well as communicating the message of a merciful and generous God. (The final event ideally is the sacrifice of a sheep, recollecting Abraham's sacrifice of a sheep instead of Ishmael.) The hajj then is not so much a journey to a place, as a way to remind oneself that all are pilgrims in this life, on their way to a heavenly home.

The caliphate of all believers

As a member of the *umma*, the believer is thereby committed to being God's servant (*'abd*) and trustee (*khalifa*), one given vice-regental supervision of the material universe; therefore, believers must realign the behavior of their lives profoundly. This language of *khalifa* is quite significant. In this tradition, the vice-regency power is the capacity for judgment and knowledge. Humans have an executive power given to them by God, as his vice-regents; and the nature of this obligation is quite powerful. In the Qur'an, humans are offered it – called "the trust" – only after the mountains and heavens were offered it, and rejected it (33:73). Humans are distinct, in all of creation, in having the autonomous power to work as God's helpers, or not to work as such – and so to ensure for themselves a destiny of eternal bliss in Paradise, or a destiny of eternal torment in Hell.

The human's reception of this duty is not simply a fact about them as agents, it sets rolling the great drama of creation. As the following Qur'anic passage suggests, it was this gift from God which provoked Satan – whose proper name in the Qur'an is *Iblis* – to rebel, and thereby inaugurate the story of fall and redemption:

> Behold, your Lord said to the angels: "I will create a vice-regent on earth." They said: "How can you put someone there who will cause damage and bloodshed, when we celebrate Your praise and proclaim Your holiness?" but He said: "I know what you know not."
>
> And He taught Adam the names of all things; then He showed them before the angels, and said: "Tell me the names of these if you are right."

They said: "Glory to You! We know only what You have taught us. You are the all knowing and all Wise."

Then He said: "Adam, tell them their names." When he had told them, God said: "Did I not tell you that I know what is hidden in heavens and earth, and I know what you reveal and what you hide?"

When We told the angels: "Bow down before Adam," they all bowed. But not Iblis, who refused and was arrogant: he was of the disobedient.

We said: "Adam! Live with your wife in this garden. Both of you eat freely there as you will, but do not approach this tree, or you will run to transgression."

But Satan made them slip, and lured them from the state they were in. We said: "Get out, all of you! You are each other's enemy. On earth you will have a dwelling, and a livelihood for a time."

Then Adam received [some] words from his Lord and He [God] accepted his repentance: He is the oft-Relenting, the Most Merciful.

We said: "Get out, all of you! But whenever guidance comes from Me, as it surely will, those who follow My guidance need not fear, nor will they grieve.

But those who reject the faith and deny Our signs [*ayat*] shall live in the Fire, and there they shall remain." (2:30–39)

This vice-regental task is not merely negative, a matter of stopping evil-doers. It obligates the believer to promote the good in certain ways, as well: in classical terms, Islam demands that the faithful "command the right and forbid the wrong" (3:104). It is equally important, that is, that believers understand that they are under an obligation not only to do the good, *but also* to see that others do it too. God's command to do the right is not simply a command that we are to hear and obey; it is one that we are to inhabit and communicate to others ourselves.

So comprehensive a vision may sound quite oppressive to Western-liberal ears. But "oppression" opposed to what? To reform and rehabilitation. Ah, but a traditional Muslim will tell you, all of Muslim society is organized around reform – all aspects are concerned with the moral perfecting of persons. It is entirely understandable for people born in Western liberal democracies to worry that there is no privacy in Islam. But it is more complicated than that; there is a real respect for different spheres of life, and a differentiation of ethical rights and duties pertains to those different spheres. (So, for example, those who are outside a household should not interrogate what happens in that household, among other things.) Furthermore, a traditional Muslim might say, you cannot appreciate the worth of such a system, because your Western-liberal institutions have surrendered this obligation. Indeed, you treat the criminal more peculiarly and invasively than we do, because we treat *all* in society with the same reforming zeal. So, for both sides, questions of the meaning of punishment are connected to broader questions about the nature and purpose of society. The violation of ethical boundaries speaks of a larger breach between the individual and God, and the individual and the community.

Such an exchange reveals two implications of Islam's vision of the moral life. First, this picture of the good life implies that moral laws are internal to the human's true flourishing. This is palpable even in the Arabic words used to talk about the moral life. The word for "penalties," for example, is *hudud*, or boundaries. The point is not to suggest a juridical or extrinsically punitive vision of ethics, but rather a vision of morality in which morality is an organic dimension of the well-lived human life.

Second, this vision assumes people roughly know what the good is, and so the tradition, from the Qur'an forward, spends its energy urging hearers to do good, but without really spending much time determining what that good is. This reflects what I pointed out in talking about Christianity – that Islam, like Judaism and unlike Christianity, does not have as dramatic a picture of the human's moral calamity. Islam assumes that people have more capacity to know the good and act to realize it, and does not trouble itself as obsessively as does Christian thought with the idea that the world as we have it is fundamentally deceptive.

In general, then, the five pillars constitute the overall shape of *islam*, submission to God's will. Beyond the five pillars, there are also laws governing worship – *ibadat* – and laws governing relations with other people – *mu'amalat*. But the five pillars are basically the structure that organizes Muslim life, and give a particular shape to the Muslim believer, who thereby comes properly to be a vice-regent (again, *khalifa*) and to thereby participate in the *umma*, the caliphate of all believers.

And all of this, many Muslims would say, is meant to cultivate in believers several virtues. First, it is meant to deepen *iman* or faith in God, in the prophets, the angels, the holy books, the day of judgment, and (as part of faith in God) in God's fore-knowledge of all things, the fact that God foreknows all that will happen. Second, *ihsan*, a distinctly spiritual virtue, whereby a deep intimacy with God is cultivated; those who have *ihsan* seek, as they do all things, to imagine that they see God before themselves, and that God sees them. By coming to see that in your life you do all things standing before God (through *ihsan*), and by understanding who God is and what powers God has (through *iman*), the pious and virtuous Muslim comes to be reformed into a new disposition or character, which is what we use to translate the Arabic word *akhlaq*. A *hadith* reports Muhammad saying, "I have been sent to complete the best of *akhlaq*."[9] Another has Muhammad commanding his followers to "anoint yourself with the *akhlaq* of God."[10]

What all this does is quite rigorously shape human life into a pattern of discernible holiness. The outer person is brought into alignment with the inner person, the individual is reconciled to the community, the believer's experience of space and time is given determinate sanctifying shape. In all these ways, and more, the pillars of Islamic practice are meant to transform the self from a bundle of loosely aligned drives and streams of thought into a coherent self, serving God by working for God's cause here on earth.

The Theory of Islam

As we have seen, the practice of Islam is primary. But Islam is far from anti-intellectual: the practice of the faith demands that the believer seek knowledge (*ilm*) of God and guidance (*hidayah*) for human behavior. Thus, it is no surprise that the faith has given rise to multitudinous theories and interpretations of itself, and provoked many questions.

From early on there has been profound and searching Islamic theological inquiry. The best word for Islamic "theology" is *kalam*, which (when joined with "science" or *ilm* is *ilm-al-kalam*) means "science of speech" about God – that is, in this science Muslims do not study the nature of God, properly speaking, but rather the character of right speech about God. (This is not far from what much Christian theology does, though few contemporary Christians realize it.) Another word for this field of study is *ilm al-tawhid*, "the science of [the divine] unity," because it is a study of the unity and singularity of God, and all that that unity implies.

Yet in another way, theology was important early on in ways decisive for Islamic ethics. For a theological debate arose about the question of divine determination and human free will. The Qur'an explicitly affirms both that God is sovereign over all things, and that humans will be held responsible for the choices they make to worship God or to rebel against God. How can both these claims be true? Furthermore, does God determine what is good and evil by divine fiat, or are good and evil objective features of reality itself?

Over the next several centuries a number of Muslim intellectuals and their followers, who became known as the Mu'tazilites, developed a thorough view in which humans know good and evil, which exist objectively, and God allows them to choose between them. For the Muslim, the Qur'an can help humans discern what the objective moral order of the universe is, but fundamentally that book is a complement or supplement to humanity's innate – that is, God-given – reason, which at its best can discern the moral order of the cosmos on its own. This discernment is the Mu'tazilites' project of profound theological systematization – of working out, with philosophical rigor, the normative implications of traditional Islamic commitment.

Against this view stood a group that understood itself to be more rooted in the tradition, called the Ash'arites. The Ash'arites argued that God established good and evil through sheer divine command, and that God's command is thus the source of moral rectitude. Values are in essence whatever God commands, and they can be known ultimately only by receiving God's command which itself is accessible to us only through the tradition – though reason can be used, in subordinate ways, to extend the tradition. Furthermore, they argued that God does foreordain all to their choices, but humans still "acquire" responsibility for what they do. While the Mu'tazilites lost the debate institutionally, their views have remained available for Muslim scholars ever since; and so they and the Ash'arites have remained the two major schools of Islamic ethical thought.

But, much like Judaism, the central form which traditional reflection about Islam has taken is not theology. Rather, it is ethical and legal interpretation. To evaluate actions, an Islamic code of law, an external code – Shari'ah – developed very quickly, emerging by the second half of the second century AH (ca. 800 CE). The centrality of this code to enquiry about proper Muslim practice suggests something of the character of Islamic understandings of the human moral life. By it, ethics became fused with jurisprudence, and morality came to be understood as obedience to the law. In the systematic legal form, human acts of heart and body are organized into five categories: expressly forbidden (*haram*); expressly enjoined (*wajib* or *fard*); disliked but not prohibited (*makruh*); recommended but not enjoined (*mandub*); and those undiscussed, hence permitted through silence (*mubah*). By reference to these five categories, Muslim jurists have sought to explicate the full shape of human life in Islamic terms.

Some might worry that so "legalistic" an account of the moral life would be especially susceptible to a dessication of reflection on that life, finally ending up in a stale legalism. But that did not occur because the legal picture carried within itself a set of assumptions about the necessary dimensions of human character that must be developed in order rightly to obey Shari'ah. Certainly, it is true that humanity is created with freedom to choose, but also with the obligation (*amr*) to observe God's commandments. Furthermore, human behavior is morally saturated; intention is crucially moral, and crucially human – there is no distinctively human action without intention. Therefore, to inhabit this world righteously, one must be able to see reality and hear God's call in it. Because of this, sensitivity to one's conscience, and awareness of the law, must be cultivated so that we develop a moral and spiritual awareness and sensitivity – in Arabic, *taqwa* – which, when fully inhabited, is a disposition of near-saintliness.

The tradition's emphasis on dispositional attunement is not only central to its understanding of the right inhabitation of the law. The scholar interpreting the law also needs to be properly oriented in his character; he needs *fiqh*, or "discernment," the interpretation and application of the law, close to what we could call "judgment." Thus, both in its concrete application and its theoretical interpretation, Islamic ethics is not stale scholastic legalism, but a living and vibrant tradition.

This explains the crucial role of education, which is historically so powerful (if at times narrow) an element in Islamic civilization; you must be trained in the Qur'an in order to know fully what to do, how to be just. It also resonates with the tradition's deep social message of *change* and reform, which sought to create a worldwide society with a universal ethical and legal system.

On the other hand, conscience – one dimension of what the Arabic word *fitra* implies (it means more generally "the natural way") – is a source, within humans, of accountability or responsibility, and it can guide humans in their own nature. It is fundamentally sound, and always should be heeded. (Even if a legal scholar issues an informed opinion, the individual who hears it must subject the opinion to the judgment of their conscience.) Hence, humans have an in-built capacity to evaluate their actions. Indeed, to do wrong is to sin against yourself; God aims for humanity's flourishing: "whoever does right benefits his own soul and whoever does evil does it against his own soul: nor is your Lord ever unjust to his creatures"(Q. 41:46). This is so because God knows what is best for humans, as God is radically intimate with the human condition; as the Qur'an says, "we are closer to him (the human) than his jugular vein" (50:16). The idea that God's commands might be fundamentally *extrinsic* to the human being – that, in other words, God's most basic wishes for us might not coincide with our own best interest – is ruled out from the beginning on this account. Islam makes no sense unless it is for the well-being of all humanity.

Conclusion

We end this chapter with the same reminder that began it: namely, that Islam – a creed professed and a *din* practiced by a billion people today, and for countless more in the past 1,400 years – is a mosaic, not a monolith. Almost every statement made in this chapter can meet its contradiction in some part of the Islamic world, past or present. Nonetheless, there is some use to the general statements this chapter has advanced, if only to begin to suggest something of the scope, ambition, and internal coherence that Muslims find in their faith.

It is also possible to suggest some comparisons now between Islam and Judaism and Christianity. While Islam is, like Christianity, universalistic, it lays less stress than does Christianity on some perennial tension between God's plan for creation and the willingness, or capacity, of creation to fulfill that plan. This is often formulated as the idea that Islam does not recognize a fundamental opposition between the church and the world – no tragic, potentially paralyzing sense of inescapable corruption in the human heart. But this is not exactly true. Practically speaking, there has always been some inherent tension between the *'ulama* – religious authorities – and the actual political powers, historically embodied in the sultan. The major traditions of Islamic jurisprudence, Sunni and Shi'ia alike, fully and frankly recognize this tension. In this way there can be a rough, functional analogue to separation of church and state. Nonetheless, there is something to the idea that Islam, like Judaism, has a vision of the human situation as less dramatically, even drastically compromised than does Christianity; but like Christianity and unlike Judaism, it has a fairly universalistic ambition, a call for all humanity.

Comparisons are not only useful (if ambiguous) on the macro-level of questions about the status of "the world;" they are also useful on a more individual level. The question of whether Islam promotes an understanding of the human as the *imago Dei*, like Judaism and Christianity, is a charged one. Certainly, there is a deep resistance to any suggestion that God has any even minimally adequate physical representation on earth. But on the other hand, humanity does have some important contact with God that the rest of creation does not, as God's vice-regents of creation, and the human does receive the spirit of the divinity. Then again, Islam is deeply hostile to the principle, central to the Christian tradition, that humanity and God can be "partners in godhead" (as Q. 42:21 alludes). The human person as created is in some important way a suitable vessel in which divinity can be manifest in some sort of decisive way (this is the metaphysical principle that Christian theologians backed into when they decided that Christ was in fact God on earth); Islam has traditionally recoiled at the idea that the finite creature can bear the infinite

Creator. So while a profound respect for the human person is palpable in the Islamic tradition, the tradition is quite skeptical of any attempt to fuse or combine or invest the human's dignity with divine weight. Here, theological compunction circumscribes what the traditions sees as humanity's tendency towards anthropological or ethical over-exuberance.

And this gets at something profound, and profoundly important, about the theological vision of Islam as it developed: its absolute and radical insistence on the absolute and radical sovereignty and transcendence of God. Among the 99 names of God are "the Compassionate," "the Merciful," and "the Protector," and certainly those are no less properly descriptive of God than are names like "the Creator," "the Maker," "the Majestic," "the Judge," and "the All-Knowing." But God's care for us as humans is first and foremost gratuitous, an excessive generosity on God's part which we in no way deserve and which obligates us all the more seriously to align our lives with the way of God, in whose path we will find the life-giving waters of holiness and truth.

Part II

Personal Matters

5

Friendship

We turn now to a number of distinct issues and try to understand how they are addressed in the traditions we are studying. Again, as I said in the Introduction, it is important to be clear about the significant diversity in how these different traditions – and different figures and strands in each tradition – describe the issues we are studying. These differences in description are so important, in no small part, because they represent the issues under analysis in crucially divergent ways, and these differences in emphasis make different issues morally or religiously more or less prominent and problematic. Again, the important matter here is not simply that people have different views on these matters, but that these views may be more or less useful for thinking, and that they may not all be compatible with one another.

In this chapter we will look at several ways in which we can understand the moral problems associated with friendship – the edges, both the beginning edges of friendship; how friendship begins, what constitutes it – and the farther edges of friendship – when friendship becomes something else.

The Problem of Friendship

Now, you may be suspicious about the very idea that there are moral problems with friendship. I mean, what's the problem with friendship? And even if there are problems, who would conceive of them as *moral* problems? One answer is obvious, to some at least. As Aristotle argues, to be a good friend one must be – well, good. Those who believe this think that the best, most stable forms of friendship are between people who enjoy one another's company – and the most enjoyable people are good people. So there is something distinctively moral about friendship.

But there are other questions as well. Must friendship always be conceived as on a continuum with romantic relationships – that is, whether or not friendship is its own sort of thing, or whether it is something like a vexed or underdeveloped or atrophied or stunted form of marriage or sexual relationship – even between heterosexual members of the same gender? That is to say, in asking questions about friendship, we are asking questions about some fundamental issues – questions of the moral significance of the distinctiveness of certain particular relationships, questions, that is, about and what are known as "special attachments." Furthermore, there are questions about what sort of things one owes to one's friends, and about whether one ought to favor them over others – whether caring about one's friends violates our obligations to treat all fairly. (We will talk about this more later on.)

Why are these problems? Well, how much do we really understand what friendship is? What sort of limits go into friendship? Are friendships really as casual as we seem to think them to be? We think about our relationships a lot, but we don't really ever give a lot of thought to what a relationship is – what relationships are about. Once again, I argue, we can come to see that our ordinary life is rich with moral complications. So it is with friendship. As C. S. Lewis once put it, friendships are the most unnatural form of basic human relationship; they are not marriage, parenting, group identity. And yet they are among the most common forms of human interrelation, and among the most valued. They are, in a way, beautifully useless.

A significant part of the problem here, I think, is caused by the fact that our culture heavily emphasizes one model for what a relationship is, to the detriment of other models – and that model is a committed romantic relationship, typically one of marriage. In other words, our culture makes it hard for us to understand the full diversity of our relationships. We live, that is, in a very reductively sexualized culture, one that is very appetite-driven. (This has something to do with the reality of advertising, which is, please realize, a relatively new fact about our lives, but one that is increasingly pervasive.) It is increasingly hard to say "friends" without extending it with "with benefits." And in thinking about friendship through the register of our appetites we significantly obscure what is most distinctive about it.

As we will see, to be good friends, we have to learn also, and simultaneously, how to be good lovers – *and* we have to learn the differences between them. One problem many face today is a confusion about what it means to be a good lover – though perhaps this is not a problem unique to our age, but a condition of relative innocence from which all humans, more or less, begin (and all too many end in it – though by then for most it is no longer innocence, but rather culpable ignorance). Indeed, some have argued that college students don't know what eros is. Some suggest that students engage in binge drinking because they do not know how to handle sexual issues, and so hide from them by losing themselves in alcohol and thus escaping the need for control (and the attribution of responsibility that is implied). Samuel Johnson is reported to have said of drunkards that "he who makes a beast of himself gets rid of the pain of being a man;" but students such as these seem to want to avoid not any existentally profound grasp of the fragility and absurdity of human existence, but simply the conditions of being a responsible adult, pure and simple.

But what are friends, after all? In general there are at least four factors that combine to make friends. First of all, there must be nearness, and persistence over time. You need to be *near* each other – at some point at least. Not really necessarily physically close, because you can be friends with someone you have never physically met. (One of my favorite books, and movies, is *84 Charing Cross Road*, the story of the friendship of an English bookseller and an American writer who never meet and who communicate entirely by correspondence – sending letters across the Atlantic – but who nonetheless become quite genuine friends.) (This prerequisite underscores the importance of contingencies, accident and circumstance in friendships.) And development takes time; as Aristotle says, "the wish to be friends can come about quickly, but friendship cannot." Second, there must be relevant similarities. You need to share some interests, value commitments, or common convictions to become friends; you must have some basis on which your friendship will stand. This can be small at first, but the depth of the friendship seems to be correlated with the extent of the similarities. (Or is it?) Thirdly, there must be reciprocal enjoyment. You need some mutuality in affection. You must resonate with one another in ways that extend beyond the merely explicit common interest. Those with common interests may be allies, or colleagues, or partners; but they need not be friends. Not all friendships become so intense that the partners see each other as an "other self," but there is something of that in the relationship. Friendship enriches us profoundly – not just with the other person's skills, gifts, and knowledge, but with the other person simply as another – to have an equal, an "other self," is deeply and irreplaceably rewarding; our friends take us beyond ourselves in significant ways. Fourth and finally, both must be willing to be with one another in a way distinct from the way each one is before the undifferentiated "public." There must be a modicum of self-disclosure, and a relative degree of exclusivity. Something about a friendship must be private, reserved for the friends alone, hidden from general access. You need some level of mutual intimacy, some ability to put down the mask or persona one wears in public, and simply be yourself. In sum, friends are simultaneously their own individuals, yet deeply magnified by the other's presence in their life. You must be a self to be a partner, but your selfhood cannot be sealed off from the other. Neither wholly alone nor wholly needy and dependent, a friendship assumes independence even as it rewards mutual vulnerability.

Thus friendship is a kind of "dislocated community" – a community that arises not because of where you began, where you were born or what you inherited, but rather because of where you went, where you got to or what you became. Yet it is not quite right to call this a chosen community. The problem with "choice" is that it does not capture the way you never simply *choose* your friends. There is a prevoluntary, or supra-voluntary, dimension to friendship; you find yourself more engaged with some people than others, more resonating with them, more at ease with them. We do not choose our friendships, so much as we feel chosen by them.

There are, of course, imperfect forms of such friendships; the wicked and imperfect do not lack for comrades, and none of our friendships perfectly manifest the essence of true friendship. But by and large the criteria here delineated capture the central norms of a wide range of human friendships. They provide, that is, a first sketch of the phenomenon.

So we have looked at the beginning edges of friendship; how friendship begins, what constitutes it. Friendship is a significant aspect of our lives, but that it is one that we do not often try to understand, and when we try to understand we see that it's much stranger than what we first thought, and has problems hidden within it. My worry here has been that our vocabulary to understand relationships has become too coarse to distinguish between the varieties of significantly different relationships in which we find ourselves.

Now we must consider the farther edges of friendship; when friendship becomes something else, and whether friendship must always be conceived as on a continuum with romantic relationships – that is, whether or not friendship is its own sort of thing, or whether it is something like an underdeveloped or atrophied or stunted form of marriage or sexual relationship – even between heterosexual members of the same gender. Furthermore, how are we to relate friendship to other forms of relationship? Can we have many friendships? Even if we can have many *friends*, can we be in several different *networks* of friendship? What happens to friendship when we fall in love and get married? It is notoriously difficult for married people (especially men) to retain friendships with others once they are married; how can we negotiate this transition to marriage more healthfully for the full range of our attachments and affections?

It is probably best to ask these questions in turn. When we do, one worry immediately presents itself. Does this account help us distinguish friends from lovers? It would be easy to think of friends primordially as "chaste couples," intimate pairs who merely do not have sex. Is this what a friendship is? This is a question about the ontology of friendship, as it were – that is, the nature of friendship as a reality. Is friendship a distinct reality, or is it merely a stage towards another kind of human relationship – for example, a sexual relationship? Do we have good reasons for not going to bed with our good friends?

C. S. Lewis again suggests something here. Friendship is not just a form of eros, because it is differently ordered: "Lovers are always talking to one another about their love; friends hardly ever about their friendship. Lovers are normally face to face, absorbed in each other; friends, side by side, absorbed in some common interest."[1] If this is so, then there is some essential difference between friends and lovers. A friendship that was simply turned in on itself would be self-consuming. Friends are partners, engaged in some common tasks.

Of course, people can be friends and lovers, and with the same people; but the obligations of the two types of relationship are distinct, and each needs to be distinctly cultivated. Furthermore, and equally importantly, even if friendship is relatively exclusive, it is still not absolutely exclusive to two; couples are not perhaps even the best model for friendship. Rather, what is important is the mutual enjoyment of the friends, not primarily in one another, but in something beyond themselves. Nonetheless, while it need not be exclusive to two, it is "an affair of the few," for a small group of people, set apart from the mass of humanity.[2] Like love, real friendship is rare, a scarce commodity, and needs cultivation, to be sustained. It is a distinct and precious good.

But is it a religious good? That is a more complicated question. In its very freedom, its detachment from natural relations with family and clan, friendship points to the possibility for a spiritual dimension to our existence, even as it itself cannot be the complete description of that existence – cannot itself, that is, be a good model for our relationship with God. This is because our relationship with God completely lacks the equality and symmetry that characterize friendship. Furthermore, the presence of friends in our life multiplies our attachments to the world in ways that may well come into conflict both with our attachment to God and our commitment to God's purpose of equal regard (whether defined in terms of love, as in Christianity, or in terms of just respect, as in Judaism and Islam).

So both in itself and religiously, friendship can cause problems – first of all, because it seems to contradict our obligations towards equality, secondly, because it can tempt us towards thinking that friendship is itself religiously or spiritually satisfactory. Each of the traditions in different ways troubles the straightforward endorsement of friendship as simply ethically good. It is always more complicated than that, they seem to say; there is more at stake here than you initially realize. We will see how next.

Judaism

Of the three traditions, Judaism has the strongest, least conflicted attitude toward friendship. Because of the strong community identity of the People Israel, and the recognition that the religious community exists in a non-universal way among many other communities, the tradition has always been fairly comfortable with special attachments and local affiliations. Judaism affirms the good of certain cultural forms, as evidenced in the fifth commandment, to honor your father and mother. Indeed, at times, friendship has been more or less directly commended; so, for example, the medieval Jewish thinker Moses Maimonides thought that the highest form of charity is to go into business with a poor man, thereby recognizing and preserving his self-respect and dignity.[3] The command to respect others means that one more immediately sees the value of cooperating with them.

This raises the question of the relationship between respect and friendship in Judaism. A language of respect is needed as a way to see others as other selves, and thus possibly as friends. And yet Judaism always affirmed the legitimacy of a language of affection alongside the language of respect, and seems rarely to have been tempted to try to fuse them together. Friendship may be morally, even spiritually a good, but it is always supererogatory, never obligatory.

Nonetheless, there are strands of Jewish thought that created forces that could lead to the idea that humanity's destiny might include something like universal friendship beyond Israel and for all humanity. Most obviously, the universal eschatology of Judaism, developed especially in the Prophets but carried forward through the Rabbinic era and medieval Judaism into modern Jewish thought, transformed the scope of moral concern from the group to all of humanity. In modernity this is formulated even in Kantian terms by modern Jewish philosophers such as Hermann Cohen, but it has perhaps its most vivid formulation in the prophet Micah:

> In the latter days it shall come to pass, that the mountain of the Lord's house shall be established on the top of the mountains, and it shall be exalted above the hills; and peoples shall flow unto it. And many nations shall go and say, Come ye, and let us go up to the mountain of the Lord, and to the house of the God of Jacob; and he will teach us of his ways, and we will walk in his paths. For out of Zion shall go forth the law, and the word of the Lord from Jerusalem; and he will judge between many peoples, and will decide concerning strong nations afar off: and they shall beat their swords into plowshares, and their spears into pruning-hooks; nation shall not lift up sword against nation, neither shall they learn war any more. But they shall sit every man under his vine and under his fig-tree; and none shall make them afraid: for the mouth of the Lord of hosts hath spoken it. (Micah 4:1–4)

This eschatological picture of friendship as a universal possibility haunts Judaism, as it haunts Christianity and Islam, precisely because it seems so distant from the reality of the world as we experience it today. It goads all who hear its prophecy to imagine that the things that separate humans one from another may well not be the ultimate truth about us, and in this way every friendship made between people, whether strangers or neighbors, underscores the power of this prophecy, even as it convicts us of our failure to fulfill it.

Christianity

Christianity is deeply ambivalent about all worldly forms, so it is no surprise that it is ambivalent about friendship as well. On the one hand, the tradition's apocalyptic hostility towards worldly attachments makes it suspicious of friendship, and works as a corrosive acid on any affirmation of particular attachments to particular people here on earth. Two scriptural texts well exemplify this. First, consider Romans 3:22–23: "there is no distinction, for all have sinned and fallen short of the glory of God." Here, all are equal in their sinful distance from God. Second, consider Galatians 3:28: "There is no such thing as Jew and Greek, slave and freeman, male and female; all are one person in Christ Jesus." Here, in contrast, all are equal in redemption. Both of these principles – of the equality of humanity in fallenness and in redemption – are complemented by a third, namely, the sheer distance between a holy God and created humanity, whether fallen or redeemed. The distance is too great for interpersonal differences to matter in any significant way.

The key is that both as fallen and as redeemed, there is a radical equality among all humanity. This equality partly underlies the tradition's suspicion of special attachments. Christians are supposed to be friends with *all* people – so the tradition is not hostile to friendship *per se*, but simply to (what it implies is) humanity's typically improper restriction of friendship to some people to the exclusion of others. And yet it inevitably puts pressure on particular relations.

On the other hand, Jesus calls his disciples friends, and suggests they can become friends of God. As John 15:13 quotes Jesus as saying, "there is no greater love than this, that a man should lay down his life for his friends." Here, then, eschatological ambition seems to rebound against the mundane "natural" use of the term. Some later thinkers, especially in the middle ages, did develop this idea – that our relationship with God might well and fruitfully take the shape of a friendship. Here, then, this-worldly friendship seems to raise some suspicion, but it is supplanted by another kind of friendship, friendship with God. The form of friendship is retained, even as it is given a radically different content.

If our relationship with God is the proper norm of friendship, how will our ordinary friendships not be seen as somehow disappointing, even defective? There is a tension where a metaphysical weight is placed on what looks to be an ordinary this-worldly form, and disappointment can all too easily be the outcome.

For these reasons, then, Christianity's worldview and values may, in subtle ways, put interesting and possibly damaging forms of pressure on Christians' particular friendships, even as it presses them to treat all people as friends.

Islam

The situation in Islam relative to friendship is somewhat more obscure. Certainly, the tradition recognizes the legitimacy and even propriety of special attachments. And yet Shari'ah recognizes few groups or associations beyond the family as religiously relevant, and in fact raises worries about some of the most powerful such associations in the world of pre-Islamic Arabia. To be sure, the "Companions of the Prophet" were a select group and are still honored as such today. But a struggle against another kind of local attachment has marked Islam from the time of Muhammad forward, and can still serve in a way not entirely dissimilar to Christianity's approach, to shadow and trouble Muslim friendship in interesting ways.

That other kind of local attachment is *'asabiya*, which signifies a form of group cohesion of the tribal and/or familial sort. Muhammad himself preached against the dangers of *'asabiya*; there is a *hadith* recorded by Abu Dawud: "He is not of us who proclaims the cause of *'asabiya*; and he is not of us who fights in the cause of *'asabiya*; and he is not of us who dies in the cause of *'asabiya*."[4]

The danger Muhammad seemed to see here was manifold. On the one hand, *'asabiya* stood behind all the blood feuds that made the pre-Islamic Arabian peninsula so brutal and cruel a place. But more deeply than simply as a motivator for feuding, *'asabiya* corroded the fundamental Islamic idea that there is truly only one community – the *umma* of the submissive – and that all other communities are sickly and fractious parodies of it. Were a true Muslim to attempt to incorporate into his faith his membership in the Banu Quraish, for example – or as an Arab, or a Caucasian, or anything of the sort that would exclude some of humanity from the definition – that person would be deluded about the true bases of his identity. The worry here seems to be putting a lesser cause at the center of your life, and not being willing to leave kin and kith behind if God calls you to do so. As Abraham was called on to shatter the idols of his family's household gods, so one must leave behind one's own household gods when one undertakes the life-long pilgrimage that is the true faith.

The challenges, and moral and spiritual qualms, about friendship here are not hard to imagine. For friendship is not only creative and fruitful, it is exclusionary, drawing lines between people that cause them to see themselves as separated. Furthermore, friendship so understood offers a certain and inescapably *local* good – a good available only to the few fortunate enough to find it. As such, it can seem to present a rival good or source of flourishing to the good of submission to God. It is no wonder, then, that Muhammad saw attachments of the sort represented by *'asabiya* to be profoundly inimical to the faith. And every Islamic understanding of friendship must struggle with this most severe condemnation in thinking through the place and limits of friendship in the Muslim life.

Conclusion

Far from being a simple matter of sheer, obvious positive goodness, then, friendship is a powerful moral reality that demands serious ethical and religious reflection for all three of our traditions. Because of the way it raises questions about its distinctiveness from sexual and marital relations, because of its capacity to split the religious community into groups of "friends" and "not-friends," and because ultimately of its complicated and ambiguous similarities (and dissimilarities) to the relationship that believers are supposed to have with God – for all these reasons, and more, all three traditions treat friendship as a very serious matter indeed.

Hence, all three speak about the limits of friendship. They all ask after the *edges* of friendship, both what goes into the making of friends, but also and more importantly, they ask about the far side of friendship – how ought we to think about how to relate friendship to marriage, to communal identity, or to religious piety, in various ways? In all these questions, what the traditions find especially important about friendship is the way in which properly "this-worldly" human relations may bear, in powerful and unforeseen ways, on the relationships established between humans and God. Tendencies towards messianic universalism, or towards friendship as a model for the human-divine relationship, or careful and wary assessments of the power of friendship to destroy religious community, all testify in different ways to the serious power of this most ordinary, even mundane, of human realities for humanity's ultimate destiny. This is just one way in which the traditions bring a moral and spiritual seriousness to their reflections on ordinary life.

In future chapters, we will see how far this seriousness extends in other directions as well.

6

Sexuality

Everyone agrees that sexual behavior is important. Most people would agree that it is morally important. But why? What reasons have we for thinking that sexual activity is a morally significant reality? Children? Well, we seem to think that sex is important irrespective of whether it results in children – we seem to think that sex is important because of what it does to *us*, those who engage in sex. Irrespective of any offspring, we seem to invest a great deal of meaning in sexual behavior and attitudes towards sexual behavior. (Indeed, sometimes we seem to invest more meaning in our attitudes towards sexual behavior – especially other people's behavior – than we do in our actual behavior itself.)

There is an immediate, bad sense in which sex is so important – for we live in a world in which sex is used for commercial purposes, to sell products. This reinforces the way that we approach everything as an object to be consumed, as a device for our self-pleasuring. (There's an important difference between "ecstacy" and pleasure.) We live in a world in which sex and consumerism have become intertwined. In this world, everything from anti-perspirant to yogurt to laxatives to condoms is sold by appeal to some sort of sexual attraction. This debases the goods being carried, but it also debases sex – for it reduces it to a neat and self-contained commercial exchange. It makes all of us whores. We live, that is, in a powerfully vulgarizing society. And in this society, thinking morally and religiously about sexuality, its pathologies and its healthy forms, is an urgent task.

But that is not the most important reason. The most important reason is that sexuality is an ontologically significant reality. What do I mean by "ontologically significant"? I mean that it has implications for how we understand the nature of the cosmos, the nature of being itself. The world is sexual. Something about our understanding of the structure of reality is revealed in our sexual behavior and beliefs. For our self-understanding and our conception of the world are intimately related. How we see the world affects how we see ourselves, and vice versa. As we grow from infancy into adulthood, who we are and what we understand the world to be changes, and the changes are correlated to each other in complicated ways.

This process of co-creation gives determinate shape to our picture of the world in ways we may not fully acknowledge. (This is a deep insight of the field of developmental psychology of the past century.) And this co-creation of self and world is in important ways inaugurated and guided by drives which are crucially *sexual* – or rather, that our sexual drives are themselves manifestations of or aspects of a broader sort of affective relation to the world. "Sex" becomes just one form of love, an energy driving us to identify with, and perhaps unify ourselves with, others. As Sigmund Freud said:

> The nucleus of what we mean by love naturally consists … in sexual love with sexual union as its aim. But we do not separate from this … on the one hand, self-love, and on the other, love for parents and children, friendship and love for humanity in general.… Our justification lies in the fact that psychoanalytic research has taught us that all these tendencies are an expression of the same instinctual impulses … language has carried out an entirely justifiable piece of unification in creating the word "love" with its numerous uses.[1]

Sex, seen as a form or developmental stage of a basic principle of love, reveals to us then that we are part of the world, a world that we are able to love; and that the world must be, in some sense, a loveable world. But because a world is loveable only because it gives us the capacity to love in the first place – a giving which is itself identical with what is given – this means that the world is itself a loving world. Sexuality is importantly related, then, to the nature of creation itself.

Because of this, it is important to inject a high level of deliberateness into sexuality, for the intensity of its effect on the whole shape of our lives is quite profound. Sex is a basic force for life – it is not just what *creates* life, but what also *sustains* it. Nor is sex something that can be quarantined from the rest of your life – it always involves itself in all of your relations. Sex is one manifestation of a basic urge that drives you to make yourself more fully connected to other people and the world as a whole.

And that is the theme of this chapter. Sexuality is important for the ontological constitution of reality, as well as our own constitution. Few dimensions of human life have the capacity of sexuality for radical selfishness or genuine engagement with the other. Because of this, sexuality is, or can easily become, a moral problem for us that has a great deal of importance for our overall lives. And the religious traditions all have rich and powerful ways to think about it.

The structure of this chapter is simple. I want to get clear on a variety of views on sexuality that have been held, and continue to be held, by many thoughtful people – positions that are not as well thought-through, I will suggest, as their adherents think they are. Then we will look at the arguments of some Jewish thinkers, who argue that sexuality has always been viewed as an enormous good and an equally enormous power in Jewish law (which carries over into Christian and Muslim thought as well, in different ways) – and that the very high value the Jewish tradition has placed on sexuality is what has led to sex being treated with enormous moral significance and a great deal of reflective care. We will then turn to some Christian arguments, which emerge out of an originally quite apocalyptic attitude toward sexuality, but which became, over the centuries, less whole-heartedly negative towards humanity's sex drive. Finally, we will look at some Muslim arguments of Abdelwahab Bouhdiba for an Islamic picture.

Throughout this discussion, we will also look at the moral status of homosexual acts in these traditions, exploring the reasons different thinkers have had either for condemning such acts, or for arguing that they ought to be understood as just another manifestation of human sexuality that, when governed by appropriate moral strictures, can be conceived of as good. Our focus is on homosexual *acts*, because before the twentieth century, there was no concept (or no concept that appears in major theorists) of a homosexual *person* – one oriented towards sexual relations with members of the same sex.

Common Misconceptions About Sex

There are three bad ways of thinking about sex, ways of thinking that are quite common today and that we need to overcome. It will help to enumerate these here. First, some fixate on the negative power of sexuality, which underscores the disruptive and "contaminating" character of sexual activity, and the way that sexual intercourse can have implications, physical and emotional, that alter the fundamental shape of our lives. But to focus on this dimension alone is inadequate, for it is only partial; and even the negative consequences of sex are not all that sex is, and we must take care not to confuse the abuse of an activity with the activity itself. The religions emphasize the dangers of sexuality precisely because it is so vulnerable to abuse, not because it is in itself an inherently demonic force.

Secondly, others go to the opposite extreme, and attempt to divinize sex – to make it the most proximate human experience of the divine. Now, to be clear, this is not to say that such a view commands absolute promiscuity. The view of sex that sees it as theologically potent does not promote sexual promiscuity – it is seen as a sacred encounter, supernatural or magical in its reality and its effects. This feeds our culture's longing for authentic intensity, so that recently this has become a powerful option in consumer culture, with its interest in extreme experiences, so that it treats sex as an "extreme sport," like Base-jumping or other liminal activities. But the core idea is simply that sex is of *absolute* value, as our most intense experience of the Holy, or the Real.

But we ought not to expect too much from sex. If we invest the bare act of intercourse with more weight than it can bear, we threaten to disappoint ourselves and our actual partners by replacing her or him with an ideological projection of what we expect them to be. Furthermore, such visions of sex as extreme render sex an escape from an otherwise boring and humdrum reality, which is a terrible calumny about our ordinary lives. This is deeply corrosive of long-term sexuality in stable marital relationships. The problem is that such relationships inevitably and I would say properly domesticate sex, and our consumer culture does not want such domestication.

There is a third kind of danger here. It is all too easy to recoil from this vision of sex into a banalized picture. Here the temptation is what we could call the ironist's temptation: to avoid making things matter in the wrong way, by making nothing matter much at all. While this approach may tempt us with its charming promise of our superiority to the activity by refusing to grant it any sovereignty over our lives, in fact its charm for us suggests how deeply terrified we are of acknowledging the very real grip our sexuality can have on us. It is not a sign of the sophistication and maturity of our particular cultural moment, but is rather one more symptom of the particular pathologies attending this moment.

Of course, there is some value to this ironic approach. Sometimes sex is merely a form of playfulness. In these situations we should accept it as such; not all sexual activity must be monumentally great; not every kiss should make you rethink your life. But no one particular example of an activity can exhaust the full meaning of the activity. Also, it ignores the inevitable complications of most sexual relationships, and encourages an unhealthy resistance to recognizing that sexual life is significantly integrated with the rest of our life, especially our emotional life.

We have seen several ways in which sexuality is prone to misconstrual in our culture. But what positive help can we find to think about a proper understanding of sexuality? More specifically, what resources do these traditions offer us to guide or critique our sexual behavior? We turn to that next, beginning with Judaism.

Judaism

Historically, most Jewish thinking about sexuality begins by affirming the fundamental good of human sexuality and its profound significance for flourishing human lives. But it goes on to insist that the human is not merely or exclusively a sexual creature, nor even a sexual and social creature; along with the communion we possess in sexual and social relationships, there is another spiritual communion we possess, with God. (This is part of the point of humanity's creation in the image of God, for Judaism.) These forms of communion are not wholly distinct, but do not collapse into one another either. For this tradition, elucidating the relationship between them is a central issue in much of its thinking about sexuality.

Sex in general

In Judaism, as we will also see with Christianity and Islam, sex is crucially related to marriage, and to the idea of a lifelong relationship of morally serious weight in which sex finds a natural role. One can almost say that there is no singular concept of sex as an isolated event in traditional Judaism – that in fact what we know as sex is divided among several different categories, the most prominent of which is "consummation," the consummation of a marriage bond which has no independent identity outside of the institution of marriage. Another is "adultery," which is sexual activity outside the bonds of matrimony. But properly speaking, sex takes place in a context defined by a lifelong marriage, and when discussed in isolation from that context, it is prone to be misunderstood.

This does not mean that direct discussions of sex cannot be properly pursued. Often they are, especially in legal discussions of pure and impure sexual acts (often related to women's menstrual cycles) and what acts are shameful, and what not. But those discussions, and the acts under analysis therein, should be understood as part of a marriage, not as something only accidentally connected to it. When seen in that context, as part of the overall shape and texture of married life, sexuality is seen as a way of *ecstasis* – of realizing transcendence – not in a momentary fleeting experience, but the whole shape of a lived life. In this way, sexual congress is a sacred act in Judaism, so much so that Orthodox Jews understand it to be a *mitzvoth* for married couples to have sex on the Sabbath.

It is only through marriage and the family that sexuality can support human sociality. Historically, the main basis for this association of marriage with sexuality does seem to be a certain construal of the import of marriage and family for social stability; were these institutions threatened, the worry seemed to be, the future of the People Israel would be in danger. While this concern has not disappeared, it has been supplemented (and at times supplanted) in the last few decades by an insistence on the moral well-being of the individual as the rationale for keeping the tight connection between sexuality and marriage. (As we will see later, it *is* historically unusual, to say the least, that even many parents today would rather see their children at twenty single and with an active sex life than married at twenty.) The idea here is that marriage *channels* sexuality, organizes our otherwise rather disorganized loves and helps us to use sexuality to develop into morally mature persons.

Why is this so important? It is so because humans are not momentary or punctual creatures, but creatures who perdure over time, and thus have histories. As Eugene Borowitz puts it, "a person must live one's life not only in the present, if one would be a self, but into and through the future as well."[2] We have responsibilities to the future and the past, as well as to the present. We ought to have, as it were, historically minded sex. Our sexuality is not only about ourselves in the punctuality of this moment, but for our lives as a whole. A marriage is not only a relationship for now, it is a relationship designed to become part of the permanent fabric of the cosmos – something in the context of which people can change, and grow, and mature, and grow old. Marriage is not just a relation, it is an institution – an institution that must bear the weight, most centrally, of two human lives. Sexuality plays a crucial role in keeping that institution healthy, and offering an exclusive set of goods to the partners therein.

More particularly and distinctly Jewish understandings of sex focus on the Covenant. Sex is understood in relation to marriage precisely as part of the Covenant, and the Jews' obligations under it. That is to say, Jews' sex lives take place in the light of the covenant, and sex has as one of its most crucial aims the propagation of children – continuing the People Israel. For this reason the question of sexuality bears, in Jewish understandings, not just on interpersonal faithfulness and the propriety of certain acts, but also on the relationship between the Jews, as individuals and as a community, to God.

So here is part of the answer to how sexuality and spirituality relate. Sexuality is *instrumentalized* for fulfillment of the covenant. But also, sexual relations themselves are powerful experiences of the other as an other self, and the experience of sexuality as fulfilling God's commands in the most existentially and experientially powerful way imaginable. So sex, by being instrumentalized for the covenant, is also given back to the People Israel as a venue, in itself now, structured by marriage, for a powerful experience of the Holy.

Judaism on homosexuality in particular

Judaism's views on homosexual acts appeal to the above themes in manifold ways. There are at least two possible views, one more traditional and one more revisionist, though the revisionist view is due to new thinking about the nature of choice and orientation.

The more traditional account would see homosexuality as a violation of God's will for creation and the created order of sexual distinction. While some versions of this seem to root this argument in an understanding of a law of nature, most are content to enumerate God's commandments about homosexual acts and stories from the Bible as a basis. They appeal to verses like Leviticus 18:22, which says "you shall not lie with a male as one lies with a woman; it is an abomination." (Significantly, Leviticus 18:23 concerns bestiality, thus associating homosexuality with sex with animals.) They further point out verses such as Leviticus 20:13, which suggests that "if a man lies with a male as one lies with a woman, the two of them have done an abomination; they shall be put to death; their bloodguilt is upon them." Finally, they appeal to the stories of Sodom and Gommorrah, in Genesis 18–19.

The key is that, on the traditional account, one's sexual acts are not only one's own. They speak to what God wants and expects of us. We are accountable to God, and homosexual acts seem like wanton, willful violations of God's order – flagrant and voluntary perversions of the way God wants creation to go, perhaps one of the greatest forms of rebellion there could be.

Thus, traditionally in Judaism, homosexual acts have been construed as willful and voluntary chosen acts of rebellion against God, and punished accordingly. But what if homosexual orientation is *not* wholly a matter of choice? How might that change in our understanding obligate us to alter our understanding of traditional condemnations of homosexual acts? Perhaps significant adjustments are necessary.

For a long time many who want to defend the legitimacy of homosexual sex in Jewish communities have been stymied by the tradition's apparent concern against it. In light of this they have either argued effectively that homosexuality is a tragic condition for which the community ought to feel sympathy, or they have suggested that Jewish *halakah* is outmoded and we need to recenter our moral lives around the commands of love, dignity, and commitment.

More recently, some thinkers have suggested that we try to find a way to interpret *halakah* in such a way as to be more welcoming of homosexuality. It is clear that *halakah* is mutable, as it involves human understanding and judgment. Perhaps, these thinkers suggest, there are resources in the tradition to reinterpret homosexual activity as something other than the abomination it was traditionally taken to be.

As regards this issue, the flaw in human understandings, some argue, lies in the received picture of homosexuality as *sheerly* volitional. Today, many believe that homosexuality is in part internal to a significant minority of human desire-structures – an expression, as some say, more of diversity than of perversity. Because of this, these thinkers argue, there may well be opportunity for more rethinking of the tradition, to disentangle the idea of homosexual behavior from wanton rebellion against God. If it can be seen not as rebellion but again as a form of legitimate human difference, inscribed into the fabric of creation, then possibly homosexual activity can eventually find its way into faithful Jewish practice.

The Jewish tradition, in sum, is clearly historically hostile to homosexual acts, though it is unclear how important and how much moral concern was given to such acts traditionally. Today, in any event, it seems possibly amenable to developments that could be hospitable to homosexual persons. We will see that in Christian ethics both parts of that claim are harder to establish.

Christianity

Christianity has a long and complicated relationship with human sexuality. Its views on sexuality are in some ways more fraught than are Judaism's, because its apocalyptic tendencies are more powerful. These tendencies lead Christians to amplify the moral calamitousness of our present condition, on the one hand, and thus come to see human sexual behavior as in some sense disordered due to original sin; and, on the other, to view anything that attaches us to the world as sinful. (After all, sexuality ties you to the world in terms of your partners and possible children; but if the world is ending, why would it be wise to be so tied?) Over time, the Christian tradition developed a more grudging acceptance of the idea that human sexuality has a deeply positive role to play in human sanctification, though there are still tensions and contradictions at work even today. We will see the details of this below.

Sex in general

Traditionally, the normative picture of the sexual act was defined as heterosexual, potentially procreative, and practiced within a permanent, monogamous relationship. This traditional account gives rise to five norms of sexual activity: it must be heterosexual, open to procreation, concerned with the satisfaction of sexual desire, and performed as an expression of love between husband and wife. These norms were fairly stable for many centuries, and up to the Reformation in the West, they were complemented by a picture of celibacy as that mode of human life which was best suited to bring the self to God – both because celibacy required a lifelong struggle with one's own sexual desires, and because it secured the person from the "cares" and "distractions" which were seen as the inevitable accompaniment to marriage, and detrimental to the development of one's relationship with God.

Only with Luther did the idea of marriage as a site for positive value for the self's encounter with God become an ecclesially endorsed reality, at least in the Christian West. For Luther, Christian marriage and human sexuality became a way of disciplining the self's passions and teaching the person something about the gratuitousness of God's love for fallen humanity. Sexuality, like all other dimensions of ordinary human life, became a site of positive significance in the divine economy of salvation. Luther, a former monk, *monasticized* ordinary life: that is, he urged ordinary Christian laity, in their everyday lives, to inhabit their every moment with the acute theological and moral self-scrutiny that previously only monks had been taught to employ.

The consequences of this were complicated. After the Protestant Reformation, Protestants were more positive in some ways about human sexuality, no longer privileging celibacy as a superior form of human life. But the temptation to identify sexuality as a particularly powerful vehicle for human sin remained, and in some ways was amplified as the monasticization of the laity led to a renewed attention to human sexual behavior, and sometimes to a more articulate and well-communicated hostility to sex as part of the created blessings of human life. Roman Catholicism, following its own developing path after the sixteenth century, also increased attention to marital sexuality, but in practical terms the consequences were roughly the same: sexuality still seemed more centrally a site of peril from sin than a possible locus of graceful blessing.

More recently, and especially in the second half of the twentieth century, Christians, especially those in the West, have moved to reassess their attitude towards sexuality. Today, personal fulfillment in a rich and mutual interpersonal relationship has become the preeminent criterion of sexual morality, for both religious and unreligious people alike, and Christians typically frame their understandings of sexuality in those terms. But there are more particular criteria that some contemporary Christians have tried to develop to interpret sexuality in light of the Christian drama of Fall, redemption, and sanctification, and those Christians would offer something like the following as a moral matrix within which to understand and evaluate sexual activity. First, sexuality is not about autonomous, self-seeking pleasure – it expresses our will to human communion, and genuine relation to God. Second, sexuality is not the only relevant dimension of love; love is also affection and emotional attachment, and a flourishing sexual life rewards these dimensions in turn. (Humans are embodied, and yet that embodiment is in deep and mutual relation with human spirituality.) Third, the fundamental sexual sin is alienation; concomitantly, sexual salvation is wholeness or integrity, a recovery (or achievement) of integration of all parts of a person's life. In sum, sexuality is not just about deep communion with the partner; it is also part of the self's ongoing salvific struggle with God. Far from being a uniquely charged site of sin, sexual life is an especially dense location of grace.

This revolution in sexual theology has large implications for homosexuality. Insofar as sex is now seen not as good only because of procreation, homosexual acts become less immediately and obviously immoral. Addressing this possibility has unleashed a series of debates, and made the last few decades in Christian thought the most exciting and innovative on matters of sexual morality since at least the time of Augustine. We turn to that next.

Homosexual acts

Historically, Christianity has shared with Judaism a profound condemnation of homosexual acts, though it has seen them not simply as signs of individual humans' rebellion against God, but as evidence of the perversity of humanity in general, and indeed of all creation, after the Fall.[3] Christians have traditionally employed one of two approaches to address homosexual acts, both of which regard homosexual acts as wrong, though for interestingly different reasons. Natural law accounts understand the moral problem with homosexuality in terms of an account of human *nature*, and what it is right for humans to do in order to flourish in the natural realm. Divine command accounts understand the moral problem with homosexuality via an account of how God has told the human to be, in order for the human to be in right relationship to God. (This is a fairly stereotypical representation of the differences between Roman Catholic and Protestant views, but for our purposes it will have to do.)

One might argue that homosexual behavior is wrong from a basis of "natural law." This is what Aquinas did; he argued that homosexual acts, and other illicit sexual activity, are bad because they go against the natural order. For Aquinas, sex is good, but disordered in its nature due to original sin. (Our experience is very important to understanding what is morally acceptable, and what is not; but we cannot naïvely accept the witness of our experience because it is skewed by sin.) The forms of sexual disordering can be gathered in two groups. The first group consists of those acts in which the substance of the act is proper, but other conditions are mistaken – this includes sex out of marriage, incest, adultery, that sort of thing; the sexual act occurs in such a way that it employs all the physical parts of the body (not just the sexual organs – there is no physical violence here) as they are meant to be employed, according to Aquinas, but the situation surrounding the acts is somehow misordered. The second group consists of those acts where the substance is wrong. These Aquinas calls the "unnatural vices," where the word "unnatural" is not just rhetoric but a weight-bearing term – sexual acts that are contrary to nature. Now, in this group, homosexuality is ranked as the next to worst sort. (The rankings of unnatural vice, from least bad to worst form of unnatural vice, go like this: masturbation, bestiality, "sodomy" (which means here homosexual activity), and "not observing the natural manner of copulation" – oral sex, anal sex, etc.)

For Aquinas, it is clear that the second group of "unnatural" vices is a much more serious kind. This makes masturbation a far worse sexual crime than adultery, rape, or incest. Why is that, you might ask? Why is unnatural vice so bad? Presumably it does not hurt other people, as rape does, right? Why wouldn't it be worse if it were a violation of charity, against the neighbor? Well, for Aquinas, while it is not a crime against a human neighbor, it is against God, because it is a "corruption of the principle on which the rest depend," a violation of the laws of nature which God has ordained; therefore it is disobedience of God.[4] A person *is* hurt by it – namely, God.

This raises an interesting question about natural law accounts, such as Aquinas's, regarding why homosexuality is wrong. It may also quite severely indict other sexual acts in ways that make many people uncomfortable. Does this mean that for Aquinas the least worst kind of "unnatural vice" is still *more* offensive to God than the worst kind of natural vice? – That, in other words, masturbation is a graver sin than rape?

Natural law accounts are not the only kind Christians have had recourse to over the centuries. There is another sort of account with which one might argue that homosexual behavior is against the declared will of God for creation. This is what Karl Barth offers. This sort of argument is structured quite differently; here, homosexuality is not bad so much because it is against the natural order, but because it is against the relationships into which God is calling us to enter. Homosexuality, much like celibacy, is a violation of God's command to enter into community and become what one truly should be. This is what Barth means when he says "the male is male only, but precisely, to the extent that he is with the female, and the female likewise."[5] So homosexuality, for Barth, is wrong because of its effects of mis-gathering the wrong – same – sorts of people.

But then Barth also, like Aquinas, goes where many today do not want him to go. He argues that all "male or female seclusion" (including celibacy, and perhaps fraternities and sororities) are wrong – because they are attempts to be alone, without the other gender, to be wholly self-satisfied in oneself, not to reach out to the complementary otherness of the other gender. As he puts it: "the decisive word of Christian ethics must consist in a warning against entering upon the whole way of life which can only end in the tragedy of concrete homosexuality."

Liberals have tried to employ a new interpretation of the meaning and theological significance of sexuality in a way that renders homosexuality less immediately illicit. Typically, they do so by redescribing the crucial characteristics of sexuality less in immediately bodily terms, thereby downplaying the literal physicality of sexual activity, in favor of a description of sexuality that focuses moral significance on the interior experience of the participants. We experience our embodiment through the understandings and experiences we have had; we are never merely or purely "carnal" creatures, with our embodiment absolutely determining our experience; insofar as we are also fundamentally spiritual creatures, our spiritual make-up (in the broadest sense) must be factored into our experiences of sexuality from the beginning.

Because of this, liberals insist that the whole question of homosexuality is in fact much more complex than earlier condemnations of it will admit, both in terms of what the Bible and tradition say, and in terms of our own deliberations on these matters. The witness of scripture and tradition, they argue, is *ambiguous*, and evinces no comprehension of the idea of homosexual behavior as an orientation rather than a set of discrete, willfully rebellious acts. What Christians must look to, they argue, is their own experience of homosexual persons, and here they suggest that most Christians, no matter how theologically conservative, will allow that the homosexuals they knew are in fact living out what they experience as a genuine orientation, not a willful perversion of their God-given nature. For them, a "liberal" approach to Christian sexual ethics is more attentive to the ways that individuals, especially women but also men, have been mistreated by the sexual norms of the past – but this liberal approach offers this attitude *through* appropriating the sexual norms of the past.

Most fundamentally, they insist that we cannot, we do not, simply "read" the Bible and uncover its unitary and straightforward meaning. Rather, any act of reading is always situation-specific. The Bible must be read in light of *our* experiences, in light of *where we are*. But this is not relativism; rather, it is simply the recognition that our sense of a text's meaning is shaped by our own previous experience.

In many ways Christianity shares profound similarities with Judaism on these matters. For example, as with Judaism, one central issue here is the nature of sexual attraction. Is homosexuality most fundamentally a matter of individual voluntary acts – of "choice" – or is it rather a matter of pre-voluntary orientation, before an individual's agency is exercised? In a way, the question of homosexuality is so fraught for us just because debates about it hang on questions which our picture of the human ill-equips us to answer. We like to think that who we are is simply a matter of our direct choices and that if we do not "do" something, then it must be that we are *helpless* before it.

In another way, however, Christianity's views of sexuality are distinctive, because they are charged with more direct theological weight, as they exhibit the human's drama in the struggle of sin and redemption. For a long time, human sexuality was commonly seen as especially suggestive of human fallenness. More recently, it has been interpreted as part of our calling from God. Whether seen as exemplary of sin or of grace, however, Christians have always interpreted sexuality through the cosmic drama of sin and redemption. For Christians, every act of sex bears in it faint traces of the Last Judgment.

Islam

In thinking about Islam on sexuality, it is powerfully tempting to imagine it as a religion of sexual repression – of heavily bearded men, and women in large, bulky, body-shape hiding robes, seeking to erase human sexuality from the world. But in fact the story of Islamic thought about sexuality is far different from that. This is evident from the fact that, up until the mid-twentieth century, the above sterotype about Islam would have seemed absurd; then – that is, from Islam's first emergence in Christian imagination until around 1960 – the sterotype of Islam is of a religion of uninhibited libidinal desires – of harems, assignations in moonlit oases, of sheiks of Araby and the like. The fact that the stereotype of Islam has undergone a 180 degree reversal over the past few decades should tell us something about how much these pictures owe to Westerners' own debates, and how little they owe to the realities of Islam.

Despite the need to hack through a thicket of stereotypes, we can indeed find a rich and vital history of reflection on the meaning of sexuality for Muslims. Because of the slenderness of general Islamic orthodox doctrine, however, these discussions have been carried out in the discourse of legal debates (focusing on what is illicit sexual activity) or in the various speculative metaphysical and mystical discourses of individual thinkers. So Islamic thought about sex is on the one hand codified in different ways with the various legal systems of the various socieities in which it finds itself, while on the other hand it is found in the irreducibly individual and therefore inevitably somewhat idiosyncratic speculations of various thinkers and mystics. Nonetheless, these two sources of thinking can give us some idea of the range of Islamic thought about sexuality, though they cannot ultimately delimit it for future interpretation.

Sexuality in general

In Islam sexuality is not rooted in the covenant, as for Jews; nor burdended with the ambivalences and ambiguities of Christian apocalypticism and the idea of original sin; it is rather rooted in the dynamism of divine creation. As such it is the most speculative, metaphysical, and mystical account of sexuality. On this account, sexuality is an unmitigated good – a cosmic and theological good. Creation itself is the core context out of which human sexuality emerges, and God's act of creation was in a complicated way sexual – so that sexuality is a sign of the divine will and the divine power.

Sexuality is social, and related to shame and the dichotomy of private/public. It is a way of *fusing* society, keeping it coherent. But more deeply than that, some Islamic thinkers have suggested that sexuality is quite profound because it is about the copulation of complementary opposites – the bringing together of things that are different and whose difference is determined in part by what they are different from – namely, each other. "Male" and "female" on this picture are different because they are meant *for* each other, and meant for each other precisely because *they* are different.

So the sexual differences are signs, significant of a larger duality and complementarity, and the performance of the reunion of these complementarities is a good that God expects, and that God rewards with pleasure. Sexuality recapitulates creation, not only in procreation, and not only in the reunion of opposites, but also and equally deeply in the pleasure the creators take in their creativity. Furthermore, sexuality is total, an all-encompassing reality. As the contemporary Tunisian scholar Abdelwahab Bouhdiba puts it, sexuality is a mediator "in this universal process that begins with opposition, continues through alternation and becoming, and culminates in prayer."[6] (Imagine what it means to say that sexuality culminates in prayer. Most of us would suspect that prayers, and begging, mostly take place before sexual activity, particularly for teenagers, except in cases of contraceptive failure.)

Sexuality is significant, and it is significant of significance. Bouhdiba calls it a "sign of signs" – that is, it always is about more than the immediate physical relation of bodies, whether holding hands or having sex, but bears a meaning because of the larger relations and emotional attachments that both parties bring to it. Moreover, the fact of this significance is itself significant – for it reveals that even at its most naked, the erotic energy that is the source and center of creation always expresses a meaning that is not captured by itself – that is, in a word, *transcendent*. The fact that sex is meaningful is itself meaningful; it means that reality itself is meaningful of something beyond it.

That gives you some idea of what significance human sexuality and sexual relations can take in traditional Islamic thought. It also illuminates the tradition's general suspicion of homosexual behavior. The metaphysical speculations underpin a powerful hostility to homosexual activity.

Islamic thought on homosexual acts

In Islam, traditionally speaking, anything that violates the order of the world is a grave disorder, a threatening source of evil and anarchy, and homosexual activities are a paradigmatic instance of violating that order. As with Judaism and Christianity, traditionally Islam, particularly in the Qur'an, has seen sodomy fundamentally in terms of rebellion. As Lut – the Quranic "Lot" who confronts the Sodomites – says, "Among all the creatures in the world, will you lust for males, and abandon the mates whom God has created for you? You are transgressing all bounds" (Q. 26:165–66). And so in traditional Islam, as in traditional Judaism and Christianity, the sexual nature of creation is decidedly heterosexual.

Because of this, homosexual acts are traditionally one of the few things that have been understood to warrant the death penalty, and as one of only three sexual deeds so worthy (the others being rape and adultery). These acts, the traditions imply, are an affront not so much to God's law as to the ordering principles that God has instituted.

Interestingly, however, the relevant Qur'anic passage does not specify a particular punishment; it merely says "punish them":

> If any of your women are guilty of lewdness, call four witnesses from among you; if they testify to their guilt, confine them to home until death comes to them or until God ordains to them another way.
>
> If two men are guilty of lewdness, punish them both. If they repent and amend their ways, leave them alone–God is Oft-relenting, Most Merciful. (Q. 4:15–16)

The need of four witnesses for women, and the perpetual possibility of repentance for the men, both speak to the caution of traditional Islamic law on these matters. The presence of mercy in the Qur'an, given the ever-present possibility of "turning" away from the condemned practice, means that in fact this punishment was not inevitably exacted. Nonetheless, the tradition is clear on this. Homosexual action is fundamentally *unnatural*, and suggests a revolution against the order of nature that God has clearly ordained. While the condemnation may be practiced mercifully, it is still fundamentally a condemnation.

Nonetheless, there is – perhaps – a latent Islamic argument for the Qur'anic validity of homosexual acts, based again on the argument that in earlier ages there was no way to understand homosexual acts as other than a wildly perverse expression of human will, revolting against a natural order that governed each person in the same way. When Lut says to the Sodomites, "you are transgressing all bounds," in the Qur'anic passage discussed above, it is clear that the core problem is the character of these acts as "transgressing all bounds." But today we think that not everyone experiences homosexual desire as a rebellion against their nature; again, for those oriented towards same-sex attraction, it would be totally licit, socially affirmed heterosexual acts that would seem against nature. Because of this, to "submit" to God's will in the sexual sphere, for some people, means to accept that God has made them to be attracted to others of the same sex.

Whatever the view of homosexuality taken in Islam, however, its overall vision is set within a context of profound affirmation of human sexuality – Islam's vehemence against other forms is precisely because of the importance that it attaches to what it sees as proper sexuality. While Islamic thought is unanchored in a concern for a particular people (as is Jewish thought), and yet not troubled by world-denying apocalypticism (of the sort that has so haunted Christianity), it offers a way for its faithful to think about sexuality as both religiously and metaphysically profound and positive, and also legally and ethically quite seriously prescribed.

Conclusion

In a way, the ultimate question of this chapter is simple. What is sexuality *for*? How does it fit into our overall lives – and not just our individual lives, but the lives of our societies, and our lives before God? Answering these questions helps enormously in determining how properly to assess sexual behavior for its propriety or impropriety.

Sexuality is inescapably an embodied phenomenon, but it raises questions about how we ought to understand our embdodiment as part of our moral and spiritual lives – how our embodiment both enables and constrains us in our longing for the Holy, and our quest to be good. Insofar as our bodies relate to God, part of that relation must be through our sexuality.

One deep issue that is especially revealed in the debates about homosexuality is that perhaps all the parties are, in part, expressing a dissatisfaction with our received understanding of agency – a picture of us as wholly voluntary beings. Love and its manifold experiences are misconstrued if we think about them purely on the model of voluntary choice. And yet that seems the only plausible account to us, at least as we currently understand human agency. Perhaps we will have these debates until we find some new manner to think about the complex character of human action in more supple and complicated ways.

At the end of this discussion, however, another question presents itself. Why have these traditions decided that the family and marriage are the right focus of all sexual activity? The next discussion – about marriage – should help here.

7

Marriage and Family

The previous chapter tried to argue that sex is so important morally, not only because it can have dangerous moral consequences, and not only because it is pro-creative of children, but also because sexuality is important to us in deep and profound ways. Sexuality tells us about the world and our relation to it in ways unequalled by any other activities or spheres of life.

Thus marriage becomes important here, because marriage is the context in which humanity has, for the last few millennia at least, lived out its struggles with sexuality and with the consummation of human community. Marriage is the most acute experience most humans have of another person. This chapter will argue that marriage is not so much *a* moral problem as it is *the* fundamental form in which most of us experience the moral concern of otherness upon us. (By "fundamental" here, I mean not the earliest form of moral concern, but the most profound, persisting, and massive form.) Furthermore, understandings of family and marriage are deeply intertwined with larger social and political issues. Therefore, marriage is not adequately assessed merely as a private matter between two people; we should also acknowledge the social and political realities within which any actual marriage exists.

Things are different today. Today, marriage is a far more voluntary institution than ever before. This makes the risks of it greater, but also the self-conscious rewards can be greater as well. Statistics show people are less likely to marry today, and fewer people expect to stay married than ever before; yet the numbers who think a good marriage is "extremely important" have increased slightly in the last two decades. The average age for first marriage is older (24 for women, 27 for men), and divorce is far more frequent. In 2001, the National Center for Health Statistics reported that, in the United States, 43 percent of first marriages end in separation or divorce within 15 years.[1] So a good marriage seems both more important to people today, and faces new challenges as well.

It is odd to think that young people aged 20 today consider themselves so much less naïve and innocent of the ways of the world, less morally prudish, than their grandparents' generation at the same age. It is odd because far more of their grand-parents were *married* at the age of 20 than they are. Many even had children already. So who is really more innocent of the ways of the world?

Part of the challenge for successful marriages, it seems safe to assume, lies in our large-scale uncertainty as to just what marriage is all about. There are, broadly speaking, two tendencies in our contemporary public discourse about marriage. Marriage, we are told, is all about sex, or it is all about equality. Either it is effectively an institution for the satiation of all our desires, or it is to be approached warily as if it were a tidal vortex, threatening to suck us into a condition where we "lose our selves" in a larger agglomeration of mass consumption.

Much is ignored by such definitions. Much is also avoided – most importantly, how to relate the various goods of marriage. Indeed, while there is a great deal of moralistic talk about marriage, most of the time we find that marriage itself is not presented as a moral challenge, because we do not want to think about marriage as hard, as work – as happening in time, and the concern of fundamentally temporal beings.

Our topic is vast and fundamental, and as with earlier chapters we will study it by attending to how the three traditions have tended to think about it. Following that, we will look at the vexed question of homosexual marriage as two of these traditions confront it. (Because of the limited amount of attention that this issue has been given in Islam, we will not discuss that tradition here.) Here we ask, what do these traditions have to say about the possibility of ordaining a specific way to recognize and legitimate same-sex marriage? The value of studying this issue is that it will help us articulate the various reasons and convictions that all of us – whether we are members of these traditions or not – have that stand behind the positions we hold, and thereby help us improve our understanding of marriage, both as the traditions represent it and as people experience it. Thinking about homosexuality and marriage helps us get clearer on what we think is essential to marriage, and what we think is *in*essential to it. It make us all (even those who are, and remain throughout, in principle opposed to homosexual marriage) think more seriously and sustainedly about what marriage is, and why homosexual marriage should or should not count as a legitimate form of it. Again, as elsewhere, argument is an educational tool, not a device for indoctrination.

Throughout, we will see that the key question is always, what is *essential* to mar-riage? What *is* marriage, after all? Ultimately, we will see that, while all three tradi-tions see marriage as centrally important, each explicates its religious and moral significance differently.

Judaism

Judaism's understanding of marriage is deeply covenantal. In Genesis and Leviticus, marriage is represented as a matter of establishing and protecting social relations. Genesis defines marriage as leaving one family for another, while Leviticus determines marriage in terms of a list of rules about prohibited sexual conduct (which is, in general, a fairly depressing list of crimes, especially when one reflects on the thought that these probably all happened, as they do today). The key issue here seemed to be the stability of a social order in a clan-based society. Yet even in this early stage, there is a sense that the value of social stability and of the institutions (such as marriage) that support it, is explained in part by the People Israel's commitment to the covenant.

There is a story in the Talmud that underscores the significance of marriage as the rabbis saw it. Once, a Roman matron asked Rabbi Jose bar Halafta, "From [the creation of the world] until now, what has God been doing?" The rabbi replied that God "is occupied in making marriages," and "every marriage is as difficult for the Holy One, blessed be He, as the dividing of the Red Sea."[2] The story is revealing in several ways. First of all, the image of a marriage here is of rescue, a route to sanctity – but this is a sanctity long deferred by the 40 years in the wilderness. Perhaps God is trying to make humans worthy of marriage, and perhaps that effort can only work if we take the time necessary to do it – in the story, 40 years.

The rabbis continued developing this tradition. But it is more than just a good thing for human flourishing. For the Jews, the rabbis say, marriage is part of the prophetic task of Israel. The rabbis see marriage as a form of completion, a sanctification of Israel. In fact the liturgy of marriage formulated in rabbinic times and still used by Jews today echoes the scriptural themes of divine creation and the rebuilding of the destroyed Jerusalem.

Because of this history, Judaism has a theologically profound and ethically realistic assessment of the goods of marriage. Understandings of family and marriage are deeply intertwined in Judaism with larger social and political issues. Thus, marriage cannot be thought about as merely a private matter between two people, but must acknowledge the social and political realities within which the individuals exist. Because of the traditional view of the male as the one who works outside of the domestic economy of the household, this means that duties and rights differ for men and women. Traditionally, men are required to marry, but women are not; men make all the promises in the marriage vow; the woman makes none.[3] Furthermore, divorce is relatively easy in traditional Jewish law: the mutual agreement of the partners is required, and the husband must give his wife a *get*, a divorce document (thus undoing the promises that he made at the wedding to institute the marriage).

The realism of the rabbis toward the state of marriage means that marriage is seen as a state in which expectations must be chastened, but that chastening must be chastened as well. In Judaism it is good to have children, but sex is important to marriage outside of whether children are born from it. It is considered a natural good of marriage, and an obligation. So sex is a theologically charged reality; marital intercourse is connected to the highest expressions of holiness of which most people are capable. Nonetheless, sexuality has only a limited place in marriage. On the other hand, the rabbis insist that individuals' "private" sexual activity is not merely private, but takes place in a communal context to which it is held accountable. Central to such accountability is the question of how sexual activity builds up, or hinders, the Jewish people's commitment to fulfilling the covenant with God.

Thus, marriage is important because it is both an ontological and a political reality – it suggests how much we can be with people, and how much our sociality is something we are willing to strip away. Traditional Jewish understandings of marriage recognize our need to be with others, and yet they also recognize the danger of seeing a marriage as exclusively about children; they recognize, that is, the necessary selfishness of the couple *qua* couple, and the individuals who compose that couple. It also recognizes our need for God, alongside recognizing the fact that not everything should be ruthlessly oriented toward God.

In the modern era, traditional understandings of marriage have undergone significant challenge and revision. In one way the modern focus on the individual has made marriage more about voluntary content and fulfillment. In another way, however, the rise of gender equality has made many think that the received tradition is too male-focused in its attention to marital rectitude.

The possibility of homosexual marriage in Judaism is in principle perhaps less fraught than in Christianity, if only because the question of marriage in general is less fraught. Given the centrality of the covenant to Jewish understandings of marriage, and the traditionally matrilineal character of Jewish identity, one can reasonably anticipate that much of the resistance to homosexual marriage may focus on the inability of same-sex couples to reproduce naturally. If the nature of Jewish identity is reconceived, however, so that adoption becomes more fully normalized, some of the most powerful arguments against same-sex marriage in Judaism may well become defunct.

Christianity

As was the case with sexuality, Christianity has had an ambivalent relationship to marriage. On the one hand it sees the good of marriage, and even amplifies that good by talking about the communion of the Christian church with God as a "marriage." But on the other, its apocalyptic leaven makes it structurally suspicious of any human community which is not immediately organized around worship of the Christian God.

This ambivalence is present in the tradition's scriptures. Along with the Old Testament, it has the New – and it interprets the Old through the prism of the New, often in ways that quite dramatically affect the sense of the earlier texts. This is especially prominent in Christian understandings of marriage. Most central among the New Testament texts for Christian discussions of marriage are the letters of Paul, and in particular the first letter to the Corinthians. In that letter, Paul distinguishes between what is "from me" and what is "from the Lord" and most of what he says about marriage is from him – marriage is a bother because it brings worries and divides cares, so should be avoided if possible. It is easy to see the apocalyptic character of his teaching – all in light of the fact that the world is soon coming to an end.

In contrast to this glancing and, to some degree anyway, contemptuous view of marriage, the early church used a certain "spiritualized marriage" metaphor to explain the relationship of Jesus Christ and the church. So the idea of marriage was quite powerful from early on, as a model of how Christ and the redeemed community relate; and because of this, marriage eventually became a *sacrament*, a sign and means of God's grace, from early on in the Christian churches' history.

Hence, Christians have historically had a powerfully ambivalent view of the place and significance of marriage in the life of the believer. Today, Christian understandings of marriage still carry that ambivalence, though often quite covertly. There are more "liberal" and more "conservative" Christian understandings of marriage abroad today, and they also undergird substantially different understandings of what is going on in the question of same-sex marriage. We will look at versions of each. Then we will look at an approach that takes a deeper historical view, seeking more traditional resources for Christian life.

Many liberal arguments will begin by noting the historical relativity of the forms of the family, while affirming the absolute social and political necessity of the family as a force for transformation and salvation in creation. The family is both relative and absolute: it is relative because the family structure has changed throughout history – nuclear families are nineteenth-century inventions; hence, family structures that are different from the nuclear family are not wrong just for being different. And yet the family is necessary, not only for childrearing (which is far more difficult when it is a single parent's job than when it is a couple, or a number of adults together), but also because the family is about transforming ourselves into beings who more fully inhabit our being, which is our capacity for love, and this capacity is increasingly attacked in our culture.

Why is this so? For liberals, here is an opportunity for cultural critique: our culture, they fear, is replacing love with desire, rejecting a view that sees marriage as a project of coming to see another person for who they are and to value them as who they are, in favor of a project of seeing others as "completing" you, fulfilling your needs – or else unworthy of your continued fidelity.

To resist this instrumentalization, marriage must be seen as profoundly contingent on the partners' commitment to it. Marriage is a process of becoming, and in its "processional" character it desperately needs the involvement of God to direct it in the right ways. Therefore, marriage is never, for such liberals, just a relation between two, but always refers to a third that is essential to their flourishing. And this relation between the two and God, takes place in an inescapably *temporal* fashion.

This description of marriage and its challenges is in no way restrictive of marriage to heterosexual unions. In fact, liberals see no substantial reason to so restrict marriage. If marriage is in fact about the communion of two people with God in a project of training the participants in love – and if that training is an attempt to live out a life in integrity that is authentic to one's own calling into sexual personhood – it is not only *not* surprising, but expected, that some will find that calling to take the shape of a same-sex marriage. If, as many believe, some not insignificant proportion of humans are oriented towards sexual attraction to the same sex, then those people will find their calling in same-sex marriages.

In contrast to liberal Christian depictions of marriage as contingent, Christian conservatives typically emphasize the need for stability in marriage as a bulwark against the fickleness of the humans who are putatively committed to it. Such conservatives worry both about the liberal emphasis on contingency and about the picture of the human that they think lies behind it – a human with a will that they can easily command, a will they must autonomously align in order for the marriage to be real. For conservatives, this gets things backwards in two ways. First of all, people should be able to rely on the marriage being stable even when they themselves are not. Secondly, the vision of the human here is far too focused on the individual will, to the denigration of the person's various enmeshments in community and their inevitable embodiment as male or female. But it is precisely these constraints that are significant; unless we acknowledge the important physical differences between men and women, we cannot understand marriage's purpose.

Hence, Christian conservatives worry that these assumptions misconstrue marriage and the human person, and make it hard to see how marriage is the site wherein most of us encounter, in the profoundest and most immediate form, what it means to be finite, and sinful, yet blessed with love and communion. In this way, these thinkers suggest, marriage plays, for most people anyway, a crucial salvific function. Because of this, they worry about the future of marriage in quite fraught, even apocalyptic terms. They worry that Christian liberals are really seeking to escape the inescapable condition of embodiment; they think that that desire to escape bleaches away the distinctive goods of marriage, which can only be appreciated ascetically – that is, by a practice of disciplined transformation of our passions and dispositions to align them properly with what God wants. As Gilbert Meilaender, a contemporary American Christian ethicist, says, marriage serves "a healing purpose. It is, among other things, a divine ordinance intended to bring our wayward desires and passions under control, intended to begin to shape them in accord with the pattern of God's faithfulness."[4] Marriage is healing or therapeutic – not because we have been victimized, but because we are sinners; and if we do not confront its challenges in these terms, we will fail not just to understand marriage, but the Christian gospel more generally. There is inevitably a *sacrificial* dimension to Christian marriage, a dimension of marriage that invites genuine painful suffering on the part of the participants as they suffer the transformation of their affections. (This is hard to deny: There is something profound revealed in the fact that in Eastern Orthodox marriage services, the bride and the groom wear crowns – not the crowns of royalty, but of martyrdom: of those who must suffer, and whose suffering is sanctified because it is significant of a life lived in humble obedience to God's call, and following in Christ's footsteps to the cross.) For conservatives who emphasize this sacrificial motif, it is saerilicial precisely the liberals' inability to see the meaning of such conversion, and such sacrificial suffering, in terms of the inflexible reality of male and female bodies that makes liberals find same-sex marriage unobjectionable. For these conservatives, then, liberals fail to see homosexual desire as a challenge given by God, to some, with which they are called to struggle – a challenge in some ways relevantly like a physical handicap.

Note that, in this debate, the conservative and liberal positions use many of the same words, even the same categories, but construe them in significantly different ways. For example, they have quite different fundamental conceptions of sin, or at least different emphases about sin. For the liberal, sin is primarily a matter of incoherence in ourselves, a form of inauthenticity, where the loss of integrity reveals a flawed picture of the self. For the conservative, in contrast, sin is primarily a matter of our wayward desires, which need to be reordered in proper fashion, to be aligned with the external moral order. Both of these accounts, when pressed, will accommodate the other's insights, to a degree; but both subordinate the other insight to their primary one. These different pictures of sin motivate different accounts of good action and bad action, and offer differing pictures of the moral nature of homosexuality therefrom.

To be frank, most of the arguments about homosexual marriage, whether "liberal" or "conservative," have typically relied on some extension of the views we see above. "Conservatives" think homosexual acts are wrong on natural-law grounds, or on divine-command grounds, and tie that to a vision of marriage as disciplining the self, and these components reinforce a condemnation of homosexual marriage. "Liberals" do not think that homosexual acts are morally charged in the same way, either because they dismiss the viability of natural-law accounts, or because they read the divine commands in Christian scripture differently, and they in turn tie this to a view of marriage as a process of discovery and exploration, and these components reinforce an acceptance of homosexual marriage. In both cases, the views are pretty clear and predictable.

Recently, a third understanding of Christian views on homosexual marriage has begun to emerge, one that is deeply traditional and like the conservative position in insisting that the fundamental sin is a matter of our wayward desires, which must be brought into right order by ascetical practices. Yet, like the liberal position, this view argues for the propriety of same-sex marriage in the tradition. The most powerful exponent of this view is the American theologian Eugene Rogers.

For Rogers, a proper understanding of the propriety of same-sex marriage must take a step back, and understand the meaning of marriage itself. He understands marriage to be more central to Christianity than just a lifestyle for some people. "Christianity … enacts a nuptial mystery;" that is, the Christian faith itself *is* a marriage. (I pointed out earlier the importance of the idea of sacrament for Christian understandings of marriage; Rogers is getting at that theme here.) On his understanding of the tradition, marriage is "a way of participating in the divine life not only by way of sexual satisfaction but by way of ascetic self-denial for the sake of more desirable goods … marriage is not primarily for the control of lust or procreation. It is a discipline whereby we give ourselves to another for the sake of growing in holiness."[5] This understanding of marriage is, as he says, *ascetic* – it is a form of moral training in order to prepare its adherents to live a certain kind of life. And for Rogers, all of the Christian moral life is ascetic, because Christianity is all about training its adherents to become certain kinds of people. (In this, Judaism and Islam are ascetic traditions as well.)

What is the nature of the moral transformation that this asceticism seeks? For Rogers, it is not most fundamentally a reordering of our wayward desires – though that is an appropriate general description, it is not specific enough. No, the key is not simply our having the right desires, but learning to see ourselves *as* desired, as wanted. God loves humans and humans must learn to see themselves as loved, and as created to be loved. In light of this, marriage is not a site primarily designed for the satiation of our desire for the other, but rather for the other's desire of us; instead of both parties entering into marriage in order to *get* something, Rogers suggests they should both enter into marriage in order to allow themselves to be *gotten* – and thereby to "use" marriage as a training site for their larger pattern of coming to accept the fact that they are loved by God. The disciplines of asceticism in the Christian life, for Rogers, are all ways of making humans vulnerable to, susceptible of, and watchful for, God's ever-pursuing love.

Marriage and monasticism both undertake this asceticism differently, on Rogers' account. Monasticism is for those who find themselves transformed and sanctified in the direct desirous perception of God. But marriage is for those "who find themselves transformed by the desirous perception of another human being made in God's image."[6] In such settings, sexuality, disciplined by and into marriage, becomes one way in which God draws humans into communion with a loving Triune God.

Rogers ties this vision of asceticism and the meaning of marriage to an argument about the diversity of creation itself. Creation is diverse. And the diversity of homosexuality is more outrageously diverse than heterosexuality: "if bodily differences among creatures are intended to represent a plenum in which every niche is filled, then the burden of proof lies on the other side."[7] That is to say, those arguing against homosexual marriage need to show that homosexuals do not participate in this creative diversity. Normally, such opponents do argue in this way, by suggesting that homosexuals are unnatural, not part of the order of creation, but a "swerving" from it. But Rogers wagers that most Christians arguing against this will not take that route. They will argue that homosexuals are part of the created order, not simply an effect of the Fall.

If this is so, Rogers says, "for gay and lesbian people, the right sort of otherness is unlikely to be represented by someone of the opposite sex, because only someone of the *apposite*, not opposite, sex will get deep enough into the relationship to expose one's vulnerabilities and inspire the trust that healing requires. The crucial question is, What sort of created diversity will lead one to holiness?"[8]

In sum, then, Christian arguments about marriage, and about the possibility of same-sex marriage, must confront and work through the same tangle of tensions and arguments as does Christian ethics as a whole. The tradition seems to deprecate this-worldly existence, while yet also insisting on its sacramental nature; it seems suspicious of human sexuality as a privileged conduit for sin, yet also insists that sexuality will be part of the redeemed human being, as it was part of the created human being; and it seems suspicious of the institution of marriage and family because of their tendencies to make us favor some people over others, while the tradition yet insists that humanity as a whole is one family, and that the best model for humanity's relation with God is one of a "mystical marriage." We will see next that Islam's account, and its challenges, are quite different.

Islam

The status of marriage in Islam is a bit surprising. To overstate it only slightly, marriage has no distinct theological or religious status. In Islam, marriage is a legal contract – it is not a sacrament. It requires the mediation of no special religious authority; it is a legal contract between two partners, the man and the woman. Indeed, in classical Shari'ah handbooks, laws on marriage are located together between laws on oaths and laws on commercial activities. It seems, that is, to have no special theological significance.

Of course, the lack of a sacramental vision of Islamic marriage is not because the institution of marriage is not saturated with religious significance, but because it bears no *special* significance, because all of reality is homogeneously saturated with religious significance, and all is regulated through Shari'ah, religious law. We can therefore understand marriage's non-sacramentality in Islam in two different ways. On the one hand, it might be seen as an example of the tradition's indifference to marriage, its treatment as incidental to the great struggle inside the soul of the believer and between the believers and unbelievers in the world as a whole. But on the other hand, it can be seen not as contemptuously indifferent but as audaciously indiscriminate – as underscoring Islam's insistence that *all aspects of life* are religiously charged.

So marriage's ordinariness and mundaneity in Islam does not mean that marriage is unimportant. On the contrary, it is very important, though its significance lies wholly in the worldly realm of human social life. There is a very popular *hadith* in which Muhammad is reported to have said, "When a Muslim man marries, he has fulfilled half the religion."[9] And this is because, as Lois Lamya' Ibsen al Faruqi puts it, marriage offers "a balance between individualistic needs and the welfare of the group to which the individual belongs."[10] Thus the benefits of marriage are, from the supercharged perspective of Islam, quite mundane. It provides a controlled forum for sexual behavior and procreation, a stable space for childrearing, and a secure form of economic sustenance for the mothers of children. Furthermore, it offers a distinct kind of "emotional gratification" for both women and men.

On this understanding, marriage is not made a sign of the relationship between the community of humans and God; it is essentially a human social form, one in decisive ways placed under the overarching structure of the extended family. In fact one can say, with only a little exaggeration, that in Islam the central category for marriage has historically not been the couple, but rather the family. The reasons for this have something to do with culture, but also something to do with the traditional Islamic sociopolitical imagination. In general in this tradition, the family is isomorphic to society – a well-ordered family is the private "model" of the public "model" of a well-ordered society. Family life and social life are two spheres in which the human submits to God's will, and thus proper family order is quite crucial in traditional Islamic thought. This is important – for we in the non-Islamic, post-Christian "West" think first and foremost about the couple (thus I framed this chapter as "marriage," not "family"); but in most traditional Islamic cultures, the family is given more fundamental consideration as the crucial fact about marriage.

Because of this, divorce is possible, for both men and women, so long as the family structure remains intact. (Thus, Islamic law has given considerable space for reflection on childcare issues.) A divorce does not threaten the divine-human relationship as it does in Christianity, nor does it put the future of the community in peril, and thus threaten its covenant with God, as in Judaism. A divorce, in Islamic thought, is simply a sign that a purely human relationship has failed, and the main concern is to contain the consequences of that failure to the couple involved, and manage its effects especially on the children, so that social stability is ensured and the children are raised in a context of security and love.

For all these reasons, the question of same-sex marriage in Islam has simply not come up as a major topic in the tradition, and while there are some Islamic thinkers in the West today exploring this idea, the profoundly non-religious character of marriage in Islam makes it difficult to construct an explicitly Islamic argument for same-sex marriage.

None of this is meant to deny that there is no serious and profound Islamic theological enquiry into human love as reflecting something of the God-humanity relationship. Of course, there is, especially in Sufism, a wide range of reflection on how human longing for the beloved reflects, or should reflect, humanity's quest for God. But the Islamic legal tradition's explicit denial of any sacramental or religious weight to the institution of marriage means that marriage *qua* marriage is not the central focus of this tradition of reflection.

Conclusion

Clearly, the issue of marriage is a rich and complicated topic. And today, more than ever before, the debate about homosexual marriage is a live one, and one to which we are well advised to attend, no matter our views on the practice. After all, those debates raise questions about the character of marriage and its role in society, as well as even broader questions about society and how we understand ourselves and the reasons we have for entering into marriage.

The deep question here asked is simple: is love an end or a beginning? Cultural appearances may deceive. If marriage "resolves" one set of issues, it opens up a host of others, at least for the couple who are undertaking it. Too often in our culture, we find ourselves debilitated in thinking about marriage, because we find ourselves unable to imagine love *domesticated*. To "domesticate" love seems to us to kill it. We believe – or are told by the media and our consumer culture again and again, anyway – that real love, authentic love, is extreme, savage, wild, anything but domesticated.

And yet marriage is nothing if it is not an attempt to domesticate love, to bring it out of the wilderness and into the home – in Latin, the *domus* – into the family. It is, in this way, one more form of how these traditions all attempt to sanctify the mundane, here at least in the erotic sphere. This is a difficult challenge in any setting, but our culture does not make it any easier.

I have argued that marriage is not so much *a* moral problem as *the* fundamental form in which most of us confront the moral concern of otherness upon us. But we have seen here that that formulation, even if it may possibly bear up under scrutiny, still does not get at the full range of significances for marriage in any of these traditions, and may even obscure important parts of it. For marriage in each of these traditions is oriented towards significantly different ends, and these ends recursively affect each tradition's understanding of the nature of marriage. Because, that is, of the differing stories that the traditions tell about humanity and God's dealings with humanity, they have different understandings of what marriage most basically *is*.

As I have argued, one crucial dimension of moral consideration of marriage is time – how we inhabit time and what we understand the meaning of time to be. All too often our culture depicts marriage as the end of the story – the goal, the conclusion, the *finis*. But any real marriage is actually a matter always of beginning again, of renewing the covenant, of going forward, from this moment, now, in life together. It is no accident marriage has been linked to birth. Both are experiences of newness. Insofar as we are always new beings, we have to fight against end-ism, against summing up, against conclusions – against death. We want to control things, but this means to end them. And that is suicide. In contrast, truly to live is always to live bravely. In these ways, then, marriage is one way that ordinary time becomes significant, for some traditions perhaps even sacramental.

These perhaps stratospheric theological concerns should not obscure for us the ground-level fact of the sheer ethical and personal *difficulty* that marriage entails. Marriage is the great opponent of selfishness. But all three traditions – indeed, all of the relatively sane persons whose acquaintance I have made in my life – would recognize that we are nothing if not deeply selfish creatures, in some ways good, in others bad. Marriage challenges this selfishness, makes us uncertain of how or who or what we want to be, because it takes us out of ourselves in surprising ways. Still, marriage can also destroy real human individuality – it can be a person-crushing experience. It is the most intense expression of the claim of moral otherness upon us that most of us face, and we should think about it not simply in terms of love, but also in terms of commitment, and in terms of commitment that are importantly *moral*, and also (for some of us) importantly *religious*.

The moral of this story is simple. Our private acts are crucially public, our personal commitments are inextricably related to larger sociopolitical ones. Far from being a purely personal discussion, the act of becoming married, and the ever-renewed act of staying married, is also perhaps the first virtue of our political existence.

8

Lying

The previous chapter, about marriage, revealed something about the moral status of everyday life. Marriage, I argued, is not so much *a* moral problem as it is *the* fundamental form in which we experience the moral concern of otherness upon us. This is because marriage is never a purely private matter between two people, however much one might like to believe that; it must acknowledge the social and political realities with which it is implicated.

The moral form of the discussion about marriage, then, was that the most profound moral challenges emerge precisely from the center of ordinary living. And this is one of this book's most basic points: for these traditions, and I would argue for human life itself, morality is not a matter of the extraordinary or heroic, but of the mundane. It is in the everyday that we find ourselves challenged by the deepest moral perils imaginable.

Insofar as most of us encounter genuine good, or genuine evil, we do not encounter them in scenes that would appear in movies. And yet we do, I think, encounter them. It is part of our challenge to see that the everyday touches on the deepest challenges we face.

This is certainly true about the topic of this chapter: lying. Like marriage, at first, lying looks like a wholly individual, fairly innocent, amoral matter. But each of these traditions has thought a great deal about it, and each insists that this most "harmless" of behaviors actually has serious public and theological implications. (It is worth noting that when we call something "harmless" we normally implicitly recognize that it actually is harmful.) Far from a trivial matter, each tradition thinks of lying, and the ethics of speech more generally, as a crucial dimension of their traditions.

Thinking about lying in fact brings us face to face with several of the deepest themes this book asks us to confront: the problem that different traditions frame issues in very different ways and therefore understand moral issues quite differently; the question of whether moral conviction becomes so absolutist as to be moralistic

– that is, more interested in judging the rightness or wrongness of actions in a spectatorial manner rather than attempting to guide a genuine human life; and finally, the revelation that some of the most profound moral and spiritual issues that humans can face lie not at the extremes of human existence, but at its ordinary center – in the mundane everyday muddles of daily life.

In this chapter, after an initial attempt at getting clear about what lying *is*, we will look at each of our traditions to see what we can find therein.

A General Picture of Lying

To begin with, what exactly do we mean by lying? Here is a rough definition: lying is the intentional act of deceiving someone. This rules out questions of whether you have a malicious purpose in lying, or whether you think you are telling a lie for the person's own good; it also rules out the question of the truthfulness of your own beliefs, so that even if what you present as false (or true) is in fact false (or true), if you believed that it was true when you sought to convince someone that it was false, you have, on our definition, lied. In other words, you lie when you know you deceive someone.

Now, lying is obviously something that most of us, if asked, would say is morally wrong. But if we probe our behavior even a little bit, we see that there can be times when lying may seem morally harmless, necessary, or even perhaps beneficial. Examples of this are not hard to find:

- How many times a day do we walk by someone else who asks us, "How's it going?" We know the right answer is "OK" – even when we're not OK, even when we're deeply sad or upset about something. In such situations it may seem like etiquette compels us to lie.
- Alternatively, what about those times when you're talking to a family member on the phone, and they ask how you are doing; in such situations you may well lie to them if you don't want them to worry about you.
- What should you tell your children, if you have any, about Santa Claus?
- What about those situations where someone asks you to do something with them (not even a date), and you lie to get out of it; or you lie to get an extension on a paper, or to explain why you missed class. (How nervous must college students' aunts and uncles and grandparents be! For I must tell you that, anecdotal analysis of email from my college students shows that such relatives are quite likely to suffer a sudden tragic accident or illness, or even death, at a rate much, much higher than the rest of the American populace, and oddly, just around exam time.) You could have told the truth, and maybe received a lower mark, or had the person be a bit upset at you; but instead you looked for the easy way out. But is it so easy?
- Imagine you live in occupied Holland during World War II, and you are hiding a Jewish family in a secret basement. One day, the Nazis come to your door and

demand if you know where any Jews are hiding. Do you tell the truth or do you lie? What if you say, "They're under your feet!" – hoping that they will take offense and storm out; and they do. You succeeded at deceiving them while telling a literal truth; but isn't this both lying in a deeper sense, and being too morally fastidious (because you are anxious to avoid the surface appearance of a lie)?

These examples suggest that we have a more complicated attitude towards truth-telling than we typically tell ourselves we do. And this in turn raises questions about the purpose of all our moral posturing about lying. It raises questions at the heart of the distinction between morality and moralism. Morality is moralistic when it focuses on judging people to the exclusion of understanding and helping to direct (and at times correct) them. Are we asking ourselves *how can I act not to be blamed*, or *what is the good thing to do here*? So while we generally think lying is bad, at other times we feel that things that seem to be legitimately called lying can be at times be socially useful, perhaps even morally right. Are there times when our concern *not* to lie may become itself immoral? When our excessive interest in remaining ethically immaculate or morally pristine may in fact allow, or even cause, actual positive wickedness to happen?

These are questions fundamental to the human condition at any time. But there are also challenges specific to our particular day. Today, it seems increasingly hard to tell the truth, as our culture moves toward accepting a kind of dissembling, a form of "spin" in all aspects of life – in important part because of the increasing complexity of our lives, and thus a deepening sense of the difference between the many roles I play in society, and the "real me." The meaning of deception and its moral character is thus both a perennially fundamental and a presently urgent matter.

But precisely why, we might wonder, is lying distinctly bad? That we do think it bad seems a simple fact revealed by our behavior: lying requires a reason, but truth-telling does not. Lying must be excused. And we only need an excuse when we have done something out of sort. What exactly is wrong with lying? Here there are several possible components to an answer. First and most personally, there is the damage that lying can do to the individual who lies. (The primary damage to the individual who is lied to, I take to be axiomatic and obvious.) Consider your own experience of lying, and in particular what some thinkers call the "two-sided experience" of lies, the fact that we want sometimes to be able to use them, but we want no one else ever to be able to use them. Why should we want something occasionally that we do not want anyone else ever to use?

Consider the psychological perils of telling lies. After all, lying is like a spider-web; as someone said, it is easy to tell a lie, but hard to tell only one. To begin to lie is to enter into a maze of your own making, in which it often ends up being more work to keep the deceptions straight than it would to tell the truth from the first. Lying is an attempt to control; and by and large attempts to control lead to more situations where we feel the need to control. A trick we use to try to escape becomes an even more powerful trap for us.

Lying brings with it another, I think more profound, cost to the individual. I propose to you an odd sort of introspective activity. Pay attention to yourself the next time you lie, or reflect as best you can on a recent lie you've told. Somewhere, deep down at the bottom of that experience of lying, I wager you will find something a bit surprising. I bet you will find that a certain experience of terror accompanied your lying. Yes, certainly some of that was fear of being caught. But another part of it was something else – fear of being believed. It is deeply upsetting, I wager, to tell a lie and find that people accept it as the truth. When we lie, that is, a little bit of us realizes that we can make the world go wrong, and know we are doing so. There's a phenomenological experience of vertigo there, as if one had a glimpse of the bottomlessness of human interaction. Perhaps it's lies all the way down. A bit of our trust in the world dies when we lie; and if we think the world is worthy of trust, that is a kind of real damage.

Along with the individual perils, there are social perils to lying. And these are many. Our society is built on the implicit trust we give one another and assume in others; without it, we're in deep trouble, and quickly. Think about driving on a major street in a city, undivided in the middle by any barrier save a strip of paint, you zipping along blithely indifferent to the other cars whizzing by you in the opposite direction, with maybe three feet between you and them, both lanes running 50–60 miles an hour, but in opposite directions. What is to stop someone from swerving? After all, it happens from time to time – mostly accidentally, occasionally on purpose. But these are accidents, the exceptions that prove the rule that we all trust each other in enormous, and largely tacit, ways. As society grows ever more complicated – as you find yourself more and more frequently giving people you've never met and will never meet, thousands of miles away in calling centers, your mother's maiden name, and not giving it a second thought – as this happens, the trust becomes more entangling, more essential to our lives. But this makes our lives all the more vulnerable to temptations to break that trust. To lie attacks this trust directly (in the lie itself) and indirectly, because it calls attention to how much we rely on this trust – and this attention can work, like acid, to undo it.

There is a third level of damage, at once both individual and social. People who routinely lie do not only make their acquaintances mistrust them; they learn to tolerate themselves by normalizing their behavior, and so begin to assume that everyone else is lying as well – thus making all human interaction illusory, a mockery of itself.

Hence our intuitive conviction that lies are basically wrong is backed up by both social and psychological reasons. It is not just a bit of weird moralism that suggests lying is bad. Lying is not simply about misleading someone verbally. It strikes at the heart of our sincerity with each other, our trustworthiness and reliability. When a lie is discovered, it is typically taken as a mark of disrespect for the other; it makes the other person wonder if he or she is dealing with "the real you," or just a convenient mask for your deeper, true, self. Speech is perhaps the most common way by which we are present to each other – by which we present ourselves to each other. And challenges to the trustworthiness of speech make us worry about the reality of our presence to one another.

But sometimes lies can be plausibly seen as legitimate, because the consequences of *not* lying are horrendous. Not all lies are bad in the same way; or perhaps, we want to say, they are not all equally bad. Plato, one of the greatest philosophers of all time, thought so. In his view, we can think of ourselves as allowing them – even telling them – without falling into total moral licentiousness.

One important thing to do is to distinguish between different kinds of lies. Not everyone would allow such a distinction to be made – and we'll talk about absolutists in a moment – but many of us do distinguish between harmful lies and what we call "white" lies. Perhaps the most famous exponent of such a distinction is Plato, who in his *Republic* makes a useful – though questionable – distinction between "true" and "useful" lies. What Plato calls "veritable" or true falsehoods are, he says, "deceptions in the soul about realities," a genuine lie that deceives us. But there is a second kind of speech that only superficially resembles lying, at least for Plato. These are what he calls "falsehoods in words," which are only a copy or replica of this one – an intentional deception. Sometimes this is useful, either in deceiving enemies or friends who have gone insane (here one has the intent to deceive, but the intent is excusable because of the situation); or in "edifying" fables, which we know are probably literally untrue but still convey something both important and useful. Plato's own example of this is the famous (for philosophers, anyway) "Noble Lie" – the story of how all humanity is divided into three classes of people whose souls are composed of different metals – gold, silver, and bronze; he says the leaders of the ideal state should tell this story to both themselves and the people of the state, over successive generations, so that all come eventually to accept the social order as a given and unquestionable structure.[1]

This may sound incredibly, obscenely paternalistic, a form of thought control practiced by one part of the population over the rest (and if Plato is to be believed, by the tellers over themselves as well). But is it really so distant from our own experience? Can we imagine any noble lies we have around? Any intentional deceptions we give ourselves or one another? Yes, there's lots; we lie, in part, to provide grease for social interactions. Think about (again) Santa Claus; what are parents *really* communicating to their children there? What about the line "all men are created equal" – what does that mean? equal in strength? in intelligence? in origami skills? What about "your vote counts;" does it, in an election that can be decided by a million votes?

So there may well be situations where certain things that look like lies may be allowable, or even good to say. What might absolute prohibitionists say in reply?

Absolute prohibitionists do have a response to the fact of troubling consequences. "If one stays close to the truth," they say, "one cannot, strictly speaking, be responsible for the murderous acts another commits. To give someone what they are due in no way means that you approve of what they do with that. If we did not recognize the difference between one and another at this point, the whole edifice of moral responsibility would crumble." But have they saved their intellectual integrity merely superficially here?

Typically, people offer one of three resistances to an absolute prohibition on lying. First, we can distinguish between really bad lies and ones that are not so bad. After all, we do pardon some lies, and we seem to recognize different degrees of severity all the time; that's why we have the category of "little white lies." Second, we can appeal to what we call a "mental reservation" approach – namely, an approach where, in our minds, we interpret our outward verbal expressions in idiosyncratic ways that permit us to say we are not "literally" lying, but only telling part of the truth. (For example, if your mother asks "do you promise to pick up your room?" and you say "yes," meaning "at some point quite far away in the future, like when I'm 35," you have engaged in a kind of "mental reservation" strategy.) Third, we might say that not all are morally wicked lies – some lies are justifiable: robbers, for example, or Nazis, have no right to the truth from us, and we are allowed to lie to them. Other moral concerns may trump lying's moral badness, that there will be times when what at least looks like lying will be permissible, perhaps even obligatory, to do.

Behind all of these, and behind the various counter-arguments to them offered by those who resist them, often lurks a common presumption that unless we can immediately offer a systematic account of when and why lying is wrong, our ethical development is undeveloped in a seriously problematic way. That is to say, both "prohibitionists" and "permissivists" over-value the systematicity of their accounts, and thereby silence the ambivalences and ambiguities that actual humans feel in these situations.

On the other hand, the easy reductionism of some other moral systems – such as, for example, utilitarianism (which says that at each moment you have to deter-mine what is the right act, based on greatest good for the whole) – is too extreme. Such views rely too heavily on our ability always to foresee clearly the possible outcomes of a range of choices, and suggest that outcomes alone determine the moral worth of actions. Furthermore, they do not seem able to acknowledge our presumptive, prereflective, almost instinctive valuing of truth, and put us on a slip-pery slope towards permitting many more lies. They obscure the damage that lying does to the liar herself – personal discomfort and loss of integrity, the greater likeli-hood, however marginal, of needing to lie again to shore up the first lie; and of a somewhat diminished resistance to lying in the future. They are to that extent, and strictly speaking, *inhuman*, not designed to accommodate the messy creatures that we humans actually are.

The upshot of this, I think, is that moral systems may not always be as helpful as many of us would like to believe. They offer clarity, but at the cost of reality; they provide comfort to the anxious speculator and spectator, but little useful guidance for the person caught in a sticky situation. (Thus, as many students of philosophy have discovered to their repeated dismay, systems do not inevitably lead towards the same outcomes – different people working within a system, or the same person at two different times, may come up with incompatible practical commands from the same system.)

Nonetheless, while systems may be dangerous, they may also be necessary. Some attempt at thinking that prepares us for difficult choices – which is what systems are originally meant to do – may be inescapable. We're bad systematizers – sloppy and inconsistent – but we're systematizers nonetheless. We look for general rules, seek out fundamental principles, try to make sense of our actions not just in the moment, but as reflecting some long-term convictions we have. So it is not that systems, just because they are systems, are inhumane. To say that they are, to reject the systematizing urge too completely, is just another form of inhumanity. Much of what we might complain about as inhuman in a system's resistance to our wishes is not its systematicity but its normativity, and it merely reflects systems' inflexibility before fickle and too-often self-centered human interests. Systems give people backbone to make and stand by hard choices, even when they do not think they want to do so.

Furthermore, a person's refusal to tell a lie in a situation where there is an obvious and immediate cost to that refusal, and a cost that is on its face morally significant, is not always a matter of a moralistic avoidance of responsibility; some belief systems give us very good reasons for thinking any lying is bad. The question about lying is how to rank different moral values, what's important to us, and why it is important. Is telling the truth important because it is directly about our relationship to God? That is, because it is about whether we trust in God, we trust that God's way, which is the truth, will be the best way? And is to tell a lie to seek to wrest control away from God? Alternatively, is telling the truth important because it is the fabric of human society, and truth-telling is the ground on which society lives? If so, then truth-telling is valuable only instrumentally, as a device to secure the flourishing of human society.

Figures in each of the traditions offer arguments of these sorts. It's time to look at them.

Judaism

Jewish teaching on lying and speech is sophisticated and nuanced. Certainly, the practice of keeping faith with what one has said is a central commitment of the Torah; and the story of Adam and Eve organizes itself precisely around the breakdown of trust in words, manifest first in Eve's exchange with the serpent, and then in both Adam and Eve's refusal to offer any direct answer to God's direct question to them: "Did you eat of the tree I commanded you not to eat from?" (Genesis 3:11), and then spilling out across the scope of human history. One could write a book telling the story of God's dealings with humanity in Genesis, Exodus, and beyond, that would tell the story through humanity's duplicitous use of language, both to God and to each other. And it makes much sense, then, that the ninth commandment is that "You shall not give false testimony against your neighbor" (Exodus 20:16).

And yet Jewish thought in general recognizes the complexities of life will some-times make some forms of dishonesty appropriate. Here we have the evidence of two texts – one that may strike you as a bit lax, the other that may seem excessively rigorous. But both proceed from a common set of convictions and a shared view of the nature and role of speech in human society.

First, the Talmud – again, after the Bible, the central source for Jewish law and ethics – permits several exceptions to the prohibition of lying. In fact, there are three situations, according to the Talmud, in which lying may be appropriate:

1 *Tractate.* It is acceptable to claim false ignorance as a check against pride; so that, if someone asks a scholar if they know a certain text, the scholar can present themselves as uninformed about the text – even if they know a great deal about it.
2 *Bed.* It is allowable to use dissimulation to shield marital privacy from public eyes. Not simply in terms of straightforward sexual matters, but more broadly, what occurs between marital partners is not normally a proper object of public exposure.
3 *Hospitality.* It is permissible to deceive another – about liking a meal, or gifts – in order not to hurt that person's feelings; as the Talmud puts it, "where peace demands it, a lie may be told."

In general, as the contemporary British Jewish thinker Louis Jacobs argued, "the idea behind the above teaching is that though truth is important it must not be made into a fetish. Truth is a value which exists for the benefit of society and may, on occasion, be set aside if the well-being of society demands it." What is central here is the sustainability of existence, the idea that humans have a large obligation to cultivate a stable world, and that this obligation may outweigh a moralist's clini-cal fixation on immaculate truth-telling. As Jacobs argues, "if absolute truth were always to prevail, man could not endure … man must try to live by the truth but there are times when truth imperils man's existence and then truth must be cast to the earth." The deep point being communicated here is related to the prohibition of idols. The moral code itself can become an idol, if it is distorted into a series of absolute and always inflexible absolutes.[2]

Does this suggest that Jews are in general more relaxed about lying? More lax about ethical matters? Far from it – as the tradition's prohibition of talebearing demonstrates.[3] Ancient Judaism distinguished between three kinds of bad speech – *gossip*, *slander*, and *talebearing*. I trust you know what gossip and slander are. But what is talebearing? Talebearing – in ancient Hebrew, *rekhilus* – is the act of bearing a tale to someone – telling someone that someone else is talking about them behind their backs. To be a talebearer is to be a tattle-tale, an informant.

In ancient Israel the sin of talebearing walked in some pretty impressive company. Consider the most proximate neighbors of its prohibition in Leviticus 19:15–16; that text reads: "You shall not act dishonestly in rendering judgment.

Show neither partiality to the weak nor deference to the mighty, but judge your fellow men justly. You shall not go about spreading slander among your kinsmen; nor shall you stand by idly when your neighbor's life is at stake. I am the Lord." Here, talebearing is associated by proximity to the act of honest judgment, and to the act of letting another die for lack of your testimony. Those are two large tasks. So, even if what you would report is true, even if you'd say it with the other person present, even if the person being told already knows what was said, *even if* it will cost you a great deal, so that you must risk losing your life's savings – even if *all* these things are true at the same time, it is still not right to inform.

Why is talebearing *so* bad? It violates an explicit negative commandment, yes. But it is not simply that it violates God's explicit command – it has complex and damaging implications far beyond sheer disobedience. It's precisely in these most mudane matters where restraint can have the most effect. By the time you have to consider more momentous decisions, and undertake more dramatic acts, things have already gone too far. "What would you do if the Nazis came?" is a question that we use all the time, in thinking about ethics; but in fact it is precisely the wrong question to ask. The "Nazi problem" is *too Wagnerian*, if you will – too grandiose. If you get to the point when you're worried about Nazis, society's already frayed too far. Where we can stop a culture of lies is at the beginning, in the minutiae, the little things.

Questions remain, of course. Can there be morally good gossip? What about gossip among college women, concerning which men are sexually aggressive when they drink too much, or are violent? But would gossip be the right response to such knowledge? Presumably there are situations in which something like talebearing is permissible, just as is the case with lying. And indeed there are. The Jewish tradition says it is acceptable to lie in more dramatic moments, too. The Jewish tradition called this *pikach nefesh*, "the saving of human life." When life is threatened there is a right to break all but three commandments, namely, denying faith, killing another, or sexual misconduct (with animals, etc.). But the basic convictions here are clear: language is a profoundly morally charged reality, and we must take care in our ordinary use of it not to trespass on its fragility.

Christianity

In turning to Christianity, we will see that the ambivalence about lying in Judaism – the moderation with which it is viewed in most settings, but the concern about its infectious nature in others – has partial functional equivalents in Christian thought. But there are important differences that make the two traditions engage the issue of lying on very different bases. In order to see the particular character of Christian thinking on this, we will look at two Christian approaches, with different outcomes but similar modes of reasoning.

Absolutist: Augustine

The fifth-century African theologian Augustine of Hippo (354–430 CE) is perhaps a paradigmatic representative of an absolutist position on lying. This is a bit surprising, because on other topics Augustine is seen to have been what some have called a "realist" in ethics. On war, on political engagement, even on the nature of sin itself, he seems willing to countenance morally murky behavior. So it is surprising that he is also considered as the exemplary absolutist on the prohibition of lying – though as we will see, his reasons for his absolutism are profound and far-reaching.

Consider the example of a patient seriously ill and in danger of death, whose son has just died, unbeknownst to him. He asks to see his son; if we tell him the truth, he may well die from shock at the news. Should we lie to him? Augustine emphatically argues that we must not:

> If we grant that we ought to lie about the son's life for the sake of that patient's health, little by little and bit by bit this evil will grow and by gradual accessions will slowly increase until it becomes such a mass of wicked lies that it will be utterly impossible to find any means of resisting such a plague grown to huge proportions through small additions.[4]

Beneath the rhetoric, Augustine is making a deep point here: lying, once begun, is ever harder to stop, because it never seems susceptible to resistance: the short-term benefits of lying always remain attractive, and the individual wickedness of any single lie seems quite minute, while the costs of stopping the lies and finally owning up to the truth mount to ever-vaster magnitudes, "huge proportions through small additions." Thus, lying is a particularly insidious and insinuating form of evil.

On Augustine's view, lies are bad for society, but still more importantly they are also bad in themselves. They are bad for society because they attack the basis of social trust, and meet evil with evil. They are also bad in themselves, because a lie in itself reflects an agent's mistrust of God, a mistrust that God's truth is the right way for the world to run; furthermore, such mistrust can become a habit, manifesting itself in other, ever greater lies, and ever greater forms deception. Thus lying is an especially tempting form of the primal temptation, for Augustine: the temptation to be "like God," the temptation to which Adam and Eve, on Augustine's reading, succumbed in the Garden. Lying is an evil, pure and simple, and while it may have consequences that appear beneficial for all the parties involved, to Augustine's mind you can never knowingly do an evil that good may come of it.

For Augustine, that is, the first victim of the lie is the liar him- or herself; for in lying one succumbs to the delusion that humans are suitably well positioned in the world to know comprehensively what is best for themselves and for others, and that they have the power to produce that "best" from their wills. But this is deeply deceptive, Augustine thinks, disguising as it does the calamitous condition of the world and the perilous position we occupy within it. In contrast, to tell the truth even in the bleakest circumstances is an evangelical act – confessing our sin and the brokenness of the world, and relying on the Good News of God in Christ to save us.

What ought we to do? Well, we ought to be silent more often, and trust that God will work through the consequences of our truth-telling when it is necessary. There will come times when we must tell the truth and trust God to make everything come out right. That is the core of the Christian faith anyway, for Augustine, and we are simply practicing what we should preach in those moments.

Augustine's deep point here is straightforward. For Augustine, lying strikes at the center of human relations, and at the heart of the human's dependence on God. Even permitting little lies opens up the possibility that we are able to choose what is telling the truth and what is not. To refuse to lie under any circumstances may shock or even offend people – but it is necessary, not least of all because it communicates the seriousness with which we take the idea that the world is not rightly ordered. In a rightly ordered world, lies would never be attractive.

(Apparent) permissiveness: Dietrich Bonhoeffer

In contrast, consider the argument of the twentieth-century German theologian Dietrich Bonhoeffer. In an essay entitled "What is meant by 'Telling the Truth'?" Bonhoeffer offers a powerful Christian account that seems to countenance deception.[5] As we will see, however, Bonhoeffer does not regard it as deception, but as the righteous protection of distinct realms of life from impious and disrespectful inquisitors, and hence as a form of truth-keeping.

He begins by noting that truth-telling commences in the context of the family, and that from the beginning there are asymmetries, inequalities, built into this context: "The parents' claim on the child is something different from that of the child on the parents," he says.[6] The different kinds of truth-telling obligatory in these two roles are symbolic of a larger truth: different people have different responsibilities to one another for different kinds of truthfulness, because we have different relations to one another.

To speak the truth in this way is to speak in ways that are appropriate to the different relations between us and our differing conditions, our differing capabilities and rights to hear the truth. It is the cynic, Bonhoeffer claims, who blankly speaks the truth at all times – and in doing so, reveals their cynicism as they implicitly deny the importance of context or setting, deny the complexity of the world that God has created, and hence "denies everything that is real."[7] The cynic denies that God has indeed put each of us on the earth and given us the right to know some things and not others. It is the cynic who denies the real by refusing to acknowledge the goodness and rightness of God's providential will.

In contrast, Bonhoeffer argues, instead of such blind and cynical literalism we ought to enact "concrete" truthfulness, which entails attention to how our obligations appear in our concrete context – so we must develop a sensitivity to "reading" the real, of attending both to the particularities of the world and the particularities of God's command to us at this moment. To enact concrete truthfulness, we must fundamentally be attentive to God, alert to how God's concrete expectations for us change from moment to moment and situation to situation.

For Bonhoeffer, fundamental here (as was the case with Augustine) is a recognition of the sovereignty not of humans but of God – and the ever-powerful temptation on humanity's part to usurp to that sovereignty. Furthermore, the real is itself organized in manifold distinct subregions, so that family life and non-family life, for example, would be different. The real is both intrinsically complex as created – there are "orders of creation," spheres of society which have fundamentally different rules and regulations (politics, the household, one's professional life) – *and* the real is corrupted and broken by our sin. So our obedience to God is not to a "metaphysical idol," nor is the world we inhabit a blank field without relevantly different spaces; instead, we live in a world obedient to "the living One who has placed me in a life that is fully alive and within this life demands my service."[8] Our obligations are not to a principle or a proposition, but to a God whose expectations are susceptible of development, and even change.

The reason for this attention to God is because of what Bonhoeffer sees as the essential character of the lie, and what it reveals about language: "lying is the negation, denial, and deliberate and willful destruction of reality as it is created by God and exists in God, no matter whether this purpose is achieved by speech or by silence."[9] All this means that there will be times, for Bonhoeffer, when it is appropriate not to answer someone's question with the truth, but to refuse to answer it out of an appropriate sense of decorum – such as the example of a child being asked by a teacher about whether their father comes home drunk. In this situation Bonhoeffer wants the child to tell what the teacher might see as a "lie." (Interestingly, we can ask whether Bonhoeffer's attention to the distinctiveness of different spheres may not, in this example at least, be more problematic than he seems to realize – for one can imagine that in an abusive family, it may well be someone from outside the family who can intervene to stop the abuse from happening.) The "lie" in this case is not primarily an effort on the child's part to seize or deny God's sovereignty, but rather to protect God's sovereignty against the teacher's greedy, cynical, and curious effort to usurp it.

Bonhoeffer is alert to the danger that this proposal can sound like a simple situation ethic, where you do what you think it best to do, determined wholly by the situation in which you find yourself, and disregard or dramatically deemphasize any need for coherence or consistency in your position over time. Such a situation ethic can tempt you to assume you can judge as God does, and also slowly to shift one's criterion from "what is best to do" to "what is easiest to do." After all, we experience the real as sinners, and the real itself as sundered by sin, corrupted and ruptured. And yet Bonhoeffer thinks that the only way to address this is not by some set of principles that one would wear like a cognitive chastity belt, but rather by sensitive attention to the real, to what is going on. This may not sound like much protection at all, but at least, he suggests, it is real protection, and not the delusion of an apparently extra-personal guideline – which simply pushes one step further back the question of how such a guideline is to be followed.

Now Bonhoeffer, in comparison to Augustine, can sound a bit more even-handed, a bit more moderate, more like the Talmudic principles for thinking about lying. But are they really similar? In some ways, certainly: Bonhoeffer demands that believers judge for themselves whether someone is due this kind of truth-telling, or not, and the Talmud requires the same moral assessment by the faithful. But in other ways, maybe not: whereas for Bonhoeffer there is a sense that all our speech is marked by sin, and so we speak in fear and trembling, in the Talmud there is a sense of flexibility about what is needful for the world.

For all their differences, Augustine and Bonhoeffer do reveal some shared themes that in turn uncover some deep Christian intuitions about lying, and the use of language in a sinful world. Both share an understanding of the world as fairly radically askew. Augustine's attitude towards lying is based on his sense that refusal of the temptation to lie is a form of evangelical witness; so is Bonhoeffer's view of respecting the different contexts against those demonic cynics and others who would seek to overthrow them. The Talmud has little of their sense of cata-strophic wrongness, their sense that the world is fundamentally askew; for the Talmud, the human has a responsibility to cultivate the world, not lament its collapse. The world must be *maintained*, even *managed*, and the idea that humans ought to act in ways that underscore the calamity of our existence might well seem, to the compilers (or later readers) of the Talmud, a dangerously, mor-bidly self-obsessed concern. We will soon see that Islam is closer to the Talmud on this topic.

Islam

As is the case with Judaism and Christianity, Islam pays serious attention to one's honest dealings with others. But like what we saw of Judaism, and unlike some strands of Christianity, it seems less austere in its attitude towards truth-telling. There is no impression in Islamic sources of a moral laxity when it comes to lying; the obligation of truth-telling is very serious. As the Qur'an says:

> God does not take you to task for what is careless in your oaths, but He will for your deliberate oaths: to atone, feed ten poor people with food such as you would normally give your own families, or clothe them, or free a slave. If this is beyond your means, you should fast for three days. This is the atonement for breaking your oaths – so keep your oaths. Thus God makes clear His signs [*ayat*], so that you may be grateful. (Q. 5:89)

Clearly, truth-telling and keeping promises and covenants is a fundamental good in Islamic thought.

However, much as was in the case in certain strands of Judaism, in some situations the obligation to tell the truth can be outweighed by other considerations. There is a *hadith* in which Muhammad speaks precisely to this issue; there he is reported to have said that "lying is wrong, except in three things: the lie of a man to his wife to make her content with him; a lie to an enemy, for war is deception; or a lie to settle trouble between people."[10] There are a number of interesting issues here. First of all, what does it mean, "war is deception"? Interpretations differ here, but one might safely say that in war both sides understand the aim to be the defeat of the other, and so have already lost trust in one another's words. Hence war is itself already a form of deceit – to such a degree that the warring parties would themselves be surprised were each party to start telling the other what they were about to do, and then proceed to do it.

But the idea of dishonesty in marriage and the idea of lies in resolving disputes are more complicated and richer. In both of these situations, unlike states of war, the parties assume honesty on both sides. (Indeed, it is one of our most heartfelt bits of contemporary pablum, that marriage is all about honesty.) The *hadith* suggests that, as was the case with the Talmud in Judaism, Muhammad saw that language is not in fact worthy of being worshipped, but must serve the more fundamental goods of God. And central among those goods is the good of peace and right order. A marriage is always a matter of great truth-telling; but there can be many little lies, by and large temporary, within it, to sustain an institution that two imperfect people are trying to inhabit. And reconciliation between aggrieved parties will get nowhere if both parties remain entrenched in their sense of self-righteous grievance; and most reconciliation processes begin with both parties in such entrenchments. Here a lie by a mediator, in the sense of concealing what one party says about the other, or suggesting something that one side could say to the other, may advance the cause of peace.

We may ask questions here about the degree to which these should even count as lies. If the aim of such language is to create a relationship where none exists, or heal one that is broken, is the language being misused? Not if we see, again, that language is part of the weave that enables humans to be present to one another. If you and I are friends, and I am upset at you and say terrible things about you, is it fair to say that that is what I really believe, that that is *all* I believe about you? I think not; who I am in my anger is not my whole self; in my anger I have given way to one part of me, a small, mean, and petty part. In fact, as Bonhoeffer saw, a too-complete fidelity to literal accuracy may, in fact, actually misrepresent reality in a quite fundamental way.

Islam has thought a good deal about religious deception as well, and resists what can be seen as Christianity's emphasis on salvific suffering, favoring instead a policy of outward deception to save the Muslim from grievous physical harm. Given the centrality of the *shehada*, the profession of faith, to the first moments of a Muslim's religious life, it is clear that Islam takes the religious use of language with terrific seriousness. The attention to the propriety of certain kinds of language in the discipline of *kalaam*, or theology (again, literally "speech about" God) only reinforces this. And yet here also there are situations where the early experience of the Muslim community gave nuance to the faithful's understanding of the limits of honesty in language.

Most basically, both the Qur'an and the tradition recognize the possibility of outward deception, so long as the inner-self remains rightly attuned to God. Two Qur'anic verses in particular speak to this. First is one in which room seems to be given for vain promises: "He will not call you to account for oaths you have uttered thoughtlessly, but for what you mean in your hearts. God is most forgiving and forbearing" (Q. 2:225). Second is one concerning compulsion (presumably under violence or the threat of violence): thus the Qur'an does not condemn "those compelled to profess they do not believe, although their hearts remain firm in faith." (Q.16:106). Both of these emphasize the primary importance of truth-telling, in the inner recesses of the self, to God, first and foremost. Honesty to humans is overwhelmingly approved, but in some situations (of violence-threatened compulsion, for instance) humans have abrogated their right to expect the truth from those they threaten. Furthermore, humans have no right to punish people for holding to the true faith, and therefore God gives the faithful the right to deceive the unbelievers.

Shi'ia Islam, long suffering persecution at the hands of the majority Sunni branch, developed the notion of *taquiyya*, or concealment under threat of religious persecution, based on another Qur'anic verse: "The believers should not take disbelievers for their allies rather than other believers – anyone who does that severs himself from God – except for need of protection from them. But God warns you to beware of Him; the final good is to God" (Q. 3:28). Shi'ia were allowed, on this reading, to present themselves in deceptive fashion, in order that they not be persecuted by those who are not of the true faith. This is in a way simply an extension of the more general conviction, shared by Sunni and Shi'ia alike, that believers may deceive unbelievers for the sake of the faithful. The preservation of life, and the security of the faithful, is more important than the truth between people.

Nonetheless, even in this practice, the last word is a reminder that lying is prone to get out of hand, and so the faithful Muslim will always "remember" God, the final goal – thus shadowing the permission given for some deception with the reminder that though the path be crooked, one must never forget that it ends before God, and so the believer had better be able to give an account of every act of deception as properly warranted and strictly required to protect the life of the faithful. "My Lord never errs, nor forgets" (Q. 20:52); so lying, and other similarly permitted morally ambiguous matters, ought to be undertaken only with fear and trembling, in the believer's sure and certain faith that one day they will be called to account before the Holy One for all their deceptions.

The basic lesson here is that the interior truth is what matters, and that the believer must never be deceived in themselves about their own status before God, and of their need to beg for God's mercy. One of the deepest themes in Islam is the significance of interiority and secrecy. The radical intimacy with which the Qur'an represents God's presence within humanity (remember: "we are closer to man than his jugular") has as its cognate the idea that such intimacy between humans is attenuated and fragmentary, at best. So the idea of privacy, secrecy, and deception has been a popular theme in Islamic discussions of selfhood. And central to much of this discussion has been an insistence on speech etiquette, on the good use of language for this tradition. In one of the earliest Islamic texts on the inevitability of secrecy, the ninth-century Sunni theologian al-Jahiz (776–868) quoted a "Sage": "My son, man is nothing but talk, and so if you can, be good talk."[11] Precisely because humans do not have divine access to one another's thoughts, the question of what we owe to others in the way of such access becomes especially pointed. And so lying, and the use of language more generally, is a matter of fundamental concern for the faith.

Conclusion

What we see in these traditions' reflections about lying is on one level unsurprising. Each tradition struggles with the issue in ways that reveal how some of its deepest commitments or convictions are manifest in daily life. We also see that for each tradition the issue of lying is not merely an "ethical" issue, but touches on theological and metaphysical concerns of the greatest profundity. In a way not unlike the question of marriage, we find in this most ordinary of human foibles – the use of language to shade or alter or avoid the truth – that some of the deepest commitments are engaged.

One last thing. I suspect it is surprising to you that the issue of lying, when we attend to it with serious reflectiveness, reveals to us deep moral and religious issues that were unimagined. But that is the way with much of the ethics of ordinary life. It is often there, in the most mundane and banal and quotidian of matters, that we can find the most profound and troublesome challenges to our lives. Drama is unnecessary; indeed, what we call "drama" is mostly, actually, melodrama. The ordinary has all the moral profundity one could ever imagine.

9

Forgiveness

Lying is about trust – the reliability, the believability, of society. More deeply, the questions surrounding lying reveal the role of language as the crucial cement of society, and reveal language's role as a matter of *being present* to one another. This is why "talebearing" is so bad for Jewish thought, why Augustine thought silence might be more needed than we think it is, why Bonhoeffer thought language was so susceptible to abuse, and why some Muslim thinkers believe that language should be calibrated to the company in which one speaks.

In this chapter, we will talk about forgiveness. Forgiveness is also about community – in this case, about whether we can heal a rupture in community, and if so, what form such healing would take. And here too, as with lying, we need a working definition. Here is one: Forgiveness is a device that allows people a second chance; it affirms that, as the old adage has it, "every person is greater than their worst act."

This makes forgiveness *not* a number of things. Most obviously, it makes it not a matter of revenge, resentment, or repression. It is not revenge, obviously, because it resists the urge to pay back in kind what was done to one. It is not resentment, because it does not hold a grudge against the other (a particular kind of power over another, which makes it impossible to relate to each other as equals). And it is not repression, because it does not seek to "forgive and forget;" forgiveness is all about remembering things, but remembering them in a different light. It is real work – not a matter of just saying "I forgive you." As the contemporary Christian theologian Greg Jones has put it, forgiveness, for all these traditions, is "a way of taking the past seriously, yet struggling to witness to the freedom that God has created for a new and renewed future."[1]

In interpersonal terms, it is a way of restoring relations, recovering presence, "healing the wounds of the past," and so moving on, yet not fleeing the past. But it is more than that. Forgiveness – at least of the sort we see in our selected tradi-tions – is crucially theological, for it is tied into these traditions' beliefs about the nature of God and God's relation to the world. All can inhabit the psalmist's cry to God: "cleanse me with hyssop [a herb], and I will be clean; wash me, and I will be whiter than snow" (Psalms 51:7).

And yet forgiveness is more than just a resolution of conflict between humans or between humans and God. It is a way of inhabiting time, a way of relating to history – it acknowledges the claims of the past on the present – the relevance of the past for the present – while insisting that the past does not determine the present. It suggests that there are ways the past can be redeemed. Forgiveness, then, is about the future as much as it is about the past – it is a way of releasing us from the past by recognizing the need we have to go forward into the future.

All this can sound very hopeful, very optimistic. But there is a deep question lurking here that we should confront at once: is forgiveness always possible? Or better – because we cannot know if it is finally achievable, and so cannot really answer that question – should forgiveness always be pursued?

In terms of both the register of interpersonal presence and temporal continuity, this question has a grip on our experience. Often, we talk about not being able to "get beyond" a violation or cruelty that has "come between" two people; or we talk about the past as not being resolved, about it continuing to disrupt us in the present. I trust that readers of this book have themselves used both of these ways of talking. These questions, about the moral and even ontological meaning of forgiveness, are not even "buried" in our ordinary way of talking; they are on the surface, visible to all who will simply pause to reflect on the words they use.

Consider a parent forgiving the murderer of his or her child. Can we really say to the parent that it is their duty to forgive? Can we even say that they ought to forgive? It is hard to know what the "ought" might mean there – unless it is a cruel twist of the knife: "Yes, yes, you feel bad about your child's death, and we all sym-pathize with that, etc., etc.; but *now*, after the crime has occurred, that very crime has created *in you* a certain moral obligation, to forgive the criminal who committed it; and if you do *not* forgive, well then *you* are in the wrong." Could you imagine actually saying that to someone?

This raises a still deeper question about the scope of morality itself. We think that morality most clearly applies to interpersonal relationships (as opposed to the larger political or social realm). But even here, it seems, where morality appears most needful, it may face unbearable strain. Even here we may be right to ask whether, in the face of absolute moral horror, morality of any sort can reasonably be asked of people.

Forgiveness, History, and Modernity

Furthermore, in thinking about forgiveness in this way, we are asking about the possibility of genuine novelty in history – of breaking the chain of cause and effect, the blood feud of pain and recrimination that suffuses so much of human history. In a way, the modern world understands itself to begin with, if not forgiveness *per se*, then at least a great act of renouncing the past that bears a functional and structural similarity to forgiveness. *Novus ordo seclorum* says the Great Seal of the United States – declaring the nation, and the era inaugurated with its birth, "a new order of the ages" (somewhat perversely, this is a quotation from the ancient Roman poet Vergil).

And there is a sense in modernity of forgiveness as *easy*, as a matter of simple choice, as if we could choose to leave the past behind. As Voltaire, one of the most famous of the eighteenth-century French *philosophes*, is reported to have put it, "Tout comprendre, c'est tout pardonner" – "to understand all is to forgive all." Thus Voltaire seems to be saying that we have within our intelligence the power to grasp the motives and actions of those who offend us, and to "rise above." Yet others in modernity have a far darker sense of the grip of the past upon the present, and the depth of our entanglements in the past. "After such knowledge, what forgiveness?" asks T. S. Eliot, in a direct rebuke to Voltaire; and William Faulkner famously said "the past isn't dead. It isn't even past." For these thinkers, and others like them, the idea that forgiveness is easy, or that we can leave the past behind, is a profound moral deception, and our assent to it can only lead to tragedy, or worse.

In thinking about forgiveness, then, we are thinking about the meaning of modernity. We get to a deep conviction underlying modernity: we can *start over*, begin again, and leave the past behind. Is that true? Things close to this can be said, and are said, all the time. This situation is most dramatically faced by people in our own time who have confronted absolute evil in situations of total dehumanization. In many different ways the historical event of the Holocaust, or Shoah, has served as a privileged site for such reflection. Certainly, there are other events that are in one way or another comparable in their hideousness – the various genocides elsewhere in the world (of the Armenians, or in Cambodia or Rwanda). But the Holocaust has provoked some of the most profound writing on these matters, and so we will refer to it at several points throughout this book. This is one of those points. I want to tell the story of Simon Wiesenthal's remarkable book, *The Sunflower*.

The Sunflower

The Sunflower is a straightforward story. It begins with "Simon" in a labor camp, in the midst of the Holocaust. He notices that while the dead inmates – all Jews – are piled in heaps, the camp guards and soldiers who die are buried with sunflowers planted on their graves.

On duty one day, Simon is picked out and taken into a hospital by a nurse. Inside is a German man named Karl, covered in bandages with holes only for his nose, ears, and mouth. Karl tells him a story: when he was a soldier, he helped burn down a house with a Jewish family trapped inside. He had done other horrible things, but he focused on this event with Simon. Now that he was dying, he had asked for "a Jew," in order to confess, show his remorse, and beg forgiveness for his crime. Simon finds his story compelling, and his remorse real. But he does not forgive; he notices a fly buzzing around the room, and he silently walks out of the room.

He hears that Karl died the next day, and left Simon all of his possessions. Simon refuses the possessions, but is haunted by the event. After the war, he seeks out Karl's mother, now a widow with no living family members. She tells him how innocent and sweet Karl had been as a child – an altar boy – before joining the Hitler Youth. Simon listens but tells her nothing, leaving again without saying a word. The story ends with Simon, years later, still wondering if he had done the right thing.[2]

That last charged question has provoked innumerable responses. Some people see Simon's silence in the face of Karl as a refusal to forgive which is itself immoral. If someone is genuinely sorry, such thinkers say, we ought to offer them forgiveness. To do less is not only to fail to be good; it is to be actively evil. This seems to be Edward R. Flannery's view: to him, Wiesenthal's refusal to forgive is "a form of hate." On this view, Wiesenthal's silence simply perpetuates evil and suffering.

But perhaps sometimes it is not appropriate for us to forgive another person, for any one of a number of reasons. First of all, it may be unclear that a person is in the proper position to forgive. Perhaps, properly speaking, no one is left who can forgive. After all, who can forgive a crime against another? Can God forgive crimes against others? In the Jewish tradition, that is impossible; only the one who was wronged can forgive. Jewish thought recognizes that it is far too easy for us to enact a pseudo-drama in our own heads where we imaginatively come face to face with those we have wronged and solicit from them a quick forgiveness; it wants to resist such slippery imaginations as strongly as possible.

And anyway, is forgiveness always a morally good thing? Perhaps, in fact, it is not – perhaps, sometimes, forgiveness is *dangerous*. This is Cynthia Ozick's argument against forgiving Karl: "forgiveness," she says, "is pitiless. It forgets the victim. … It drowns the past. … vengeance, only vengeance, knows pity for the victim."[3] Ozick, a contemporary American novelist and essayist, makes her stand on a profound claim about the nature of moral reality, indeed about the nature of reality itself. The central claim she makes is simple: some deeds are literally unforgivable. She does not mean that simply as a psychological fact about the limits of our mercy as forgivers; clearly, all of us struggle to forgive people, sometimes even for the most trivial of offenses. No, she means it as a claim about what certain acts do to the nature of reality itself. As she puts it, "there are spots forgiveness cannot wash out."[4]

It will help us understand this response to put it in context. For it speaks to very fundamental convictions about the determinate shape of moral actions in Judaism, and how to "overcome" the wrongs that one has done. On Yom Kippur, the "day of atonement," Jews learn that *teshuva*, the "turning" that constitutes repentance, has four steps. The first step is to ask the person who you have wronged for forgiveness. The second step is to ask God for forgiveness as well, for violating God's

commandments and abusing God's creation. The third step is to feel the appropriate remorse, and to repent of those deeds that you did. Here, "repentance" is a quite
particular thing; it means to disown them, to do a sort of violence to yourself and
expel that part of you from yourself, to become another person. The fourth and
final step is to ensure that you do not commit the same sin in any similar situation
in the future. This structure should make clear just how detailed and precise are
the steps to undo a wrong in Jewish thought. For healing to happen, work is
required.

But sometimes that work cannot proceed. In the Jewish tradition, recall, forgiveness can only be offered by the one who has been wronged. So some acts – acts of
murder, most obviously – create holes in reality that cannot be repaired. Imagine
a sheet torn in two. If the two sides of the sheet remain intact, then certainly they
can be sewn back together. But if I tear the sheet in two, then cast one part of it
into a fire, it is gone forever, and no such suturing is possible. Ozick's claim may
sound shockingly vehement, emotionally over-heated, and contemptuous of forgiveness – after all, who would call forgiveness "pitiless"? – but she is actually
making a cool-minded philosophical point: the claim that one party has "forgiven"
another for crimes that the second party perpetrated against people who no longer
exist, is in fact a form of forgiveness that *is* pitiless, that has "forgotten" the true
victim.

(This does not mean that Judaism is an unforgiving tradition. Far from it; the
excessive withholding of forgiveness is a mark of cruelty in the Jewish tradition, and
one must forgive after being asked by the repentant wrongdoer three times.[5] But it
is the case that Jewish thought on forgiveness is altogether more sober than some
other traditions in its expectations of the moral capacities of those who need it and
those who can offer it.)

Ozick's protest against a cheap and easy sort of forgiveness, and the larger point
about the propriety of forgiveness by someone other than the wronged party,
should resonate especially with Christians and those brought up in cultures that are
culturally, even if not confessionally, Christian. For she points to a temptation
toward easy forgiveness in the Christian tradition that does pose a problem for the
honest moral accounting of human action. All too often, Christians and secular
"cultural Christians" think that, because the drama of individual salvation looms
so large in this tradition, all truly relevant issues of moral weight are a matter of the
individual's solitary relationship with God. Christians, that is, find it a little too easy
to frame their moral failings as a wholly individual and solitary matter between
them and God, and to shunt to the side the concrete historical people who have
been wronged. The momentousness of the moral drama of the soul's salvation in
Christianity means that the all-too-human others who populate the drama too
readily become bystanders, and are easily effaced from the script.

Because of this, Christians, and those raised in culturally Christian contexts, are
tempted to think about morality as a courtroom where they stand, alone, before
God. In such a setting, having a sense, a conviction, or an experience of God's
forgiveness can seem to render any further moral concern with one's past moot, or

even morbid. Let the dead bury the dead, after all. Christians can thus find it possible to use their inner, personal experience of justification before God as a moral whitewashing, a justification to not seek reconciliation with the people in their past, and perhaps their present, whom they have wronged.

Note that I am not saying that this is a necessary consequence of Christian doctrines, properly understood: rather, this is a temptation powerfully available to Christians, though it is *not* what the tradition directly propounds. And I recognize that some would challenge my assessment of the view detailed above as morally wrong; some will certainly believe the above account to be plausible. I am simply suggesting that such an account does not respect the moral (and even theological) status of other humans. And I am not alone in this; even some of the best Christian theologians have written in express agreement with my view. For example, Dietrich Bonhoeffer, whose thoughts on lying we discussed earlier, offers a powerful critique of this temptation in his analysis of the perennial Christian temptation towards "cheap grace." Cheap grace, for Bonhoeffer, is a kind of false experience or conviction whereby one feels forgiven for what one has done without feeling under any obligation to undertake the difficult work of repentance and reconciliation. Cheap grace is cheap just because it is counterfeit: no matter how powerful the believer's conviction that they've "gotten right with God," what they have actually done is succumbed to the temptation to fabricate a false God who they then use to whitewash their sins. The temptation towards Bonhoeffer's cheap grace, then, is a particularly Christian form of a universal human proclivity towards self-deception and moral evasion. It is given a distinct form and power by certain elements of Christian doctrine and the larger Christian worldview; but it is not an inevitable component of Christianity.

So Ozick's vehemence, and the surprisingly deep challenge she presents to much of her audience, uncovers powerful moral and theological issues to which we are well advised to attend.

Others, recognizing the power of Ozick's view, nonetheless dissent from it. Milton Konvitz, for example, argues that forgiveness does not mean we do not punish people. Forgiveness need not be an act of *obliterating* the past, of erasing past crimes and making it unnecessary to retribute for those injustices. There is a difference between personal forgiveness and public or social or political justice: "Suppose Eichmann, when the charges were read to him in the court in Jerusalem, had tried to show that he was sincerely remorseful. The court would still have been bound to enter a judgment of guilt and to pass sentence upon him. Many criminals have gone to their death remorseful and penitent."[6] Here, forgiveness is understood to mean that we respect and affirm the authenticity and integrity of the criminal's remorse and repentance. Whether a thinker like Ozick would understand that to be an adequate sense of forgiveness is another matter.

Perhaps, then, the possibility exists that some moral acts are so abysmal and determinate in their consequences that no further act of repair can undo their cruelty. Perhaps some crimes are simply unforgiveable. Perhaps our desire to give people a second chance actually masks the possibility that no such second chance is available in some situations. Perhaps there are people to whom the only appropriate moral stance is one of outright repulsion, moral exile, existential annihilation – for whom it would be better had they never been born. Perhaps to treat such people as if they are in the realm of morally acceptable persons is too dangerous.

Forgiving and Forgetting

What are we to do then? If we find forgiveness impossible, yet we do not want to indulge in hate, is there a better way of responding to suffering? What about "forgetting"? When it is not appropriate to forgive someone, perhaps we ought to try to "forget" what they did to us or to our loved ones. Forgetting differs from forgiving in several ways, but the most relevant way is this: while forgiving seeks to keep the past alive, and keep history alive to us, forgetting suggests it is better sometimes to forget that history – to let bygones be bygones. It does not seek to redeem the past but rather to ignore it – to let go of it, for our generation at least, in order for us to build on our lives in a new way. Besides, is it not true that we all need to forget some things, to let past pains be past pains? Maybe that is what forgetting is.

Sound unlikely? But what about places that have *too much* history – Northern Ireland, the former Yugoslavia, South Africa (think about the Truth and Reconciliation Commission). Do we want those places to continue confronting their pasts? The question may be, for many, simply a pragmatic one – we estimate, however roughly, *both* the costs in blood and violence of the confrontations and painful remembrance that forgiving entails, *and* then the costs in repressed pain and supressed violence that forgetting might entail, and then we judge – which is worse?

Forgiving seems to have a higher moral and psychological cost than we first thought it did – it requires a recitation of the hurts received from others. But who would want to hear a full recitation of the pains they have inflicted upon others? Who can stand to hear just a little bit of that – even one description of how you were cruel? Who can bear to see themselves as others have seen them, with all one's own selfishness, indifference to others, and duplicity laid bare and unmissably visible?

The Wounds of the Martyrs

So real forgiveness is hard work. Whatever complications or rival interpretations Christianity and Islam give to the practice, in these essentials they agree with Judaism. But the differences are real, and important, and we should come to terms with them before going forward. So now I want to turn to some complicating facts about Christianity.

The first complicating fact – and this is one that Christianity seems more basically to affirm than either Judaism or Islam – is that for Christians the primary forgiver is *God*. God forgives humanity for its sins, and beneath all our local forgivenesses of one another, humans are called upon to see themselves as first and fore-most forgiven, and enabled thereby to extend that forgiveness to others who have wronged them. So in Christianity, unlike in Judaism or Islam, it is God who is the central agent of forgiveness.

This may sound nice, but it raises a series of problems for Christians that few have ever paused to consider, problems about whether *any* concept of God worth its salt can accommodate *anything like* a concept of forgiveness at all.

This is the argument of the contemporary Canadian philosopher Anne C. Minas, in a provocative essay entitled "God and Forgiveness."[7] Most simply put, her challenge is that forgiveness is something humans can do, and it is made possible for us by our limited and changeable natures. When we talk about God, we normally suggest that God is perfect in a number of ways humans are not, and so God "logi-cally cannot forgive" – at least (and here Minas's argument is controversial) on a number of understandings of forgiveness we might have.

What is crucial here, for Minas, is that on our typical understandings, the divine is *perfect*. In many different ways, the perfection *blocks* God from forgiving. We cannot imagine divine forgiveness as a *reversal* of divine judgment, for God cannot change God's moral judgments, because God wasn't wrong in the first place. Nor can forgiveness be conceived of as a *modification* of judgment, an acknowledgment of an exception to an approximate moral rule; after all, God does not work with moral approximations, but with the actual, infinitely fine-grained realities. And we cannot imagine God's forgiveness as the sheer *condoning* of bad actions, for God cannot "overlook" bad action, in the sense of refusing to know it.

Nor can God forgive, if forgiveness is about simple clemency: God cannot do this because God would then be violating or overriding codes God had set down, the violation of which would make God look like little more than a "practical joker." If forgiveness is about renouncing hurt or offended feelings, because God is perfect, eternal, and immutable, then God cannot change God's feelings about anything. (Besides, Minas asks, how can a perfect God be "wronged" in the first place?) Finally, if forgiveness is about obliterating the bad deed, God cannot "wash away sins" in the sense of making them lose their character as *bad* or *evil*. This, she thinks, is little better than a childhood fantasy. In sum, for her, the idea of divine forgive-ness seems hard to render intelligible.

How might Christians – or others interested in the idea that, as the Qur'an puts it, God is all-merciful – respond to Minas's challenge? They would seemingly have to show how forgiveness, especially as God practices it, means something else than (though not something unrelated to) our understanding of forgiveness. How might they do that? It involves asking other questions about God's relation to history, and the nature of history itself. Are people's actions able to define who they most deeply are in an irrevocable sense? If so, does that place limits on the capacity of God to organize the moral order as God wills? (This opens up into the question of Hell, and the possibility of eschatological redemption.) If not, is the moral meaning of any act perpetually up in the air – and doesn't that threaten us with a profound moral unseriousness?

The deep question here is simple: can time be "redeemed" at all? Or is an act's immanent, immediate presence in the world all there really is to the act? Is forgiveness, that is, in some metaphysical sense impossible? Each of the traditions thinks not; each, that is, preaches the possibility of forgiveness, and forgiveness as a real transformation in the nature of our bad acts. For each, eschatology is their escape hatch. Judgment day is a salvific blessing. For it permits the possibility that the final, ultimate sense of all our acts, and thus the final meaning and sense of our whole lives, is yet to be determined. And if that possibility remains open until the end of time, there is no reason to despair of our own, or another's, ultimate redemption, for the faithful in any of these traditions.

But if forgiveness *is* possible, *how* is it possible? We have seen something of how Jewish thought imagines forgiveness and prescribes its proper scope. But what about Christian and Islamic understandings?

Consider Christian forgiveness here. Christian forgiveness is distinctive, both in terms of the object requiring forgiveness and the agent providing it. As to the agent, the particularly Christian identification of Jesus as the Christ and the Messiah, and the Christian understanding of God as Triune, make for a distinct understanding of forgiveness, and through this, the meaning of history itself. This is so because Christ is understood to be in a way the party most profoundly wronged in all human history, and yet on the cross (the tradition believes) Jesus asks God the Father to forgive all a request that Christians believe is granted in the resurrection. Furthermore, the Triune God is described as Triune both in order to name God's proper autonomy from and non-neediness of creation, and to provide a way to talk about the Christian God's mission to save the world from its self-damnation. And that gets to the second point; namely, that the wrongdoing that Christianity understands forgiveness most fundamentally to confront is not the multitudinous individual-interpersonal faults of each of us, but instead the fundamental rebellion of humanity as a whole against God – a rebellion that lies at the root of all the interpersonal cruelties we inflict on one another.

Because of this, it is only a slight exaggeration to say that Christians never forgive. Rather, they *participate* in God's forgiveness. Christians do not forgive on their own, it is not their proper possession to give to people. This is another way in which grace is so important. Recall that I earlier insisted that Christianity is not about justice, but about love; this is a manifestation of that belief. Christians should believe that they live in a wholly "gifted" world – a world that is not ultimately a matter of merit or desert, but is finally a matter of gift. We live in sin, and so assume that for one to win, someone else has got to lose. But this is not the way that grace operates – grace is offered unconditionally and unlimitedly. It is not a zero-sum reality. And Christians should understand their own capacity, and right, to forgive anyone to be grounded in the gratuitous gift of God's own forgiveness, which is always and unconditionally offered.

But this again raises a worry about cheap grace. By shunting off the act of forgiving onto a God who is guaranteed, even before the deed is done, to forgive the deed, does not this account make forgiveness both too easy – because guaranteed – and ultimately the responsibility of a divine and all-competent other, thus avoiding the unpleasantly troubling question of whether a concrete and fallible humanity has it within its power actually to forgive in the concrete cases that they face?

Christian answers to this question have largely focused on the person of Jesus. Grace is supremely manifest in Jesus's life, death, and resurrection. Both death *and* resurrection are important here. The grace of forgiveness is both judgment and mercy. Christ's resurrection, for Christians, does not cancel the crucifixion or amount to a metaphysical "do-over." The Christ in whom Christians confess belief is not Christ uncrucified, but the Christ crucified and risen preached by Paul. Christian forgiveness is not a matter of obliterating misdeeds, but of showing how God has used them in surprising ways. As Joseph says to his brothers in Genesis, when he confronts them after their betrayal of him, "you meant it for evil ... but God intended it for good" (Genesis 50:20). This is not to say that this forgiveness is easy, let alone cheap; as the crucifixion signifies, for Christians it comes at a price. Mercy will be given to at least some at the end; but all will have the wrathful judgment of God pronounced against them. In Christian terms, real forgiveness requires suffering.

This understanding of forgiveness is perhaps best exemplified by an image that the Christian thinker St. Augustine discusses near the end of his massive work *The City of God*. In talking about questions about the bodily resurrection of all humans at the Last Judgment – what age will we be resurrected at, will men have beards, etc. – he spends some time on what seems on first glance a fairly esoteric issue: whether people will be resurrected with the scars they have suffered in their lives, or if those scars will be erased in the resurrection. Augustine does not directly answer this question, but he does say something interesting: we can know, he says, that the wounds of the martyrs – those who died for the faith – will not be effaced, but will be transfigured and turned into "marks of glory" on their bodies. How can we know this? Augustine's answer is interestingly based on his understanding of Christ: because the gospels report that Jesus kept his wounds after he was resurrected (Luke 24:39; John 20:20, 24–29), we can know that God will retain at least the marks on all human bodies that were suffered for the faith.

Just as the wounds of the martyrs matter in some ultimate sense, so Christians can say that forgiveness is not the effacement of the past – what Minas calls its "obliteration" – but its transfiguration, a task of laborious effort.

That is to say, for Christians at least, God does not simply dismiss the charges against humanity; instead, God offers humans the strength to work through them, to face those whom each of us have wronged to beg their forgiveness, undertake proper repentance, and so be returned to healthy and well-formed relationship with them; and God *demands* the conversion of all human victimizers into penitents in the end.

Conclusion

We live in a world that is profoundly morally compromised. And in living in this world we not infrequently do wrong. Given this, the question of the possibility and character of forgiveness will almost inevitably appear as a pressing one. In asking this question, many people will want to ask about how morality (and again, focusing especially on forgiveness) is or can or ought to be connected to what some of us think is its supra-worldly source – namely, God. What sort of theological underpinnings does our understanding of forgiveness entail? If we are right that our moral energies for forgiveness come from God, what sort of God gives us these energies – and what do we learn about how those energies should be employed by learning about this God? What kind of God would invoke forgiveness? And what would this forgiveness look like? These are, as I hope is now clear, real and vivid questions in each of our traditions, and among them as well. But none of them offer simple or straightforward answers; if anything, each merely makes more acute the need to ask these questions, in a morally and spiritually serious way. To do more than this – to offer something like a complete theological and moral answer – may well compound the moral and spiritual faults that those who offer it are seeking most diligently to heal.

Part III
Social Matters

10

Love and Justice

The previous part of this book explored issues that might be categorized as more or less issues of *personal* morality – moral issues that affect us in our private lives. But once we have discussed marriage, lying, and forgiveness, we stand at the threshold of issues that are at least as much of social concern as of individual interest. Marriage, as we have seen, is in many ways a transitional matter, because the traditions typically understand the institution of marriage as part – and a crucial part – of the social world. Therefore, this part of the book discusses matters of *public* morality – concerns about moral issues in which we may not have much personally invested, matters involving not only our friends and acquaintances, but often involving strangers. We will talk about the very idea that there should be moral concerns in public – both whether there should be at all, and on what grounds should we think about such moral concerns. And we will see that, as before, the traditions are on multiple sides of these debates.

When asked, most people say they think that morality can and should be a public concern, that it does have a public role to play. Because morality involves caring about people, and because such caring is typically connected to love, we think that love has something to do with public actions. (Here, and throughout this chapter, I use "love" as a general term for each tradition's particular form of pious filial devotion that should motivate the tradition's members in all their actions.) But the fact that most people say this does not of itself lead to any consensus about precisely how morality should be operative in public – how, that is, moral commitments should inform our public and more particularly our political actions. Once we allow that love does have something to do with it, that is, we still have to ask: precisely *what* does love have to do with it?

Given the many questions this and the following chapters will address, this is the question that lurks behind them all. There are at least two relatively distinct dimensions to this question. Let's call them the challenges of pluralism and of realism.

Each deserves our separate attention here, for any attempt to be moral in public must face each of them.

First of all, consider pluralism: here we confront the question of how moral convictions and concerns should be manifest in a context of moral murkiness and conflicting interests, agendas, and visions. It is hard enough merely to be morally decent to members of our own immediate families; it is far harder for us to be morally decent in our vast and ethically pluralistic modern societies.

Second, consider realism: here we face the question of the place of moral convictions in public affairs considered in general. What role should morality and moral arguments play in public deliberations? Given that our societies are so pluralistic, how can we know if or whether our particular moral convictions – those convictions that we profess guide our actions, give them their rationale and their particular shape – how can we know if or whether those convictions are not being imposed on others who do not share them, so that they are forced to participate in a quasi-religious practice that they find deeply objectionable?

And yet more pointedly for our purposes, what role should the various *religious* moralities play in public deliberations? This is actually a twofold question: on the one hand, it is about the civic etiquette of speaking out of one's particular religious convictions in a setting where not everyone shares those convictions; on the other, it is about the practical application of those religious convictions to issues of public import. We will study all these issues, though focusing more specifically on the latter, on *what* religious traditions have to say on these matters, rather than on *how* they should say it.

Here we begin with the question of the place of love in a world where love may not be all you need. More specifically, I want to explore this issue initially through some classic discussions of it in Christianity, particularly around that tradition's long discussion of the vexed question of the relation between love and justice. These terms are of course enormously complicated, and the debates about their proper meaning are vast and unending; but here are two quick ways of beginning to understand their distinctiveness from each other. Love looks *at* a person, and is concerned with what's best for them in themselves. In contrast, justice looks *around* a person, at their context (however broadly that is construed), and compares them with others, and is concerned with fairness and equality. Love asks how to *help* others, how to advance their good; justice asks how to *respect* them, how to secure what is right for them.

Here, we will look at two positions in this debate, positions that disagree due to differing understandings of the relationship between justice and love – namely, those of Reinhold Niebuhr and Stanley Hauerwas. We'll ask two questions. First, what is love, and what do we mean by justice, and how have those concepts been used to develop complex moral systems? Second, how ought we to understand our duty to act on our commitments to love when we live in a world where such love may not be a "simple possibility"? These are our questions; let's get to them.

Love and Justice: Definitions

Few categories have had as much philosophical investigation as the concept of love, particularly in Christian ethics. After all, love is both demanded of Christians and recognized as among the most powerful – if not the most powerful, in the guise of self-love, or over-attachment to some people in distinction from all others – sources of human wickedness and weakness. The Christian tradition typically distinguishes three kinds of love, namely, *eros*, *philia*, and *agape*. *Eros* is sexual love – the all-consuming sort of attachment that threatens to voraciously consume the other person with one's desire. *Philia* is friendship, which is (as we saw earlier in this book) a potentially quite profound but essentially non-consumptive affection for another, typically based on common interests. *Agape* is self-giving and absolutely unself-interested love, self-sacrificial love. Since saying that does very little to clarify matters, it will be useful to explore what exactly the category of *agape* has meant in Christian moral thought.

Agape has several distinctive characteristics. First, it is (potentially) universally inclusive. That is to say, it seems in principle not to be something that admits of partiality and favoritism. One cannot choose to show agape to some, and not to others, and expect your behavior to go uncondemned by the tradition. Agape has an intrinsic ambition to reach all people. Second, it is (oftentimes) primordially unilateral. One who is governed by agape does not wait for another to ask for help, much less for them to show any worthiness to receive it. Agape is preemptive, running to the other's care and heedless of evils or flaws in the other's character. Third, it has a trumping character over other sorts of commitments. Agape presents itself as a superior obligation to parental love, or marriage, or friendship, or patriotism, or any kind of social group identity. We cannot violate others to favor our own attachments to our particular loved ones or friends.

So understood, agape can seem a powerful moral force – indeed, so powerful that some Christian thinkers have tried to build their whole vision of morality around it. Others have worried it is inadequate, in various ways. Is this enough as a moral program? What are its problems? How can it be embodied? Historically, the tradition has identified two basic challenges to enacting this agape in human life. First is what we can call the problem of *self-love*: does agape leave no space for the psychological fact that we come to moral consciousness primarily concerned with, and attentive to, ourselves? One would think that agape would simply dismiss self-love. But it ought not to do that, because self-love is a powerful and generally recognized good, and one that bears within it deep analogies with the structure of *agape*, analogies that can help us understand what it means to love another person.

"Love your neighbor as yourself," said Jesus (Mark 12:31), and he called it the second greatest commandment. Most theologians have taken him to mean that in our own self-regard we have a clue as to how we should love others. There are three dimensions to self-love, each of which can become the basis of an overall view of self-love to the dangerous exclusion of the other insights:

1   Self-love is good, because it is love of one's concrete particularity, and can lead to loving others' particularity, their particular quirks and characteristics. We understand what it is to respect another – we understand what it is to follow the Golden Rule "do unto others as you would have them do unto you" – precisely because we understand how *we* would want to be treated, how we think we should be valued. And that sense is in part based on our self-love.

2   Self-love can be acceptable, insofar as it is a "prudent" self-love. We are charged, after all, with special responsibility for our own moral deliberations and decisions, actions and responses, and we ought to attend to our moral status in a particularly attentive way. This is not egotism, in fact recognizing it is the first step towards curing our egotism; one just is responsible in a special way for taking care of oneself.

3   Nonetheless, and perhaps most famously, self-love is still quite clearly dangerous, because we easily forget (some would say, not without evidence, inevitably) and become self-absorbed in powerful ways. Just because of our curious immediacy to ourselves, we easily efface the presence of other people in our moral consideration.

All three are dimensions that any assessment of self-love must account for.

The second challenge to living a wholly agapic life emerges in the question of what is known as the problem of "special attachments," those particular loves we have with particular people. We typically do not talk about a general kind of love for people in general, but usually about the *loves*, plural, that we have – in all their particularity, variety, and non-interchangeability.

We have lots of particular loves, and love begins locally, with the local attachments we have with particular others. We build outward from those particular love attachments toward "larger," more general and abstract affiliations. I don't simply love my infant son in the abstract; I love the furrow that appears on his brow when he's puzzled, I love the dreamy way he smells after a bath, I love how his eyes follow his big sister around, and I love the way he looks at me when he's going to sleep. In all of these dimensions what I love is not just one person but *this particular* person, and I love him in a way that is not interchangeable with other affections. All this is understandable, perhaps even approvable, in a parent. But in ethical terms, it causes problems, because, even when we are fully mature moral agents, certain special bonds of attachment remain, and these sit uneasily beside agape's demand that you should love your neighbor as yourself.

That is, we may run into conflicts between the moral command to treat all equally, and the reality of our affection for especially loved ones close to us. What if there are two people drowning in the sea, and you have only one life vest to throw them? Can you legitimately throw it to your beloved without casting lots to see which should get it? What if the other person is a young mother struggling to keep her and her infant's head above water? In itself, the commandment to "love your neighbor" offers us no straightforward guidance in such matters, no straightforward way to determine how to negotiate our multiple and conflicting loves in these settings.

How can we translate the command to love into a coherent and publicly workable moral system? How can it avoid simply devolving into sheer sentimentality? Some thinkers have argued that the problem is the religious formulae in which it is set; and once it is recast in the sobrieties of sheerly secular philosophical prose, such thinkers hope, the pith of the tradition can be rendered admirably coherent and practical. Two secular philosophies in particular present themselves, in part, as attempts to help us answer this question: utilitarianism, which locates the core of love in the commitment to impartial concern for the greatest good; and Kantianism, which locates it in the idea of respect.

Utilitarianism's similarity to the love commandment consists in its impartiality and beneficence, its insistence that all must be considered equally in making any decision, and its insistence that the decision must be determined solely or at least crucially on the basis of the effects of the system. This account certainly does justice to the impartiality of the second commandment. But it seems to be inadequate because it doesn't appear to set any absolute limits on what we can do – it does not allow for the idea that some actions are just forbidden. Considering things wholly on the basis of impartiality does not rule out the idea that, if some person somewhere must be tortured for the rest of us to live happy lives, that there is still something morally wrong about torture.

In contrast, Kantianism's similarity to the love commandment consists in its emphasis on respect, on its insistence that all people are irreducibly ends in themselves and hence invested with absolute worth. But it does not seem to usefully add anything to traditional formulations of the love commandments; that is, it seems to simply repeat, in a fairly inelegant Teutonic-academic prose, the command to love your neighbor as yourself. Furthermore, insofar as it claims to move away from a theistic grounding, its arguments seem no more convincing to skeptics than a bare appeal to God would be to them – which is to say, not convincing at all.

This is a problem with any attempt to account for any dimension of human life, moral or otherwise, in abstract theoretical terms. Such theories are good as models, but practically they always attempt to seduce us into confusing the model for the reality.

Love and Justice: Relations

So you can see that "love" may be all you need, but you need to understand it in very specific ways for it to be really adequate. And when you understand it in those ways, you come to see that you are also thinking about the meaning and role of justice in an ethic based on love.

To generalize wildly, there are two ways in which people have spoken about love and its relation to justice. The first way is to relate them, as it were, dialectically. By this I mean that such thinkers understand justice and love to be organically related, with one flowing naturally into the other, but also related in a critical way, so that each checks the deformations of the other. The second way is to relate them in a

sense oppositionally, where they stand in somewhat more straightforward opposition to one another, their similarities being merely superficial as they in fact contest
the same ground. On this account we should beware trusting the siren-song of
justice if it seems to conflict with the clear demands of love. And any sense of complexity in their relationship is merely an illusion we let ourselves believe in order
to avoid the hard obligation of love. We will look at these in turn.

Dialectically related

Perhaps the best example of a thinker who understands love and justice to be dialectically related is the American theologian Reinhold Niebuhr. For Niebuhr, in the
relation between justice and love, justice is *love limiting itself*. As Niebuhr said,
"Insofar as justice admits the claims of the self, it is something less than love. Yet
it cannot exist without love and remain justice. For without the "grace" of love,
justice always degenerates into something less than justice."[1] We treat each other
justly because we partly realize the worth of every person through our own
partial and particular apprehension of that worth in our local loves. Thus we treat
each other justly out of love. But we know that love is too powerful for its
own good sometimes, and can lead us to trample over or smother someone's
good in our self-professed care for them; so we limit our ability to love, in order to
protect the people we love from ourselves. And this activity, of love limiting itself,
is justice.

An example is not hard to find. Most parents love their children more than
anything else in the world. They want nothing more powerfully than they want their
children to flourish. And yet, as a thousand novels, movies, and sitcoms make clear,
it is precisely that invasive, overwhelming love that is the cause of a great deal of
misery for many children, particularly as they grow up. Self-aware parents realize
this (if only through reflecting on their relationships with their own parents) and
try to learn not to overwhelm their children. They limit their love, not because they
lack love or have a limited love, but precisely because they love so much – even
when it feels like they will burst from not telling their children what to do, they
manage, out of love, to restrict love. (And trust me, among the hardest things to
do in the world is *not* to do something for your children.)

What worried Niebuhr most in his day was the powerful temptation towards an
escapist sentimentalism on the part of his fellow Christians – those Christian moral-
ists who thought love was, as Niebuhr famously put it, a "simple possibility." So he
said that, while the "law of love" is the "final law" of human existence, things are
more complicated than that. Our activities cannot be straightforwardly governed
by the law of love, because we cannot simply decide to love everyone. Love is not
something we can will into existence; it is either there, or it is not.

Well, can we try to treat one another with the moral equivalent of love – say,
self-giving justice, perhaps? Even this is vexed, however, by what Niebuhr sees as a
second fact about us – namely, that we are irremediably self-interested. This is the

problem with typical claims to love one another: as Niebuhr put it, they "still tend to smell of sentimentality in our day because the law of love is presented without reference to the power of the law of self-love."[2] Because of this, "moralistic Christianity" has two problems in dealing with justice. First, it assumes that being Christian is identical with the possibility of "consistent selflessness." Typically, we think that morality is a "simple possibility" for us. But this is not so. Were perfect selflessness "a simple possibility," then "political justice could be quickly transmuted into perfect love," which it manifestly cannot be.[3] It is, in short, naïve.

Second, such a naïve moralism misunderstands the nature of our situation, and misapprehends the challenges we face as moral agents. It does not theoretically acknowledge – that is, it does not work into its theoretical account of moral deliberation – the fact that conflict is often not between selfishness and care for others, but rather among competing cares for others, competing moral claims. Choices between family and friends, or friends and nation, or nation and world, or one's commitment to human rights and the quality of life in third-world countries and one's commitment to the global environment – all of these can come into conflict; and it doesn't help answer these puzzles to say that we need to abrogate our self-interest.

Because of all this, the dialectical position suggests that love and justice are complexly related. We should not try to meet the challenge of selfishness only with direct resistance; meet it indirectly. As Niebuhr put it, "A simple Christian moralism counsels men to be unselfish. A profounder Christian faith must encourage men to create systems of justice which will save society and [our]selves from [our] own selfishness."[4] What we need, that is, is a way of understanding the urge to justice emerging from the law of love, but emerging from love only to turn round on it and check its excesses.

Niebuhr never thinks that this is easy or simple; sometimes, indeed, it may be more or less impossible, and lead us into tragic situations. The danger of tragedy was not merely hypothetical for Niebuhr; morally self-conscious Christians would invariably find themselves caught up in these sorts of tragic contradictions, simply because of the moral complexity and incoherence of our world. Sometimes, he thought, there would be inescapable conflicts between goods which could not be reconciled; sometimes moral choices carry a cost in genuine goods foregone, and sometimes lesser evils are accepted in the face of greater evils we mean to resist. But this does not mean that Christians should not do this; rather, it entails that they can only engage in life through faith. For Niebuhr, recognition of the necessity of such tragic choices should throw Christians back on their faith, and in particular on their faithful hope that God, not humanity, will solve the contradictions of history. "No possible historic justice is sufferable without the Christian hope. But any illusion of a world of perfect love without these imperfect harmonies of justice must ultimately turn the dream of love into a nightmare of tyranny and injustice."[5] There is a powerful connection between a proper understanding of love and justice, and a certain construal of the Christian faith, where the two sides of that equation interlock and mutually support one another.

Profoundly opposed

Niebuhr's account of the relationship between love and justice is not the only option, however. Some would say that dialectical thinkers like Niebuhr are wrong – that "tragic wisdom" is not the deepest kind of wisdom, that it is in fact a certain kind of consolation, an evasion of love's profound challenges to the way we live our lives. For such critics, love demands more than the dialectically minded thinkers seem to recognize. It is a harder calling, and ends not so much in tragic contradiction, but in the stark message of the cross, and the hope of the resurrection.

Perhaps the most voluble such critic is the contemporary American theologian Stanley Hauerwas. Hauerwas jumps on Niebuhr's affirmation of the role of Christian hope, seen above, and accuses Niebuhr of not taking hope seriously enough. When we do take it seriously enough, we see that it's not that morality and religion must conflict with politics, but rather that morality and religion can go on as if there were no importance to worldly politics, as if that politics did not matter anymore – because, from Hauerwas's perspective, it simply does not.

Hauerwas's disagreement with Niebuhr is straightforward: "Reinhold Niebuhr was mistaken in suggesting that the tragedy which marks our existence follows from realizing that the limited good we can achieve can only be accomplished ultimately through coercion and violence" – in short, through injustice.[6] For Hauerwas, it is wrong to resist violence with violence; it is better to allow violence to have its way with you than to participate in the disease of violence yourself. He does not recommend this because he thinks it will be an effective way of dealing with the problem; he does not think in terms of effectiveness at all.

Against Niebuhr, Hauerwas argues that the peaceableness Christians seek is not an "impossible ideal," but a "present reality" – because he conceives of peaceableness not as the tranquility of an entire social order, but as the stance out of which Christians can act, in faith in, hope for, and love of Jesus Christ. Such a peaceableness may seem mysterious to many, but in fact it is not an inner condition of tranquility of soul, but a simple decision to join a church, practice its non-violence, and live according to its gracious discipline. Peaceableness for Hauerwas is not first and foremost a perfection of individual character (that is impossible to realize, in this life), but rather a practice of living in a certain kind of community, however imperfectly.

For Hauerwas, the peaceable practice of love cannot be an individual perfection, because in the present we are caught in a powerful self-deceptive pattern of sin; as Hauerwas puts it, "all social orders and institutions to a greater and lesser extent are built on the lie that we, not God, are the masters of our existence."[7] Because of this deception, we find a real call for peace quite threatening. What we want instead is stability, quiet, order; and we get those, we think, only through control. In this context, real peace creates instability, because it subverts an order built upon violence, the violence of avoiding the stranger (who is ultimately God).

On this view, Christian love does not lead to a certain attitude of wistful regret at the costs and consequences we must accept as part of running the world, while yet accepting responsibility for running the world; rather, it is a radically different way of life that stands in contradiction to the received way of the fallen world. Its stark opposition means that Christians must accept suffering, because they must accept that humans are not in control. Yet Christians are joyful in the recognition that God is in control, even in the midst of their recognition of the misery and suffering which often surrounds them. Of course, such a joy is different from happiness: "happiness is too shallow a notion to characterize the disposition of the Christian, it too often suggests merely the satisfaction of desires determined by ourselves.… The joy that characterizes the Christian life is not so much the fulfillment of any desire, but the discovery that we are capable of being people who not only desire peace but are peaceable."[8] "Happiness" reflects our desire to be self-controlling, to satisfy our wants. Joy is something we get when we realize that we are not in control: "Joy is thus finally a result of our being dispossessed of the illusion of security and power that is the breeding ground of our violence."[9] Joy is not a reward for achieving a non-violent attitude for Hauerwas; rather, joy is simply another description of the act of surrendering the desire for control that is at the root of our reflexive violence as fallen creatures.

For Hauerwas, then, love does not so much coordinate with justice as replace it. The command of God is captured in the scriptures. Unlike Niebuhr, for whom some compromise of Jesus's exacting example and commandment is necessary in order that Christians accept their responsibilities in the world, for Hauerwas it is precisely Jesus's example and commandment that free Christians from the delusion that they should ever have thought that they had any responsibility in the world beyond giving witness, with their lips and in their lives, to the joyful message of humanity's salvation by God in Jesus. The demands of love need not heed the call of justice at all, for Hauerwas.

Conclusion

On its surface, this chapter has been only an intra-Christian debate. But to some degree the lessons, and the arguments, can be carried over to the other traditions, who face similar issues concerning the particularistic demands of their traditions and the question of how those demands will shape life in the world as we find it. This problem is of course manifest in different ways in the different traditions, but each of them must confront the tension between its ideals and the fact that the world does not simply allow those ideals to be realized in any straightforward way. Christianity may face this problem most overtly, but the other two grapple with it no less.

As for the specific questions of this tradition, to my mind this is still the most interesting fundamental debate in Christian ethics. Both sides echo the apocalypticism of the tradition in different ways. Niebuhr suggests that the world is so riddled by sin that only God will perfectly fix it; Hauerwas argues that the world is so riddled by sin that Christians, just because they are fallen humans, cannot trust their own moral intuitions. Both affirm, that is, some of the same deep convictions that the tradition assumes, even as they take those affirmations in very different, indeed incompatible, ways.

Whatever you think of that claim, however, it is indubitably true that this issue will shadow the following chapters in this part, because they all ask fundamental questions about the application of moral rules to particular cases, and one of the questions that they all must ask is about whether any application inevitably involves a religiously and/or morally troubling compromise. This question, in turn, raises the issue of whether such a compromise is acceptable or not within the strictness of the tradition; and so we will see the debates of the following chapters return again and again to analogous restagings of the disagreement between Niebuhr and Hauerwas explicated here.

Simply put, the world is always far too complicated for any humanly organized system of morality, however ingeniously designed, and the attempt to live a moral life strictly through the framework of any such system invariably leads to situations where crisis or compromise is inevitable. The question of love and justice, then – their ordering and relation – is a question any serious moral and religious tradition of thought will have with it so long as it submits to life in a world not designed, first and foremost, to congratulate humans for their cleverness. And from all the evidence of human history we so far have, we can say that the world has little interest in proffering such congratulation.

11

Duty, Law, Conscience

Once we have asked the question about how love and other particular motivations should play a role in our social ethics, we can turn to the central concepts that social ethics typically employs. When we do that, we are likely to think about social ethics by relying on a set of concepts that we rarely if ever question. Central among these are the three concepts of *duty*, *law*, and *conscience*. Together, these three are among the most fundamental building blocks of ordinary received morality, especially "public" morality, where we cannot assume others will share our more particular languages of faith or morals. When we think about our social obligations to one another, we tend to think about them in terms of our *duties* to one another. When we think about the proper shape of our social order, we tend to think about *law* as the way to articulate that shape, and provide its moral skeleton. And when we think about the power of the individual to apprehend and fulfill their own duties, and to follow or disobey the law, we think about that power in terms of the individual's *conscience*. Duty, law, and conscience are the basic building blocks of our typical imagined social ethics.

But what if our understanding of these concepts is deeply flawed? That is the disturbing suggestion this chapter pursues. By focusing especially on conscience, the chapter suggests that these concepts are far more ambiguous than we often think they are, and that we may need to rethink them in order to allow ourselves to keep using them.

I want to share with you a problem, a problem with our language of conscience. I want to get you to begin to see this by giving you an image, telling you a story, and then trying to show some ways of thinking about it. This image is of a group of soldiers, ordered to commit atrocities, and most doing it, for fear they will be seen as cowardly; and the story is of a man – Adolf Eichmann – who insisted that, in organizing and running the Holocaust, he was merely obeying the law.

Here is the story of the soldiers. They were German soldiers in World War II; tough, hard men, the men of a Reserve Police Battalion 101, men drafted into the army from the Hamburg police force – cops, men who had seen the worst of humanity and fought for the law, however imperfectly, in the decades before the war began. These were not Hitlerite fanatics, or twenty-year olds who had had Hitler as *der Führer* for their entire conscious lives; these were older men, many of them fathers, with a wide range of experience of humanity, in a great and cosmopolitan city. And then one day, they were invited to participate in one of the greatest crimes ever known to humankind:

> Around 2 a.m. the men climbed aboard waiting trucks, and the battalion drove for about an hour and a half over an unpaved road to Józefów [a small Polish village]. Just as daylight was breaking, the men arrived at the village and assembled in a half-circle around Major Trapp, who proceeded to give a short speech. With choking voice and tears in his eyes, he visibly fought to control himself as he informed his men that they had received orders to perform a very unpleasant task. These orders were not to his liking, either, but they came from above. It might perhaps make their task easier, he told the men, if they remembered that in Germany bombs were falling on the women and children. Two witnesses claimed that Trapp also mentioned that the Jews of this village had supported the partisans. Another witness recalled Trapp's mentioning that the Jews had instigated the boycott against Germany. Trapp then explained to the men that the Jews in the village of Józefów would have to be rounded up, whereupon the young males were to be selected out for labor and the others shot.
>
> Trapp then made an extraordinary offer to his battalion: if any of the older men among them did not feel up to the task that lay before him, he could step out. Trapp paused, and after some moments, one man stepped forward. The captain of 3rd company, enraged that one of his men had broken ranks, began to berate the man. The major told the captain to hold his tongue. Then ten or twelve other men stepped forward as well. They turned in their rifles and were told to await a further assignment from the major.[1]

The Holocaust began at a million individual places, when individual men and women were told to do particular things. For these men, Józefów was the beginning of the Holocaust. (For their victims, of course, it was the end.) They were invited to participate in a horrifying mass murder. They had spent their adult lives on the side of law – on the side of the law as the authorities of Hamburg interpreted it, surely, but certainly there was some self-respect and sense of dignity about protecting individual humans from humankind's criminal predations. And here they were ordered to become criminals; and almost all of them did.

In the next year and a half or so, the 500 men of Reserve Police Battalion 101 shot approximately 38,000 Jewish men, women, and children, and sent approximately 45,200 more to Treblinka. These 500 men were responsible for over 80,000 murdered innocents. And it all began on one morning, in the small Polish village of Józefów – when their commander had actually invited them to refuse this service.

Why had so many of them not refused to participate in massacre? What made them (or worse, enabled them) to do it? Interviews after the war suggested a disquieting answer: for these soldiers, to refuse to engage in mass murder seemed to them to signify cowardice, frailty – in short, moral weakness. Even most of those who had stepped out of ranks described their decision not to participate directly in the Holocaust as a moral failing. Think about that: even decades after the war, after what the massacres had meant had become clear, these men still saw their refusal to shoot women and children as a shameful mark of their weakness. It should communicate something of the depth of the depravity in place here, that when the perpetrators of such crimes reflect on whatever minor escapes from complicity they were allowed by fate, they cannot help but think of those escapes as moral failings on their part.

This incident should give rise to thought. The point is not simply to reiterate our astonishment at the multitudinous pathologies and malices that went into the making of the Holocaust, no matter how weirdly satisfying that may be. Instead, we are after larger game: we are after what incidents such as this teach us about the language of conscience as we use it today. We turn to this topic next.

Conscience

To get to why these are important images for me, however, we should think about conscience for a moment. Our ordinary understanding of conscience is fairly straightforward. We picture it as internal – a voice – that typically is inflexible and indubitable. As Thomas Jefferson wrote in a letter to his daughter Martha:

> If ever you are about to say anything amiss or to do any thing wrong, consider before hand. You will feel something within you which will tell you it is wrong and ought not to be said or done: this is your conscience, and be sure to obey it. Our maker has given us all, this faithful internal Moniter, and if you always obey it, you will always be prepared for the end of the world: or for a much certain event which is death.[2]

It is not insignificant to recognize, alongside these fine sentiments, the rather unmelodious note that Jefferson was a slaveholder, who fathered children with one of his slaves, and which children – his own children – he then kept as slaves on his plantation.

The marks of conscience, traditionally conceived, are all here. Conscience is an interior sense, relatively autonomous from our consciousness, in some sense "outside" of us, even as it exists within us; and by that quasi-independence given authority to judge our actions.

But where does the conscience come from? What is it about humans that makes them susceptible to moral claims of this type? Historically, we can sort answers to these questions into three distinct groups of theories about the source of conscience. The first is what we can call the metaphysical theory, held by thinkers like Thomas Aquinas, Plato, and possibly Mr. Jefferson. On this theory, the source of moral norms is absolute and comes from outside oneself. It is a sort of metaphysical signal receiver that instructs us as to the moral rules of the universe. A second model is available. In this model we understand conscience not as an externally grounded source, but an internally based one, one arising from the inner logic of our own free agency itself. It affirms that moral norms are absolute, but come from inside oneself, from the fact that one knows one is like other people and so one must treat them as one would want to be treated. The point is that conscience does not come from some outside source, like God or an objective moral law; rather, for these theories, conscience arises from something intrinsic to being moral agents. Preeminently this is Immanuel Kant's approach, but many others in recent centuries have suggested variants of this. Third and finally, we have those cluster of theories that do not think of conscience as a fixed moral guide, but rather as psychologically, socially, or culturally constructed. We can call this group of theories constructivist. For theorists in this vein, the source of moral norms is contingent upon human societies, and is not absolute but is internalized by socialization and psychological dynamics.

Whatever theory of the origins and nature of conscience to which we ascribe, it is especially important to recognize that it is a sign of responsibility. That is to say, it is something to which only we can attend, and something that is experienced as both inside and outside us – both intimate to us, and somehow transcending us. This is why even Christian thought on conscience insists that the conscience ought never to be disobeyed. One must always obey one's conscience; if one does not, one is in outright rebellion against oneself.[3]

These are the traditional contours of our idea of conscience, a category with a long and distinguished pedigree in the West, and most certainly a category at home, albeit in different ways, in all three of the traditions we study in this book. But beyond, or alongside, its many benefits stand some profound challenges that have become increasingly unavoidable over the past century.

I suggested that the fact that a slaveholder such as Jefferson could pen such noble thoughts as he did about conscience, while yet keeping other humans as pieces of property, should give rise to some thought about whether those words are really adequate to the phenomenon they self-congratulatively purport to represent. I want to explore this question below, through two examples, one drawn from America's experience with chattel slavery, the other from the European Holocaust.

The Curious Case of Huckleberry Finn

The first example is from one of the great works of Western literature, *The Adventures of Huckleberry Finn*, and concerns the main character of that work, Huck Finn himself. Mark Twain is often understood today as a corn-pone storyteller, but in fact he was a tremendously powerful moralist, a quite acute diagnostician of the sins of his age. In the figure of Huck Finn – a tremendously clever, deeply "unsivilized" young man of the pre-Civil War era – he created his masterpiece, and the crown jewel in the masterpiece is perhaps the story of Huck's tormented relations with his friend Jim, who also happens to be a slave.

Huck's crisis is easily described. Huck and his friend, the slave Jim, are travelling along the Mississippi. Huck effectively helps Jim escape from Miss Watson, his owner. After he does this, he comes to believe that he has "stolen" Jim, who would be worth $800 as a commodity; what's worse, now that Jim believes he has his freedom, he means to go back and help his wife and children escape – which Huck understands to be more theft. (Huck says, upon hearing of Jim's plans to rescue his children from slavery, "I was sorry to hear Jim say that, it was such a lowering of him.") Huck, that is, comes to believe he has committed a massive crime against Miss Watson, a person who cared for him and trusted him.

What should he do? The crucial moment of Huck's realization comes in chapter 16:

> Jim said it made him all over trembly and feverish to be so close to freedom. Well, I can tell you it made me all over trembly and feverish, too, to hear him, because I begun to get it through my head that he WAS most free – and who was to blame for it? Why, ME. I couldn't get that out of my conscience, no how nor no way. It got to troubling me so I couldn't rest; I couldn't stay still in one place. It hadn't ever come home to me before, what this thing was that I was doing. But now it did; and it stayed with me, and scorched me more and more. I tried to make out to myself that I warn't to blame, because I didn't run Jim off from his rightful owner; but it warn't no use, conscience up and says, every time, "But you knowed he was running for his freedom, and you could a paddled ashore and told." That was so – I couldn't get around that no way. That was where it pinched. Conscience says to me, "What had poor Miss Watson done to you that you could see her nigger go off right under your eyes and never say one single word? What did that poor old woman do to you that you could treat her so mean? Why, she tried to learn you your book, she tried to learn you your manners, she tried to be good to you every way she knowed how. THAT'S what she done."
>
> I got to feeling so mean and so miserable I most wished I was dead.

Much later in the story (chapter 31, to be exact), Huck has a second chance to do what he thinks is the right thing – that is, to turn Jim in; and again he discovers the terrible (and to his mind immoral) power of his affection for Jim:

> I felt good and all washed clean of sin for the first time I had ever felt so in my life, and I knowed I could pray now. But I didn't do it straight off, but laid the paper down and set there thinking – thinking how good it was all this happened so, and how near I come to being lost and going to hell. And went on thinking. And got to thinking over our trip down the river; and I see Jim before me, all the time, in the day, and in the nighttime, sometimes moonlight, sometimes storms, and we a floating along, talking, and singing, and laughing. But somehow I couldn't seem to strike no places to harden me against him, but only the other kind. I'd see him standing my watch on top of his'n, stead of calling me, so I could go on sleeping; and see him how glad he was when I come back out of the fog; and when I come to him again in the swamp, up there where the feud was; and such-like times; and would always call me honey, and pet me, and do everything he could think of for me, and how good he always was;

and at last I struck the time I saved him by telling the men we had small-pox aboard, and he was so grateful, and said I was the best friend old Jim ever had in the world, and the only one he's got now; and then I happened to look around, and see that paper.

It was a close place. I took it up, and held it in my hand. I was a trembling, because I'd got to decide, forever, betwixt two things, and I knowed it. I studied a minute, sort of holding my breath, and then says to myself:

"All right, then, I'll go to hell" – and tore it up.

It was awful thoughts, and awful words, but they was said. And I let them stay said; and never thought no more about reforming. I shoved the whole thing out of my head; and said I would take up wickedness again, which was in my line, being brung up to it, and the other warn't. And for a starter, I would go to work and steal Jim out of slavery again; and if I could think up anything worse, I would do that, too; because as long as I was in, and in for good, I might as well go the whole hog.

Some readings of the novel present this episode as a triumph of conscience over a wicked set of social mores – as if Huck understands himself as a heroic rebel. But that is manifestly false. Huck understands himself to be a moral *failure*, a calamity for not following the moral law. The conflict here is between what Huck sees as his pre-rational, problematic sympathy and the proper morality (which Twain suggests is actually a horrific hypocrisy). Huck sees himself as weak, because he takes the social norm as the only possible standard of conscience, no matter the violence it seems to do to his feelings (and really, we can see, to his whole psyche). The upshot of this situation is that Huck rejects morality, and becomes not so much immoral as amoral.

The moral of the story, such as it is, is oblique: we must not ever let "morality" float too free from ordinary human empathy, lest our agency become wholly captive to unreal abstractions at the cost of attending to the real world. Conscience needs to be fed both by rigorous, abstract, skeptical argument, and by concrete realities brought to our attention by our vital human affection. The danger is in not seeing that any one version of morality may need to be changed, and if it is not changeable, we may end up, like Huck, jettisoning our concern about morality altogether.

The fictional story is powerful, and the irony of the telling suggests it is an exaggeration. But recall the men of Reserve Police Battalion 101, the ones who refused to kill the Jewish men, women, and children of Józefów: they too, like Huck, understood their refusal to participate not as a sign of moral heroism, but as a sign of moral weakness. (One suspects Twain would not be pleased to be proven so literally prescient.) One century's fiction may well be the next century's fact.

And this is where we transition to our second story, that told by Hannah Arendt in *Eichmann in Jerusalem*. Arendt's worry about conscience is similar to Twain's, but with a twist – she is worried that, in extreme situations of large-scale societal moral perversity, conscience can work against its proper purpose – that is, that conscience, improperly internalized, will not resist evil, but aid it.

Eichmann on Doing One's Duty

Arendt's story centers around a single figure, a personage not without interest in the bestiary of human malice. Of all the Nazi leadership caught and prosecuted after he war, Eichmann is in many ways the most interesting, if only because his case seems the most troubling for our received views of evil and wickedness.

On many levels, Adolf Eichmann is a surprising figure to have risen so high in the Nazi hierarchy. He had been, of all things, a vacuum-oil salesman in the early 1930s, then joined the Nazi Party and the SS in 1932 and began to ascend the ranks. His remarkable facility with bureaucratic matters, and his unquestioning devotion to work, made him increasingly valuable. By 1942 he was given the job of "Transportation Administrator" for the Nazi genocide against the Jews, which put him in charge of managing a large part of the logistical bureaucracy of the Holocaust. He carried out his duties with relentless, unimaginative efficiency.

His criminality as the central bureaucrat of the Final Solution would certainly be enough to convict him of crimes against humanity. But his case is made more curious, and his soul seems all the more suspicious, because of a surprising event in the closing months of the war. As it became clear that the war would be lost for the Nazis, Heinrich Himmler decided to stop shipping prisoners to the death camps. He ordered Eichmann to stop sending the trains to the camps. Eichmann, however, disobeyed this direct order, and the trains kept running. Why? This is the mystery around which the prosecution at the trial in 1961 based its case against Eichmann.

Arendt, however, thought that asking this question was horribly misleading. In fact, for her, the trial revealed that we lack the resources in our ordinary moral vocabulary to allow us to confront the problems that the Holocaust presents to us. We do not have quite what we all need, and so we have to attend to the particularities of the experience in order better to understand it, and be able to respond to similar situations should they happen again. Arendt, that is, challenges the *moral and legal concepts* which organized the war-crimes trials and argues that they need to be rethought. To judge the Holocaust on the old moral concepts, she thinks, is cowardly and dangerous: "To fall back on an unequivocal voice of conscience … not only begs the question, it signifies a deliberate refusal to take notice of the central moral, legal, and political phenomena of our century."[4] For Arendt, the Holocaust trials in general were actually failures, because they did not come to terms with what was before their eyes.

This is revealed by a troubling fact about Eichmann that the prosecution ignored but upon which Arendt seized. It turned out that, under questioning, Eichmann revealed that, in the disturbing episode at the end of the war (and indeed throughout the war as a whole), he thought he was doing his duty – not just obeying orders, but the law. This is crucial, and Arendt builds her argument around it. For her, this fact reveals the perils of conscience-language – namely, that the energies of "conscience" can be retained even while its aims are horribly misdirected. Eichmann, it turns out, had read Immanuel Kant's works – at least his *Critique of Practical Reason*, his central ethical work – at least enough to achieve a rudimentary understanding of it. His analysis of Kant is disquieting; he does not think he rejects Kant, at least at first, but subtly alters his argument. He keeps the intensity and fervor of Kant's idea of duty, where "doing one's duty" goes beyond mere obedience; you do not only obey the law – whatever it is – but you do so with *devotion* to it. This version of "doing one's duty" provides Arendt with an alternative account of why Eichmann sought until the end to carry out the transports to the camps. He did so not out of "fanaticism, his boundless hatred of Jews," but out of duty: "It was not his fanaticism *but his very conscience* that prompted Eichmann to adopt his uncompromising attitude duing the last year of the war."[5] In this context, Eichmann "did not need to 'close his ears to the voice of conscience,' as the judgment has it, not because he had none, but because his conscience spoke with a 'respectable voice,' with the voice of respectable society around him."[6] Like Huck, Eichmann's context framed reality in such a way that being decent to Jews seemed to be immoral to him. Eichmann was simply "better" than Huck, if that is the word for it, in his capacity to resist succumbing to his bare human sympathy – largely because he had no sympathy at all within him.

This may seem like a fantastic vision of the moral insanity of the Nazis, but support for it comes from a study of some things that Heinrich Himmler, Eichmann's superior, said earlier in the war. In Poznan, Poland, in 1943, Himmler gave a speech to a group of SS leaders that is among the more remarkable events in the history of human moral existence. In that speech, he said:

> I want to tell you about a very grave matter in all frankness. We can talk about it quite openly here, but we must never talk about it publicly. I mean the evacuation of the Jews, the extermination of the Jewish people. Most of you will know what it means to see 100 corpses piled up, or 500 or 1,000. To have gone through this and, except for instances of human weakness, to have remained decent, that has made us tough. This is an unwritten, never to be written, glorious page of our history.[7]

Himmler was right that the Nazis who carried out these crimes suffered; many suffered from ulcers, alcoholism, stress, and other bodily injuries. Their very bodies revolted against the monstrous crimes they committed. (None of that should generate sympathy for the Nazis, of course; but it is a sign of the monstrosity of their deeds that bodies actually rebelled.)

For Arendt, the Eichmann case reveals the problem with relying solely on the received language of "conscience." Conscience motivates us to disobey orders *only* when they go against the law's normality. As Arendt says, "unlawfulness must fly like a black flag above the orders as a warning reading: Prohibited! … And in a criminal regime this black flag with its warning sign flies as manifestly above what normally is a lawful order – for instance, not to kill innocent people just because they happen to be Jews – as it flies above a criminal order under normal circumstances."[8] Eichmann's story shows us what can happen when conscience exists within a framework of deep evil – we get not moral anarchy but *moral inversion*; as Arendt puts it:

> Just as the law in civilized countries assumes that the voice of conscience tells every-body "Thou shalt not kill," even though man's natural desires and inclinations may at times be murderous, so the law of Hitler's land demanded that the voice of con-science tell everybody: "Thou shalt kill," although the organizers of the massacres knew full well that murder is against the normal desires and inclinations of most people. *Evil in the Third Reich had lost the quality by which most people recognize it – the quality of temptation.* Many Germans and many Nazis, probably an overwhelming majority of them, must have been tempted *not* to murder, *not* to rob, *not* to let their neighbors go off to their doom …, and not to become accomplices in all these crimes by benefiting from them. But, God knows, they had learned how to resist temptation.[9]

None of this is meant to exonerate or excuse anyone in Germany. For after all, others in Germany in these years – even some on the front lines of the Holocaust – did know it was a tremendous evil, and tried to fight it.

Arendt's ultimate point was far from exculpating Eichmann, even though almost everyone acted as he did. Nor was her point to praise those rare few who did not, who retained something of their humanity in extraordinary conditions. Her point was that such heroic people are invariably not the norm; they are unusual, even rare. And yet appealing to the language of "conscience" as a bulwark against such genocidal events across a whole society, in practice amounts to a hope that most societies have enough such heroes to stop the massacres from commencing. Unfortunately, history teaches us that no society has enough such heroes even to alter the massacres' course in any real way. So to rely on extraordinary moral heroes to keep our societies sane is a deeply intellectually and morally evasive strategy, not to mention one doomed to fail.

Conclusion

For Arendt, then, conscience can easily become a "false friend." It is quite possible to believe we are being extremely moral and yet objectively to do horrendous evils. And on the other hand, it is possible for remarkable acts of decency to appear at first in the guise of moral failure or weakness. Simply to hope that in extreme moments individuals, who are rarely heroic in ordinary life, will suddenly snap out of the malfeasances they have hitherto found so attractive and pull back from the ultimate malice, is delusional; and to suggest that such self-knowledge is perpetually available in such a way that, after such events, we can assume the agents of such evil were in all relevant ways in morally similar conditions to ourselves – to hope or assume any of this, Arendt suggests, is a horrific mistake, and a moral failure on our part.

None of this, of course, is to suggest that the conscience cannot be a real force for good. In some situations it clearly is the only thing that allows some people, anyway, to stand up to horrendous evil, when most of the rest of us have gone mad. Arendt's deepest point, and the one that she shares with Twain's depiction of Huck, is more profound than that. Both teach us a very old lesson: that ignorant idealism and ignorant cynicism are equally escapist, morally disreputable strategies of evading coming to terms with the hard facts of our situation. An unremitting cynical hostility to the language of conscience is just as mistaken as a naïve reliance on it. Both seek to excuse us from the hard task of thinking about our condition as moral agents in the world as we find it, and so both are to be avoided. To believe one could do less and still be properly moral is to think of oneself not as a human, but as a sort of robot. Insofar as we take ourselves, and not our programming, to be responsible for our deeds, we must expect more of ourselves than that.

12

Capital Punishment

If there is a central moral problem with American higher education, it is the infantilization it perpetuates on its inmates. Students call themselves "boys" and "girls" without thinking about it; yet they can vote, they can legally marry without parents' permission, and can serve in the military. Sure there are grades; but really, society has designed things so that the institution of higher education rarely lets its inmates feel the weight of reality.

This is not a problem just with higher education, however. It is part of the condition of being modern. Reality is messy and difficult, and it slows us down. So we develop ways of avoiding it. Technology is the knack for arranging life so perfectly that we manage, by and large, to avoid it. Much of our lives are technologies, in this sense.

In fact the roots of technology's allure for us lie even deeper in us than in our condition as modern humans. For this is a fundamental human fault – namely, escapism. As far back as human history goes, our basic strategy, when confronted by reality, is to *avoid*.

This truth is a direct challenge for a book like this, just because this sort of evasion of reality is at root a moral failing. One of the things that studying ethics should do for people is render less avoidable the fact that we live *in* reality, not at some distance from it, and our lives matter in some sort of absolute sense – in the only sense of absoluteness, indeed, that we have unambiguous access to, in this world, anyway. And in the matter of capital punishment, this is especially important, because in fact for those readers who are Americans like myself, you and I are killing people, deliberately and directly, even today. As citizens of a republic, within which ultimately sovereignty and thus responsibility, rests with we the citizens, we are finally accountable for these killings; and so it behooves us to think seriously about whether or not we wish them to continue.

Why don't we show executions on TV? After all, we see lots of made-up murders and deaths. What's so horrific about seeing a real one? Why spend so much time making fake ones realistic? After all, you and I are the "producers" of capital punishments. Why are we so squeamish about avoiding the fruits of our labor?

This chapter explores the meaning of punishment, and in particular capital punishment.

This is an especially pointed problem, because of the horror about the objective reality of killing, whatever you think about the context of the actual execution; we all, I think, experience a horror of, and I would argue a *prima facie* moral command against, killing. (By a "*prima facie* moral command," I mean a command which presents itself to us on first sight (*prima facie*) as a command, when we first encounter it, but which may be overridden by other obligations we feel to be more important.) This *prima facie* command against killing is manifest in some of the most surprising places. War, for example, is often about *not killing* – in war, we kill, but because we are worried about further deaths that will result unless we stop some state from doing worse things. In this regard, capital punishment, by being about direct killing itself, is in a more morally intense location than war.

Furthermore, capital punishment is also a powerful way to excavate and assess our convictions about the meaning and nature of punishment itself. Attempting to understand capital punishment means we ask questions about the point of punishment itself. That is what we should do here.

Punishment contains, or can contain, three distinct aspects. First, it has a punitive, retributive, or restitutionary aspect; in this dimension, the punishment is supposed to reply to the crime in some sort of reflective manner, so that the wrongdoing that the perpetrator inflicted is in some curious way "matched" by the harm or damage inflicted upon them. ("An eye for an eye" is a relatively straightforward way of talking about this punitive aspect.) Second, it has a deterring aspect, whereby the punishment is supposed to communicate to other potential perpetrators that the society as a whole will not tolerate it, and will seek out offenders and punish them – thus hopefully deterring others from committing such a crime in the future. Third, it may contain a rehabilitative aspect, so that the punishment helps, or at least does not hinder, the criminal's moral progress towards that condition in which they will no longer be interested in being criminal. (Thus many prisons are called, perhaps optimistically, "correctional facilities.")

These three aspects raise a further question about the purposes of punishment: are they "merely" social or somehow more fundamental, perhaps even metaphysical, restoring some sort of balance to the nature of the cosmos itself? Is punishment, especially perhaps capital punishment, a wholly this-worldly practice, or does it serve a different sort of purpose, one not so much extra-legal but in some way *supra*-legal?

The Secular Debate about the Death Penalty

Two strong secular views offer arguments about capital punishment in ways that raise precisely these points, and make us ask ourselves what exactly we care most about in morality. Abolitionists argue from what they see as two facts. First, capital punishment does not deter crime, and second, the death penalty, as it is currently applied, is unfair and inequitable. In contrast, proponents of the death penalty counter that there is evidence that it does deter crime, and the unfairness of the death penalty's application does not speak to the justice or injustice of the death penalty itself.

To get clear on these views, we should map out their disagreements on three contested points: capital punishment as deterrence, the moral inequity of capital punishment, and the moral depravity of execution itself.

On the matter of deterrence, abolition proponents argue that there is no real evidence of the death penalty's deterrence value, and deterrence is hard to establish because the application of the death penalty is not consistent. In fact, they argue that, even as regards rational criminals, the death penalty may be too much, for long-term imprisonment is a severe enough threat to make rational actors not want to murder. Furthermore, deterrence only works for premeditated murders, but the vast number of capital crimes are crimes of passion. For all these reasons, advocates of abolition say, the death penalty should be renounced.

But proponents of the death penalty have their own responses to these arguments. First of all, they argue that deterrence seems to have evidence in favor of it, historically speaking. Furthermore, they suggest that without a further penalty – namely, the death penalty – those who are convicted of life sentences without parole have no reason to behave well, even in prison. And as regards the abolitionists' charge that most murders are "crimes of passion," and so undeterrable by rational threats, they argue that abolitionists are arguing from the absence of evidence – which is not the evidence of absence. If the majority of murders are in fact crimes of passion, and thus not strictly rational and "premeditated," death penalty defenders argue, then that may well suggest that the deterrent power of the death penalty against premeditated murders is in fact quite potent – because there very well could be more of them if there were no death penalty. The only ones who are not deterred, that is to say the only ones who do commit murder, are those for whom no threat would be potent enough.

On the matter of the moral fairness or unfairness of the death penalty, the abolitionists say, there is an especially important point. The death penalty is applied in a racially discriminatory manner. (In 2005, for example, fully 40 percent of death-row inmates in the United States were African American.) If it is not applied in a relatively equal manner, they argue, it is unjust to apply it at all. The death penalty may be *retributionally* satisfactory, but fairness and equity in punishment are of at least equal moral weight to the moral obligation of retribution; and the clearly uneven distribution of the punishment among different racial groups suggests that we should be hesitant to allow the death penalty.

Again, however, advocates of the death penalty think that these arguments are unconvincing. They insist that capriciousness of a punishment's application does not make the punishment itself unjust – it only means we must try harder to apply it justly, that is, by applying it to a broader group of perpetrators. Capricious application does not tell against the penalty itself, but merely its application; we do not argue that because the police do not catch all speeders, they should not issue any tickets. Capriciousness is a good reason for ceasing to employ a punishment only when a punishment is randomly meted out to both guilty and innocent alike, not when the punishment is disproportionately applied to a subset of the guilty. The proper response to this disproportion is not to abandon the punishment but to apply it more vigorously and fairly – that is, to execute more people who are found guilty of execution-worthy crimes.

Furthermore, these advocates insist, this demonstrates that we must distinguish between justice and equality. Justice and equality are two different moral criteria, and they insist that concerns about justice ought to trump concerns about equality – so that, if we can catch and punish only some of the offenders, we ought to punish them anyway, and not worry that our treatment of the class of offenders is unequal. Ernest van den Haag puts this well: While "Unequal justice is morally repellent," nonetheless "unequal justice is justice still. What is repellent is the incompleteness, the inequality, not the justice."[1] Equality, they insist, is concerned with making sure that justice is applied *equally*, and is not itself a direct concern of justice.

The discussion on this point would quickly move to large fundamental questions. Opponents of the death penalty would counter the advocates by asking about the propriety of a punishment that is unequally distributed but not in merely random ways. If a punishment falls disproportionately on a group already the subject of significant discrimination, at what point does the punishment's cost in increased social tension and resentment outweigh its propriety as a means of justice? Advocates of the death penalty reply by arguing *never* – the crime committed, they aver, must be punished, and to withhold punishment for fear of increasing a certain social cynicism about the justice system among a minority is wrong. Abolishment would accomplish that aim only at the cost of increasing a society-wide cynicism about the justice system being used as a tool of social policy. In turn, opponents of the death penalty would reply that the justice system is *already* effectively a tool of social policy – just one that the advocates refuse to see as such.

The questions brought to the surface by this debate are profound. How concerned should we be with the question of fair distribution? If we cannot catch and equally punish all criminals, should we not punish those we can as severely as we can? Should we care about the indirect effects on "social capital" – on individuals' attachment to their larger community and their commitment to work and perhaps sacrifice for the common good – of a part of the justice system that delivers justice unequally? Do we believe that justice should be a tool of social policy, or not?

Beneath all these debates, furthermore, there is a final, deep moral issue at stake on both sides: whether life is so absolutely sacred, valuable in a way that entails that no life should ever be deliberately and intentionally taken, or not. Abolitionists argue that it is simply not appropriate for a morally civilized society to kill anyone; it is barbaric. Execution is not simply retribution – it is far more cold-blooded than a murder, because it is so premeditated and carried out by the state – by all of us, collectively. (Furthermore, execution is irreversible – what if we kill someone and they are innocent? We have committed a heinous crime that can never be mitigated in this life.) A government that practices this punishment debases itself, and its citizens, and can be expected to cultivate in them an insensitivity to moral horrors of this sort as well as others.

Defenders of the death penalty take a different tack. For them it is precisely the value of life that is at issue, and that they are at pains to defend. Is there anything worth dying for? Is there anything worth killing for? Is life the basic value that can never be trumped by any other value? Some defenders of the death penalty go farther, and suggest that abolitionists suffer from "failure of nerve" about justice – they cannot have faith in their ability to judge people, and think that others should not judge them either. For such defenders, the attempt to undo the death penalty is part of a larger cultural practice of challenging the idea of moral absolutes; arguments about the death penalty are really displaced arguments about the culture wars.

So we have seen how two views, formed without explicit recourse to religious reasoning, still have absolute and non-negotiable commitments concerning the sacredness of life and its value relative to other values. In a way, both are governed by commitments which they cannot convince the other side to share, but which shape their own views in powerful and fundamental ways. Their arguments, that is, are built importantly (though not exclusively) around different assessments of whether death is ever right. Both, that is, are rooted in "acts of faith," absolute values about what is morally basic. For abolitionists, life is an absolute good that ought never to be taken away, at least when there are other ways of handling the person who would otherwise be killed. For defenders of the death penalty, life is a good, but it is not so absolute that we cannot imagine dying for something, or killing for something; life is part of a hierarchy of goods, and stopping moral abominations can be more important than one's own life. They give us the problem, but do not help us find a solution.

A stalemate exists here. The only way to overcome it, it seems, is to explain the fundamental presuppositions of both sides, and to determine how to assess their validity. In doing this, we will be helped by views from the religious traditions, which are more self-conscious about how their overt ethical stances rest on metaphysical or religious convictions that not everyone shares. We will turn to those next.

Judaism

In the Jewish tradition, questions about the death penalty connect up with arguments about the nature of crime, the purpose of this-worldly punishment, and the role of the People Israel in history. Because of the range of issues involved, the tradition has a complicated view of the death penalty. At their heart, however, most

Jewish assessments of capital punishment, for and against, circle around the primordial conviction of the unique and unquantifiable value of each individual, murder victim and murderer alike.

In the Hebrew Bible, capital punishment is commanded for a variety of different violations of the Law, especially within the People Israel, living under the covenant – but murder is treated differently, first of all as a sheer crime of humanity against humanity, but then also as a certain form of pollution. Because it is murder that centrally concerns us here, we can focus on that.

The story of murder begins early, with Cain and Abel; but it has its most profound statement in the covenant God makes with Noah after the flood. There God says, after forbidding humans to eat the blood of animals (which the text understands to be vampiric),

> For your own lifeblood, too, I will demand an accounting: from every animal I will demand it, and from human beings in regard to their fellows I will demand an accounting for human life. Whosoever spills the blood of a human being, by a human being his blood will be spilled; for in the image of God has the human being been made. (Genesis 9:5–6)

Here the prohibition seems twofold. First of all, the "blood" of a human – like the blood of animals – is especially precious; it is the locus of their life-force. One who consumes animal blood is a vampire, and this is wrong; and one who spills human blood is a murderer, and this is wrong too. Indeed, "wrong" does not quite capture the horror of the event, nor the inevitability of the consequences that flow inexorably from it. Even the language of this passage communicates that. The rhetorical character of the central verse here – the first part of Genesis 9:6 – "Whosoever spills the blood of a human being, by a human being his blood will be spilled" – is a *chiasmus*, which is a technical term for a figure of speech which relies on a rhetorical reversal of structure to underscore the point of the statement. Here the chiasmic structure of the statement suggests something natural, inevitable about the consequence of the murder. Murder does not most basically break a positive law, something that needs to be explicitly promulgated to be understood and obeyed; here, murder is presented as part of a series of actions that end in the death of the murderer. The very structure of the language here suggests the inevitability of this end, the naturalness of such a punishment.

What makes the murder of a human even worse, however, is the explicit connection to "the image of God." In killing a human, their blood not only cries from the ground, as God reported to Cain that Abel's did; it is also a direct affront and insult to God that one who bears so striking a resemblance to the Most High would be so savagely and contemptuously treated by another bearing that same resemblance.

After the covenant, the nature of murder as a crime worthy of capital punishment gets a new meaning for the People Israel, and the theological dimensions of this crime become even more prominent:

You shall take no ransom for the life of a murderer, who is guilty of death; but he shall surely be put to death. And you shall take no ransom for one who has fled to his city of refuge, that he may come again to dwell in the land, until the death of the priest. So you shall not pollute the land wherein you are: for bloodshed pollutes the land, and no expiation for the land can be made for the blood that is shed therein, but by the blood of him who shed it. And you shall not defile the land that you inhabit, in the midst of which I dwell: for I am the Lord who dwells in the midst of the children of Israel. (Numbers 35:31–34)

Here there are at least two innovations on the earlier Noahide Covenant. First of all, it is possible for one who kills another by accident to flee to a "city of refuge" (effectively a form of exile) from which they cannot be taken and killed. Thus for "accidental manslaughter," we might say, capital punishment was not mandated. But exile is still important, and the reason for it illuminates the new quality that adheres to murder for the People Israel – namely, the fact that by making the covenant with God, Israel has become God's holy people, and their land is now holy land, and a murder on that land defiles or "pollutes" it. The covenant has infused a new kind of holiness that the People Israel bear, and part of the glorious burden of that holiness is a new kind of obligation to keep themselves pure, in the most minute details of their mundane lives, and in the most dramatic violations of the fundamental human agreement to live together. Murder is not just an assault on a human, or an attack on human society, or an insult to the Image of God in humanity; it is also a profound violation and pollution of the covenant, the identity-conferring marker for both God and Israel, and puts the true nature of both of their beings into question.

In the Rabbinic era, things changed more than is at first apparent. First of all, the rabbis were firmly in continuity with earlier Jewish thought about capital punishment, even as they explored some of the legal and religious questions arising therefrom. The key is the rabbinic emphasis on law as the command of God, and the human as fully autonomous and therefore capable of observing the law. The rabbis developed the character of murder's punishment as regards to positive law, but kept the primordial character of murder by incorporating it into the legal system. Murder does not most basically break a law, it is what Genesis said it was – an assault on the nature of creation, on the human social order, and on God's created Image, that must be retributed for by humanity. They add to this the insistence that the pollution must be overcome.

Yet at the same time, the actual practices of capital punishment were not something Jewish communities could mete out. The Diaspora meant that they were small communities in nations not under Jewish law, so the issue of capital punishment remained fundamentally a theoretical one for the rabbis. Often, in fact, the issue of capital punishment served as a site to explore the differences in Jewish understandings of God and the human in contrast to Christian and Islamic accounts.

In the modern age, Jewish thought has largely come to terms with legal systems as fundamentally *secular* realities and as such not properly designed to bear the weight of theological justice. (Even the legal code of the modern State of Israel bears the marks of this recognition of secularity.) Nonetheless, the question of capital punishment remains a live one, and there are rival options for today, all of which still emphasize (1) the reality of the individual lost; (2) the social nature of the crime and thus the punishment; and (3) the role of Israel's God in this. However, they do offer significantly different approaches, to which we now turn.

Some would argue for the death penalty, insisting that God's fundamental interest in organizing human society is equality, and a just society; this justice entails the perpetual presence of the death penalty as the last recourse in situations of egregious injustice. For such thinkers, proportionality matters enormously: the punishment must fit the crime, as exactly as is possible. But in the case of physical harm, no perfect equalizing process is in fact available – there is no way to restore physical damage, nor to equally compensate for it. If I put out your eye, taking out my own does not put yours back. And what is the case with relatively minor bodily injuries is even more the case when it comes to murder. There simply is no way to compensate for a death. Atonement is possible for a murderer, then, only in some attenuated sense, and only by their own execution as well. In a way, society is forced into execution by the murderer's own deed. But in another sense, it also affirms (however paradoxically) the value of human life by responding in so dramatic a manner. Capital punishment is therefore not only a deterrent to future potential murderers; it is also an expression of ultimate outrage at this most basic violation of the human person, an expression owed not only to the victim, but to society itself as composed of other potential victims.

Such pro-death penalty thinkers see contemporary society as paradoxically *too* merciful. For them, the problem with "forgiveness" is that it rejects equality, and tolerates murder by not treating the murderer as having committed the crime that they actually did, as if we gave out jaywalking tickets for rape. (Recall Cynthia Ozick here, with her concern that "forgiveness is pitiless.") Totally to overcome vengeance would be to lose the sense of the individual's absolute and irreducible moral worth, and of equality; it would suggest that individuals matter only insofar as society deems them to matter, which would be morally unacceptable. We must never lose sight of the actual victim of the crime – the man or woman, boy or girl, of flesh and blood who is no more.

Others, in contrast, would argue against capital punishment, arguing that while God's aim is justice, God also seeks mercy, and in today's society mercy can be operative where before it could not – because of changes in the social order, and because the opportunities for punishing criminals have expanded. For them, there are three overarching reasons for punishment: (1) realignment of the relationship between God and creation, (2) retribution, and (3) deterrence. They think that extreme caution should be taken with the death penalty, just as the rabbis were very cautious about it, even in abstraction. Furthermore, modern societies have an alternative that the ancient Israelites didn't have – prison. (The issue of whether contemporary American prisons are ideal for such rehabilitation is of course different from the question of whether they could be.) Life in prison without parole, these thinkers suggest, is an adequate alternative to the death penalty in all cases. Essentially, in fact, this punishment retains the death penalty; it simply leaves the moment of execution up to God. Most fundamentally, they appeal to the same principles that proponents of the death penalty do – namely, the principle of the uniqueness of each individual's life. How can it make sense, they ask, to punish one for taking life by taking their own life? For these reasons, they think, the death penalty should not be used.

No matter their conclusive views on the propriety of the death penalty, what is important across all of these disputants, by and large, is the degree to which *justice* on this earth can be satisfied. Little concern, at least relative to Christianity, is given to the idea of deferring to a fundamentally eschatological justice, the "Last Judgment" of God. Moral seriousness is *immanent*, not eschatologically deferred. We will see that in Christianity things are often quite different.

Christianity

Like Judaism's understanding of capital punishment, Christian views have developed over the centuries. Early on there was not a great deal of attention to an explicitly Christian approach to capital punishment, first because Christian reflections on governance were slow to get going in general, and second because capital punishment was considered a quite normal part of the powers of government. Nonetheless, at least by the fifth century CE, a theologian like Augustine could write letters to political authorities urging mercy to convicts facing the death penalty. Still, such urgings were always in the context of a general acceptance of capital punishment, the clear majority view among Christian thinkers up to the twentieth century.

Today, things are a bit more complicated, and so we will look at some contemporary Christian views on capital punishment. To understand these issues, we have to see the full range of the dimensions of the debate. This will involve us appreciating, first, the various understandings of Christian teaching as regards this-worldly government's obligations; second, the nature of Jesus's mission as decisively revealing God's intentions for humanity and God's means to humanity; and, third though most immediately, the differing assessments of the metaphysical nature of crime and punishment. Different positions view these dimensions differently, and prioritize them differently as well.

Here we will look at three different views. The first, exemplified in several of the statements by the United States Roman Catholic Bishops, argues that God's purposes for us can at times allow for capital punishment, but the present conditions of our society do not justify *our* system of capital punishment. Furthermore, Christians' endorsement of capital punishment suggests a misunderstanding about the nature of the crime, the nature of the state, and the nature of the sort of justice available in this world. A second view dissents, suggesting that the current temptation to reject capital punishment categorically and absolutely is philosophically incoherent, theologically anathema, and socially problematic. A third view, in contrast, suggests that Christ's death on the cross has forever cancelled out all need for retribution; we must advance the cause of God by affirming that that cancellation has occurred, and that the first task in that undertaking is the renunciation of the sort of violence that the death penalty exemplifies. We begin with the first view.

In their several statements regarding the death penalty over the past several decades, the US Roman Catholic Bishops have offered a powerful and well-worked out view regarding the death penalty and the nature of punishment in modern societies in general. They recognize the legitimacy of the deterrence argument. The state must protect society, both from outward enemies such as other nations and dangerous extra-national forces (as is handled by the logic of just-war theory, which we will study in forthcoming chapters) and from interior ones such as criminals (which is the logic of punishment). The state serves to keep society and all its individuals flourishing. Fundamentally, it does this via its policing function, but in the last century or so it has extended those functions to include cultivating and protecting some structures in the society against the encroachment of other structures (so that Roman Catholic social teachings have insisted on defending the integrity of civil society, the family, and the dignity of the human person against the predations of excessive capitalism ever since the papal encyclical *Rerum Novarum* in 1891). Nonetheless, the security of its inhabitants is the state's fundamental justification; if it cannot by and large secure that, then serious questions about its legitimacy, even viability, may be raised.

For the bishops, then, capital punishment is therefore possible in situations of extreme social danger (such as martial law). But today, they think, is not one of those situations. Society is not in that situation of grave danger, and therefore the urgent rationale is not operative. Furthermore, the way the death penalty is practically employed actually does harm to the social order. Apart from the very real possibility of a mistake in judgment (what if you execute the innocent?), the long and unavoidable delays make the penalty seem very remote, and yet the extension of the time between conviction and execution creates anguish – not only for the guilty, but for innocents who love the guilty (e.g., their families). Furthermore, the publicity and apparent discriminatory character of the death penalty actually work to intensify social conflicts. For these reasons, the bishops urge that capital punishment should be rejected as a viable tool of good governance for modern societies.

They add to this a cultural critique of the role the death penalty has played in American politics in the past few decades. Recognizing that questions of capital punishment are never purely about capital punishment, but are always part of a larger political discourse, they lament the political manipulation of the death penalty to increase social and political tensions for individual political actors' self-interested political purposes. They recognize that the death penalty came back, in the late 1970s, in a period of deep anxiety about crime among the populace – an anxiety partially legitimate, but also partially illegitimate, as a camouflage for racism.

Furthermore, they think that abolishment would be both socially and evangelically useful. It would, they argue, break the cycle of violence in society – it would show that we no longer are engaged in a blood feud, but can step beyond the immediate need to retribute, and offer a genuinely new response. It would also demonstrate the value of each person and so connect with other commitments (such as the bishops' opposition to abortion) that also highlight individuals' value. Furthermore, the abolition of the death penalty would demonstrate the basic good of life as a fundamental theological principle, reinforcing the idea that each individual is to be respected, with possible spillover effects in other parts of society. They think it is consonant with the example of Jesus, and thus enables people to take more seriously the command to follow Jesus than they presently seem able to do. Finally, they couch their opposition to the death penalty as part of a larger social proposal, namely, that we collectively rethink and restructure the correctional system, "in order to make it truly conducive to the reform and rehabilitation of convicted criminals and their reintegration into society."[2]

While it may seem that the bishops are aiming solely at rejecting capital punishment, in fact their ultimate aim here is a non-apocalyptic understanding of the function of the human political state. The state does not aim to produce absolute justice, but serves the purpose of this-worldly harmony. For the bishops, "this is not the era of retribution" – we are not meeting out the *final* judgment, for to do so would be to usurp God's role as judge.[3] It is up to God to retribute fully; vengeance is mine, sayeth the Lord (Romans 12:19). Rather, "the forms of punishment must be determined with a view to the protection of society and its members and to the reformation of the criminal and his reintegration into society."[4] This reveals the importance of the bishops' understanding of and commitment to a certain construal of the common good. That is to say, punishment by the state in this theological era – the era between the resurrection of Christ and the end of the world (a fairly long era, as it turns out) – is primarily about protecting society, not balancing the cosmic books on the backs of those few murderers who are caught and convicted. Yes, the state has a right to extreme self-defense under extreme threat, and that is when the death penalty is permitted. But punishment by the state is not about the victim *per se* – it is about the danger done to society. In strict legal terms, the victim's suffering is not the problem; the violation of proper order is the problem.

Some thinkers, following the bishops, offer a further rationale for this view. Such thinkers, like the contemporary Roman Catholic Joseph Bottum, worry that the desire to see the state mete out absolute justice is simply part of our growing tendency to see the state as the ultimate metaphysical actor in the cosmos, and as the provider of all our existential, metaphysical, and ultimately spiritual and theological needs. That is, such thinkers worry most about an unacknowledged growing *statism* in our society. For them, the state is an overwhelmingly this-worldly reality, and permitting it any part in divine justice is to give it too much power and majesty – a gift that is especially dangerous given the character of the modern state. To fantasize that cosmic justice is possible is to suggest that the state has a cosmic role to play – and the modern state, as a wholly secular entity, with no pretentions to divine authority, cannot, ought not, make such claims.[5]

The bishops allow that there is a place within Roman Catholic moral reasoning for the idea that executing criminals might be permitted. Some Christian thinkers worry that this too easily obscures the importance of justice. Others worry it diminishes the import of Jesus's example for Christians. We should appreciate both.

For many of those Christians committed to keeping the death penalty, the key fact for them is the import of *justice* and keeping an explicit focus on justice alive as a part of social and political life. Retribution is the primary purpose of just punishment; the restoration of justice is good in itself. Of course, this view allows that a too-simple view of retribution is problematic, as the Roman Catholic bishops make clear. But such thinkers insist that some genuine retributive justice is realizable in this life – there is some degree of moral realism available to us. As J. Budziszewski – one thinker who makes this case – puts it, "The sentences of human magistrates cannot be, and are not meant to be, a final requital of unrepented evil; that awaits the great day when Christ returns to judge the quick and the dead. But they *foreshadow* that final justice, so that something of the retributive purpose is preserved."[6] The crucial word here is *foreshadow*: the punishment meted out in this world still stands at some distance from God's ultimate judgment of the crime, but it anticipates that judgment in the nature of its punishment in the here and now. This-worldly justice can have a genuine concern with the ultimate meaning of our acts. In meting out justified punishments, therefore, humans can participate *proleptically* in God's judgment – they can serve as "partial delegates" of God.

Furthermore, speaking societally, Budziszewski argues that capital punishment, the demand to keep capital punishment as a possible penalty, brings home to our minds the seriousness of what justice and the law are all about – and thus brings home to our minds the importance of caring about justice, and possibly makes us more serious about the reality of absolute moral laws. That is to say that, for Budziszewski, keeping capital punishment a live option serves an evangelical purpose for the Roman Catholic Church: "if we who recognize this standard [of a transcendent order of justice] do not act as though we believe in it, then no one will be brought by us to believe in it."[7]

Apart from this pro-death penalty argument, there is another Christian argument, this one affirming with the bishops' argument that the death penalty be abolished, but really arising from a more absolutist anti-death penalty view. These Christians – many (but not all) of them pacifists – take a much more absolute line against the death penalty than do the bishops. For them, *any* sort of death is absolutely forbidden, and cannot ever be contemplated as an appropriate option to take.

Such thinkers often argue from what they see to be the example of Jesus. For them, Jesus declares the death penalty wrong indirectly, by insisting that executioners be sinless; as he is reported to have said in the instance of the woman caught in adultery, "let him who is without sin cast the first stone" (John 8:7). But it is not just in the example of his life, but in the event of his execution that Jesus demonstrated an absolute commitment to non-violence, and one that is normative for all who claim to live in his name. For many of these thinkers, the story of Jesus's crucifixion and resurrection ends all need for retribution and sacrifice. It was this deeper lesson to which the example of his life was pointing. As Christianity bears as its central symbol the image of a man crucified, executed by the state for his purported crimes, so Christians should, these believers feel, never allow that memory to be forgotten: believers must work as hard as possible to ensure that no one else suffers Jesus's fate.

This contrast is not meant to be merely a private one; it must be communicated and shared with the wider society within which Christians live, a society composed both of Christians and non-Christians alike. Thus, this opposition to the death penalty becomes an evangelical principle for these believers. Bearing witness to what they see as this great injustice is a means of giving testimony to their faith – and not just a provisional or optional type of testimony, but one close to the center of what they take to be their Christian faith.

This is so because they see such execution as the classic form of compromise, merely the tip of the iceberg of bad faith. The basic worry of this group is that Christians today remain far too comfortable in their collaboration with the "worldly" powers around them. As we saw earlier, some pragmatic opponents of capital punishment are concerned about the growing power of the state, its encroaching on what they see as properly God's turf; and some defenders of capital punishment worry about an incipient cultural relativism and collapse of moral order reflected in the jettisoning of ultimate punishment. Against both of these, absolutist opponents see what they take to be a deeper problem than either of these – not the danger of the culture decaying, but that Christians could ever have imagined that they have a responsibility to *run* or master this culture at all – for it is "worldly" and not something of ultimate concern.

This has implications for our understanding of the relation between this-worldly justice and divine justice, and the nature of politics and political institutions in this world. God's justice is exhaustively manifest in the merciful forgiving of evil. God would never "order" through violence, through force or the threat of force. Human political structures are always potentially, and often actually, seduced by the demonic temptation to be in control. In such situations, it is inevitable that Christian "political" activity will be largely oppositional and fugitive, a matter of giving witness more than proposing any positive program of civic action. Positive and constructive action will be needful, of course, but efforts to undertake it will always need to be haunted by a skeptical alertness to the danger that one could cross over to collaborating with the powers that be rather than witnessing to their announced and inaugurated overthrow.

We've now seen some Christian views of capital punishment, grounded on religious claims about God and the way God wants the world to be run. Now I turn to two Islamic views on the death penalty, to see how Muslim religious convictions can cash out to defend the death penalty as a legitimate and justified social device, or as something we may need to rethink.

Islam

The Qur'an treats murder very seriously: "If anyone slays a person, unless in return for murder or spreading corruption in the land – it is as if he slays all mankind; while if any saves a life it is as if he saves the life of all mankind" (Q. 5:32). In particular, two crimes are worth death: deliberate murder and "spreading mischief in the land" (*asad fil-ardh*). In the case of murder, forgiveness and compassion are strongly encouraged. The murder victim's family is given a choice to either insist on the death penalty or to pardon the perpetrator and accept monetary compensation for their loss (Q. 2:178). While the Qur'an does not prejudge the choice, the tacit presumption as it develops in the legal literature seems to be for mercy.

"Do not take life, which God has made sacred, except by way of justice and law" (Q. 6:151). Islamic law is quite clear. In the case of "spreading corruption," the categories are treason or apostasy (when one leaves the faith and turns against it), and the use of violence and force outside of the authority of the state (a class that in the legal tradition includes terrorism, robber gangs, and piracy, and rape, adultery, or homosexual acts). Here the logic is that such acts, in traditional Islamic societies, strike at the basis of social order and thus peace, and therefore threaten the whole social fabric; as society is valuable in the same way as (though not more than) are human individuals, it must be defended as vigorously.

Executions are expected to be public – indeed, as used to be the case in many Western countries, they are meant to be exemplary, teaching all the faithful the consequences of violating the Law – the law of humans, but also the Law of God. Punishment is seen not as *replacing* God's punishment, but as in Judaism though not in Christianity, the continuities between this-worldly punishment and divine judgment are less troubling for Islamic thinkers. There is less of the opacity separating the will of God from the events of creation, as we understand those events. The judicial arm is a relatively clear and straightforward agent of God's will on earth, and so punishment is warranted for both this-worldly reasons of social order and harmony and for diverse reasons of what actions are pleasing to God and what actions are not.

Despite all this – the clarity of approval of the death penalty, its place in Muslim thinking about social order, and its proper publicity – the tradition seems to urge, however tacitly, that those who can show mercy *should* show mercy. The criteria for confirming adultery in particular seem designed to make it hard to convict someone, and the tradition makes unmissably clear the ever-present availability of divine mercy in all cases where punishment is merited. God can well forgive up to the last instant (Q. 79:35–41; 39:53), and it is suggested that God's mercy is something that all the faithful should copy.

Conclusion

Debates around the death penalty bring to the surface some very fundamental issues for these traditions. The issue is important not just because it discusses the handling of certain especially heinous crimes. More broadly, it reveals the vision of the role of government, and the scope and purpose of human community.

Clearly, each tradition has thought hard about this, and there are respectable strains of each for which capital punishment is clearly not just thinkable, but at times morally the right thing to do – just as there are also respectable ways of using the traditions' commitments to argue against the death penalty. In unpacking the thinking on these matters, we see that this issue touches not only on the understanding of the shape and function of human society, but also on the character of human history and the nature of each tradition's understanding of God.

We turn next to an issue deeply related to the death penalty, namely, the question of war. We will see some of the same issues arising there.

13

War (I)

Towards War

This chapter and the next study the reality of war and violence as a moral problem. They look at the possibility of morality in and around war, and the way that religions have thought about war in the past.

Not that long ago, a topic like this would have seemed antiquated. When I began teaching in the 1990s, the idea that major wars would preoccupy our world was fairly far-fetched. Oh sure, there were short, sharp conflicts in far-off lands, in which the "developed nations" (developed enough not to make war against each other, that is) might or might not take an interest, like Olympian deities.

I hope now everyone understands the force of the quip, often falsely attributed to Leon Trotsky, that while "you may not be interested in war, war is interested in you." We live in an age of wars, and rumors of war. Students who sat in chairs in my classes a few years ago have now experienced war in Afghanistan and Iraq; and at least one, Humayun Khan, UVA class of 2000, a Captain in the United States Army – and a Muslim, by the way – has died in one.[1]

War is thus an urgent concern today. It is also one of particular interest to those concerned with religious ethics. Some think that religions are the cause of wars. Others claim that only religions offer us the resources to stop the wars scarring the face of the earth. The truth is somewhere in between. Throughout history, religious beliefs have been mobilized to permit or prohibit involvement in warfare. No religious tradition is purely militant, nor purely pacifist; all struggle with the ambiguities of the apparent necessity and obvious cruelties of warfare.

Furthermore, there has developed a tradition of thinking about war called the "just-war" tradition, a tradition that argues that there are possibly *rules* which we ought to obey in war. These have been applied both to going *to* war, and to activities *within* war. In this chapter and the next we will look at these issues from several different directions. This chapter explores these debates by looking at the three traditions' thinking about war, and in particular at how their understandings of divinity, and of the present status of creation *vis-à-vis* what God intends, shape attitudes toward use of force. Effectively we are asking, how do these traditions' various understandings of the nature of God and God's plan for creation illuminate their understandings of war? And what, in contrast, do these traditions tell us is the meaning of peace? By necessity, this chapter will also explore the development of the just-war tradition, historically Christian but recently formulated in secular terms as well, especially its mode of reasoning about when it is right to go to war – what is called the question of *ius ad bellum*.

We begin by looking at positions developed in early Judaism, focusing on how war was understood as part of God's governance of the world and in light of the mission of the People Israel both in their pilgrimage on earth and in their eschatological goal in *shalom*, God's peace. The chapter will then look at how Christian thought has struggled with the complex inheritance of the Christian faith on what is for it the clearest case of a situation where our moral commitments come into conflict – namely, the case of the use of the sword, or violence, in political activity. Ought Christians to accept the use of violence as sometimes legitimate, or ought they always to shun it? Then this chapter will look at the history of these debates in Islam, noting the complicated inheritance of the Qur'an and the various interpretations of that inheritance, especially around the notion of *jihad*. In all three traditions, the role of religious belief in motivating people about war is complex, and raises questions about whether we think war can be a positive good or not.

Judaism

There is no single, simple, coherent picture of Jewish thought about war. This is due both to the fact that this is a tradition that is more polyphonic than creedal – a tradition that possesses multiple competing authorities rather than one authoritative voice – and to the fact that there was little need for sustained Jewish reflection on war for most of the past two thousand years, until the establishment of the State of Israel in 1948. In fact there have been significant changes in Jewish thought about the ethics of war in the past century – more changes, perhaps, than had happened in the previous two millennia. From the time of the Romans' destruction of the Temple in Jerusalem in 70 CE until the establishment of the State of Israel, Jewish political thought was the thought of a people without much expectation of political power, and without much expectation that they would be charged with ruling themselves as a fully sovereign political community.

And yet the tradition carried within its scriptures the memory of political rule, and thinkers in the tradition never stopped reflecting on the problems associated with governance, even if they often formulated those thoughts in messianic forms. In the deep history of the tradition there were wars and rumors of war; and at least from Abraham forward, the Patriarchs were reported to have waged wars when commanded by God (e.g., Genesis 14). (Indeed, it is ironically the case that whereas Christianity, as we will see, began with a larger emphasis on non-resistance, and had to "spiritualize" its commandments to "resist not evil" and "turn the other cheek" in order to authorize the use of violence, Jewish thinkers after the end of ancient Israel had to spiritualize their tradition's literal language of violence and warfare to make it relevant to Jewish life when the People Israel were no longer a distinct political entity.)[2] In the Rabbinic era, when the Jews seemed furthest away from self-governance, in Babylon and the Mediterranean Diaspora, the rabbis developed an account of the "Three Vows," a line repeated three times in the Song of Songs: "I make you swear, O daughters of Jerusalem, by the gazelles and by the hinds of the field, do not wake or rouse love until it is wished." The rabbis interpreted this as a radical criticism of all attempts to bring the Messiah to earth by direct human action. The rabbis understood the Three Vows to (a) forbid large-scale return to the land of Israel and to (b) forbid the Jews from rebelling against the rule of the Gentiles; in return for the Jews keeping these vows, God vowed (c) to ensure that the Gentiles would not persecute the Jews "too much."

However, the two great events of the twentieth century for Judaism – the Shoah and the establishment of the State of Israel – forced major changes. Both, in very different ways, focused many Jewish thinkers' minds on the practical constraints and logics of international warfare from an explicitly Jewish perspective. So since 1948 there has been a renaissance of Jewish political thought, and questions of war and peace have become topics of considerable practical interest for Jewish thinkers, largely as a matter of discerning how to relate traditional legal codes and modes of thought to the new conditions of modern war and the democratic Jewish state.

In general, the heritage of ancient Israel was rich in examples of God both demanding and delimiting violent behavior. There is no evidence of principled pacifism or the idea of non-resistance in Judaism; that would conflict with the demand, in almost all situations, for strict justice. A Talmudic line is crucial for understanding the nature of self-defense, personal and social, in Judaism: "if someone comes to kill you, kill him first" (*Sanhedrin* 72a). The Israelite code of warfare in Deuteronomy 20 was quite brutal, and commanded genocidal violence against those peoples closest to the Israelites – the Hittites, Amorites, Canaanites, Perizzites, Hivites, and Jebusites and the Gigrashites – and horrific violence against others. But even in these texts there are boundaries to violence, and boundaries which are significantly tighter in this setting than other peoples of the same era would permit.

What is crucial here, as it will be for the other traditions, is the idea that war is a *divinely* governed activity: not an activity that God sets in motion and then turns away from, indifferent to its outcome, leaving humans to behave as they will, but an activity to which God devotes serious attention, over which God watches, and on which (and through which) God exercises judgment.

Because of this, the rabbis classified all possible wars in terms of God's attitude toward them. The Mishnah categorized Israel's wars as permitted or obligatory (*Sotah* 8:7). Permitted wars – *reshut mitzvah* – were ones that were allowed, but which human discretion was given authority to instigate; in permitted war, the enemy nation must have violated, and have been shown to violate, at least one of the seven Noahide commandments. Obligatory wars – *milhamot mitzvah* – were required in situations of existential defense of the People Israel, or versus the Amalekites and the idolatrous seven nations in the conquest of Canaan. Indeed, against those who have shown themselves hardened enemies of the People Israel – certain Canaanites and the Amalekites – certain kinds of unlimited war were viable, perhaps even obligatory.

Within this relatively militarily permissive picture, however, the final aim of war was always peace. One conducts wars justly in order that the consequent peace may be as righteous as possible. And that righteousness is manifest in the peace upon which a just international order is built. But there is a fundamental recognition that *shalom* – peace – is an eschatological and messianic ideal. The root word suggests completion and perfection, wholeness. No such perfection is available before the Messiah returns. So we are never in this life fully able to lay our weapons down. True *shalom* exists in history like a promise always lingering on the horizon, never getting closer. And yet it is the duty of all faithful Jews to work for the approximation of that peace, in themselves and among all nations.

Christianity

Christian thought on war begins within the matrix of Judaism. But because the early Christians seem to have expected a quick return of Jesus as the Messiah, and because the first several centuries of Christian history are the centuries in which Jewish political entities went into eclipse, Christians did not spend a great deal of time developing their own Jewish resources about the meaning of human politics in general, and the proper use of violence in the service of social ends in particular. When, in the fourth and fifth centuries of the Christian era, Christians began to feel the need to think through the idea of war in a religious frame, they drew on their familiarity with the Hebrew scriptures, and certain forms of more recent Jewish thought; but they were also deeply informed by their acquaintance with classical Greek and Roman sources on the meaning and nature of political life and the moral shape of war.

Many Christians assume that the Christian New Testament is a fundamentally pacifist text. (At times such assumptions are implicitly connected to assumptions that the Old Testament, the Hebrew Bible, and the Qur'an are just less developed on these matters.) But in fact the New Testament itself is less purely anti-war than it is a text that speaks of war in a different way than what Christians came to see as the Old Testatment. In general, we can say that it is not *mundane* war that is the first kind of war that these texts imagine, but cosmological war. The New Testament's vision, especially in the Book of Revelation but elsewhere as well, is about cosmic war, between God and Satan. Christians are depicted by and large as witnesses, bystanders in a war between supernatural powers in which heavenly forces fight for humanity.

So the New Testament texts required a good bit of exegetical gymnastics to be made useful for thinking about the propriety and morality of war. Nonetheless, even in these writings there were moments of literality as regards human war that mainstream Christian interpreters seized upon. For example, the author of the letter to the Hebrews says that figures in the Old Testament such as Samson "conquered kingdoms through their faith" (11:32–34). In Acts 10 the centurion Cornelius is baptized by Peter, but there is no record of him leaving the service of the Roman empire as a centurion. And famously Romans 13 seems to command obedience to the sword of the authorities.

Even Jesus's example is complex. We all know the passages where Jesus says turn the other cheek, do not resist evil with evil, and the like (e.g., Matthew 5:38–42; Luke 6:27–31). But there are other passages that do not fit this story, passages in which Jesus commands the disciples to buy swords (Luke 22:36), where he drives the money-changers out of the temple with a whip (Mark 11:15–33; Matthew 21:12–27; Luke 19:45–48; John 2:12–25), and in which he says "I come not to bring peace, but to bring a sword" (Matthew 10:34). It is not because they did not read the New Testament that medieval Christian rulers saw themselves as imitating Christ in his stern role as *pantokrator*, "ruler of all." To say that the New Testament portrays Jesus as a pacifist pure and simple would be almost as mistaken as to represent those stories as depicting Christ as a "motivational speaker."

Christianity seems to present, then, two conflicting moral movements: one shunning, even fleeing, the use of the sword, and the other willingly accepting, even commanding it. What are we to make of this? More importantly for our purposes, what did Christians make of this? Christian thinkers drew quite different conclusions from almost the same arguments – we must see why the arguments are so interestingly and importantly different. Most basically, some of them developed an account of war that has become one of the bases for a great deal of international law. Others rejected or modified this account. Let's look at these in turn.

The just war

One of the most powerful traditions of reasoning about war in Christianity is the just-war tradition. This tradition is very ancient. On some understandings it predates Christian reflection, for it has roots in Cicero (106–43 BCE), especially his magisterial work *On Duties*. But it gained its most famous "founding father" in the thought of St. Augustine (354–430 CE), not only in his *City of God* but in several of his letters and scriptural commentaries, particularly those defending the theologically positive significance of the Christian Old Testament against those, such as the Manichees, who wanted to discard it as a radically flawed text. (We will see that the insistence on the theological and moral relevance of the Old Testament is a crucial point for many just-war theorists, against many of their opponents who overtly or (especially in recent years) inadvertently support a supersessionist reading of the New Testament over against the Old Testament.) Later thinkers developed this tradition more fully, especially Gratian in the twelfth century and Aquinas in the thirteenth, both of whom systematized and deepened the tradition. In the sixteenth and seventeenth centuries, new challenges emerged for the tradition, and Roman Catholic thinkers such as Francisco de Vitoria (1492–1546), Luis de Molina (1535–1600) and Francisco Suarez (1548–1617), and Protestant thinkers like Johannes Althusius (1557–1638), Hugo Grotius (1583–1645), and Samuel von Pufendorf (1632–1694) developed the tradition further by applying it to the new conditions of early modern nation-states and global war.

In the eighteenth and nineteenth centuries, the tradition seemed almost to disappear, mocked as an archaic tradition by anti-traditional Enlightenment rationalists and overwhelmed by the new mass nationalistic total wars of the Napoleonic era and after. But it was rediscovered in the twentieth century by religious and secular thinkers alike, and its influence today is profound.

Bellum and duellum

The tradition of just-war reasoning implies a distinction between two types of violence, one that is legitimate and one that is not. This distinction is captured in Latin by the distinction between *bellum* and *duellum*. *Bellum*, which is roughly coterminous with the English term "war," signifies the idea of the authorized use of force by a legitimate collective power (the state or some other similarly politically legitimate body). Interestingly, this category is at least adjacent to, and possibly continuous with, the political body's *policing* duties. (It is worth noting that the idea of a distinction between a police force and a military force is a relatively recent development.) *Duellum*, from which comes our term "duel," signifies the illegitimate because private or personal use of violence between non-politically legitimate agents. Anything from piracy, robbery, or illicit rebellion, to actual dueling, is captured in this idea.

The distinction between *bellum* and *duellum*, legitimate and illegitimate uses of force, can be conceived, in a way, as the beginning of distinctively political life in its most basic contours. What that distinction identifies is not so much the idea of legitimate war as the more basic idea of political legitimacy – the idea that there is some way in which people can distinguish between the brute use of force, with nothing standing behind it but further use of force, and the brute use of force which understands itself to be authorized by and in turn accountable to some other standard, which is irreducible to further force. So this distinction between "private" and "public" violence is really quite foundational to human civilization.

Just-war theory uses this fundamental distinction to explain how the use of force can be legitimated. Two principles emerge out of the assumption that it is possible to legitimate war, namely (1) the principle that war *can* be an instrument of justice, and (2) the consequent principle that, nonetheless, not all is fair in war – there are some things that are wrong, even if the overall cause may be right.

Over the centuries, as moral and religious reflection on war developed, two different clusters of concerns began to be formulated as distinct questions. The first set of concerns was clustered around the question of when it was right to go to war.

The second was clustered around the consequent question, what are the rules that should govern conduct in war, or is war not governed by such rules? These concerns are formulated typically as concerns about *jus ad bellum*, or "the right to make war," and *jus in bello*, or "the right (conduct) in war." They have each developed distinct criteria for evaluating the legitimacy of particular wars. The criteria of *jus in bello* are discussed in the next chapter, but the criteria for *jus ad bellum* we should discuss here.

Jus ad bellum

As the questions around the *jus ad bellum*, or the legitimacy of war-making at all, became clear, thinkers worked out a series of criteria whereby a properly formed moral agent (just who that is, is importantly obscure) can, given proper information, determine the legitimacy of any war. There are three major criteria. First, the party deciding whether to go to war must be a *legitimate or lawful authority* – that is, one publicly recognized (however that is determined) to have the right to make such a decision. Second, the party must be able to show *just cause* – the violation of, or attack upon, the strict rights of some party. Historically, this was usually (but not always) referred to one's own rights, but more recently the judgment has expanded to recognize the possible rights of another party. Third, the party must possess, and manifest, *right intention*, both in terms of cause and in terms of motives. The intentions which motivate the act of going to war must be just, that is to say, appropriate to the end intended; most basically, war must not be waged for immoral motives, like revenge. Peace or justice must be the aim.

Beyond these three basic principles are four more criteria, which are sometimes called "prudential guidelines," for there is need, in determining whether or not they have been met, of "judgment calls" that rely on the decision-maker's prudential assessment. First is the establishment of *last resort*. On this principle, a reasonable person must be able to determine that war is the only reasonably possible remaining means of righting the wrong. Note that theorists do not mean here to say that if there is *any* step that could be taken, it should; rather, it is a matter of assessing – inevitably contentiously – that if any reasonable step remains to be taken, it should. It is not a matter of what Michael Walzer has called "metaphysical finality." Seeking such finality is not a principle for discriminating right action from wrong, but a recipe for paralysis when confronted with the question about any action.

Second is the determination of *relative justice*. The "relative" here is important; the tradition typically is profoundly skeptical of any claims to perfect righteousness in a cause, but rather asks for an assessment – again, inevitably guided by individuals' prudential judgment – that one can claim relative justice in the case under contestation. If one cannot claim that there is some justice in one's underlying warrant for war, it is properly speaking impossible to engage in legitimate war. Note here that this criterion suggests that both sides can claim relative justice. This points to a larger concern of the just-war tradition: it is unmoved by the classic modern view that one side in any fight is the "good guys" and the other is the "bad guys." When just-war theorizing was under development, the wars that it attempted to inform were not total wars between worldviews or ideologically or religiously incompatible nation-states; war was a "normal" activity and thus did not have the rather radically exceptional character it increasingly does for people today.

Third is the determination of the *proportionality* of the war, the need to balance the forseeable costs of a war against its expected benefits; the costs must not out-weigh the benefits. Perhaps there has been a violation of one party's strict rights, but is the violation egregious enough to warrant risking the lives of combatants, and possibly non-combatants, in combat? Some situations are harder to tell apart than others; examples of dubious decisions for war include the "Cod Wars" fought between the UK and Iceland from the 1950s through the 1970s, the 1969 "Soccer War" between El Salvador and Honduras, and the 1933–3 "Chaco War" between Bolivia and Paraguay. Others may be seen in the successive steps of the United States toward a decision to intervene militarily in South Vietnam in the period 1961–5 (an option the Eisenhower administration had been offered, and refused, in 1954), and German Chancellor Theobald von Bethmann Hollweg's reputed response when he learned that Great Britain would enter World War I because of Imperial Germany's violation of Belgian neutrality, where he famously said, "You are going to war over a scrap of paper." (Presumably, by 1918, some significant part of Great Britain's population would have felt sympathetic to von Bethmann Hollweg's words.)

Fourth and finally, there must be a clearly *reasonable hope of success* or victory. One cannot engage in a suicidal war without hope of victory, though this can be overridden in situations of existential self-defense; and it is up to the actors engaged to determine when such a situation has been reached.

If all these criteria are met, then just-war thinkers argue that service in war is not only permissible, but that it might be *morally good* – that there might be such a thing as not only a (regrettably) justified war, but a properly *just* one – a righteous, good, virtuous, perhaps even holy war. Christ's "offices" – his various functions, the work he accomplishes in and for creation – underwrite this view, especially the "office" of king. Christians can, then, "follow Christ" by fighting and killing. They can do so, however, only if they can intelligibly articulate the connections between the love that should motivate their actions and the activity of war. Only if we can understand war as a manifestation of love, can we understand war as rule-bound, and thus as existing within morality; as the Protestant Christian ethicist Paul Ramsey (1913–88) famously said, "the justice of sometimes resorting to armed conflict originated in the interior of the ethics of Christian love."[3]

In these ways, the just-war tradition insists on a crucially moral dimension to political authority and political activity. It implies that political authorities are concerned not with the neutral technocratic distribution of goods among funda-mentally independent agents. Rather, they are concerned with the ordering and cultivation of genuinely public or *common* goods, and behind them and encompass-ing them all, some sort of construal of a "Common Good" shared by everyone.

Politics is not simply the agglomeration of manifold private interests; there is a way in which it appeals to something "higher" than self-interest. The just-war theory may sound bloody, but in fact it possesses remarkably idealistic dimensions.

And yet there is a puzzle here. For how can an act of force be a manifestation of love? The tradition argues that force is an act of love insofar as it participates in God's use of force. This is both a positive proposal and a negative proscription of certain forms of violence; after all, it means that acts that are intrinsically evil – for example, deliberately murdering innocent people – are ruled out. But what does this mean? For sometimes God's use of force may seem less than discriminatory. Think about Jericho:

> The people shouted, the trumpets sounded, when they heard the sound of the trumpet, the people raised a mighty war cry and the wall collapsed then and there. At once the people stormed the town, every man going straight ahead; and they captured the town. They enforced the ban on everything in the town: men and women, young and old, even the oxen and the sheep and donkeys, massacring them all. (Joshua 6:20–21)

One may say that God commanded all would die, because all were guilty in God's sight. But of course for Christians, no one is righteous in God's sight, no, not one – except Jesus: so, as Clint Eastwood's character William Munny says in *Unforgiven*, "we all got it coming." Second, a skeptic may point to this and say: murderousness often cloaks itself in religious fervor and the mantle of divine righteousness, and what was reported of Jericho was reported also of Jerusalem during the Crusades, when rivers of blood were said to flow out of the gates of the city. Why, then, should anyone give credence to the wishful thinking of scholars, when the realities seem to tell so terribly against their wishes?

There are two ways to take this disquiet: realism, which wonders whether Christians ought to suspend what it sees as the gospel's morality in order to wage war, and pacifism, which urges Christians to jettison war in order to retain what it sees as the gospel's morality. We will talk about them in turn, not only for their views on war, but also for what they reveal about their understandings of Christian ethics.

Complications: Realism

Christian realists worry that the just-war tradition is being applied too literally in some contexts, and does not recognize the tragic character of our need to engage in war. Reinhold Niebuhr is a good example of one thinker who represents this worry.

In his writing, Niebuhr tries to navigate between what he sees as two false claims: first, that non-pacifism is an *apostasy*, a denial of the gospel; and, second, that pacifism is a *heresy*, a profound misconstrual of the Christian message, leading those who believe in it into the depths of Hell. Niebuhr rejects a simple-minded pacifism that thinks that the world *can* be governed by non-violence. Such people, Niebuhr thinks, do not act out of properly Christian reasons at all, but rather out of a naïve optimism quite at odds with the heart of the Christian message: "They do not believe that man remains a tragic creature who needs the divine mercy as much at the end as at the beginning of his moral endeavors. They believe rather that there is some fairly easy way out of the human situation of 'self-alienation.'"[4] This sort of pacifism proclaims that humans can realize some sort of end point within history, that humans can progress until they have achieved some real stable end state at the end of history. For such pacifists, religion is a technology to get what they want; their deepest belief is their faith in progress, in the inevitable maturation of the human race away from crude violence and towards resolving all disputes with reason.

Niebuhr thinks this is neither plausible nor particularly Christian: "The New Testament does not … envisage a simple triumph of good over evil in history. It sees human history involved in the contradictions of sin to the end." The conflicts of history will mount, not resolve themselves, as time progresses. For Niebuhr, Christianity is about us *not* being in charge of our lives or of history: "The Christian faith believes that the Atonement reveals God's mercy as an ultimate resource by which God alone overcomes the judgment which sin deserves."[5]

But realism is not called realism merely because it is opposed to pacifism. Rather, it is so called because it holds a certain view of the role of morality in political affairs, and particularly in war. Like the just-war tradition, realists like Niebuhr derive the legitimacy of the use of force and violence "from an understanding of the Christian gospel which refuses simply to equate the gospel with the 'law of love.'"[6] However, a realist such as Niebuhr departs from the tradition of just-war reasoning at this point as well. Recall that the just-war tradition sees the obligation to fight as itself emerging from Christian love. Niebuhr sees no such coherent view; instead, he thinks that the necessity to wage war in order to protect the innocent is in frank contradiction to the heart of the gospel command to love one another; yet what warrants it is the fundamental message of forgiveness that Niebuhr sees as equally central to the Christian message. "The good news of the gospel," he says, "is not the law that we ought to love one another. The good news of the gospel is that there is a resource of divine mercy which is able to overcome a contradiction within our own souls, which we cannot ourselves overcome."[7]

It is important to recognize that "realists" see themselves as such not because they *choose* to be such; rather, they think that a "realistic assessment" of the actual facts in any situation of war compels an honest thinker to qualify and render more ambiguous the moral stance they took before they entered the situation, in order that their moral thinking represent "realistically" the very ambiguity of that situation. What is important here for Niebuhr is a fundamental recognition of sin on the part of the reflective actor. Christianity recognizes not only the law of love, but the fact of sin – a fact that pervades all human endeavors, and that that fact makes all human activities, even those putatively in support of God's word, implicitly in part also opposed to God. Yet the recognition of sin does not alleviate our responsibility to love the neighbor, and that love for the neighbor can compel us to use violence to protect our neighbor from those who would prey upon them. But even in that instance, Niebuhr says, we are likely to be sinning, at least in part, in the use of violence, and so still in need of divine forgiveness and mercy.

Nevertheless, Niebuhr also argues that morality is not simply a moralistic illusion. Indeed, even pacifism is not a heresy, for it expresses "a genuine impulse in the heart of Christianity" towards perfection: "It is a reminder to the Christian community that the relative norms of social justice, which justify both coercion and resistance to coercion, are not final norms, and that Christians are in constant peril of forgetting their relative and tentative character and of making them too completely normative."[8] That is, it serves a prophetic purpose, witnessing to the church for its true ideal, which it cannot forget.

This is why Christian realism is still not amoralism. Its vision of the political world is profoundly *dialectical*, that is, emphasizing two extremes without trying immediately to reconcile them. In this case the dialectic is between sin and forgiveness, and between the command to love one another and the obligation to protect one's neighbor, both the need to acknowledge our responsibility and the final truth that God, and not humanity, is in charge of history. This helps realists come to terms with Christianity's tendencies towards apocalypticism while yet offering what they see as a practical proposal for life in this world.

Instead of an apocalyptic answer, then, realists like Niebuhr propose dividing the challenge up into a properly eschatological question about how evil will in principle be overcome – a question best addressed in directly and strictly theological terms, as the explanation of the faith's understanding of the end times – and a more complicatedly practical problem, the problem of how, before the end of history, "men are to achieve a tolerable harmony of life with life."[9]

In the context of this second question, Niebuhr thinks that there are useful things to be said about how Christians can use the law of love in a world where it is at best only imperfectly followed, how Christians can allow their ideals to have some play in governing politics. He thinks there are three ways in which the law of love can have a place. First of all, it has a direct constructive role. The law of love *is* really the law of life – it really is a power present and active in history. As Niebuhr says, justice requires power, but without love motivating it, justice would become intolerable (recall Niebuhr's reflections on love and justice, which we studied earlier). Secondly, it serves as a principle of what Niebuhr calls "indiscriminate" criticism. The law of love operates to condemn all of our activities insofar as we are sinful in them – thus it compels us to confess our own imperfection and wickedness, chastening our pride. Thirdly, it serves as a principle of "discriminate" criticism. The law of love gives us a way of evaluating the relative achievements of justice – or, perhaps better, the relative amelioration of injustices – and of deciding which is the most appropriate among them for our situation.

So Niebuhr argues most fundamentally against a simple moralism, which cannot accommodate the complexity of our own motivations, and insists that we must be entirely right or else we are entirely wrong. This vision cannot accommodate the complexities of our moral world, and so blinds us to the real costs of action in a world where action is often imperfect at best and leaves us with dirty hands. But this is not the only option; a tradition of pacifism still exists as a powerful voice in Christian thought, and deserves attention.

The challenge of pacifism

Another challenge is embodied in the tradition of Christian pacifism. In our day the most influential voice espousing this position is Stanley Hauerwas. Niebuhr's rejection of pacifism as a political proposal is entirely open to the idea of pacifism as a religious witness. Hauerwas's position is constructed in response to Niebuhr's, though it is founded on a vision much closer to Niebuhr's than it may at first appear. I turn to that now.

Hauerwas's proposed pacifism is not the kind of pacifism Niebuhr critiqued – the sentimentalist world-transformative vision of those who sing "all you need is love." Hauerwas agrees with Niebuhr that this kind of pacifism is bad, but for different reasons. Niebuhr thought it was bad because it was pragmatically ineffective – that is, it wouldn't work. Hauerwas thinks it bad because it is *theologically* inappropriate, not true to the gospel. It is, on his view, *Constantinian* – it assumes that the church must serve the world, that it must cater to the world's needs, must accept the place that the world has for it and not speak to the world from a position of authority over and judgment upon it. In contrast, Hauerwas's pacifism is in no way a retreat from the world. Furthermore, its resistance to Constantinianism Hauerwas thinks, allows it more richly and more fully to engage the world than do more "collaborationist" approaches. So Hauerwas's pacifism is part of a larger "Christian social ethic" which presents itself as quite critical of the world we inhabit, and outside of which it is unintelligible.

The theological key to this social ethic is God's action in Jesus Christ as the embodiment of God's will. For Hauerwas and those who think like him (such as John Howard Yoder), Jesus is not just the victor over evil in history; Jesus's life is a model, a paradigm, a path that we are called to follow. And in a world where that victory over evil is still in the making, that path may well lead to our death. We follow Jesus by imitation, which leads to the cross. As Yoder put it, "the very essence of the incarnation, the meaning of the victory of the resurrection, and the subsequent form of the Christian life is that God deals with evil through self-giving, non-resistant love. The meaning of the cross is the rejection of political means of self-defense."[10] The Christian witness entails non-resistance because non-resistance is the way that God has chosen to transform the world.

This is then a form of Christian ethics which gets its norm not from success in the world but from obedience to God. As Yoder says, "The good action is measured by its conformity to the command and to the nature of God and not by its success in achieving specific results."[11] And obedience to God's command is found through a reading of scripture, especially the New Testament texts.

The main thing that this kind of pacifist learns from such a reading is the profundity of the perpetual temptation to seize control of history from God. They agree with Niebuhr on one basic claim: perfection is not realizable in the world; God, and not humans, will save the world. But they disagree about what Christians ought to do in the meantime, in the period inaugurated by Jesus Christ's life, death, and resurrection and the last day when Jesus's kingdom, they believe, will come in its fullness. Concomitanatly to this, they agree on another basic claim: war is essentially a bad thing, an evil. They differ on whether it is a "necessary evil" or not. For them, every warlike act is at best a tragic necessity, or a necessary evil.

In some ways, then, both realists and pacifists agree in opposing the just-war tradition. But the just-war tradition can reply to their charges as well. Against realists, this view argues that war cannot be understood as simply morally evil; that would suggest that there are no final boundaries to what can or cannot be done in war, and this tradition does say there are boundaries – no intentional killing of the innocent, for example – for precisely the same reasons that war may be a good thing to do. Against pacifists, the tradition assumes that a proper understanding of Christ, and Christ's several roles – prophet who fortells the end times, priest who reconciles us to God, and king who rules the universe – helps us understand how, against pacifists' assumptions, "following Jesus" cannot be simply replicating everything he did. That suggests that we would have to replicate redemption, and we cannot and should not attempt that.

Behind all these debates, one question looms: what is the *point* of war? What purpose could justify it? Here the tradition has answered "peace" – but what that word means is deeply contested by many different thinkers. In fact, Christian notions of war and peace have been used to critique pacifism itself. Writing from very different political and ecclesial perspectives, George Weigel (a conservative Roman Catholic) and Rowan Williams (the progressive Anglican Archbishop of Canterbury) have both argued that too often a wholly "secular" notion of pacifism is allowed to govern anti-war movements, even for Christians.[12] On this understanding, the main aim of pacifism is to oppose all uses of military force. While Weigel and Williams differ in the scope of acceptable pacifism, they agree that the mere opposition to the use of force is insufficient; Christian pacifists must not be mere reactionaries "against" violence in the state system, they must rather be *for* peace, and being "for peace" raises all sorts of questions – about which manifestations of violence to protest most vehemently, about what violence actually is, and about what the promised end of "peace" really means. It is at least questionable, Weigel says, to focus so much on Israelis' attacks on Palestinians without recognizing the far more gruesome civil war in the Sudan; it is pointless to say that Christian pacifists in the US should only protest violations in which their own government is complicit. Christians should have broader horizons than what their passports permit them to have. Similarly, Williams argues that it is not right for pacifists to condemn the use of violence among nations without thinking hard about the nature and presence of violence *within* nations; furthermore, such pacifists do not see that much of the obstruction to true "peace" comes not from people with guns but from people's indifference to one another. Jesus's peace, for Williams, is powerful, but absent from the world. There is no peace for the "Son of Man" on earth, though Jesus *is* peace; but he is a different kind of peace. This is not a worldly peace – rather, this one involves being seen and judged. Our peace, the world's peace, is often the peace of indifference, of being left alone – the peace of privacy, of being at home. Our contemporary notions of privacy are, on this reading, eschatologically problematic here. For Williams and Weigel, then, proper Christian pacifism is a universal act, and so stands at some distance from national structures and this world's political understandings, and must critique them and our imaginative captivity to them.

Even in its pacifism, then – perhaps especially with its pacifism – an impatience with the structures of the world mark Christian reflection on war and peace.

Islam

The mainstream of Islamic thought, Sunni and Shi'ia alike, is that there is no argument in the tradition for pacifism. Instead, the tradition assumes that some wars are not just permitted but obligatory, required by God, and concomitantly that the use of force outside those contexts is forbidden. While this is not quite identical to the tradition of Christain just-war reasoning, or with Jewish thinking on war, the similiarities are interesting and significant.

Islam and *jihad*

The rationale for Islamic thinking about war has its basis in the fundamental categorical structure of Islam itself. Because the world is divided between submission to God's will and rebellion against God's will, the fact of conflict is inevitable. (Note that I do not say between believers and unbelievers – that would be too Christian a categorization, and it would obscure the way that this conflict occurs even in the heart of the ordinary Muslim, as she or he struggles to be properly and fully submissive to God.) In this way, the fundamental logic of war is couched in theological terms of obedience to God. Humans are naturally designed to be peaceful and live in harmony with each other and all of nature. But some have chosen to rebel and resist the proper sovereignty of God, and their rebellion places them in an act of war against God and nature (and themselves). Those who still submit to God's will must be prepared to fight to defend God's order, and – when the requisite authorities deem it proper – to fight to expand the dominion of God across the whole globe. The ultimate aim and expectation is universal conquest; as one of the most historically significant verses in the Qur'an suggests, Muslims are enjoined to "fight [the unbelievers] until there is no more persecution [or seduction] and worship [*din*] is devoted to God" (Q. 2:193). Here the goal seems to be conversion and submission, though as we will soon see the testimony of the Qur'an and the evidence of the tradition suggests a far more ambiguous picture.

The general category through which Islamic thinkers, historically and today, have thought about war is through the category of *jihad*. Obviously, this is one of the most politically charged and religiously fraught terms in the world today, so it will behoove us to examine it with some care. The career of the term has paralleled the career of the term "crusade" in English; what was originally an exclusively religious category has become secularized over the past few decades (so we can talk about a "political crusade"). But it is its theological meaning that concerns us here.

The basic meaning of *jihad* is "struggle towards a worthwhile end," and in Islamic thought this is the struggle to bring those who do not submit to God into a relation of submission to God. Though it has been used most frequently to refer to warfare, war – literally, *qital*, or "fighting" – is simply the last step in the "ladder of escalation" in the effort to conduct *jihad* in the *dar-al-harb*; it was the way in which Islam would be brought to non-Muslim lands, if those lands would not allow more peaceful means of bringing Islam. *Jihad* is in a way simply the reality of the tension and irresolvable conflict at the border separating the *dar-al-Islam* and the *dar-al-Harb*. Early in Islamic history, engagement in this struggle, in some way, became spiritually meritorious for Muslims: "Those who believe, who have journeyed and strive hard in God's way with their possessions and their persons ... they are the ones who will triumph" (Q. 9:20). Some would say that *jihad* applies as much within believers as between believers and non-believers, that the struggle is as deeply interior as interpersonal.

The category of *jihad* and its history is deeply ambiguous. Early in Islam, it seems, many believers understood the struggle against the unbelievers to be an individual duty, leading early legal scholars (most influentially al-Shafi'i) to articulate and codify the principle that *jihad* was not obligatory for every individual Muslim, but only for those who are needed by the Caliph. Thus, offensive *jihad* is a collective duty – *fard ala al-kifaya* – in which enough people *must* enlist, but no one in particular is obligated (and it explicitly denies universal obligation). Defensive *jihad*, on the other hand, is a universal duty, in which all able-bodied Muslims must serve.

Once this principle was in place, the ethics of war in Islam were effectively governed by a code of law not completely unlike Christian just-war theory, and at times in apparent intellectual interchange with it. Indeed, just as with Christian pacifism, in fact there is a powerful "minority report" in the tradition that interprets the meaning of the term as centrally focused on the inner struggle of the self against its own unbelief, its own rebellion against God. This is normally done by distinguishing the "lesser *jihad*" of outward struggle against unbelievers from the "greater *jihad*" of the internal struggle. Such a view is supported by certain *ahadith* in which Muhammad is reported to have made this distinction. This distinction does not seem to have been attended to by Muslims for the first few centuries, and its widespread recognition as significant seems to have happened several centuries into the history of Islam, concurrent with the growth of Sufism as a mystical tradition in the tenth century. But it could not have happened were there not earlier suggestions in the tradition that such a view could be proper. One source for that is found in the "peace verses." We turn to those debates next.

The "peace verses" and the "sword verses"

This interpretation of *jihad*, as primarily a struggle within the individual believer, is real and powerful. But the main account of *jihad* has focused on it as a geopolitical reality for war between believers and non-believers, and we should understand it as such. There is a large debate about what the Qu'ran commands as regards the "sword verses" and the "peace verses." The question of the proper prioritization of these verses, and how they should be understood in relation to one another, has been a central issue for Islamic thinking about war.

The peace verses seem to say that, if others want peace, you can accept them as peaceful even if they are not Muslim. For example, the Qur'an says "fight in God's cause against those who fight you, but do not transgress limits [in aggression]: God does not love transgressors" (Q. 2:190; see also 4:75, 4:84, 4:90–91, 8:39, 22:39). As this example indicates, the peace verses suggest that force is only permissible in self-defense, and do not seem to leave much space open for offensive wars aimed at converting the infidel.

The sword verses, in contrast, suggest that mere peace is not enough – that their bare status as non-Muslims means that you must fight perpetually against them. Examples of the sword verses include the following: "when the forbidden months are over, wherever you encounter the idolaters, kill them, seize them, besiege them, wait for them at every lookout post" (Q. 9:5). And: "You who believe, fight the unbelievers near you and let them find you severe; and know that God is with those who fear Him" (Q. 9:123; see also 4:76, 9:29, 9:36, 9:41). This more vehement attitude carries over into conduct *during* warfare, as one might expect. For the peace verses, it seems that capacity to fight is the selection criterion for those who are legitimate targets of attack – so that old men, women, children, peasants, slaves, and hermits are not legitimate targets; whereas for the sword verses, belief is the criterion, so that, except for women and children – explicitly identified as non-combatants by Muhammad – all others are legitimate targets of attack. Because the sword verses were revealed in Medina and later than the peace verses, which were revealed in Mecca, the sword verses are often taken to be normative, or even to have "abrogated" (revoked) the peace verses.

What is interesting, though, is how even in its more militaristic forms of the sword verses, the Islamic doctrine of *jihad* does not seem to have committed its faithful warriors to engage in wars of mass conversion. Historically, Islamic armies sought conquest but not conversion; in the early centuries especially, conversion seems to have been discouraged. Particularly with the other "Peoples of the Book" – that is, Jews and Christians – the economic benefits of taxing non-Muslims (the *jizyah*, tax on non-Muslims) meant that the early Islamic Caliphate stood to lose valuable streams of funding were too many of their subjects to convert to the religion of the Prophet. Furthermore, the Qur'anic adage that "there is no compulsion in religion" (Q. 2:256) seems to have been heeded throughout the history of Islam. Unlike Christianity's insistence on self-consciously accepting (or experiencing) the grace of Christ, from the beginning Islam recognizes the possibility of salvific efficacy in the other Abrahamic faiths – that is, so long as people are properly submissive to God, they are properly Muslim. Because of this, it felt less pressure to seek to convert others for the sake of their immortal souls.

What we see in Islamic thought on war, then, is something with remarkable similarities to Jewish and Christian thinking. Common prejudices aside, this should not be surprising. The traditions share the same convictions about God's general will towards the world, the divine abhorrence of bloodshed, and the conviction that one cannot become sanctified without a serious ethical analysis of one's own acts. Furthermore, like Judaism and Christianity, Islam possesses a scriptural heritage that seems decidedly of two minds when it comes to thinking about the propriety and proper limits of war. For all these reasons, then, Islam seems in a functionally analogous place to Judaism and Christianity when it comes to war.

Conclusion

Clearly, the challenges for thinking about religion and war are profound – historically deep and in our contemporary world quite broad. Irrespective of your own religious beliefs, or lack thereof, as inhabitants of the modern world and citizens of its polities, we have higher demands for political thoughtfulness put upon us than ever before, and nowhere is that clearer than in cases of war. And much of the moral understanding we have of war comes from these religious traditions and their interpretations of war, developed over millennia.

As we have seen, the nature of traditional understandings of the relationship between religion and war is enormously complex and contested, with no tradition offering a single voice on what is to be done. Moreover, the challenges that our contemporary situation puts upon us, both its promise and its perils, are real and momentous. Whether we can meet them may well depend on how deep our understanding of the historical heritage of thinking about these matters is.

But all these challenges are not the only ones we face in thinking about war. There are other, in some ways deeper, questions about the nature of war itself, about whether its very profanity is so extreme as to put the lie to any ethical assessment, religious or otherwise. The next chapter explores these questions, and the question of whether morality can apply in war itself.

14

War (II)

In War

Early in April of 1999, General Wesley Clark, Supreme Allied Commander Europe (SACEUR) and military chief of the NATO alliance, sat in his underground war room and came face to face with a problem that had been building over the past two weeks. Clark was leading a military campaign against the rump Yugoslav – mostly Serbian – government in an attempt to drive the Yugoslav army out of Kosovo, a province in the south of Yugoslavia that had enormous historical significance for Serbs and a majority Muslim population that was engaged in a bloody and brutal insurgency against the Serbs, who the majority saw as occupiers. The war began on March 24 and was conducted entirely by airstrikes, with weapons launched from a very high altitude to protect against casualties.

By early April, expectations of a quick resolution had faded. Once the bombing began, the Yugoslav Army had begun a massive "ethnic cleansing" campaign in Kosovo, driving tens of thousands of Muslim refugees into nearby Macedonia. NATO warplanes were striking Yugoslav military targets, but their strikes seemed to have little effect on the ground.

NATO political and military leaders had to decide what to do in response to the ethnic cleansing campaign and to complaints in the media, and by rival politicians in their own countries, that their war was profoundly ineffectual at best, and perhaps making things worse. A number of military leaders, Clark among them, urged a broader campaign of airstrikes. After several days of ugly controversy among the NATO member nations, the alliance agreed to do this.

Slowly, the target list lengthened. On April 21, SACEUR expanded the target list to include the Socialist Party HQ in Belgrade (with a high casualty estimate of 50–100 government and party employees, and up to 250 civilians in neighboring apartments which could be destroyed or significantly damaged by the blast). On April 23, Serbian TV (a major propaganda force) was hit, with at least ten employees killed. On May 3, NATO launched its first strike on Serbian targets where carbon filaments were used, shorting out power lines; and on May 24, NATO forces upped the pressure by targeting directly Serbia's power grid, and particularly that of Belgrade. The strikes did little physical damage, but most of the city, and a great deal of the country, lost electric power, with severe consequences for hospitals and many others. By the time the war ended on June 11, many of the targets initially forbidden by the political authorities had been hit, as part of the general, and perhaps inevitable, escalation that occurs in war.[1]

The Kosovo war raised a number of questions for those interested in thinking ethically about war. Central to these questions was a general recognition that the war, such as it was, represented a watershed moment. For the first time in history, tactical decisions about where exactly bombs could be dropped were taken out of the hands of the soldiers in the field and made the object of deliberate decision by political leaders at the highest levels. (A similar experience had happened to the United States Army in the Vietnam War, but it had been generals in helicopters commanding small-unit firefights on the ground thousands of feet beneath them; in Kosovo, it was politicians, not generals.) And yet, once in the war, those political leaders seemed compelled by the war's curious necessities to select targets in an increasingly loose ethical manner. Even given near-perfect technical precision, the war raised disquieting questions about whether the whole idea of "ethical combat" was a contradiction in terms.

And that is the topic of this chapter. The previous chapter looked at the religious traditions' complex inheritance concerning war, and saw how thinkers in the same tradition came to significantly different conclusions from many of the same sources. It studied how these religious traditions can motivate and guide its adherents into war, and how those traditions inform the way their adherents view the propriety or moral and religious acceptability of war.

This chapter asks another question, from inside the experience of war. While we may want to say that at times *going to war* may be appropriate, it is altogether another thing to say that right and wrong apply *within* war itself. Is war a rule-governed activity, or is it simply a moral abyss? Is it possible that it can be moral? Or is the experience of war so overwhelming as to be of necessity extra-moral? And if it is that, what does that say about the prospects for a realistic and useful morality, religious or otherwise? It raises the question of *moralism*, which we turn to next.

Moralism

The challenge of moralism begins from a simple question. Is it possible to conduct modern war in a morally acceptable fashion? Many have their doubts. Wars are signs of social organization, but organization oriented towards profoundly anti-social ends – namely, the infliction of destructive violence upon an enemy. As Frederic Manning, a veteran of World War I, wrote, "war is waged by men; not by beasts, or by gods. It is a peculiarly human activity. To call it a crime against mankind is to miss at least half its significance; it is also the punishment of a crime."[2] Can we say, do we want to say, that there ought to be rules that operate in such situations, or should we say that all rules are, or should be, abolished during war?

This is made more complex by the realities of modern war, which seems importantly different from the sorts of wars that the just-war tradition has historically reflected upon. Modern war has become more intense and more psychologically all-encompassing, more *total*. First of all, modern war is different – more extreme and potentially less rule-bound – than the paradigm of warfare that just-war theorists had in mind. Technology and global reach have meant that wars are no longer waged primarily by neighbors, but by strangers, and strangers are notoriously less prone to see one another as fellow humans worthy of mercy. Second, modern war is waged by modern states – which are not usually ruled by kings, but are typically participatory democracies of some sort or another – populated not by a king's *subjects* but by a state's *citizens*, all those who collectively share ultimately in the sovereignty of the state. Thus, wars rely on the implicit reflective support of ordinary folk. Thus, there is clearly no appeal to "obedience" to the higher authorities in modern states; each such appeal, in a democratic age such as our own, is immediately suspect. Third, and as a consequence of the first two, modern war is more total – it can involve destruction of national resources not directly related to the war, and can involve a more total commitment of national resources to the war than earlier wars. In this context, to argue that there are rules that should govern the act of warmaking – that human beings placed in such situations can be held accountable to ethical considerations of the sort that compel them to distinguish between civilians and soldiers – is to court ridicule.

And indeed the idea of rules of war that apply within war does seem an idea honored more in the breach than in the observance. Terrorizing a population has become a useful military tactic in recent wars; often in recent wars, civilian populations have become the primary target of military operations, which has inverted the military to civilian casualty ratio from 8:1 (eight military casualties to every one civilian casualty) in wars around 1900 to 1:9 (one military casualty to nine civilian ones) in the wars of the 1990s.[3] For all our "civilization," advanced society seems far more barbaric today than we were a century ago.

All of this raises a fundamental question about the scope of moral claims. Given these challenges to proper human behavior, are we forced to conclude that morality has edges, that there are dimensions of human experience that are beyond good and evil? Do we think that assessments of action as right or wrong are simply too artificial, too avoiding of the facts on the ground, the real conditions of human behavior, to apply? Who are we to judge humans put in these situations? Isn't moral assessment in such settings simply reduced to sheer moralism?

The term *moralism* may sound like rhetoric, but it can serve a weight-bearing purpose in thinking about ethical deliberation, and it's worth pausing to reflect on it for a moment. As a rule of thumb, let us stipulate that morality becomes "moralistic" when it focuses on judging people to the exclusion of understanding and helping to direct (and at times correct) them. Moralism is, then, merely a spectator sport – a way for people to amuse themselves, voyeuristically, at the expense of any actual understanding of the human situations in which others find themselves. Often, it over-dramatizes some moral deeds, illegitimately amplifying the moral weight of minor foibles or morbidly fixating on some dimensions of a problem while ignoring the larger context of the acting agent, in an improper interest in the self's absolute moral purity. Trafficking in sheer abstractions and absolutist maxims, allergic to any consideration of reality when such consideration threatens to smudge the previously crisp lines of moral judgment in which the moralistic mind so delights, it makes morality more of a parlor game than a useful guide for life. As such, moralism is always a temptation for ethical thinking, and one to which we should be highly sensitive.

But the experience of war makes us wonder whether there is any space for morality within war at all – whether morality is revealed, in war, to be wholly *moralistic*. After all, it is easy, in reflecting on war, to judge the situation, but it is much harder to do something like justice to the motivations directing people within it. The closer you get to the experience, the harder morality seems to be to apply. As Paul Fussell, a World War II veteran who has reflected seriously on these matters, puts it:

> Those who actually fought on the line in the war … constitute an in-group forever separate from those who did not … there is the accidental possession of a special empirical knowledge, a feeling of a mysterious shared ironic awareness manifesting itself in an instinctive skepticism about pretension, publicly enunciated truths, the vanities of learning, and the pomp of authority. Those who fought know a secret about themselves, and it's not very nice.[4]

Fussell's challenge here is simple: don't judge unless you were there, for if you were not there you have neither the requisite experience nor the moral right to do so. As General William Tecumseh Sherman famously put it, "war is all hell." The idea of rules in warfare is wrong; war is so immoral that it dissolves any rules; the only thing to do is get the war over as quickly as possible. Judging the acts required to end the war quickly is both morally and rationally wrong, reflecting in the first place an offensive moral arrogance, and in the second a sheer blindness to the realities of the situation.

Is Fussell right? Does war exist beyond moral assessment? If it does, what does that say about morality? Does reflection on war, reflection on situations of the absence of moral norms, suggest something about the nature of morality itself – that perhaps it has edges? These are the questions that must shadow our discussion in the pages to come, and to which we will return at the end.

This challenge has become more pointed in the last century with the onset of total war. There are worries that the nature of modern warfare differs so fundamentally from premodern warfare that it is not just implausible and unrealistic but positively unethical to assume moral standards can be in any way applied to modern conflict. After all, the conditions under which just-war reasoning reached its most systematic exposition were those of medieval battles between Christian soldiers, which typically lasted no more than six hours, where combat was between individuals at short distances, which had relatively confined boundaries, and in which combatants were pretty clearly distinguished from non-combatants; in some ways more like a bloody rugby match than like a modern, 24 hours a day, seven days a week battle where the killing is often done invisibly and impersonally.

Perhaps the thinker who saw this most vividly in the twentieth century was the Protestant Christian ethicist Paul Ramsey, mentioned in the previous chapter. He was genuinely concerned that modern war undercut morality in general, and thus threatened to make us all in some terrible way barbarians:

> Can civilization survive in the sense that we can continue in political and military affairs to *act civilized*, or must we accept total war on grounds that clearly indicate that we have already become *totalitarian* – by reducing everyone without discrimination and everyone to the whole extent of his being to a mere means of achieving political and military goals?[5]

Ramsey thought in fact that such action was possible, that we need not be uncivilized. And he insisted that warfare can be understood as within the domain of moral reflection, and not a challenge to it, *if* we understand it in a certain way – as manifesting love.

Worries such as Ramsey's and Fussell's are especially pointed for those who profess to be religious, and especially when they try to act out of one of the religious ethics detailed here. After all, these ethics claim a universal application – they claim to operate in all situations, typically. Even if (as is arguably the case with Jewish thought) they may only apply, at least in parts, to only some portion of the human race, for members of those groups they are still comprehensive, still meant to apply in all situations.

This is troubling. We think that morality supports religion, that appeals to our moral nature give evidence that religious claims can be legitimate. But in fact this conviction cuts both ways; problems with morality can serve to undermine our religious commitments. How should our religious commitments influence our political activities, given that they cannot be simply or straightforwardly applied? Furthermore, how should this knowledge, of the difficulty and complexity of such influence, in turn inform our understanding of our religious commitments?

This chapter will take as its case study the criteria that the Christian just-war tradition developed to guide combatants' behavior in war – what are more commonly called the criteria of the *jus in bello*.

Jus in bello

As is the case with the criteria for *jus ad bellum*, the criteria of *jus in bello*, or the character of proper conduct in war, were refined by thinkers over time. They worked out a series of criteria whereby a properly formed moral agent can determine the moral propriety of any military action (tactic or strategy) – that is, whether any particular kind of action in war is morally allowable or condemnable. What is appropriate conduct and what is inappropriate conduct in war? The criteria used to answer this question are two.

First, the action must exhibit appropriate care for *discrimination* between combatants and non-combatants. For example, for just-war theorists, a sniper cannot shoot blindly into a crowd of people, some wearing the enemy's uniform and some not; the sniper must discriminate between combatants and non-combatants, and if she or he cannot do so, they cannot ethically take the shot. The principle of non-combatant immunity is (by and large, more or less) inviolable – one cannot directly attack non-combatants (what this term means is up for debate), though there may be a distinction to be made between "intentional" and "foreseen but unintentional" acts whereby non-combatants are killed.

Second, the action under contemplation (or evaluation) must be *proportionate* to the aims sought. The benefits must outweigh the costs. For example, it is probably unethical to invade enemy islands that are of no material advantage in ending an ongoing conflict merely for the sake of keeping that territory after the war's end, especially if the seizing of that territory costs the lives of many combatants on both sides. More controversially, one cannot plausibly destroy an apartment building, inhabited by many civilians, to kill a single sniper; however, it is at least conceivable that one *might* legitimately destroy that same apartment building if (a) one knows that the enemy's main headquarters is there, containing their senior military leadership, and (b) one believes that the costs of the foreseeable (but unintended) civilian casualties are outweighed by the benefits of destroying the military leadership ("benefits" here including the measurable shortening or perhaps quick ending of the conflict, thus curtailing the further losses of civilian lives). (Some decisions of General Clark in the 1999 Kosovo air campaign seem to be analogous to this one, particularly the bombing of television stations and the main Belgrade power stations.) When it comes to assessing questions of proportionality, the dimensions of the problem are typically far more numerous, and their interrelation far more murky and complex, than are deliberations about discrimination; yet such judgments must be made.

While these criteria have been explicitly developed in the Christian just-war tradition, both Judaism and Islam have often employed similar criteria, and as we will see, all three face similar challenges. (So, for example, the Caliph Abu Bakr, immediately following Muhammad's death, gave instructions to an army heading to attack Byzantine forces in Muta, a site apparently somewhere in Syria, that they were not to cut down trees and not to kill animals except for their own food.) Effectively, anyone interested in thinking ethically about conduct in combat will have to answer questions about who to hit and how hard to hit them; which is what these criteria attempt to articulate.

These principles do leave room for complicated and murky moral assessments. Often, these assessments are made more clear by appeal to a further principle, the principle of "double effect," the idea that actions can have consequences that are not intended and are properly accidental to the intended act. The bad effect cannot cause the good effect, it can only be a by-product of it. The doctrine of double effect

admits of a fairly precise definition: under this doctrine, a foreseen evil is not imput-
able to an actor if (a) the action in itself is directed immediately to another result,
(b) the evil effect is not willed either in itself or as a means to the other result, and
(c) the permitting of the evil effect is justified by reasons of proportionate weight.
Double effect can only be applied by one who has "sound moral judgment" – that
is, it is not a mathematical formula, a program just anybody can run to see if they
can do what they want; rather, it is a practical tool for helping a well-formed moral
agent deliberate.

This doctrine can be properly used in war-fighting decisions. For instance, if an
enemy military is using civilian buses to transport its supplies to the front, and using
a bridge that buses carrying actual civilians are driving across every day, then air
strikes on that bridge can go forward – even if there is a danger that (a) a bus might
be on the bridge when it is hit, and (b) it is an authentically civilian bus, carrying
non-combatant passengers. In that case, the air strike has had two effects: the
destruction of a valid military target (the bridge) and the destruction of a civilian
bus, killing the innocents aboard. But the doctrine of double effect says that the
decision to hit the bridge does not mean that the pilots in the planes, or the com-
manders who sent them there, are morally responsible for the deaths of the civilians
in the same way; if anything, the argument can be made that the opposing army is
responsible, for acting in so risky a fashion.

But this doctrine is easily misused as well. The area bombing of German cities
by the British and American air forces in World War II was sometimes defended
as an attempt to "de-house" factory workers, with the foreseen but unintended
effect of killing a large number of them and their family members; but in this case,
as so often with morality, the moral category was misused in such a way as to make
the moral crime more horrendous by easing the conscience of those who undertook
the deeds. (The American air forces bombing Japanese cities in 1944 and 1945 did
not even attempt to offer moral justifications of this sophistication; sheer revenge
and a determination that the whole Japanese nation was a suitable target were sufficient in these cases, where racial hatred (on both sides) clearly played a far deeper
role than in the Western Allies' treatment of the Germans and Italians in Europe.)

The criteria for *jus in bello* suggest that morality exists where we may be surprised
to find it – in the horrifically "inhumane" environment of combat. Indeed, the claim
is that war can be a moral activity – not simply one hedged about with prohibitions
of the *most* horrific acts, but an activity that can positively contribute to a relatively
good outcome. Central to this is the idea that wars can be fought in relatively moral
ways, and can thereby contribute to a morally satisfying outcome, understood as a
"just peace." As Augustine put it, in a letter to Boniface, the (Christian) Roman
military leader in North Africa, just warriors are called on to "be peacemaking warriors."[6] The tradition makes the audacious claim that human beings can be considered morally in environments of extreme – perhaps, as I suggested above, in some
important ways *inhuman* – pressure.

It is worth pausing over that audacity. Is it plausible and realistic? It is somewhat
telling that many of the most thoughtful analysts of the just-war tradition are in

naval and air forces, and less so in ground forces. (And conversely, some of the sharpest skeptics of the tradition are "dirt soldiers," infantry exposed to the most brutal and intimate forms of combat.) Nonetheless, defenders of just-war reasoning argue that moral evaluation of combat situations, whether at the level of statecraft or in the trenches (or cockpits) of combat situations, can matter enormously, both in the situations at hand and for those who survive – and who have to live with the consequences of their actions for the rest of their lives.

Discrimination and proportionality: understanding how these two sets of criteria work helps those committed to it to develop a morally articulate understanding of war. These criteria can be powerful analytic and evaluative tools for thinking morally about armed conflict. Yet some consider them insufficient at best and inadequate at worst. Traditional representatives of each tradition would argue that these criteria, in themselves, are inadequate to understand the nature of war as waged by believers. Indeed, they have urged deeper religious appropriations of the categories of the tradition. Understanding these concerns is our next topic.

Rival Interpretations of the Just-War Tradition

Part of the problem is that the just-war tradition is not self-interpreting, and requires a certain level of application to become fully useful; and there are debates about how best to interpret and apply it. Central here is a debate between those who find the tradition to reflect a "presumption against violence" and those who see a "presumption for justice."

Those who see the tradition as motivated by a presumption against force argue that a basic negative judgment against violence is palpable in the tradition. For them, the use of violence to compel appears against nature or against justice. The key here is that there is what we called in chapter 12 a *prima facie* case against violence; that is, that we experience ourselves as having a *prima facie* duty not to use violence against others. Humans experience a *prima facie* command against using violence against another person; and these thinkers argue that the just-war tradition is about when that command can properly be overridden in the political realm.

Others dissent from this view. They worry about the loss of integrity of the historical Christian just-war tradition, both as regards the understanding and evaluation of war, and as regards the more general ordering of human society, both nationally and internationally. For them, just-war thinking does not begin from the presumption against war, but from the presumption *for* justice, from the proper obligation of public authority to pursue the peace of right order. On this view, the concern of the sovereign to care for right order is deeper and more fundamental than the concern the sovereign should have to avoid violence. On this account, that is, justice is more fundamental a concern than peace; or rather, justice is a precondition for proper peace; lacking it, the cessation of violence does not by itself constitute peace. Such thinkers imagine that the tradition does not authorize any presumption against war. No such presumption is visible in the tradition; it does not think of war as fundamentally a moral horror or abomination, albeit one whose prohibition may at times be legitimately overridden. Instead, on this view, war is continuous with the logic of good or just governance, the just exercise of authority. As regards the social order, this view requires that we recover the idea of the sovereign as importantly moral, as speaking about the genuinely public or *common* good. Politics is not simply the agglomeration of manifold private interests; there is a distinctly moral quality to it. Good government is, in the end, just that: good.

This is a rich and vital debate that is continuing among just-war theorists, and one that shows no signs of abating. Given current trends in humanitarian intervention, in fact, these debates are likely to move more to the forefront in coming years.

Conclusion

Is peace the appropriate end of war? How might it be? War is clearly not an end in itself, but rather a means to an end – a peace enriched by justice. But we cannot overly value the good of peace, because it may induce us to acts of moral horror in order more quickly to end a war. The just-war tradition believes that rules must govern war all the way through; so sometimes, it says, peace must be delayed for moral norms to be obeyed. A peace bought at the cost of profound evil is no true peace at all, but only a truce, made all the more uneasy and fragile by the moral compromises undertaken to accomplish it.

That is also the peril of the just-war tradition. For the insistence on rules applying in war runs straight into the challenge posed by the experience of those caught up in war itself. For many of them – often including those with the most intimate experience of war – war's reality is too terrible to be rendered intelligible, let alone manageable, by any set of codes. Furthermore, they think the attempt to apply such codes will inevitably serve only to extend the suffering of those caught up in the maelstrom, on both sides. All such codes do, these critics insist, is reassure those who live far from the realities of combat that nothing need trouble their strictly speaking spectatorial faith in the straightforward viability of moral norms to all situations.

But this is not entirely fair to the just-war tradition. At its best the tradition is attempting honestly to grapple with the full reality of the experience of war – and the very angry vehemence of the critics of the tradition suggests that they are launching, as it were, a moral critique of the idea of the morality of war. They are angry not just because they think such a morality is grotesquely inapplicable or inapt; they are angry because they think it is *wrong*, they think it is (morally) unjust to apply these norms to reality in this way. The best of the just-war tradition tries to show them that it too is opposed to such clumsy moralisms. But it refuses to accept that such a moralism is the only alternative to a nihilistic amoralism of the sort often presented as the only viable account.

One way to get at the difference for the just-war tradition is to distinguish as it tries to do between regret and remorse. The experience of regret is inevitable in war. Terrible things happen inadvertently, even when all appropriate care is taken. Sheer awful randomness takes a toll in any battle. No one who has seen combat leaves it without wishing devoutly that they could have done a thousand things differently; and whether they are fair to themselves or not, they will spend the rest of their lives with each and every one of those memories instantly available to themselves. In this way they never really leave the combat zone, they have only taken it into themselves. Regret is theirs because they wish they had done other things than the things they did.

Remorse is different. Remorse is theirs because they wish primarily that they had *not* done the things they did. Remorse is theirs when what they have done is not only accidentally or incidentally horrible, but intrinsically so. This is the killing of prisoners when one fears an immanent ambush; calling in artillery on a village on the suspicion of enemy troops, without taking due care to protect civilians; firing indiscrimately into a bus with suspected insurgents, but mixed in with civilian refugees. These memories are not only cause for regret, but also remorse – an ever-deepening retrospective horror at what one has done, and a recognition, however tacit, however unspoken, that the world has been made worse, not by the accident of what one has done, but by the direct and intentional act itself.

The just-war tradition is committed to the idea that one ought never knowingly and intentionally to do evil that good may come of it. The idea of a "necessary evil" is anathema to the tradition, and it is anathema just because when one does evil, and deems it necessary, the apparent "necessity" of it over time may become less obvious as the palpable urgency of the decision wanes; but at the same time, the recognized evil of the act is likely to grow. The just-war tradition means to make combat morally survivable for veterans, not only physically so; and one of the ways it seeks to do that is by ensuring, as best it can, that while soldiers may later feel regret for what they have done, they need never feel remorse.

Whether this conviction will satisfy critics of the just-war tradition – indeed, whether it *should* satisfy them – is a question for them to answer over time. For our purposes, it is enough to understand something of the stakes that both sides see riding on the debate. And these stakes – for those soldiers caught up in the maelstrom of war, and in a far different way for all of us who must ponder these matters simply as citizens of democratic polities, whose sovereignty is held in common possession by all of the people – are high indeed.

15

Religion and the Environment

Few doubt that we live in a very perilous time ecologically. The global ice-caps are melting; smog is oppressive in much of the world; rivers are poisoned; we are chopping down the last great forests; global warming has begun, and in general we seem to be reaching the end of the tether in terms of how much human life the earth can sustain – at least, human life lived as people in America like to live it.

So we have to save nature. But everyone is always on nature's side; people simply cannot agree on what is "natural" and what is "unnatural." That is, we face a problem in understanding "nature" – are we part of it? Is it something outside of ourselves? What is "nature," after all? The fact that we can even intelligibly ask that question is a sign of our distance from the mode of life our ancestors once inhabited. And that distance is substantial. More than ever before, advanced society seems disconnected from nature. How many of us have killed our own meat? How many of us have grown our own food? We increasingly live artificially. And the artificiality is best seen in the distance we feel between ourselves and the given rhythms of nature.

Not all of our ancestors' acquaintance with nature was unabashedly good, and not all of our distance from it is manifestly bad. By and large, by distancing ourselves from the natural rhythms of the world we have brought more power under our control, and most of us are unwilling, upon reflection, to give that up. (And many of us who persist, even after reflection, with a desire to "return to nature" may well think better of it when one of our children needs antibiotics in a hospital.) There is a real rationale for why humans might want to dominate, master, and subdue nature, and we do not serve ourselves well, morally and spiritually, if we do not recognize the attraction and intelligence of that desire. And yet our success at these tasks has brought with it a new set of challenges, gestured at above.

Arguments about the environment raise deep questions about the sorts of creatures we are – what does it mean to say we are "natural" creatures? – and about the sort of universe, the sort of "nature" we live in – what characterizes the proper functioning of the universe? Is death an inevitable part of nature? In what way might one say that, or dissent from it? In general, how should we act in respect of nature?

Well, what factors are shaping that relationship now? Many people think that blame can be placed on the religious heritage itself, and especially on Christianity; furthermore, they suggest, the modern socioeconomic system which we inhabit is itself rooted perhaps in Christianity, which causes more blame to be laid on that tradition. In contrast, others argue that while the traditions offer beliefs that let us disparage nature, they also offer powerful resources that work in the opposite direction. For them, these traditions provide vocabularies to bring environmental problems more fully into view, and narrative structures that can motivate humanity to work to help the environment. Perhaps, they suggest, deep theological conviction *can* work just as much to value the environment as to disvalue it. Whatever side one takes, it is clear that the religious traditions provide a unique and perhaps invaluable perspective on debates about the environment, both because of the answers they give to these questions, and because of how they help us ask those questions themselves.

More fundamentally still, these issues raise for us, albeit indirectly, the deep question of *otherworldliness* – whether religious traditions lure us away from thinking about our world, and towards thinking about another, "higher" world somewhere else. In philosophical-theological terms, all this raises the question of the relation between immanence and transcendence – between our "this-worldly" interest in doing good and caring for each other and the world, and potentially "otherworldly" concerns about doing justice to a transcendent God. This is a basic and interesting question with which much contemporary religious thought is concerned, and one in which environmental issues provide a particularly powerful case study of "otherworldliness's" possible reality and potential implications.

This chapter thinks about the complicated relationship between humans and their natural environment today, especially in light of the ambiguous heritage of our selected religious traditions. In doing this, we will ask two questions about the environmental crisis. The first question is concerned with the immediate matter of causality and responsibility for humanity's depletion and pollution of the natural environment. The second question is possibly more profound, for it asks about the role that these religious traditions have had in shaping the meaning of terms like "nature" and "natural" for our thinking. Throughout this discussion we will see that the religious traditions stand on both sides of these issues – simultaneously motivating distinctively moral and religious concern for humanity's treatment of the non-human environment, but also offering resources that allow their adherents to understand humanity's relationship to creation in ways that may aggravate the environmental challenges that they themselves otherwise try to alleviate.

We turn first, though, to a famous indictment of the religious traditions regarding the environment.

The Environmentalists' Indictment

What is the relationship between our religious heritage and the environmental crisis? This is the fundamental question, and it was given powerful shape by a single essay, Lynn White's "The Historical Roots of Our Ecologic Crisis," published in the journal *Science* in 1967.[1] White's essay has been so decisive that it is worth laying out its arguments for a paragraph or so. White argues that "the present increasing disruption of the global environment is the product of a dynamic technology and science which [originated] in the Western Medieval world ... and in turn their growth cannot be understood historically apart from distinctive attitudes toward nature which are deeply grounded in Christian dogma."[2] That is to say, the problem lies in the presuppositions underlying science and technology, presuppositions that are fundamentally *Christian* in their origins, and profoundly pernicious.

In particular, White identified three central themes of Christian belief as providing the fundamental roots of our problem. First, he identified a profound anthropocentrism pervading Christian belief. "Anthropocentrism" simply means "human-centered," and it implies that humans are the center of creation, and the drama of humanity's Fall and redemption are the spinal story of all of the world; as he put it, Christian anthropocentrism presumes that "no item in the physical creation had any purpose save to serve man's purposes."[3] Second, White noted a powerful and motivating strain of anti-animism in Christian belief. Due to Christian concerns about idolatry (though these are fully Jewish and Islamic as well), Christians are deeply anxious about the possibility that people will identify the transcendent Divine with some part of the Divine's creation, and so fall into idolatry. Because of this, Christians have historically emphasized the transcendence of God to a fault, insisting that God is elsewhere, not here, and thus all things in this world bear no intrinsic divine significance (an insistence that quite easily slides over into a disparagement of value in the world at all). White formulated this quite vividly: "To a Christian a tree can be no more than a physical fact. The whole concept of the sacred grove is alien to Christianity and to the ethos of the West. For nearly two millennia Christian missionaries have been chopping down sacred groves, which are idolatrous because they assume spirit in nature."[4] Third, and somewhat paradoxically given the anti-animism, Christians are motivated by a gripping "natural theology," an insistence that they can and should come to know God by deciphering the traces of God's presence in creation. (White noticed the powerful presence of Christian beliefs in some of the progenitors of the scientific revolution, such as Francis Bacon and Isaac Newton.) Thus they are often committed to a project of reading the nature of God off of the world precisely for religious reasons. This is a dangerous energy to release.

Is White right? Are religions to blame? Some argue that White's condemnation of traditional Christianity is excessive; for them, the real problem lies not in traditional forms of Christianity, but in the various secularized heterodoxies of modernity. (And indeed White himself noted some alternative paths for a religious environmentalism inspired by the tradition; he especially sees some resources in the example of St. Francis, particularly his non-anthropocentrism, his humility, and his sense of connection to the rest of the world.) For such critics, White does not see the complexity of the traditions, and especially as regards Christianity, its insistence that because creation is the handiwork of God, and because we are all fallen, we are supposed to be more careful than we are.

Traditionally, human beings were understood to be pilgrims, traveling across the face of the fallen world, but not becoming too attached to it. Traditional Christianity, that is, is fairly otherworldly, and its otherworldliness may be a block to overly intensive ecological invasiveness on the part of humans. Ironically, that is to say, these critics of White see the real problem to stem from the decline of a richly *otherworldly* religious belief, alongside the retention of some of the moral commitments and expectations of traditional religious belief – most especially, that humans are meant for a perfect, suffering- and death-free form of life – which contribute to ecological depredation. If people lose faith in the otherworldly goal of traditional Christianity, it becomes increasingly important to master and dominate the natural world – to bend it to our will – in order to secure the moral utopia which retains an overwhelmingly tenacious grip on believers' moral imaginations. That is to say, traditional Christianity's otherworldliness may encourage a less invasive attitude towards the world; but it may do just the opposite, because it devalues the world in itself, and hence silences any concern we may have regarding what we are doing to the world. So the Abrahamic religious traditions, White's critics suggest, may be more useful than he allows. Those traditions may do better than many alternatives, insofar as they insist on the intimacy of God's involvement with the world, and the integral relation of the divine to humans.

In sum, these critics of White suggest, the traditions can help bring into focus the full range of these challenges, and they offer significant resources to help construct practical responses to it. Seeing just what this is, is our next topic.

Judaism

The first thing to note about the Jewish tradition on the environment, as in so much more, is the radical theocentrism of the tradition, which includes but is not limited to a radical non-anthropocentrism. As the Psalms put it, "the earth is God's and all that it holds, the world and its inhabitants" (Psalms 21:1). Furthermore, as God's speeches out of the Whirlwind in the Book of Job demonstrate, the universe is not designed for human comprehension, nor is it governed in order to promote human felicity. This is not an anthropocentric but a theocentric cosmos; one where God, not the human, lives at the center of things, and not all things exist for the sake of human beings.

The general theme of scripture, at least as interpreted in later tradition, was stewardship. Care and attention to the world is part of piety to God, because the world is God's creation. People are to have dominion over creation. "Dominion" is a word used twice, in Genesis 1:26 and 1:28. At times this term has been construed to mean domination, and read in line with the word "subdue," in a way that authorizes violence and ultimate authority. But the tradition has largely argued that it should be interpreted via God's command to Adam in Genesis 2:15 "to work [the garden] and take care of it." In light of this, "dominion" should be understood not as a brutal overlordship, a turning of all things to our immediate purposes, but as a matter of cultivation, of bringing the flower out of the seed, of helping all of nature become what it is meant to be. (This is exemplified in the fact that, in the original command to Adam and Eve in Genesis, animals are not to be eaten. Eating flesh, it turns out, is only permitted after the flood; and even then, you can never eat blood, because that is understood to be the "life force" of the creature, and we are not called to be vampires, sucking the life from one another.) Furthermore, the "lower animals" are supposed to be treated with dignity and mercy in the Jewish tradition; animals are supposed to rest on the Sabbath day, and even when animals are slaughtered, the rules of kosher slaughtering are meant to be as merciful as possible.

This emphasis on stewardship is complemented by – or perhaps, to use a less harmonious phrase, alloyed with – an emphasis on purity, and a care for the self, a care that the self be pure. (So there is concern for keeping clear of environmental pollution, and thus for creating latrines outside of camp (Deuteronomy 23:12–14).) Over the centuries the emphasis on purity has tended to be more visible and the focus of more attention, but only perhaps because, in a world where they did not rule, Jews had fewer opportunities to exercise dominion and thus stewardship. More challengingly, however, the enjambment of concerns with purity and a commandment to stewardship creates a tension that must be perpetually renegotiated; for the obligation to be pure may well create duties that conflict with stewardship, especially given that the latter often amounts to a command to "get your hands dirty," sometimes literally.

Stewardship is complicated because it is not simply static preservation. It involves care for the whole creation and includes pruning, sometimes so that some parts must die for the whole. Most basically, the idea is that non-human nature has a claim on humanity's moral attention. Concomitantly, any human (and especially Jewish) failure to fulfill these duties, will cause nature to cry out to God about the condition of the earth:

> Hear the word of the Lord, you Israelites, because the Lord has a charge to bring against you who live in the land: "There is no faithfulness, no love, no acknowledgment of God in the land. There is only cursing, lying and murder, stealing and adultery; they break all bounds, and bloodshed follows bloodshed. Because of this the land mourns, and all who live in it waste away; the beasts of the field and the birds of the air and the fish of the sea are dying." (Hosea 4:1–3)

The story of the development of the idea of *bal tashit*, "do not destroy," is a parable for the development of this consciousness. The phrase comes from Deuteronomy

20:19–20, which proscribes the cutting down of fruit-bearing trees even in sieges. But as time went on, this principle was expanded by the rabbis, first, to forbid all sorts of gratuitous damage to an enemy's means of livelihood in war, then to explain that plants and animals are themselves not directly combatants and so cannot be part of the legitimate targets in war; and then more generally still, to a principle of how humans should treat the natural world in all circumstances. What is especially troubling for this principle is the common thoughtlessness of human destruction. At times destruction and death may be necessary for protective or productive purposes, but often such violence is thoughtlessly casual. As it was in war, so should it be with all of humanity's (mis)adventures; the non-human realm should not be made to pay for our malicious follies. How *permissive* this exemption is, of course, is heavily debated; but its normativity, however it is interpreted, is widely affirmed.

Alongside and in some ways intrinsic to the principles of stewardship and preservation is the idea of temporal rest, reflected in the traditional practices of Sabbath years and Jubilee years. In these traditions, every seventh year was a Sabbatical year, in which the fields were to lie fallow, and after every seventh Sabbatical year (i.e., every 50 years) there would be a Jubilee year, where not only would the land lie fallow, but property would be restored and Israelite slaves given their freedom (e.g., Exodus 23:10–11). Such practices as these command the fundamental interruptions of time in order for the world to care for itself, and be cared for by humanity. These practices also "reset" the world as a *gift*, not humanity's proper possession, but properly owned by God.

Yet *bal tashit* and the Sabbath were *not* about private property; the point was not to respect each individual's private goods, but to honor God's proper ownership of *all* things, and to serve God's purposes by helping creation to renew itself. The point for the tradition was not that non-human nature has some intrinsic value, but rather that humans are called to treat God's gifts to them with respect. "Nature," insofar as that is a category in Jewish thought, is really just another word for the manifold gifts of creation with which God has blessed humankind. Thus, natural things are valued not "in themselves," but for what they signify about another's relationship to them. Whether this account would be something that thinkers like Lynn White would approve of, or whether they would find it alarming in other ways, is hard to know.

Christianity

Like Judaism, Christianity sees the world as the gracious gift of a creative God. And yet more starkly than Judaism, Christianity thinks that humans have deeply damaged creation through the Fall. So the tradition continues the exhortative alarmism of Hosea with the more brooding ruminations of Paul:

> For I consider that the sufferings of this present time are not worth comparing with the glory that will be revealed for us. For the creation waits with eager longing for the

revelation of the children of God. For the creation was subjected to frustration, not willingly, but because of him who subjected it, in the hope that the creation itself will be set free from its bondage to corruption and obtain the freedom of the glory of the children of God. For we know that the whole creation has been groaning together in the pains of childbirth until now. And not only the creation, but we ourselves, who have the first-fruits of the Spirit, groan inwardly as we wait eagerly for adoption as children, for the redemption of our bodies. For in hope we were saved. Now hope that is seen is not hope. For who hopes for what he sees? But if we hope for what we do not see, we wait for it with patience. (Romans 8:18–25)

In this passage, eschatological ambition and apocalyptic ambivalence are mixed in almost equal amounts. "The whole creation has been groaning together in the pains of childbirth until now." For Paul, while our full apprehension of the suffering of creation after the Fall awaits our recognition of the meaning of Christ's mission on earth, what we realize is that creation has been "groaning" all along. Creation has always been on the precipice of catastrophe; indeed, in one way it plunged into the abyss with the fall of the first humans. In fact, it is because of the profundity of the revolution in reality that Paul thinks Christ effects, that Christians (he thinks) should come to darken their apprehension of the flawed character of the created order we currently inhabit. The glory of Christ's redemption – announced and inaugurated in his resurrection but waiting for its completion in his Second Coming – throws into sharper relief the tragic and broken character of the original created order, the "old creation" that Adam and Eve ruined. Christians should care for the world, to be sure; but that "care" is a matter of apprehending its decrepitude and eschatological longings, while hoping for its restoration in the Second Coming.

Inevitably, this eschatological ambition and ambivalence manifests itself in a complicated attitude toward the kind of practical stance Christians should take. For Christians, as God has given humans authority, what we do with these things reflects our obedience to God – and so they are morally and religiously significant, they are not morally neutral. They are part of the covenant, in a way. So stewardship is important here, as in Judaism. Yet note the trajectories towards what some see as "otherworldliness" in the Romans text as well. We are waiting for our salvation; and that salvation can sound as if it is redemption as rescue, or even escape. It is not necessarily this – after all, Paul says we are hoping for creation to be set free of its decay, and that sounds like all of creation – but you can see the tendency set up, to look at the world we live in as somehow contingent, not essential to our being. This is what White's essay picks up on.

So the radicality of the Christian message may well encourage apocalyptic hostility to the world. But it can also enable a radical critique of the status quo. And for some Christians it has done just that. One person for whom this is true is the contemporary American essayist and Protestant Wendell Berry. Berry emphasizes stewardship; for him, "the ecological teaching of the Bible is simply inescapable; God made the world because he wanted it. It is his world; he has never relinquished title to it. And he has never revoked the conditions, bearing on his gift to us of the use of it, that oblige us to take excellent care of it."[5] But Berry's practical advice on how to do this focuses first of all on human intentions and dispositions, not outward action. For Berry, the Christian's first responsibility to creation is to "*safeguard God's pleasure in his work*."[6] We do that by safeguarding our own pleasure in creation – by treating the world not as what we have *earned*, but rather as a gift, as itself grace. Berry, like most other Christian thinkers, insists that creation itself is gratuitous, a gift God has created out of nothing, from the sheer excess of divine love.

Because creation is God's gift, and not our natural right, humanity must treat it carefully, as stewards of a landlord, not as those given free reign to exploit it. The term often used to designate this is *usufruct* – a curious combination of the Latin words for use and enjoyment, signifying the right to enjoy the temporary use of (but not ultimately possess) someone else's property, so long as that use does not cause permanent damage or irrevocable and harmful change to the property.

What is proscribed, and what prescribed, if we imagine creation to be a gratuitous gift? For Christians, the consequences are considerable. Below are two ways that this theme can be developed, one from the more "natural law" approach of Thomas Aquinas, and the other from the more "divine command" approach of Karl Barth. Despite their differences, we will see that both share a profound conviction that one's treatment of the natural world is based on one's relationship with God, and properly speaking not on one's direct apprehension of the immediate and intrinsic value of the natural world in itself.

Aquinas's discussion of private property may seem an odd place to begin from, but it is appropriate because of what it reveals about his understanding of how humans can rightly be said to "own" worldly things, and how easy it is to misunderstand the nature of human "ownership" as far more absolute than it properly is. Together, these points speak to Aquinas's understanding of the status of non-human creation in an especially pointed way.

Recall again our earlier claim – in the discussion of homosexual activity – that Aquinas is generally read as offering a broadly "natural law" account of the Christian moral life. In this situation, this means that he begins from a doctrine of creation in which an ethical prescription is grounded on the basic claim that because all can know that the world was created by a God, so all can also know that this God has those rights to the world that are properly due to a thing's creator. That is to say, for Aquinas, people "own" things so long as God has no better use for the things. Thus a person does not have absolute ownership of goods to dispense with as they choose, but they only have those goods as it were on loan from God, in a way like the Qur'anic idea of the vice-regental role of humans in regard to creation as a whole.

This is seen in an especially vivid way in the situation of dire need. Consider a case in which a person who is starving comes upon the orchard of a rich landowner, the boughs of whose trees are groaning with the weight of their ripe fruit. What may the starving person do? In fact, in all cases such as this, what *ought* those in dire need do? Aquinas's answer is interesting:

Things which are of human right cannot subtract from natural right or Divine right. Now according to the natural order established by Divine Providence, inferior things are ordained for the purpose of meeting man's needs by their means. Therefore the distribution of things, that is based on human law, does not preclude the fact that man's needs must be remedied by means of these very things. Hence whatever certain people have in superabundance is due, by natural law, to the purpose of succoring the poor…. Since, however, there are many who are in need, while it is impossible for all to be succored by means of the same thing, each one is entrusted with the steward-ship of his own things, so that out of them he may come to the aid of those who are in need. *Nevertheless, if the need be so manifest and urgent, that it is evident that the present need must be remedied by whatever means be at hand (for instance when a person is in some imminent danger, and there is no other possible remedy), then it is lawful for a man to succor his own need by means of another's property, by taking it either openly or secretly: nor is this properly speaking theft or robbery.*[7]

In cases of "manifest and urgent" need, then, God's providential design for worldly things overrides parochial human property rights. Thus, taking food from another's orchard when you are starving is not theft, it is proper use of lower things for higher ones. This is what the tradition means by talking about "usufruct." The human's fundamental relation to the natural world – or more properly speaking, the rest of the created order – is for Aquinas encapsulated in this idea.

Consider a second example. While Aquinas bases his account on the idea of natural law, Karl Barth offers an entirely different approach to thinking about ethics, one based on the idea of a particular history of divine action towards the world, an approach often described as a "divine command ethics." In environmen-tal terms, this means that Barth grounds his discussion of humanity's duties towards the natural world not on a natural commandment stemming from convictions that ethical reflection by any human can uncover, but rather on a particular event of crucial importance to God's particular history with humanity, namely, the life, death, and resurrection of Jesus Christ. That is to say, instead of basing this ethic on the doctrine of creation, as Aquinas arguably does, Barth bases it on Christology.

Barth does think that humans must act responsibly in regard to non-human life, most basically because our treatment of animals and plants (especially animals) reflects the way we understand our life in this world and before God. As he says, "respect for the fellow creature of man … means gratitude to God for the gift of so useful and devoted a comrade, and this gratitude will be translated into a careful, considerate, friendly, and above all understanding treatment of it."[8] He does make a distinction between killing an animal and the "harvesting of plants and fruit." Plants grow back, but animals do not. Killing an animal annihilates a unique indi-vidual creature; "the peace of creation is at least threatened and itself constitutes a continuation of this threat."[9] Barth lived in a world – unlike the world most readers of this book inhabit – wherein many people knew and cared for the animals that they then slaughtered and ate. They did not find most of their meat shrinkwrapped on a refrigerated shelf in a supermarket. It was not wildly unusual for a farming family to eat an animal for the evening's dinner that they had called by name to the slaughter-block that morning. The uniqueness and individuality of that animal could not be avoided, for them; for us it is much easier, but no less wrong.

Because of these facts, Barth thinks, "the slaying of animals is really possible only as an appeal to God's reconciling grace, as its representation and proclamation. It undoubtedly means making use of the offering of an alien and innocent victim and claiming its life for ours."[10] This is a frankly Christological fact, for Barth: in killing a lamb you are indeed killing a lamb of God, who is sacrificed for the hunger of the world. Therefore, do not "murder" animals – that is, slaughter them in a thought-less and heedless manner, as if they were your *property*, as what you deserve or something to which you have a right. Instead, understand the killing of an animal as an act, done in fear and trembling, of the sacrifice of another individual for your own sake, as part of the enormous generosity and grace of God – and look forward to the day when all such killing is no longer necessary. It is for these reasons that Barth says, "The killing of animals ... is a priestly act of eschatological character" – that is, it recognizes the brokenness of the world as it is, repents of the need to kill animals, looks to the past by acknowledging that the world was not meant to be a place where we annihilate things for our survival, and looks to a future when such killing will no longer be needful.[11]

Out of the work of theologians like Aquinas and Barth, a certain kind of episodic or fragmentary Christian approach to environmental concern is possible. But is this enough? Some more recent thinkers demand that Christians do better – that they offer a systematic vision of how to care for creation. These thinkers argue that Christianity can offer an ethic of "eco-justice" to guide environmental decision-making. This ethic is typically composed of four principal commitments which collectively enable Christians to evaluate the environmental morality of their behav-ior. The first criterion is *sustainability*, a concern for the future and planet as a whole; here and now is not the only relevant moment in creation. There are two theological sources for this, one in creation (built around the idea of receiving creation as God's gift), the other in covenant (built around the idea of treating creation in light of the promises we made to God).

The second criterion is that of *sufficiency*, the idea of "enough," the simple thought that we might imagine that there could ever be enough, that we could be sated in such a way as to quiet our desire. There are two things to note about this. First of all, it is surprising how difficult it can be for many of us to *imagine* "enough," to imagine that there ever could be a limit on the amount we should properly consume. We do manage to imagine that so far as food is concerned, but not of other consumer goods like music, books, clothes, or shoes. Secondly, however, the category of gratuitousness itself relies on us having some sort of category of the sufficient; that is, there is at least an argument to be made that the Christian doctrine of grace requires for its own intelligibility that we do in fact have a prior under-standing of enough, if only because it is such a concept that enables us to say that grace is *more* than enough.

The third criterion is the criterion of *participation*, by which thinkers mean that all must be included in considerations – and *all* includes *everyone* – not just future generations, but animals and all life; thus this criterion is fundamentally about empowerment. (Here, attention is brought to prophetic calls for justice, for a "preferential option" for the endangered and poor, and a commitment to identify and critique what we may call "the logic of domination," the large ideological frameworks that undergird the varieties of social injustice in the world.) Fourth, those who insist on an ethic of eco-justice argue for attending to these deliberations, and evaluating Christians' decisions, on the basis of the *solidarity* it reveals Christians to assume – undergirding participation is an insistence on identifying our good with the good of all, a lack of selfishness.

By such developments as these, some contemporary Christian thinkers are developing a systematic ethics of environmental care and attention. It is interesting, however, how similar – and if anything more pro-environment – are some of the bases on which Islamic ethics thinks about the environment; and we turn to that next.

Islam

As in Judaism and Christianity, in Islam the central premise is the sovereignty of God and the vice-regency (*khalifa*) of humanity. God is indubitably the owner of the world on this view: as the Qur'an says, "the earth is God's, and He gives it to such of his servants as He chooses" (Q. 7:128). And this generates a predictably similar overall view regarding the general status of the human use of nature – namely, that, as Abu al-Faraj, a (Sunni) Islamic legal scholar of the Hanbali school (1114–1201) said, "people only enjoy the right of *usufruct* of things, which are properly owned by the creator."[12]

But *usufruct* here is employed differently than in Christianity, or its tacit use in Judaism. Here it reveals the fundamental responsibility of humanity to creation, not most fundamentally (as in Christianity) because God gave creation to humans as a gift, but because, as heirs of Adam – of he who accepted from God the "names" of all creation (Q. 2:31–33) – we have a responsibility to care for it. Our status as Adam's heirs and God's vice-regents means we must care for God's creation as God wants it cared for; we are essentially God's groundskeepers, as it were.

After all, God has purposes for nature beyond the "gifting" of it to humanity. That is to say, there is a more strident critique of the potential anthropocentrism of other concepts of usufruct than is readily available in Christian doctrines of grace, more akin, perhaps, to Jewish doctrines of *bal tashit*. Caring for creation is more a responsibility than a gift in Islam.

The scale of this responsibility is brought home by the radical theocentrism of Islamic understandings of creation, and the more fundamental independence of creation from the drama of humanity's fall and redemption. God cares for things on their own account; God revealed to the bees where to build their hives (Q. 16:68). Humanity is not the only thing that God cares about in creation; there are other "nations" or "communities" (Q. 6:38). Each species is its own "nation," and all of them exist to give praise to God.

But creation in Islam is not only theocentric in a distinctive way. It is also more powerfully *theophanic*, more "revealing of God," than is the case in Christianity. One *hadith* reports Muhammad as saying "the whole of the earth is a mosque that is a place of worship." Furthermore, nature is not just a passive site of merely human worship; recall that to be *muslim* is to have submitted to God's will. In this light, the whole of "nature," apart from humanity, is naturally *muslim*, and it is also giving glory to God itself: "everything in the heavens and earth submits to God: the sun, the moon, the stars, the hills, the trees, and the animals? So also do many human beings. But for many others punishment is justly due." (Q. 22:18). All of nature, individually and in its systematic coherence, is unified and exists for praise of God. To cultivate and defend nature is to cultivate and defend what God has created as signs of God's goodness; hence to protect nature, to preserve its value as a sign of the Creator, is to undertake a defense of God's evangelical message.

These commitments are absolute, and not simply instrumental; creation ought to be cultivated as long as we are able. A *hadith* reports that Muhammad said "when doomsday comes" if someone has a palm shoot in his hand he should plant it."[13] Because of this, there are limits on what humans can do to creation. (For example, there is a proper limit to animal suffering – a limit possibly violated by contemporary industrial "factory farming" practices.) Creation is available for human use, but its significance is not exhausted by human needs. Because of this, environmental obligations in Islam are fundamentally conservationist in form, not cultivationalist. Perhaps this is because the language of "cultivation" is too easily bent towards becoming a legitimating device for human exploitation pure and simple. Or perhaps this is in part because in Islam's original context of the Arabian desert, the enframing conditions of desolation underscored the precarious character of life. Whatever the reason, humans are fundamentally supposed to be the maintainers of the due balance and measure of creation.

This is why the Islamic concept of *haqq*, which in this context translates roughly as "duty," applies as much to non-human creation as it does to human artifice. We have a *haqq* to respect all things, as they were intended to be there by God and so have significance for God and to God. We might almost say that nature has rights in Islam, rights given it by God and violated by humans only at the displeasure of God. That is why the *balance* of the universe must be preserved; the environment is for all of time, and not just for the present; contemporary humans have obligations to generations as yet unborn.

Yet in this activity of responsible conservation, divine worship occurs. The human's proper relation to creation is not adequately described solely in terms of subjugation and exploitation; nature is valuable for us in itself, as a reality well-pleasing to God and delightful for us to contemplate, in itself and in how it leads us on to ponder God's awesome and mysterious powers. Indeed in Islam, creation seems more theophanic than either Judaism, which sees God revealed in history, or Christianity, for which God is revealed in the work of Jesus Christ, but is elsewhere obscured by human sin. In Islam, all creation sings out praise of God's magnificence. As mentioned earlier in this book, in the entire Qur'an there are only about 200 verses directly commanding believers to pray, but three times that number commanding the believers to reflect, to ponder, and to analyze God's magnificence in nature, plants, stars, and the solar system. The Qur'an says that all things are signs or portents (*ayat*) of God, and so creation is the bearer of a divine significance, sacred but not themselves divine. And part of the Muslim's duty is contemplation of God's *ayat*. After all, humanity is part of creation, not fundamentally separate from it, and we find our flourishing in the context of nature. Nature nourishes not only physically, that is, but also spiritually.

Conclusion

The growing awareness of ecological crisis challenges the received views of our three traditions on at least two levels. First of all, it raises concerns about whether these traditions, and Christianity in particular, promote a dangerously instrumentalizing vision of the world. We have seen that the traditions try to resist this worry, by pointing out how they contain clues to an overall environmental ethic concerned with conserving or cultivating the created realm as part of the human's duties before God, even as that obligation is formulated in significantly different ways by the several traditions. Those difficulties should not overshadow the insistence common to all that humans do have duties to care for nature.

But there is a second and in some ways deeper question that the burgeoning global consciousness of the fragility of the environment puts to our traditions. By picturing God as radically transcendent of the world – by picturing God as a radically sovereign Creator – do these traditions threaten to degrade or diminish the value that their adherents ascribe to the created order? After all, if God is not ultimately "in" creation, then God must be calling the faithful "out" of it as well. And if that is so, then creation is merely a dispensable backdrop to the drama of God and humanity – a stage whose value is wholly a matter of the opportunity it provides for the actors, one which can be discarded once the drama is ended. To put it bluntly: do not all three of these traditions tell us that the world is *not our home*? And if they do tell us that, does that not raise real questions about the status of the world for these traditions, even in the present moment? Clearly, this is a question with ramifications that strike to the heart of these faiths.

Yet we have also seen that each of the traditions seems at least dimly alert to this worry, and at least semi-consciously, or partially, tries to resist it. After all, Adam and Eve were not exiled from Heaven into creation in Genesis, but from one part of creation – Eden – into another; and early Israelite prophets insisted that when the Messiah comes, he will make the barren lands fruitful (Isaiah 11:6–9, 51:3; Amos 9:13–15). In Christianity, Jesus's material resurrected body seems to suggest some real value inheres in the created material realm; and it is clear that the Islamic paradise is one that God has created, full of material joys and delights. Whatever else they are, these traditions are traditions of life in *this* world.

Part IV

The Last Things

16

Pursuits of Happiness

Labor, Leisure, and Life

The previous parts of this book have studied a variety of fairly discrete moral issues, and analyzed how a number of religious or quasi-religious commitments play different roles in endorsing certain courses of action and condemning others. These last chapters get a little harder. We'll look at two final, altogether different issues, issues that seem, on first glance, to have very little to do with the topic of "religious ethics and moral problems." I want to end this book by asking questions about how we might be able to take the things we have been reading about here and more fully weave them into the fabric of our everyday lives. (People talk about the humanities not being "practical;" but this humanities book, anyway, wants to be quite practical.)

These last two topics are really quite general, though in different ways. The second of them – good and evil – seems too abstract to have much of a bearing on particular moral problems and the role religious ethics can have in informing reflection about those problems. We will talk about that in the next chapter. In contrast to that topic, however, the first of these – the meaning of work and vocation – seems quite the opposite: it seems too concrete, too homey, to have much of a bearing on these moral problems. After all, what's the moral problem with work?

This raises a question: just what is a moral problem? Must it be one we readily recognize as such? Perhaps it is all the more dangerous if we cannot see it as a problem. This is one of the claims that I want to defend here. I argue here that the "moral problem" of work is a problem in part precisely because we do not see it as a problem – and we do not see its problematic character, in part, because of our "religious ethics" – because some particular religious commitments – expressly avowed by some of us but tacitly assumed by all of us, irrespective of our professed religious beliefs – make it difficult for us to see it *as* a problem. What I mean by that should become clear in due course.

This chapter begins with a simple question: what does an ethically mutilated life look like? Certainly, when I was 22, I knew the answer quite clearly. It involved the commission of a great crime, or an act of profound betrayal – of a friend, a loved one, my country, a cause, or my own better self. In any event, I knew what moral calamity looked like, I knew that avoiding that was the fundamental challenge of living a moral life, and I thought I knew how I could avoid it.

Now, in my 40s, I am not so sure, of several things. Now it seems the great, alp-like crimes that loomed ominously over the moral landscape of my youth have receded, worn down by the indifferent vagaries of time. But the erosion of those monstrosities has not left me feeling more morally secure. Far from it: now I feel that the crimes of childhood are hardly worrisome at all, when compared to the more subtly insidious manifold wickednesses that worm their way through ordinary life. These little ills make up in patient potency all that they lack in dramatic gran-deur. Indeed, the absence of the drama may well be a necessary condition for their potency. By the time one reaches one's 40s, it has become clear that the real moral challenges for most of us never take the shape of heroic adventures. Our moral challenges are multitudinous, but minute.

And that is precisely the problem. For we lack a workable language, one that can be self-consciously appropriated and inhabited in the world we live in, to provide a morally nuanced and richly textured assessment of the moral status of ordinary life. Such a language would not be a vehicle to mark the dramatic crimes and heroics, the moral peaks and abysses of our lives; rather, it would measure and assess the everyday character of our lives, with their innumerable little decisions and indecisions, refusals to do anything, silences, evasions, purportedly harmless jokes, petty little envies, unspoken ambitions, spoken cruelties – all the manifold micro-scopic minutiae of life that occupy 98 percent of our time, and thus also form 98 percent of our moral condition. We lack, in short, a way morally to illuminate the everyday business of human life as we ordinarily live it.

Even though it may be difficult for college students to appreciate the magnitude of this problem, hints of it are visible in their mode of life. Sometimes, in my undergraduate classes, I bring a frisbee into class and hold it up so that all can see. "What is this?" I say. "Good – a frisbee. I'm surprised that you know what it is, actually. It was an important part of my college education; I should have bought one with my first set of academic books. But so far as I can tell it has no role in your education at all." Mr. Jefferson built into his design of the University of Virginia a number of beautiful fields and lawns, spaces that are perfect for tossing a disc. And yet these fields are far more typically empty than filled with people; and when there are people in them, they are typically studying.

There is something sick about the pathological captivity of many undergraduates – at least the ones that I know – to the urge to achievement. Even their parties are intense and hard work. I think some people get involved with fraternities and sororities for the contacts it brings them, of course, but also for the potentially marketable skills they develop in organizing parties, designing drinking games, etc. I expect they even schedule time for their orgies. The vices of bacchanalia have been turned into the skill-set of the young corporate striver. All too often, students spend their whole time at college preparing to leave it, and only then, at the end, as gradu-ating seniors, they regret not enjoying it for what it was in itself.

Of course, complaining about undergraduates' work habits is a waste of breath, however momentarily satisfactory it may be. To understand what is going on, we need a deeper, serious analysis of the matter at hand. For it is not the case that undergraduates, for all their inventiveness (especially when it comes to excuses) came up with this strategy all on their own; they learned this behavior from others, most notably their parents, and are habituated into it, long before they get to college (indeed, as a prerequisite to *getting into* college) by their teachers and schoolmates. And if they did not learn it from them, they would most certainly learn it from us, their college teachers, for we manifest this pathology as much as anyone else.

The general form of the problem is that we are powerfully in the grip of an ideology that promotes a total devotion to our work. We have a hard time relaxing without a guilty conscience; it's hard to spend non-productive time – with family or friends or just by ourselves – without trying to make that time spent somehow *useful* in terms of our work (e.g., "recharging our batteries"). Short of having a heart attack, the commonest excuses for not devoting all our energies to our work are that we lack the necessary talent or admit to being lazy. We are seemingly caught on an unstoppable treadmill of "pursuing happiness."

We face this problem because we're enmeshed in a peculiar socioeconomic system, one that exists in part because some of our ancestors – our "cultural" ancestors, even if not our genetic ancestors – once thought that it was appropriate to make work a certain kind of religiously significant activity, and in part because the economy today tries as hard as possible to make you want more, and we seem to have no way of imagining what it would be to have "enough." That is to say, our understandings of labor and leisure, work and consumption, are arguably confused in terribly distorting ways.

These distortions emerged out of a history that still grips us. It is the burden of this chapter to explore this history, identify some of its religious roots, and suggest how our three traditions offer resources for living in a different, and more sane, manner. These traditions offer us a range of resources by which we could bring our pathologies, in this regard, to intellectual articulation, and begin to think about what to do about it. Here I will not fundamentally be talking about how the traditions offer distinct answers to this challenge, but rather I will explore how they all offer different variations on diagnoses of and responses to our situation. For all of them, what is ultimately at issue here is the relationship between work and joy, merit and grace, labor and gift.

Perhaps unsurprisingly, then, they are uniformly dismayed at what they see as the dimensions of a fundamentally ungenerous way of life in our existence, and they wish to alter our behaviors and beliefs the better to enable a deeper and more all-encompassing generosity of spirit.

The Crisis of Work

The nature of work today is very different than it has been in the past, both in the amount of work we do, and in our understanding of its significance for our lives.

Let us begin with some facts – some simple numbers, concerning the nature of our lives as regards work.[1] In the post-World War II era, there has been an explosion in amount of work done, and its effects on our lives have been dramatic. Americans enjoyed a decline in work time from the 1850s until the late 1940s. Since then, things have changed dramatically. In the twenty years between 1969 and 1989 – a period of especially dramatic social change among men and women – the average hours of paid employment per worker increased by 163 – an extra month of work. In that time men increased their work time by 98 extra hours per year, while women increased their work time by 307 extra hours. The velocity of change has continued; in 2000, an average American put in 1,880 hours on the job, 200 more than they did in 1980. And these changes are as much about the cultural specificity of the United States as they are about the West as a whole, for today the average American works nine weeks – 360 hours – more than workers in Western Europe.

Some scholars contest the validity of these statistics. They argue that work time has actually decreased for lower-education and lower-income workers. But they too allow that there has been an enormous explosion in work time for higher-income and more educated workers. Oddly, that is, the "working class" may be working less, while the "leisure class" may be working more. So perhaps it is safest to say that these changes are not evenly distributed across the population; those with more education, and higher up the income and wealth levels, are disproportionately experiencing its pressures. The "crisis of overwork" seems precisely a white-collar crisis.[2]

The consequences of this change on the shape of life for those caught up in it have been dramatic. In the period from 1973 to 1989 alone, free time seems to have fallen precipitously, by over 40 percent, from 26 hours per week to 17. Today, many people suffer from a sleep deficit; most non-retirees in the United States get between 60 and 90 percent of the sleep they need. Increasingly, people are losing their attachments to civic associations – bowling leagues, bridge clubs, veterans' groups, men's and women's assemblies, all have suffered precipitous declines in membership numbers and the quality and quantity of engagement by the members they do have. We become increasingly creatures of home and of work, and of little else.

What has caused this explosion of work? Many thinkers suggest that the problem is, in the words of contemporary American sociologist Robert Wuthnow, "rooted in the way we *think* … in the moral frameworks we use in ordering our priorities and deciding how to lead our lives."[3] Work has an absolute value for many of us – beyond money, it is how we value ourselves. When we ask "what do you do?" we often invest answers to that question with a great deal of existential weight; and we are increasingly supposed – perhaps expected – to find our dignity, autonomy, and value precisely in our paid work. (Incidentally, this is especially pointed for upper-middle-class women, who often have internalized two different and conflicting belief systems – one about the value of work and another about the value of motherhood.)

In turn this has two causes – some relatively more superficial changes due to consumer culture, and deep changes due to capitalism. First of all, our work obsession is related to, and proximately encouraged by, the postwar spending spree – we have all the goodies in the world, and we want more; we think happiness is always just beyond the next purchase. As Juliet Schor put it in her book *The Overworked American*, we are participating in a pattern of "upscale spending" deeply shaped by the media; we measure ourselves against people much wealthier than we are, and we consume accordingly. The average American's spending grew somewhere between 30 and 70 percent (after adjusting for inflation) between 1979 and 1995, and has continued to rise since. Today, Americans spend almost exactly what they earn – that is, our savings rate, on average, is very close to zero. In part that is because our expectations rose dramatically as well; between 1986 and 1994, for example, the "dreams-fulfilling" level of income for Americans, as measured in polls, rose from $50,000 to $102,000. More ominously, we are increasingly defining happiness in material terms; polling data suggest a steady increase in the ratio of material to non-material components in answers to questions about what constitutes a "good life."

What has caused this? Obviously, there are many causes. But some are more powerful, and possibly more amenable to change, than others. Most relevant here is the fact that advertisers have learned how to influence human *desire* through the media. As General Motors Research labs general director Charles Kettering said back in the 1950s, contemporary companies aim to create a "dissatisfied consumer" in order to sell their goods; hence much money is invested in the "organized creation of dissatisfaction." Since then, of course, advertising has become only more insidious. Creation of dissatisfaction makes us work more for more money, which we can then spend on more things. And this is especially due to our habits of watching television and the advertisements they convey to us; for every hour of television they watch each week, Americans spend an extra $208 annually.

But "capitalism" is not just victimizing us like an external tyrant – it is rooted in decisions our ancestors made long ago, and which we unreflectively endorse every day about what is the *religiously* appropriate way to inhabit the world. By "capitalism" I mean something like the free market system, the economic system that we inhabit, in which goods are relatively freely produced and traded for prices relatively freely set by individuals. (This is not a perfect definition, merely a useful one, for now.) When this system of capitalism got going in seventeenth-century Europe, it reduced leisure time precipitously. Before the seventeenth century, the average person performed 1,500–2,300 hours of work per year (which is between 4.1 and 6.3 hours per day over the whole year). Since then the work load has increased substantially.

What causes this? In part, it is the structural realities of capitalism. Once a full market economy gets going, the crucial object of every actor is to maximize their profits, without limits. Now we no longer have a subsistence-based system, now we have a surplus-based system. There is no longer a belief that "enough is enough," for there is always more profit to be made. In part, it also developed out of technological innovations (rationalized means of keeping time, double-entry bookkeeping, etc.).

But technological and structural innovations are in part based on another, deeper, ideological change – namely, the transformation of work into a religiously significant reality. The so-called "Protestant Ethic" was so named by the great German sociologist Max Weber (1864–1920). In brief, this ethic made work into a means of either creating or exhibiting virtue (some thought work created virtue, some thought it just exhibited it). It made work a spiritual exercise, and made people focus on transforming themselves into more efficient workers for the sake of some higher calling – it made them all "ascetics," people who deny themselves a certain range of goods for the sake of some other good or set of goods (typically more long term and immaterial). The classic example of this "inner-worldly asceticism," and the one that Weber studied, is the seventeenth-century English Puritan movement, which revolutionized England and served as the core of the New England colonies. The Puritans were as focused and disciplined as any monastics ever were, though as they were living in the world as "visible saints" their discipline soon blossomed into worldly success and wealth. Because they organized their lives around a ruthless quest for holiness, in a manner not unbefitting medieval monks, they came to see their worldly occupations – as bakers, farmers, teachers, printers, wives, sons and daughters, mothers and fathers – as callings, "vocations" from God. (The word *vocation* had always been the exclusive province of monastics, by the way – as had the word *conversion*.) The spiritual and moral intensification of ordinary life that this entailed meant that, for the first time in Christian history, ordinary people saw the course of their everyday lives as spiritually significant. What they did, and how zealously they did it, now seemed to have effective force for shaping their eternal destiny in Heaven or Hell.

This change in sensibility was real and it was a powerful force for producing heretofore unimaginable wealth and health in those societies where it flourished. And the theological rationale not only mobilized people's energy in this-worldly pursuits; it also channeled and constrained those energies, rendering the pursuit of worldly goods powerful but controlled. But then, once the economic system so designed got going, it had no need of any theological motive to sustain our commitment to it – it simply became the world we inhabit. The deep theological rationale fell away, and people were left with the infinite obligation to work, but without an articulate explanation of why. As Weber famously put it:

> The Puritan wanted to work in a calling; we are forced to do so. For when asceticism was carried out of monastic cells into everyday life, and began to dominate worldly morality, it did its part in building the tremendous cosmos of the modern economic order. This order is now bound to the technical and economic conditions of machine production which today determine the lives of all the individuals who are born into this mechanism – not only those directly concerned with economic acquisition – with irresistible force. Perhaps it will so determine them until the last ton of fossilized coal is burnt. In [one Puritan] view the care for external goods should only lie on the shoulders of the "saint like a light cloak, which can be thrown aside at any moment." But fate decreed that the cloak should become an iron cage ...

No one knows who will live in this cage in the future, or whether at the end of this tremendous development entirely new prophets will arise, or there will be a great rebirth of old ideas and ideals, or, if neither, [there will result] mechanized petrifaction, embellished with a sort of convulsive self-importance. For of the last stage of this cultural development, it might well be truly said: "Specialists without spirit, sensualists without heart; this nullity imagines that it has attained a level of civilization never before achieved."[4]

In some important ways, then, the profoundly otherworldly motivations of a certain form of Protestant Christianity lie close to the heart of the mammon-obsessed materialism that, for good and ill, drives modern society even today. It is no small irony that a tradition that putatively puts so much stock in the admonition to "store up your treasure in Heaven" would have such paradoxical consequences, and many scholars argue that the evidence for it is exaggerated, and the precise claims made about it are inescapably vague; and yet there is clearly something to the thesis – there is some sort of connection between the rigors of the Calvinist "disciplinary revolution" and the vast changes – material, institutional, intellectual, and even cultural – that have shaped the modern West into what it is today.

What is more ironic still, this "Protestant ethic" is not effective only for Protestants; it shapes the whole logic of modern life, as Weber puts it, "with irresistible force." Roman Catholics, Jews, Muslims, other religious believers, and atheists and agnostics alike in our culture – they all attach an especially high value to finding one's meaning and value in one's vocation, which is ever-increasingly being equated to one's job.

What should we do about this? How are we to resist the siren-song of work?

Frugality?

Perhaps what we should do is simply recover long-forgotten virtues, such as frugality. Frugality as a virtue runs against both our inner habits and the outer social-structural patterns within which we live our lives. It suggests a proper *limit* on human desires; it rejects the popular assumption that humans are insatiable creatures, and leaves space for the cultivation of diverse forms of pleasure that would otherwise be submerged in a simple homogenized desire for always more of the same narrow band of habituated objects of our appetite.

What exactly is frugality? Frugality is not a form of austerity or a world-denying asceticism, nor is it a nostalgia for a "simple" life. It is, properly speaking, a part of stewardship – stewardship of natural resources, to be sure, but also of ourselves. Frugality is indeed a negative virtue, in that it focuses on resisting, on less; but it is negative in a complicatedly positive way. For frugality is about sacrifice, the sacrifice of one set of our desires, but only as that sacrifice is part of a larger positive act, part of a search for abundant life, a life that is more than one kind of good, more than one kind of pleasure. Frugality restricts our appetite, or our indulgence of our appetite, for *one* good, in order that we may more properly apprehend the full range of the goods set before us. Frugality is a form of sacrifice, an ascetical practice of constraining one's desires for some set of things in order to leave space for the cultivation of other pleasures, or other desires for other, more powerfully valued things.

But is this true? Is frugality properly and ultimately sacrifice? Or is it rather a reorientation towards other, higher goods that should have been prioritized all along? I think it is the latter. It may seem like a "sacrifice" to us at first, but later it will seem simply *the right thing to do* – so that we come to do it habitually, automatically. When that happens, frugality will seem like real life – indeed, like life abundant.

The moral of this story is simple. We are ill-served by strategies that give us a fundamentally negative task; we cannot resist the felt obligation to work, unless we have something at least equally important to oppose it. Fortunately, such alternatives exist, and come into view when we come to see that this problem is not simply a moral one, but also and at least as importantly a religious one: the problem is not simply a matter of a failure of prudence, but equally importantly it is, on religious grounds, a form of idolatry. All three of these traditions endorse the religious disciplining of all dimensions of our lives, and thereby encourage their faithful to turn their whole lives into works of praise to God.

But what could be as important as work? I want to focus on two sorts of attempts to answer that question by religious thinkers. First, I want to look at the activity of contemplation, and the idea that in contemplation we discover an alternative mode of being that is quieter and has rewards that incessant labor can never create. In contemplation, these traditions have found ways to sanctify ordinary life in terms of the human's experience of space, of being in the world. Second, I want to note the apparently passive practice of "sabbathing," of intentionally restricting and regularly restraining the everyday practices of work and consumption in order to disrupt these quotidian patterns, in the hope that something radically other will reveal itself in that interruption. Here it is not space but time that is used to transfigure our experience. Both of these phenomena, those who commend them suggest, reconfigure our understanding of agency and of the meaning of work and action in powerful ways.

Furthermore, both teach a useful strategic lesson. We will see that both practices are not so much directly aimed at resisting the false gods of materialism as much as indirectly organizing our appropriate appreciation for them by putting them in their place, giving them their right value and proper purpose in our lives.

Leisure and Contemplation

Consider first the idea that the reality of contemplation reveals to us a dimension of human life that goes unmet by the task of work in the material world. By "contemplation" we mean here the state of relaxed attentiveness, a reflective condition that puts the contemplator at some indeterminate distance from the world sur-

rounding them. Real focus and intentionality are normally at work in contemplation, but not always; at times it can seem more like a dream-like, fugue state.
(Contemplatives are notoriously bad at avoiding obstacles when they walk around.)
Contemplation, that is, seems to puncture the myth of the absolute tyranny of space
over the self. While the contemplative is "here," in the most literal sense, they are
also and more importantly *not here*. (One day the philosopher William James was
taking a walk with one of his students when they saw one of James's colleagues
wandering across Harvard Yard. The student remarked on the wandering professor,
calling him "absent-minded." James dissented: "He is not absent-minded. He is
present-minded, somewhere else.")

Contemplation is thus a sign that humans can transcend space, can be in some
sense "altogether elsewhere." And yet this transcendence of space is not an *escape*
from it; rather, the experience reveals deeper layers of significance within the world
– it shows us not that reality is other than the world we ordinarily inhabit, but more
than that world alone. It is a transfiguration of the world, a revelation of its sacramental quality, as the bearer of divine significance. (This is what lies behind the
Islamic understanding of creation as composed of *ayat*, "signs," of God.)

Some thinkers have seized on this capacity to suggest that such activity, if that
is the right word for it, can be profoundly nourishing of our souls, in a way that
the realm of worldly "work" cannot. The contemplative returns to our common
workaday world refreshed, often rejuvenated, if also a little disoriented by their
sojourn elsewhere. But even that disorientation may serve a purpose, as their return-
ing to familiarity may well uncover missed insights the rest of us overlooked; and
anyway, we do well to be reminded that this world with the tyranny of the momentarily urgent is not the only world we inhabit.

Perhaps the most provocative such thinker of our age is the Roman Catholic
philosopher Josef Pieper (1904–97). In his small gem of a book, *Leisure, the Basis
of Culture*, Pieper argues that our lives are illuminated by certain insights that go
back at least to Aristotle. In making this case, though he is working out of the
Christian tradition, Pieper uses "natural law" reasoning of the sort we saw used by
Thomas Aquinas earlier in this book. In this natural law setting, Pieper's ideas
emerge out of reflection on natural human life, proper understanding of
human experience, with little attention to biblical authorities or the particular revelation of the Christian scriptures. For Pieper, all that he says is a matter of
common knowledge, knowledge shared (in some sense) by the Greeks and Romans
as well as Christians, and so available also to Jews or Muslims or any secularist
today.

Pieper begins by noting that, in the loss of the concept of leisure, we see the rise
of a new vision of human – the human as perpetual laborer. Today, we think of
vacations as opportunities to "recharge our batteries." (That itself is a telling image;
are we supposed to understand our motivation to work as something essentially
mechanistic, and even detachable, as batteries are?) The notion that our work
should be for rest is actually quite difficult for us to take seriously. It seems like a
profound ethical failing. Our work is what justifies us, is it not? Pieper strongly

dissents: "Not everything is useless that cannot be brought under the definition of the useful."[5] While most of us today instrumentalize our rest to serve our work, Pieper follows Aristotle in affirming the reverse: "we are unleisurely in order to have leisure."[6]

What, then, is leisure? It is not a catatonic state of sheer unconscious rest. Leisure is a state of relaxed alertness and attentiveness to one's person and one's setting, but in a profoundly un-instrumental, non-purposive way. Leisure can involve strenuous effort – as one plays hard in a game, or delights in making a meal for friends – but the effort is not seen as essential to the aim of leisure. Indeed, insofar as effort is present in leisure, it has no essential point; it is done for the joy of the exertion itself. (Were the friends not to come for the meal, begging off because their children were sick, the experience of making the meal would have been fun anyway, though the end result might be disappointing.) More centrally, leisure is simply a state of relaxed inhabitation of time and place, in which whatever activity one is engaged in is not done for the sake of something else, but as a way of enjoying the opportunity to experience the event as a gift, a pleasure in itself, unrelated to any exterior end.

This vision of leisure suggests a certain set of not uncontroversial assumptions about the nature and purpose of the human being. On this account, the human does not find their ultimate meaning or significance in their achievements, but in their being a certain kind of creature – namely, that creature that can transcend the immediate demands of the here and now, and partake instead of a deeper com-munion with realities not so tightly tethered to the particularities of place and time. To put it even more strongly: on this view, the human is that creature who, without such opportunities to escape the demands of the instant, becomes something less than what she or he is meant to be. To become a person entirely and exhaustively (and exhaustingly) at the disposal of the immediate demands of the material moment is to mutilate one's own being, privileging part of oneself over the whole and thus becoming less than what one was meant to be.

Yet how can we cultivate this capacity for leisure? Interestingly, one place in which the idea of leisure is not completely extinguished, according to Pieper, is in the academy. The idea of school, ironically, is about leisure – as *scholia* – the root word for "leisure" in Greek – is the etymological source for the English word "school." Yet here too the "world of total work" has attempted to encroach on our experience of study. Today, we value even intellectual work in terms of its difficulty, instead of its truthfulness, or beauty, or profundity. But, as Pieper points out, why is *difficulty* so very much a marker of real value? Why is hard work the only marker of *good* work? No, Pieper says; the best kind of "study" or intellectual engagement is properly "effortless," as it comes from love, from being drawn out of oneself and towards a reality that invigorates and refreshes all the more, the deeper you go into it. The ultimate challenge here, of course, is to overcome the idea, so common among students and not a few faculty today, that there is such a thing as an educa-tion essentially free from the demands of final utilitarian or professionalist payoff – an education, as distinct from *training*.

Leisure wagers that there is such a distinct kind of education, for its aim is not technical or professional competency, but *wonder*. But this wonder is not a static state like death, but an endless, un-difficult, delightful dynamic contemplation. It is in the unfettered and fully engaged activity of the mind. For Pieper, while education is one realm where leisure is still dimly visible, he thinks its proper home is in religion, in the unforced and prayerful contemplation of divine things. This is why Pieper can translate Psalm 46:10 – commonly translated as "be still and know that I am God" – as, strikingly, "have leisure and know that I am God."

So understood, leisure offers a way of remaining in one place but recognizing the way that one's life transcends place – a way of being, as it were, here and yet "present minded, somewhere else."

And yet practices of leisure, as powerfully present as they are in the contemplative dimensions of these religious traditions, are not the only resources available. They have an alternative model, one that does not rely on rarefied and elite practices of education, but simply demands the bare practice of an everyday – or rather, every week – habit: the Sabbath.

The Sabbath

If contemplation is a practice that effectively takes us out of space, then it stands to reason that there would be another practice that takes us out of time, that disrupts our experience that time is an absolute frame for us, that time is all there could ever be. And there is. It is the practice of designating certain times as holy times, whether seasons or festivals, or just the regular recurrence of one day a week. In the Jewish tradition (and for many Christians) that day is called the Sabbath. It is part of the practice of all three of our traditions, but it is especially lucidly discussed by the Jewish thinker Abraham Joshua Heschel (1907–72) in his work *The Sabbath: Its Meaning for Modern Man*.[7]

In Heschel's Judaism, the Sabbath is the period from sundown Friday to sundown Saturday, in which God has decreed that the Jews must undertake no work or use of energy – not only themselves, but all those under their power (thus including non-Jewish workers and animals as well). As it was declared in the Book of Deuteronomy: "The seventh day is a Sabbath of the Lord your God; that day you shall not do any work, neither you, your son or your daughter, your slave or your slave-girl, or your ox or your ass, or any of your cattle, nor the alien within your gates, so that your slaves and slave-girls may rest as you do" (Deuteronomy 5:14). It is a practice of remembering God's rest on the seventh day – Saturday – once God had completed creation.

More often than not, if you are anything like me, you are too rushed to notice time – we pass through time, but we never accept it – we never seem to be given enough time, let alone given time itself, given the gift of time. The Sabbath is a restriction on how we use the world and ourselves, so that we may more palpably accept time – and through time, the world and ourselves. For, Heschel believes, "time is the heart of existence," and in the Sabbath, Judaism is revealed as "a religion of time aiming at the sanctification of time."[8]

What does that mean? What can it mean to say that time, and not being, is the true gift of existence? Well, Heschel thinks it means that the spatial realities all around us in the material world are in themselves mere props for the significant drama of our lives. "We must not forget that it is not a thing that lends significance to a moment; it is the moment that lends significance to things."[9] It is our embeddedness in a story that takes time, that gives our lives whatever meaning and orientation they have. This is a worldly as much as next-worldly aim; in the rest of the Sabbath, we learn to appreciate the ability to be joyous in the world as it is, as the site of the drama of our lives.

But what does it mean to *appreciate* the world? What is joy, after all? Heschel makes an intriguing claim: you cannot appreciate the world except as a gift, and so you cannot appreciate the world without having the experience of gratitude; and you cannot have this experience without implying the reality of a giver. Thus, joy entails gratitude, which entails some sort of relationship to a reality beyond you and the gift.

In this way, the ultimate point of the Sabbath, as mundane as it is, is ecstasy, joy, praise: "The Sabbath teaches all beings whom to praise."[10] This reveals something significant, for Heschel, about our humanity: our capacity to admire. No other animal admires; only we do. We are *doxological* creatures, designed to praise, and we find a certain kind of flourishing in offering praise. In teaching us whom to praise, the Sabbath teaches us something about ourselves that we would not otherwise discover.

How does the Sabbath do this? By its radical freedom from spatiality. The Sabbath, unlike other religious festivals in Judaism (and other religions), is "completely detached from the world of space." It is unmoored from the "natural" patterns of space and time; the weekly schedule corresponds to no direct calendrical pattern of the world. By being so unmoored from matter, it makes us attentive to time itself, as an independent dimension of reality. In doing this, it aims to help us "become attuned to *holiness in time*."[11] Unlike Pieper's more "natural law" approach, then, Heschel's understanding of the Sabbath presumes and requires the apprehension of the revealed will of God as calling people beyond the bounds of the merely natural world. If we were to rest content with what nature tells us to do, Heschel says, we would never come properly to see the Sabbath as a gift, and our apprehension of the gift-character of creation as a whole would be too unstructured, fugitive, and fleeting to shape our souls as it should.

It is meant to disrupt our ever-present temptation to just go with the flow, to surrender to the current of time onrushing. It is a form of discipline, of training the soul to hear resonances beyond those of the created order. For Heschel, the Sabbath teaches Jews that "the higher goal of spiritual living is not to amass a wealth of information, but *to face sacred moments*. ... What we plead against is man's unconditional surrender to space, his enslavement to things."[12] To become attuned to holiness in time is to become attuned to the Holy – to be able to say, at all times and in all places, *hinneni*, the "here I am" that Abraham uttered to God, just before he was asked to go and kill his son.

What is the Sabbath's goal – what is created in the faithful fulfillment of the command for Sabbath rest? To answer this, Heschel appeals to the Hebrew word *menuha*. This means not just withdrawal from labor, or freedom from work; it is a *positive* reality: "tranquility, serenity, peace and repose."[13] The ideal aim of the Sabbath, then, is peace – though this is more than the peace of the cessation of conflict, it is the fullness of harmony and joy. The word is found in the 23rd psalm, a famous psalm for both Jews and Christians: "The Lord is my shepherd; he leads me beside the waters of *menuha*." In this way the Sabbath teaches us not only a reality that is present in this life, but also one that gives us a foretaste of the promise of the next; the Sabbath is our taste of Heaven, given to us weekly.

What can we say about the prospects for the Sabbath, or a structure like it, being appropriated in the traditions of Christianity and Islam? For Christianity, things are a bit complicated; Jesus said, "The Sabbath was made for man, not man for the Sabbath, so the Son of Man is Lord even of the Sabbath" (Mark 2:27). There seems to be a way that the apocalyptic urgency of the early Christians rendered the ritual of Sabbath-keeping possibly more contingent than obligatory. Frequently since then, Christians' more urgent apocalyptic expectations have meant that patterns of behavior that aim to habituate Christians into forms of resistance to the world have been treated with some skepticism, precisely because habituation is often seen by Christians as the problem – for habituation is getting used to things, and there is a very real way in which "getting used to things" is a problem in Christian life, keyed as it is (more deeply than Judaism or Islam anyway) to an ultimate eschatological resolution of this world. That said, there are definitely practices of Christian religious practice – the Christian Sabbath, for one! – that would seem amenable sites to learn from Heschel's proposal.

Islam has retained more of its traditional rigor about regular religious rituals (so that the Qu'ran 62:9, which urges all to observe Friday as a holy day to worship God and reflect on their faith, is still largely observed by Muslims, as is the five-times-daily prayer). Its mini-sabbaths of daily prayer times, and also the experience of the month of Ramadan, means that these patterns are preserved quite seriously in ordinary Muslim lives. Indeed, if anything, the structured disruption of time is something that is more vigorously pursued in Islam than in either Judaism or Christianity; the regular round of five daily prayers faithfully engaged in, is a more frequent practice of training in attunement than anything undertaken by the large majority of contemporary Jewish or Christian faithful. So the prospects of a Heschelian-like development in Islam are, in fact, already more than prospects.

Finally, it is not inconceivable that this practice, though it is not observed so much in our world, could become more common. Its implications would be interesting to track. Imagine not buying something even two days a week – say, Tuesdays and Saturdays, for example; one wonders how well our economy would weather a dramatic decline in purchases on two days out of every seven. One wonders what

the implications would be – not just for the religious lives of the people who undertake this discipline, but for our social order in general.

Conclusion

In trying to find structures of analysis and critical leverage to resist the perpetual
temptation to become enmeshed in the everyday world of work – a world that we
all today find so alluring, or at least so unavoidably enthralling – we have returned
again and again, in these religious traditions, to the category of idolatry. And this
is not surprising. After all, all three traditions use this category. In fact it is central
to all three faiths, and it is readily applicable in illuminating when work, or other
"worldly" matters, become people's idols. Idolatry is the refusal to recognize that
legitimate longings are both horizontal *and* vertical. By condemning such refusals
as idolatrous, these traditions affirm something important about the human. That
is to say, the critique of work as a form of idolatry here effectively honors God, of
course, but secures transcendental dignity of the human – something all three of
these traditions insist upon. For to make work an idol is not only to to idolatrize
God, but to mutilate the self – to limit it improperly.

The profundity of this complaint of idolatry is matched, in all three traditions,
by the frequency with which this charge is leveled. Indeed, the frequency of such
charges in all three traditions suggests that they all believe that humans often live,
as it were, on the *outside* of life, on the surface, not yet really living it; and it is by
participating in various religious practices that flourishing life is really possible. Just
as much as idolatry is meant to protect the holiness of God from confusion with
God's creation, so it also is meant to protect humans against their perpetual temptation to undercut themselves, to reduce their self-understanding to that of a mere
machine, a cog in the wheel of a productive society. For all three traditions, idolatry
is fundamentally debasing – debasing of God, to be sure, but also debasing of the
humans who indulge in it. The *hinneni* uttered by the faithful community or person
(such as Abraham, when asked to sacrifice Isaac) is certainly the expression of a
readiness to serve God. But it is also a remarkable – indeed astonishing, perhaps
terrible – recognition that we as humans can stand apart from the structures and
conditions of the created world and ask fundamental questions of that created
world, in a kind of self-transcendence that is, in all proper senses of the word,
awe-full.

17

Good and Evil

Photo: akg-images

A picture, I offer you, of a baby. An infant, almost, not quite one year old. A boy, judging from the haircut, he gazes out at the camera in blank, innocent curiosity. Dressed in a frilly white gown popular until the middle of the past century, there is something ridiculous about the outfit, to our eyes at least; surely this baby is better clothed in a diaper, a shirt, and little else. (Why do we want to take memorializing photographs by costuming the subjects in clothes they would never want otherwise to wear?) Propped up against a dark cloth background, sitting in a chair, tottering like a tree whose trunk has been cut but has not yet fallen, this little boy gazes out at us from over one hundred years ago – innocent, startled, not adorable in his stiffness but still clearly loved and loveable, this child could be anyone – your great-grandfather. Clearly, this is a charming little tyke.

In fact it's a picture of the young Adolf Schickelgruber – Adolf Hitler – not quite a year old.

I think I know something of your response to my little revelation here. There's something extremely disquieting about the idea of Hitler as a baby. There's something wrong about that – not just wrong about the idea of seeing a baby Hitler, as if the disquieting thing about it were simply that it was the baby's cuteness – but rather about the idea that Hitler was ever a baby at all. The truly troubling thing is not to imagine Hitler as a *cute* baby, but to try to imagine Hitler as anything but the adult demonic figure that we know from history. The problem, that is, is Hitler's sheer *humanity*.

Finding any connection between Hitler and the human race is deeply disturbing to us. For after all we have come to understand Hitler, I believe, as somehow non-human – somehow suprahuman, unimaginable. That's how we tell ourselves we can tell real evil – it feels somehow different from us, alien, not human. But of course one of evil's greatest powers is its complete familiarity to us. As Albert Speer – a brilliant architect and close confidant of Hitler – said, "It is hard to recognize the devil when he is putting his hand on your shoulder." The true terror of this picture, then, is not in the baby, but in the bare idea that Hitler once was a baby, and so a human, at all. This is the sort of disquiet that can give rise to thought.

Here at the end we're asking some broader questions than we've asked before, questions too mundane or too stratospheric to be easily seen as "moral problems." I'm asking these questions because I want to end this book with questions about how we might be able to take the things we have been looking at and more fully weave them into the fabric of our everyday lives. In the last chapter, we talked about the meaning of work and vocation, and I suggested that work has become, or *should* become, a moral problem for us insofar as we find ourselves enslaved, morally captive, to an infinite obligation to work, and a bad mode of living in time. If that topic seems somehow too homey to rise to the respectable level of a "moral problem," the topic of good and evil seems too etherial, too abstract and stratospheric to have much of a bearing on particular moral problems and the role religious ethics can have in informing reflection about those problems.

Indeed, the problem may well be deeper – it may be that we have a hard time making sense of these terms in the abstract at all. We live in a culture that usually chooses to forego the judgmental language of good and evil for a therapeutic language of suffering and pathologies. As the contemporary political thinker Jean Bethke Elshtain puts it, "We no longer believe in sin; we believe in syndromes." Furthermore, good and evil are profoundly complicated concepts. They seem to sit uneasily at both the boundary separating "ethics" from "religion," and also at the center of each of them. Clearly, they are categories that are needed by ethics insofar as it is an evaluative discipline. But they seem unsatisfied to remain merely evaluative terms – they seem to point beyond their evaluative function towards a metaphysically realist dimension.

But perhaps the language of good and evil may still be a language that we want to keep around. Yet a willingness to do so is inadequate unless we can answer some questions about just *how* to keep it around. And this means coming to terms with some fairly fundamental questions about what we mean when we use the terms *good* and *evil*. What is the nature of evil and good? Are these terms that inevitably raise theological questions? Is "evil" evil only from our partial perspective? Is evil just a necessary complement or contrast to goodness – in such a way that you cannot have one without the other? Does the good play a role in evil, or is evil totally outside and opposed to the good? Is goodness itself something we can discern from the world directly, or must it be something we see only in God? How is goodness, moral goodness, related to religious sanctity? Questions about evil will lead us to ask about the nature and meaning of the good, and even God, and vice versa. These are the questions we are facing here, near the end of this book.

Evil

How can we see evil in human terms? Let us return for a moment to the puzzle of the figure of Hitler. Movies struggle to depict even the adult Hitler as *human*, as something other than a demonic force. But when they do, they are criticized for it. This is odd, because speaking abstractly, the culture seems unable or unwilling to think about evil in abstraction. And this is the problem – how to connect up the abstract metaphysical category of "evil" with the concrete reality of actual human beings. For, as the Russian poet Joseph Brodsky has said, "the most interesting thing about evil is that it is wholly human." If we cannot make sense of that, then we are seriously in trouble.

And perhaps we are. Our culture seems to be losing its ability to understand and respond to the realities of suffering and evil. A gulf has opened up in our culture between the visibility of evil and the intellectual resources available for coping with it. We are undertaking, or at least witnessing, a "process of unnaming evil." This forgetting of evil has important and potentially disastrous practical effects. We know neither how to resist nor how to suffer evil: the presence or the awareness of real evil bewilders us, leaves us speechless, unable to respond to it in any real way.

Why would we want to keep talking about evil? After all, there are reasonable worries about this language. There is a legitimate and deep challenge posed to thinking about evil – the worry is that it homogenizes what should be kept apart. We should not try to connect in a single concept the gas chambers of Auschwitz and a father who slaps his child. Essentially, this challenges the idea that the language of evil can pick out anything useful for us to worry about – whether it can do any work apart from labeling people we don't like, or acts about which we feel guilty. Perhaps, some thinkers suggest, it's best if we simply drop the word entirely. Perhaps "evil" is itself evil.

On the other hand, the language can be defended. For many criticisms of the language of evil are criticisms of its misuse, which are generalized into total rejections of this language. Certainly, it's true that the language of evil has been misused to demonize people, to warrant annihilating them, especially during wartime. But we shouldn't be so ready to demonize "evil" itself, to *jettison* this part of our moral language because it is susceptible to abuse. We must not disarm ourselves of this powerful conceptual device in our moral armory.

If that is so, how should we employ these terms? What use can they have for us? There are two dimensions to this issue that we will directly discuss. First, there is the question of the meaning, scope, and significance of the human capacity for evil – what it means that humans can be evil, and how far they can go wrong. Second, there is the question of the role of evil in the divine plan – how evil exists in relation to God, as something the divine affirms, uses, or opposes in creation. As we will see, the differences within the traditions are often just as dramatic as the differences between them.

Judaism

The etymological roots of the word "Satan" are very revealing. The word *shaitan* in the proto-semitic language originally meant "rival." In a way, the story of all three of the traditions' grappling with the idea of evil is the story of their grappling with the metaphysical connotations of this root. Is "Satan," or the evil Satan is taken to represent, most fundamentally a *rival* to God – a peer deity or equally fundamental metaphysical fact that simply opposes the deity we know as God? If so, the world is caught in the midst of a struggle between equally powerful rival forces, one good one evil, with the ultimate outcome fundamentally up in the air. The story of these traditions is the attempt to understand evil as some sort of dissent from the fundamental structure of the cosmos, but *not* a free-standing rival.

Consider the first story of evil and disobedience, in Genesis, the story of Adam and Eve. The function of this story in Judaism differs dramatically from its function in Christianity. In Judaism, the story does not bespeak the calamitous Fall of humanity into sin, it does not tell the story of the *origins* of evil, the introduction of sin into the world (Jews would say, evil was already in the world in the form of the serpent, or in the temptation to which the serpent called Eve's attention). Rather, it is just the chronologically first instance of a depressing pattern that will repeat itself throughout history, namely, the discovery that one is not as morally righteous as one thought one was, that humans can succumb to temptations that they would upon reflection resist, and the moral fallout that inevitably accompanies, even enables, that discovery. It is the story of Genesis 3:

> Now the serpent was more subtle than any other wild creature that the Lord God had made. He said to the woman, "Did God say, 'You shall not eat of any tree of the garden'?" And the woman said to the serpent, "We may eat of the fruit of the trees of the garden; but God said, 'You shall not eat of the fruit of the tree which is in the middle of the garden, nor shall you touch it, or you shall die.'" But the serpent said to the woman, "You will not die. For God knows that when you eat of it your eyes will be opened, and you will be like God, knowing good and evil."

So when the woman saw that the tree was good for food, and that it was a delight to the eyes, and that the tree was to be desired to make one wise, she took of its fruit and ate; and she also gave some to her husband, and he ate.

Then the eyes of both were opened, and they knew that they were naked; and they sewed fig leaves together and made loincloths for themselves.

And they heard the sound of the Lord God walking in the garden in the cool of the evening, and the man and his wife hid themselves from the presence of the Lord God among the trees of the garden.

But the Lord God called to the man, and said to him, "Where are you?" And he said, "I heard the sound of you in the garden, and I was afraid, because I was naked; and I hid myself." He said, "Who told you that you were naked? Have you eaten of the tree of which I commanded you not to eat?" The man said, "The woman whom you gave to be with me, she gave me fruit of the tree, and I ate." Then the Lord God said to the woman, "What is this that you have done?" The woman said, "The serpent beguiled me, and I ate."

The Lord God said to the serpent, "Because you have done this, cursed are you above all cattle, and above all wild animals; upon your belly you shall go, and dust you shall eat all the days of your life. I will put enmity between you and the woman, and between your seed and hers; he shall strike your head, and you shall strike his heel." To the woman he said, "I will greatly multiply your pain in childbearing; in pain you shall bring forth children, yet your desire shall be for your husband, and he shall rule over you." And to Adam he said, "Because you have listened to the voice of your wife, and have eaten of the tree of which I commanded you, 'You shall not eat of it,' cursed is the ground because of you: in toil you shall eat of it all the days of your life; thorns and thistles it shall bring forth to you; and you shall eat the plants of the field. By the sweat of your face you shall eat bread until you return to the ground, for out of it you were taken; you are dust, and to dust you shall return."

The man named his wife Eve, because she was the mother of all living. And the Lord God made garments of skin for Adam and for his wife, and clothed them.

Then the Lord God said, "Behold, the man has become like one of us, knowing good and evil; and now, lest he put forth his hand and take also of the tree of life, and eat, and live for ever." Therefore the Lord God sent him forth from the garden of Eden, to till the ground from which he was taken. He drove out the man; and at the east of the garden of Eden he placed the cherubim, and a flaming sword which turned every way, to guard the way to the tree of life.

So, behind (or at least at the beginning) of all three of these traditions' understandings of evil is this story in Genesis, the disobedience of Adam and Eve, their illicit acquisition of the knowledge of good and evil, *tov* and *ra*.

But we should note the mysteriousness of this knowledge as the locus of evil. This "knowledge of good and evil" appears four times in this story (2:9, 3:5, 3:17, 3:22) and is a curious location for the origins of human fault. Here "good and evil" seems to mean a kind of knowledge that encompasses all things – not just the meaning of these two terms, but more like "from alpha to omega," or for an earlier generation, "from soup to nuts." And yet the term still seems loaded with a meaning both ominous and opaque. Why is it the *knowledge* of good and evil that is the problem?

And of all the forms of knowledge that might cause a fall from grace, why would it be the knowledge of good and evil? Why, that is, is *this* the knowledge that gets Adam and Eve expelled from the Garden?

One clue is in the term *knowing* that is used here. The Hebrew root is *yd'*, or *yada*. This is not simply an abstract conceptual knowledge. This is "knowing" in the sense that knowing is used in the Bible with a sexual connotation. It designates an intimate experience, more than a merely intellectual acquaintance. Such knowledge brings with it a certain kind of maturity, perhaps; but a flawed maturity. Perhaps all such human maturity is accidental and reluctant; perhaps any real wisdom contains within itself a certain ambivalence about the cost incurred in gaining that wisdom. Very few are the 20-year-olds who want to be 80; but many 80-year-olds are at least sometimes interested in being 20 again. Innocence doesn't look so bad from the side of experience.

This knowledge is both accomplishment and burden, blessing and curse, but mostly curse. For Judaism, however, it is not in itself the actual *origin* of the metaphysical reality of evil, the singular entry-point of sin into human history (as it arguably is in Christianity). Those origins lie in the fundamental structures of human creation itself. Humans find themselves always already engaged with good and evil.

For the rabbis, indeed, this condition is signified in the scriptures themselves. In Genesis 2:7, the Bible states that God formed (*vayyitzer*) man. The spelling of this word is unusual, because it uses two "Yods" (the "y" sound in *vayyitzer*). There is also a doubled consonant in *levavekha* (Deuteronomy 6:5), "with all your heart." From these two observations, the rabbis inferred that these two letters represent two different inclinations, or "impulses" (*yetzer*), that God created in humans: a good impulse (the *yetzer ha tov*) and an evil impulse (the *yetzer ha ra*). The *yetzer ha tov* is something like what we call "conscience," an inner sense that alerts you when you consider violating God's law. (Interestingly, the *yetzer ha tov*, some sources argue, blossoms in the human at age 13, which is the point at which a Jewish boy becomes an adult man, reading from the Torah scroll and beginning to observe the commandments.)

The *yetzer ha ra* is a more murky concept. It is part of the human's created nature, innate in the human from the womb; as Genesis says, "the *yetzer* of the human heart is *ra* from youth" (Genesis 8:21). And yet – or perhaps because of this – it is not itself a demonic, utterly unnatural impulse, expressing anarchic hostility to God's creation; rather, it seems more rooted in self-interest, as an expression of the idea that creatures will naturally take special interest in their own well-being. The Talmud says that it is the *yetzer ha ra* that allows humans to build a house, marry, have children, or engage in business.

Some thinkers suggest that the language of "evil" is too loaded a category here, and that it is better translated as the "bad impulse." While we will not follow their terminological proposal, the idea behind it – that we must be very clear on the metaphysical and theological connotations of our terms – is certainly right and something we need to keep in mind. The idea here seems to be that evil is not supernatural, but wholly a function of our natural created being, which can, when unbalanced by other parts of our nature, lead us astray and cause great damage. Again, the tradition offers a quite sober view of malice: a profoundly non-dramatic, anti-metaphysical understanding, as a powerful but wholly mundane reality. Evil could serve as a challenge that humans must confront, but it would not *overwhelm* humans. In particular the Jewish people would suffer repeated persecutions, but they would never become so extreme as to threaten that people's existence. It gets at something important, something that the Jewish tradition builds on in profound ways.

On this account, evil is not so much an abstract philosophical problem as it is a practical challenge to those afflicted by it. By and large, on this understanding, evil should be faced as a challenge whose successful overcoming will strengthen and deepen the person in their wisdom and faith. Not all evil can be thus understood, of course; but in general, this is how traditional Jewish thought teaches its adherents how to confront evil.

As such a practical question, regarding our behavior, it falls within the scope of *halakah*, and thus becomes something intelligible that the tradition can interpret and govern. This is a distinctly Jewish proposal to respond to the problem of evil, one avoiding the Christian expectations of a complete and question-silencing and doubt-dissolving solution – expectations which lead Christians to valorize suffering caused by evil as a necessary good, a valorization that many Jews, among others, find to be extremely dangerous.

These worries about suffering in Christianity reveal interesting differences with Christian understandings of evil and suffering. On this *halakhic* view, evil and suffering are kept within human dimensions; it is a human issue, a challenge that humans are set and can overcome. In Christianity, however, evil always threatens to overwhelm the creature's capacities to resist it; it always threatens to become, that is, a theological problem, a divine reality. From this Jewish perspective, evil in Christianity always threatens to become melodrama.

By and large over the centuries this approach has remained a viable one for faithful Jews. But the twentieth century, and in particular the event of the Shoah, the Holocaust, radically challenged this traditional Jewish understanding of evil. Here it seemed that the old agreement with God had fallen apart, and that the persecution of the Jews had reached beyond traditional pogroms to become metaphysically eliminationist in character. Post-Shoah Jewish thought has struggled deeply with this challenge, and the struggle shows no signs of ceasing anytime soon. Indeed, one can say that the attempt to understand the meaning of the Shoah has been one of the most powerful inducements to Jewish thought since 1945.

This is not to suggest that Jewish thought about evil has been undermined by recent events, but rather to identify a profound challenge that Jewish thinkers are struggling with even today. As we will see next, Christian thought about evil has its own complexities and challenges to confront.

Christianity

It was the slowly dawning apprehension, among the earliest Christians, of the drama of the work of Jesus Christ, coupled with the particularly apocalyptic tenor of first-century Judaism, that made early Christians depict the human condition as darkly as they did, and represent the power of evil as dramatically as they could. First of all, there was a powerful sense of spiritual combat abroad, as we saw earlier in our discussions of war. In such an account, evil is simply more cosmic (and apocalypticism makes evil more palpably and determinately part of creation). Secondly, the very dramatic magnitude that early Christians perceived in Jesus's life, death, and resurrection seemed to demand some similarly powerful opponent over whom to triumph. St. Paul thus looked back through the history of Israel and found in the Adam and Eve story a narrative very different than the one the earlier tradition had done:

> Therefore, just as sin entered the world through one man, and death through sin, and in this way death came to all men, because all sinned – for before the law was given, sin was in the world, but sin is not reckoned when there is no law. Nevertheless, death reigned from the time of Adam to the time of Moses, even over those who did not sin by breaking a command, as did Adam, who was a type of the one to come. ... Consequently, just as one man's trespass led to condemnation for all, so one man's act of righteousness leads to justification and life for all. For just as through one man's disobedience many were made sinners, so also by one man's obedience the many will be made righteous. (Romans 5:12–14, 18–19)

The dramatic nature of sin in the Christian tradition, and the representation of evil as powerful, active, and seeking humanity's downfall, reflect in interesting ways the perception of the magnitude of Christ's saving act.

Later Christian thinkers, especially in Western Christianity, deepened and systematized this account of evil's dramatic presence, though never without making an equal effort to underscore the ultimate victory of the absolutely sovereign and good God. Preeminent here is St. Augustine, who for his work on this topic and on a few related matters (particularly the nature of divine grace and human freedom) is sometimes called the "Second Founder of the Christian Faith." Augustine made two fundamental claims about sin and evil. First, sin is the perversion of an originally wholly good human nature. Unlike Judaism, where the possibility of human temptation and failure is built into human nature from creation forward, for Augustine any mark of human weakness or frailty is a consequence of the primordial calamity of the fall of Adam and Eve. Furthermore, as perversion, human wickedness always bears, to those who understand it, the appearance of an intelligible good. For Augustine, it is impossible for someone sincerely to want to do evil just because it is evil; radical nihilism of that sort is ruled out. This is related to Augustine's second fundamental claim: namely, that evil is essentially nothing more than the privation of some fundamentally good reality. There is no "metaphysical substantiality" to evil – no rival metaphysical center of power and gravity named "evil" over against God. Satan is not fundamentally a rival to God, but rather God's rebellious servant, who nevertheless still serves God's mysterious providence. For Augustine, as God created all and called all good in Genesis 1 and 2, and as God is thus the source of all that is, there can be nothing – not even, for Augustine, Satan in "his" original (and still fundamental) creation – that is not good in God's eyes. Evil is not mere "appearance" on this account – the logic of perversion serves to secure its palpable reality – but evil is simply the lessening of being; the devils are small and puny creatures compared to the great and powerful angels they were first created to be. By such metaphysical maneuvers, the fundamental principles of the cosmos are rendered secure here from challenge.

Augustine's imaginative theological achievement was immense. But over the centuries, many Christians have felt that – as stated so barely above – his account did not do justice to the complex reality of evil and its role in the Christian narrative. These concerns and felt inadequacies have led to the development of compensating themes or images in Christian faith and practice. In particular they have organized themselves around two foci of great theological density: the sufferings of Christ, and the power of Satan in human history. We should look at both here.

First of all, popular and theological attention to the sufferings of Christ on the cross was a way to account for evil, especially by more mystical thinkers in Christianity. For Christians, the role of Christ's divinity in the crucifixion has always been a fraught theological topic. Christ as God must be sufficiently implicated in the Passion to be able to be salvifically effective; yet Christ's divine nature cannot strictly speaking suffer. How to relate these two axioms has caused no end of theological debate, and occasionally spiritual grief, in Christianity. Some have gone so far as to say that Christ is still dying or indeed in some way dead in the Godhead – incorporating suffering, even unto bare negation, into God's very being. (The great nineteenth-century German philosopher G. W. F. Hegel has been read as saying this.) The sufferings of Christ seem to function as a theological *remainder* in the tradition – just as in some mathematical problems, schoolchildren are allowed to use "remainders" in learning division of whole numbers. The degree to which one focuses on Christ's sufferings seems related to how deeply one feels the presence of evil in the world. The danger of this is that it can valorize a certain kind of suffering as the only proper response to evil, and makes suffering a route into knowing and being with God – an approach which certainly has its legitimate theological pedigree, but an approach which also can become excessive and self-abusive in theologically, not to mention morally, dangerous ways.

Others have emphasized the power of Satan as a free-standing force for evil in the world. (Sometimes this has shaded over into talking about the Antichrist, but for our purposes the two are essentially the same.) The function of such talk seems to be to articulate one's experience of the felt positivity of evil, a positivity some feel is inadequately represented in the traditional Augustinian picture. Often, people writing in this vein will use a language of seduction or captivity or enchantment to talk about the experience of evil. This approach vividly captures the experience of evil as a living, external power able to *overwhelm* humans, and is very useful in helping to draw human attention to evil and mobilize our efforts against it. But it may well serve also to undergird witch-hunts (literally as well as figuratively), and can just as easily obscure as illuminate the challenges humans face in confronting evil in the world.

Where Judaism seems to engage evil's challenges by focusing on the practice of enduring faithfully in a world of mixed good and evil – that is, in focusing on *obedience to the Law* – and Christianity insists in the face of evil on the fact that the sovereignty of God is mixed with the immanence of God – that is, focusing on *Christ* – in Islamic thought the focus is on human duties to resist the temptation and tendencies towards evil, represented in Satan, who is a profoundly rich figure in Islamic thought, as a locus of reflection on the nature of evil.

Islam

In the central Islamic moral command – which is what we may call the command to "do good and forbid evil" – the word that "good" translates is *al-mar'ruf*, which means "the well-known;" in contrast, the word for "evil" is *al-munkar*, "the unknown." Evil is unknown for God – that is, it is precisely that which God chooses *not* to "know," to become intimately acquainted with, what God passes over in indifference. But the fact that evil is "unknown" by God does not mean that evil is unknown *to* God – God is well aware of human sin, and the demonic rebellion that induced that sin. Rather, the character of evil as "unknown" means that evil harbors at its heart a vacuity of intelligibility. Since God has chosen not to "know" it in this rich sense, it is properly speaking unintelligible, much like the Christian account offered by Augustine – something that is fundamentally futile.

As in Judaism, and perhaps more ambiguously in Christianity, evil does not originate in any way with an extra-human agent; rather, the figure of Satan (Iblis) in Islam is simply a tempter who can take advantage of the human inclinations toward self-centeredness which can become evil.[1] The story of Iblis is a powerful representation of the origins of evil, perhaps the most direct such representation available in the sacred scriptures of Judaism, Christianity, and Islam. After all, in Judaism, evil is present from the beginning, and is therefore not described in its origins; similarly, while Christianity rereads the Genesis account and finds therein the origins of *human* evil, it insinuates a preexisting malevolent power through reading the serpent in the Garden as a disguise of Satan. Only in Islam do we get a direct representation of evil's origin in Satan, at several points in the Qur'an, perhaps most notably here:

> We created you, We formed you; and then We commanded the angels, "bow down before Adam," and they bowed. But not Iblis; he refused to be one of those who bow.
> God said: "What prevented you from bowing down as I commanded you?" And he said: "I am better than he: You created me from fire and him from clay."

God said: "Get down from here! Here is no place for your arrogance, Get out! You are the lowest of creatures!"

but Iblis said, "Give me respite until the day they are raised."

and God said, "You have respite."

And then Iblis said, "Because you have put me in the wrong, I shall lie in wait for them on Your straight path; I will assault them from the front and the back, from their right and their left; nor will you find that most of them are grateful."

Said He [God], "Get out! You are disgraced and expelled! I swear I shall fill Hell with you and all who follow you." (Q. 7:11–18)

The language of "bow" here is interesting – the word is derived from the Arabic *sjd*, which refers to the positions taken in ritual Islamic prayer, *salat*. Iblis is asked by God to worship Adam; he refuses; and from this rebellious refusal all evil proceeds.

At times Iblis is also named *ash-Shaytan*, "Satan," though at other times *ash-Shaytan* is used to refer to all the forces of evil under Iblis's leadership, and sometimes it is hard to tell. To many Muslim scholars, the apparent lexical confusion here has a philosophical point: Satan is ambiguously a personal agent in much Islamic thought – at times Iblis appears as an agent, with desires and designs on humanity, but at times Iblis seems better described as an impersonal force, a power in the cosmos that humans experience as preying on their weakness and seducing them (but is it they who convince themselves that they are seduced? who seduce themselves into believing in their own seduction?). The value of the impersonal representation of Iblis is that, as an impersonal force, Iblis is better understood to saturate all dimensions of human existence; Satan is potentially everywhere and anywhere, in our deficiencies large and small, urging us to wash ourselves hastily and to ignore the cries of those being murdered by others. Either way, Iblis is fundamentally and finally merely destructive, against all the goods of God's creation – an agent, or a force, committed ultimately, in the most literal way, to nothing.

The majority tradition in Islamic thought gives a powerful and stark depiction of Iblis as a failed creature, a once-glorious being now fallen into the uttermost darkness, a catastrophe of a creature who now seeks desperately to drag others down into that catastrophe – not so much for company as to master them, and avoid further the unavoidable recognition that this fallen angel still serves God as tempter, that – unbelievably – evil itself serves the good.

But there is another tradition in Islamic thought on Iblis, one represented by a number of early Sufi writers, and carried forward by other later thinkers. These writers suggest that Iblis was, or perhaps is, the perfect monotheist – the one angel who would not bow down and worship Adam when God created him. For them, by and large, this interpretation of Iblis is part of a larger mystical worldview where all is in God's hands. God's will for Iblis is not violated by Iblis's refusal to bow before humanity; God's will is rather fulfilled by it.

This strand can be seen as in one sense offering a "minority report" on Satan in the Islamic tradition. But it can also be seen as insinuating a complication into the main story that, for those willing to follow its thinking about Iblis, and the evil and rebellion against God that Iblis represents, offers deeper insight into the nature of evil as the faith professes it. Evil's origin here is not completely irrational, not simply a matter of excessive self-love or a rude sense of pride; rather, it is due to a misplaced but plausible sense of *right value*. After all, Iblis cannot worship what is *below* him, or what is *other* than God. Iblis is offended – perhaps for God's sake, even – that God has commanded spiritual beings to prostrate themselves before material ones, and that God has commanded anyone to worship anything other than God. It is, then, precisely Iblis's prim theological propriety that is the problem. Iblis falls, driven by a proximately noble and worthy motive – one that is not irrational, but one grounded on a misplaced assessment of the right order of values.

A General Statement about Evil in the Monotheistic Traditions

With Islam's repesentation of Iblis we have reached the end of our sketch of how these three Abrahamic traditions think about evil. But perhaps we can now notice something interesting that they have in common – namely, a powerful drive towards representing evil as something under God's sovereign, if mysterious, rule. For all three of these traditions, evil is not ultimately a metaphysical *rival* to God, but rather subordinate to God, serving God's purposes in some profound way, even while apparently in rebellion against the divine plan. This is a consequence of the triumph of monotheism, a triumph that is never fully complete in any of the traditions but is always developing. After all, the original meaning of Satan in proto-semitic – *Stn* – is simply "rival," and these traditions emerged out of a cultural melieu in the ancient Near East in which a metaphysical dualism of good and evil was always a live option. For all three of them, the choice to affirm a single God, without peer or rival, has momentous consequences for their understanding of evil – and also, as we will now see, their understanding of good.

Goodness and God

We should recognize that our reflections on evil entail that we think seriously about the nature of moral goodness and perhaps even the character of God. Is goodness an active force, or a passive object of contemplation? Is it a way to reach God, or a rival source of value that competes with God? How should we understand the relation between sanctity and goodness?

The deepest danger with losing the language of evil is that we seem inevitably to lose along with it the language of good, the language of nobility and righteousness. We lose a sense of being able to be the kinds of beings we think we are – free, responsible creatures who know what is right and can do it, at least part of the time. The battle about the language of evil is equally a battle about the language of goodness, and a battle about what kinds of creatures we are – whether morality ought to continue to be a central language we use.

The difficulty here is that the language of "goodness" may present its own problems for us to struggle with. At least, that is the suggestion of some thinkers, who we look at below.

Moral saints

In thinking about this, we face another problem. We've been talking this whole time as if religion and morality are two peas in a pod. But maybe in fact morality is made more complex by religion, and vice versa, than we have acknowledged. Some philosophers put this question to us with special intensity. They ask, in effect, whether we can worship morality in the same way we can worship God.

This puts the whole point of this book into question because it makes us wonder whether there can be a "religious ethic," whether "religion" and "ethics" fit so neatly together. Susan Wolf asks this from the perspective of ethics – ought we to pursue ethics with religious devotion? Robert Adams asks this from the perspective of religion – ought we to think that ethics is what religion is all about? Let us look at them in turn.

In her essay "Moral Saints," Susan Wolf raises the question of whether morality is the sort of thing we should aim at at all. If we imagine the ideal model that these moral theories present to us as "moral saints," we find that these saints are terrifically boring, monomaniacal (focused on one thing), and lacking all the goods of ordinary life that we think are valuable.

Consider all the things that, Wolf suggests to us, moral saints cannot do. They cannot take naps because they could be licking envelopes for fund-drives. Also they are prudes – they cannot enjoy many things that we would enjoy because of the tinge of immorality that hangs about them (they could not enjoy movies like *There's Something About Mary* or *The Hangover*, for example). Furthermore, there are real non-moral goods that we think of as equally basic – sports figures, or great chefs, or great artists, or doctors, or mathematicians, or philosophers – and the moral saint is so focused on living the moral life that they cannot pursue those goods, and must practically discourage them. Furthermore, moral saints try to live their lives *wholly* out of moral reasoning – forbidding us to have any thoughts but ones that are fundamentally moral thoughts. This is, at the least, tiresome; but it may also be deeply inhuman. Much of our life is *amoral*, and we cannot wholly moralize our lives without becoming something else.

So it seems that such people would not be very fun. But would they be useful? That is, perhaps we might want others to be such moral fanatics? Not so, Wolf says; for in making them so, we would lose the many non-moral goods that other people provide: style, flair, humor, good cooking, excellent car repair service, superior lawyering.

The problem is not with the sort of moral theory we accept, but with the way we accept it – "The flaws of a perfect master of a moral theory need not reflect flaws in the intramoral content of the theory itself."[2] What we should do instead, according to Wolf, is refuse to grant moral sainthood absolute sovereignty over our other life-plans; we ought not to require an overly moralized understanding of our selves.

Robert Adams was provoked enough by Wolf to write a response essay entitled, simply, "Saints." Adams agrees with Wolf that "we ought not to make a religion of morality."[3] But then he also points out how Wolf's account misses what he sees as some important issues. For example, to make morality into our religion is to idolatrize morality, to be, in Christian terms, a Pharisee. Saints are primarily *religious* figures, not moral. (This is why Adams resists Wolf's phrase "*moral* saints.")

Adams thinks that Wolf's account of "saints" improperly tars saints with the narrowness and vacuity that more aptly applies to prudes. Adams wants to tease apart Wolf's association of prudes and saints. Saintliness is not moral perfectionism – it is more a matter of holiness. And, for Adams, holiness is only at best obliquely related to moral goodness. Saints are not better than us, more morally perfect. If anything they are less so, or experience themselves as less so, just because they are so profoundly aware of their own sins and the need for their own personal repentance. Quite often, a person who we would see as a saint is simply operating on another frequency altogether. As Flannery O'Connor said, "Ye shall know the truth and the truth shall make you odd." Crucial to many forms of sainthood, Adams thinks, is "an exceptional capacity for joy."[4] That seems like a sheer assertion to me, ungrounded in any particular facts; perhaps it would be closer to the center of things to say that saints seem especially to apprehend the idea of participation in God's plan – and God is larger than morality (avoid the question of whether or not God must obey morality as we do – that's another issue). Saints are more alive to God, and so more vividly respond to God's call – so are more themselves in all their idiosyncrasy and less the prefabricated selves we fashion for ourselves in our consumer society.

If saintliness applies to religion and not morality (because morality is *not* religion), what does this mean? It means that religious people do not, according to Adams, live their lives merely by moral scorekeeping, but actually admit that there are other values that God (or the gods, or what-have-they) affirms *alongside* explicitly moral values. Thus one of the highest wisdoms of morality, for Adams (and also Wolf), is knowing when morality ceases to be relevant – when morality can be ignored.

Conclusion

Both evil and good, then – or more precisely the knowledge of evil and good – sit uneasily, perhaps, beside the worship of God for these three traditions. Perhaps the knowledge of good and evil is a tragic fact about us, and a contingent fact – unimaginable to us not to be without it, but in fact a sign, an ultimate sign, of our captivity to a way of living in this world that in fact didn't have to be the way we live in this world. To know of evil is to know of the way that God does not want, and does not intend, for creation to go; it is to have a certain kind of knowledge whose very possession harms us, in a way, by dislodging us from our trust in God. And to know of goodness is to know of goodness as an option, a possibility, that we must choose; it is to know goodness, in a way, as the serpent promised, to know "like God" knows, to be a rival, in a way, to God; which is one way of understanding the fundamental fault of Iblis, in God's court, at creation, at the beginning of all time, at the beginning of good and evil itself.

Far from being a simple blessing to human life religiously or morally, then, the knowledge of good and evil, *tov* and *ra*, the known and the unknown, may well be a kind of knowledge that we are not properly meant to have; a truly melancholic knowledge. And as the example of the saints teaches us, at least as Robert Adams would have them teach us, our happiness, and our blessedness, as these traditions understand it, may lie centrally in leaving that knowledge behind – not before we have acquired it, for we live in a world where its acquisition, however painful, is inevitable, necessary, and useful; but in somehow, miraculously, graciously, getting beyond it, into a fresh apprehension of God's plan for us, an apprehension that is, because the plan also is *beyond* good and evil.

Conclusion

What's So Funny 'bout Peace, Love, and Understanding?

There are no questions more urgent than the naïve ones.
  (Wislawa Szymborska, "The Turn of the Century")

We have reached the end of this work. There is much we have left undone. But of the making of books there is no end, and as regards our topic, we approach a genuinely adequate coverage only as we approach infinity. Given the amount of your time that this book has already taken, it seems the better part of scholarly propriety now at last to step back and offer some final comparative observations.

Too much of the time, humans act out of their fears rather than their hopes. Too much of the time, our hopes remain unexpressed, inarticulate, inchoate, even to ourselves. So from time to time it is worth while to stop what we are doing, step back and ask: what do we hope to see one day?

For those humans who are in religious traditions that have a conception of Heaven, this question can sound abashing. It sounds childish to talk about what we imagine Heaven to be like. But our imaginations of Heaven – just like atheists' imaginings of a perfect, this-worldly utopia – reveal much about what we value and how we order our values.

With that said, then, let me tell you about how I imagine Heaven to be. Heaven, when I imagine it, is a great dinner party. Yes, God is there, and humanity spends much of its days in direct and central communion with God. But once in a while (stay with me here) some humans go off on their own, to a small, secluded chamber, and share a meal together. It is a party of friends – maybe six or eight or so – sitting around a table. The meal begins in late afternoon and lasts long into the night, lit by candles. The windows surrounding them – open to refreshing breezes – first show the sunset, then become filled with the sparkle of a starry night, as the meal proceeds with many courses, none of which are so large as to leave the diners thinking they're too stuffed to go on. Instead, over wine for those who will have it, and fruit juice, and tea, and cool, fresh water – culminating in small glass cups of dark, sharp, spicy Arabian coffee (magically decaffeinated!) over dessert plates – the diners talk, and talk and talk, about all manner of things, ranging across the whole scale of human existence, from the best way to dry socks, say, to the ultimate and ineffable nature of God, and God's purposes in creating creation.

What may be odd about this vision of Heaven, at first glance – well, you may think there are many things odd about this vision of Heaven, but one thing that may be odd – is that there is a genuine diversity of views around the table. Not just cultural views, but in some sense *religious* views. I'm not saying that there's any wild pluralism, with dour Scotch Presbyterians sitting down next to befeathered and murderous Aztecs; but there are at least representatives of the three traditions we've studied in this book around that table. Anyone who is in one of these traditions and who has shared the conviviality of a meal with good friends who are members of another faith – a Passover Seder, say, or the feast breaking the fast of a day during Ramadan, or a Christmas dinner, or just an ordinary meal on a typical weekend – you know what I mean: it's not clear if the meal or the conversation is more delicious or nourishing.

I know what you're thinking. Only someone as truly geeky as me would find this so exciting. And that's got to be true to a degree; after all, my idea of a good time can involve snuggling up in front of a warm fire with a book on late Stoic theories of the emotions. So yes, I admit it, I don't get out as much as I should, and maybe my excessive interest in footnotes does require clinical help.

But maybe, if you think this is ridiculous, maybe part of the problem lies with you, too. Maybe you haven't been to that many truly good dinner parties.

Think about that. What are the questions you want to ask, you want to have answered, even if you don't often ask yourself these questions? In my experience no one *doesn't* think about the matters that a conversation like that would cover – the value of one's work for one's life, the nature and health of one's relationships, what brought you to belief, what challenges your beliefs, what questions remain unanswered – maybe even unasked – by you, how far we can "read" God's nature off of the details of creation – a million questions and issues appear as possible topics. And who better to have the conversation with, than good friends with sufficient distance from yourself not to be implicated too much in what you're saying to become defensive, yet committed enough to you not to find it boring? And among those friends, wouldn't you want some who are significantly different from you, just to hear their perspective on what you all talk about? Who wouldn't want that?

Anyway, an image like that has been roaming through my head throughout the writing of this book. It is a beautiful image, I think. And, if I can say it without sentimentality or mawkishness, it is something our world could desperately use.

Too often, these traditions are at odds. Too often, incomprehension, hostility, and suspicion mark their dealings with each other. Too often, they are the source of the problems we face. And we have tried to be frank about those problems in this book. But were they inhabited in a different way – were believers more able to be patient with one another, and yes, act not out of fear but of hope – what power would these three faiths, acting together in our world, possess to help heal the world in the ways that all three faiths confess God wants it healed. Of course, these are three very different traditions. But threaded together, these three "palpable histories of holiness" could make a nearly unbreakable cord. Think of all the good that could be done in the world; think of all the great joy that could be found; think of all the wonderful, fractious, endless arguments and conversations. What a rich world it would offer us.

In fact, I would say something more than that such an invigorated conversation between the three is possible; I think it is inevitable. They have too much in common to leave each other alone, especially in a world that is growing ever closer together. And yet their strengths and convictions are diverse enough never to fold into one another, as well as to enable those who are gripped by them to stand firm in their faiths.

Home: "Arguments you can't escape"

Why did you read this book? What did you think it would do for you? What did you want to get out of it? It is a presumptuous book. It tries to teach you things it presumes you already know. It presumes to tell you how you already, if only pre-consciously, think about yourself. It aims to make you more yourself – more yourself than you already are. What are you? The book is in many ways a wager, built on a certain answer to that question – that you are arguments. That is why I quoted the contemporary poet Dave Smith in the Introduction to this book: "what's home / but arguments you can't escape?"

The book has tried to teach you that who you really are is a snarl of arguments about who you should be, and what you should do, arguments which it is the task of a lifetime to untangle, understand, and evaluate. It has tried to do that by using a set of moral problems to help us explore the resources available to us in a number of traditions of religious thought. So let me say something about both the idea of "moral problems" and the idea of "religious ethics" as they've functioned here.

We have tried to look at a series of moral problems in order to better inherit these arguments we can't escape. Of course, it is slightly deceptive to call them "moral *problems*" because they are not simply a series of discrete independent problems, but are also different facets of the same problem – the problem of morality itself. The central moral problem that all of these have gestured at, is single and simple: *Is morality real?* Are we the kinds of beings who are affected properly by these sorts of cares? And are these religious traditions right in thinking that the reality of morality reflects an energy and purposiveness – a personality, a person – not immediately visible in the physical make-up of this world? And what sorts of beings are we, and what sort of world is this, if right and wrong do exist, and if the law reveals a lawgiver?

In affirming the reality of morality, we've made two claims about morality. First, we have insisted that morality is pervasive. It saturates our existence – it has something to say on pretty much everything. We are always confronted by moral issues. (Not only in our work, but even in our relaxation – as the discussion of work and leisure was supposed to make plain to you.)

Second, we have affirmed that morality is practical. Because its problems are so intimate to our lives, we struggle with them every day. So again, we have to see the explicit "problems" as connected to each other and not discrete and isolated quandaries, puzzles we are set as in a math exam.

But there may be limits on the applicability to our lives of morality in general, and the special case of "moral problems" in particular. Hence, our reflections must steer between two extremes. First of all, not all heroism is moral heroism – not everything ought to be moralized; artists can suffer terribly for their art, or athletes for their sports, or scholars for their studies, and we ought to praise them for that; but we shouldn't see such suffering as praiseworthy in a particularly moral way, not unless something of clear moral weight is involved.

Secondly, neither is morality most basically heroic – morality doesn't only appear in moments of moral heroism, though those do happen: think of the lone Chinese citizen standing against the army tanks after the 1989 Tiananmen Square massacre; or the passengers on United Flight 93 on September 11. Moral heroism is usually only required when something has gone horrendously wrong, when morality as a whole has broken down. So *pray not to be put to the test in your own lives*; pray that your own moral lives will be lived as much as possible in the ordinary routines of life, that your own "moral problems" will be those we find in our daily life and work. That's task enough.

Morality is not most fundamentally about making us moral superheroes. It is about helping us *flourish*, both outwardly (in the sense of knowing how to do the right thing) and inwardly (in the sense of being happy and well). It is about the ordinary living of ordinary people. Almost all morality takes place in quite quiet, daily living. Those activities can demand all of our moral ability, and can exercise our character to the fullest.

The religious traditions recognize this, in their various ways, as well; the etymological root of the word "salvation" is *salus*, or health, in Latin, and both Judaism and Islam find worship of God to be part of what it is that completes human nature, without which we go wrong in predictable, and predictably dismaying, ways. None of these traditions suggests that finally the human is best fulfilled by existing in fundamental contradiction to the world; of the three of them, Christianity has the most tendencies in that direction, but even there the anti-worldly tendencies do not finally have control of the tradition: they are opposed, and overwhelmed, by the fundamental Christian idea that God became incarnate in Jesus Christ to redeem humanity from their sin, and will return again to give the elect life everlasting.

All that is to say that we should think about moral reflection as an ordinary activity, something we do every day of our lives. This is why we attempt to bring our everyday lives into the light of ethical reflection. So in contrast, perhaps, to what you might have thought going into this book, I hope you can see now that moral reflection is not an occasional or special activity you engage in only when you find yourself in situations of moral perplexity. In fact, it is often the case that we get in those situations only because we have not been thoughtful enough about where we have been going.

Agency

We face the problem of being in the condition of not exercising our moral muscles nearly enough. The ancient philosopher Epicurus had it right when he said, "Most people are in a coma when they are at rest and mad when they act." Most of us live our lives outside of ourselves, in the routinization of our days, and never – or only very, very occasionally – stop what we are doing and ask what it is, or why we are doing it. We very rarely, that is, *wake up* to ourselves. There are many forces that can pressure or tempt you into assuming that morality need not be something you think about a lot. We live in a culture which seems increasingly to want us to understand ourselves either as *consumers*, choosing lifestyles the way we choose clothes, without giving thought to how the way that we live shapes our characters; or as *victims*, understanding ourselves as inescapably enslaved to our past or our physical make-up – determined either genetically or genealogically, biologically or biographically, in any event not responsible for what we do or who we are.

Both of these visions are problematic, the first because it offers us only the most trivialized and debased understanding of freedom, of what it is to be a human agent; the second because it obliterates the idea of freedom itself, propagating the faith that who I am is just what other people, or my biology, makes me. Both visions eclipse the whole idea of moral responsibility, our ability to accept responsibility for what we do – the cornerstone not only of our moral language, and our understanding of ourselves as able to choose good or evil, but also of our understanding of ourselves as free beings, creatures with a certain agential dignity that cannot be traduced.

This book has tried to help you more fully appropriate such a model of agency. And to do that, I have tried to make you more *intelligently judgmental* as well. That is to say, I have tried to make you both more *judgmental* – better able to make moral judgments, and more comfortable using a moral vernacular, and thinking with moral concepts – and I have also tried to make you more *intelligently* judgmental – more sophisticated and supple in your thinking, by becoming more aware of how complicated and contestable (from within a tradition and from other positions) your moral deliberation can be.

Real judgment, and real moral deliberation, is difficult and precarious. It is easier to be intellectually lazy, to be apathetic, to insist that all is a matter of opinion, and there is no final answer to be had. But this is incoherent; for even if one tries to restrict the indictment to metaphysical or theological views, to say that such views are merely opinion seems, on first glance, itself the sort of metaphysical claim that it means to dismiss. If all is opinion, then that statement is too.

More than that, the experience of these claims tells against them: the "all" is not opinion, as our very use of that "all" so tersely suggests. These questions speak to us in fundamental ways. We need to ask them, to give voice to the wonder they express. And we find we need to judge, for not all is opinion. Life is too serious for that.

Religious Ethics

If one good route into thinking about morality is via explicit problems, some of the richest resources for such deliberation are found in the treasures given us by millennia of reflection by philosophers, theologians, and ordinary folk, the riches of *traditions*. And most of these traditions historically, and also for most of you, are fundamentally *religious* traditions. We've tried to inherit this as well, by acquainting ourselves with a variety of visions and arguments from the religious traditions we've studied. The readings have tried to give you some idea both of the diversity among religious traditions on moral matters, and the diversity within those traditions on those same matters.

What we've seen, again and again, is that these traditions are not settled, and are not found most vividly in their conclusions, but in their questions, in the way that they carry on debates among one another and even within themselves. Think about human sexuality, or war, or lying, or the environment. We do not most basically receive settled conclusions on these matters from the traditions – we rather receive unsettling arguments. And if we are faithful, we inhabit those arguments, and unsettle them further by so inhabiting them. We become them, in an enlivening way.

Yet it is not just that the traditions are unsettled in some of their views regarding the issues that this book has discussed; they're equally unsettled as regards the *appropriateness* of this book's very approach to these issues as well. They raise the suspicion that this book's very method inevitably distorts the nature of these traditions, and at least inadvertently encourages an understanding of religious traditions as a sort of cafeteria of moral and religious perspectives, from which one can pick and choose at will. The contemporary pundit David Brooks has a good name for this; he calls it "flexidoxy." Such suspicions ultimately amount to the charge that a work of this nature, comparing traditions without explicitly privileging one over the others, is not only an exercise in bad faith – because the book's author certainly has his own views on these matters – but is also ultimately in the service of a consumeristic picture of humanity. So, the worry goes, *my* real tradition, in writing this book, and yours, in reading it, is really consumerism.

I do not pretend to have a finally satisfying theoretical response to these worries. I think they are real worries. They're forced on us by the fact that we inhabit an institution fundamentally designed for the Enlightenment, namely, the modern university. And yet many of us profess faiths whose origins lie much further back in time than that, and whose commitments this institution, and other ones just like it around the world, work, at least partially, and intentionally or not, in quite profound ways to oppose and undermine.

Yet we are children of both worlds – of the Enlightenment and of tradition – and if we are to better understand our heritage, we will have to do so from within these conflicts, not outside them. So here again, I do not propose an answer to this challenge, but I recommend your continuing grappling with it, ideally at least for the rest of your lives. Hopefully, in a way, as the rest of your lives. But that is as it should be. "What's home / but arguments you can't escape?"

This book has been about teaching you about your homes – both philosophically and religiously, your homes as moral agents, the languages of moral and religious conviction and orientation within which you reflect on what it means to flourish as moral agents, and not just as consumers or victims – and historically, your homes in particular traditions of moral reflection, many of which are religious traditions. This is what I mean when I say that this book has tried to help you become more fully yourself – the real, thoughtful selves you can be, not the kind of selves we are all too often content to be. Hopefully, this book has enriched your repertoire of moral and religious resources so that you may better struggle with these questions now and in years to come.

But I do not deceive myself, nor should you be deceived, that what this book has accomplished, even at best, has done more than scratch the surface of this task. What we have done, we have done too quickly, too glibly, often sloppily and always too shallowly. And we have left much undone; beyond the accidents of my own authorial failings, and your own failures as readers, there have been many issues and topics we have simply not discussed at all, because of the limits of space and of our own – *my* own – capacities.

It remains for you to try to continue the trajectories of thought laid out in this book – to widen and deepen them as you carry these questions forward in your life. This book doesn't "pay off" now – indeed, if this book were in any real way now *over* for you, it has failed to do what it most centrally set out to try to do. More basically than equipping you with knowledge – beyond giving you all sorts of neat arguments – I have been trying in this book to *make you think*: to wake you up to the fact that *you live in a world that asks something of you*, that asks you to be, or to become, someone you are initially not: namely, yourself.

You can go through life asleep to these demands; and I have no doubt that some of you will. I do not, I cannot, speak to you here. I speak to those of you who may one day wake up, and those of you who may already be awake. I cannot tell who of you will be awakened in this way, and neither can you. Nor can I provide any useful clues as to what causes such wakefulness. All I can do is know that for some of you these words will, today or some day, have a meaning. And you will know that you have begun to think, and to wonder. As the ancient Hellenistic philosopher Plotinus said:

> Therefore it cannot be said or written … but we [the teachers] speak and write, sending on to it and wakening from words towards contemplation, as if showing the way to [one] who wishes to see something. For teaching extends to the road and the passage, but the vision is the work of one who has decided to see.[1]

The work that is left to you, the work I cannot *but* leave to you, is the work of vision. Or, if not of seeing, of hearing – of being called to live; as Yahweh called to Moses out of the burning bush, as Jesus called Lazarus out of the tomb, as Gibreel called Muhammad to recite: "Iqra!"

The Roman Catholic writer G. K. Chesterton was once asked by a low-church woman if he believed in the practice of infant baptism. He replied: "*Believe* in it, madam? Why, I've *seen* it!" It's a joke, but a deep one. For we can see that these traditions do revivify their adherents at times – even while at other times, or for other adherents, they render them dead to the world. Perhaps the ultimate credibility of these three traditions lies in their capacity to bring their adherents back to life, from a condition that, from their reinvigorated perspective, is visible to them as nothing more than a walking death, the life of zombies.

This revivification is at least as much a religious task as it is a moral one – as much about existence, and the nature of being, as about how you treat others – for it is a work of piety, of being called to attention, to attend to what is before you. Indeed, you will not be necessarily more free – for feeling obliged may not seem like what you today take to be freedom; nor more powerful, for you may feel captive to the good, enslaved by your obligations, to a course of action that you would not have chosen on your own; but you will be more *real* as moral agents, if you can bring to thought – however clumsily, however haltingly and awkwardly – the central questions that this book has returned to again and again: what ought I to do? How ought I to live? Who or what is calling me, and in what way am I responsible to that call?

We think of answers as more important than questions. But that may be our greatest mistake. Perhaps we are most alive in living inside questions – in wondering, and in wonder. This book has been premised on the hope that that hypothesis is right. Whether or not that hope proves true depends on you.

In the first chapter of this book I said something I will say again now. This book is not about making you good, or even better. But I also want to clarify – even modify – that somewhat. If it cannot make you good, it at least hopes to try to make you less prone to be a zombie in your life, and hence more able to become good, more able to incorporate and in turn incarnate the good in your lives – or, at the least, to know what the good, and perhaps also God, *could* be.

The rest, as always, is up to you.

Notes

Introduction

1 David Burrell, *Faith and Freedom: An Interfaith Perspective* (Oxford: Blackwell, 2004), p. 257.
2 Michael Oakeshott, *On Human Conduct* (Oxford: Clarendon Press, 1975), p. 8.

1 God and Morality

1 Frederick Buechner, *Wishful Thinking: A Theological ABC* (San Francisco: Harper San Francisco, 1993 [1973]), p. 174.
2 *Euthyphro*, 10a.
3 In later dialogues he challenges the simple dichotomization, suggesting that the good and God may be more intimately interrelated than this allows. So the Euthyphro dilemma may already be superseded in its author's own lifetime.
4 H. Richard Niebuhr, *The Responsible Self: An Essay in Christian Moral Philosophy* (New York: Harper Collins, 1963), p. 20.
5 *Ibid.*, p. 27.
6 *Ibid.*, p. 30.
7 *Ibid.*, p. 34.
8 Kenneth Burke, *The Philosophy of Literary Form: Studies in Symbolic Action*, 2nd edn. (Baton Rouge: Louisiana State University Press, 1967 [1941]), pp. 110–11.
9 *The Responsible Self*, p. 35.
10 *Ibid.*, p. 35.

2 Jewish Ethics

1 Daniel Boyarin, *A Radical Jew: Paul and the Politics of Identity* (Berkeley: University of California Press, 1994), p. 252.

2 *Ibid.*, p. 255.
3 *Tractate Sanhedrin, Tosefta 13*, "Those who have no share in the world to come."
4 Daniel Boyarin, *Border Lines: The Partition of Judaeo-Christianity* (Philadelphia: University of Pennsylvania Press, 2004), p. 13.
5 *Genesis Rabbah*, 26.6.
6 *Bava Bathra*, 12a.
7 *Avodah Zarah*, chapter 1, 3b.
8 *Babylonian Talmud, Tractate Sanhedrin*, 98a.
9 See Aharon Lichtenstein, "Does Jewish Tradition Recognize an Ethic Independent of Halakha?" pp. 62–88 in Marvin Fox, *Modern Jewish Ethics: Theory and Practice* (Columbus: Ohio State University Press, 1975).
10 Menachem Marc Kellner, *Contemporary Jewish Ethics* (New York: Sanhedrin Press, 1978), p. 5.
11 *Seder Nezikin, Tractate Sanhedrin*, chapter 4, 5th Mishnah.

3 Christian Ethics

1 David Ford, *Theology: A Very Short Introduction* (New York: Oxford University Press, 2000), p. 60.

4 Islamic Ethics

1 Kevin Reinhart, "On the 'Introduction to Islam,'" pp. 22–45 in Brannon M. Wheeler, ed., *Teaching Islam* (New York: Oxford University Press/AAR, 2002), at p. 25.
2 For more on the diversity of Islam, see Reinhold Loeffler, *Islam in Practice* (New York: State University of New York Press, 1988); Clifford Geertz, *Islam Observed: Religious Development in Morocco and Indonesia* (New Haven: Yale University Press, 1968); and especially Michael Gilsenan, *Recognizing Islam: Religion and Society in the Middle East* (New York: I. B. Taurus, 2000).
3 For the historical background and context out of which Muhammad and Islam sprang, see Mohammed A. Bamyeh, *The Social Origins of Islam: Mind, Economy, Discourse* (Minneapolis: University of Minnesota Press, 1999).
4 See Sachiko Murata and William C. Chittick, *The Vision of Islam* (St. Paul, MN: Paragon House, 1995).
5 Ala'Uddin Ali al-Muttaqi ibn Hisam-Uddin al-Hindi, *Kanzul 'Ummal*, vol. 7, # 18931.
6 Quoted in Vincent Descombes, *The Barometer of Modern Reason: On the Philosophies of Current Events* (New York: Oxford University Press, 1993), p. 3.
7 See Robert R. Bianchi, *Guests of God: Pilgrimage and Politics in the Islamic World* (New York: Oxford University Press, 2004).
8 Malcolm X, with Alex Haley, *The Autobiography of Malcolm X* (New York: Grove Press, 1965), p. 346.
9 *Sahih Muslim*, # 6017.

10 I have not been able to locate this *hadith*, but it is quoted in Siraj al-Shirazi's *Tuhfat al-Muhibbīn* (1454). See Murata and Chittick, *The Vision of Islam*.

5 Friendship

1 C. S. Lewis, *The Four Loves* (New York: Harcourt Brace Jovanovich, 1991 [1960]) p. 61.
2 *Ibid.*, p. 60.
3 Maimonides, *Mishnah Torah, Matanot l'Aniyim* 10:7.
4 Quoted in Malise Ruthven, *Islam in the World* (New York: Oxford University Press, 2000), p. 79, citing Muhammad Asad, *The Principles of State and Government in Islam* (Gibraltar: Islamic Book Trust, 1980), p. 32.

6 Sexuality

1 In Freud's *Group Psychology and the Analysis of the Ego*, revd. edn., trans. James Strachey (New York: W. W. Norton, 1975), pp. 29–30.
2 Eugene B. Borowitz, *Exploring Jewish Ethics: Papers on Covenant Responsibility* (Detroit: Wayne State University Press, 1990), p. 250.
3 See 1 Corinthians 6:9 and Romans 1:27 for examples.
4 Thomas Aquinas, *Summa Theologiae*, Ia–IIae, q.154 a.12.
5 Karl Barth, *Church Dogmatics*, III/4,§ 53–4, ed. G. W. Bromiley and T. F. Torrance (New York: T. & T. Clark, 2009).
6 Abdelwahab Bouhdiba, *Sexuality in Islam*, trans. Alan Sheridan (London: Routledge, 1974), p. 7.

7 Marriage and Family

1 Matthew Bramlett and William Mosher, "First marriage dissolution, divorce, and remariage: United States," *Advance Data From Vital and Health Statistics* No. 323 (Hyattsville, MD: National Center for Health Statistics, 2001).
2 *Genesis Rabbah* 68:4.
3 *Babylonian Talmud, Tractate Yevamoth* 65b.
4 Gilbert Meilaender, *The Limits of Love: Some Theological Explorations* (University Park: Pennsylvania State University Press, 1987), p. 125.
5 Quotations are from Eugene F. Rogers, "Sanctified Unions: An Argument for Gay Marriage," *The Christian Century* 121: 12 (June 15, 2004), pp. 26–9, here p. 26.
6 *Ibid.*, p. 26.
7 *Ibid.*, p. 27.
8 *Ibid.*, p. 28.
9 Recorded by Ahmad al-Bayhaqi in his *Sunan al-Bayhaqi*.
10 Lois Lamya' Ibsen al Faruqi, "Marriage in Islam," *Journal of Ecumenical Studies* 22: 1 (1985), p. 57.

8 Lying

1 It's worth noting (something that few do) that Plato's *Republic* itself, the book in which the idea of the noble lie is first articulated, is a sort of Noble lie – a sort of fiction.
2 The quotations are from Louis Jacobs, "When, According to Talmud, a Jew May Lie," pp. 39–40 in Philip Kerr, *The Penguin Book of Lies* (New York: Viking, 1990).
3 Norman Lamm and Israel Meir Ha-Kohen, "Shunning of Talebearing," pp. 56–67 in *The Good Society*, ed. by Normal Lamm (New York: Viking, 1974).
4 Augustine, *Contra mendacium* (Against lying), § 37.
5 Pp. 601–8 in Dietrich Bonhoeffer, *Conspiracy and Imprisonment: 1940–1945* (Minneapolis: Fortress Press, 2006). All page references are to this essay.
6 *Ibid.*, p. 602.
7 *Ibid.*, p. 604.
8 *Ibid.*, p. 602.
9 *Ibid.*, p. 607.
10 *Hadith* recorded by ibn Hanbal, in *Musnad Ahmad*, Bk. 6 # 459. From *Ihya ulm al-din* (al-Ghazali), Vol. 3, pp. 284–7: "One of Mohammed's daughters, Umm Kalthoum, testified that she had never heard the Apostle of Allah condone lying, except in these three situations: For reconciliation among people. In war. Amongst spouses, to keep peace in the family."
11 At p. 25 in "Keeping Secrets and Holding the Tongue," pp. 13–32 in William M. Hutchins, ed., *Nine Essays of al-Jahiz* (New York: Peter Lang, 1989).

9 Forgiveness

1 L. Gregory Jones, *Embodying Forgiveness: A Theological Analysis* (Grand Rapids, MI: Eerdmans, 1995), p. 289.
2 Simon Wiesenthal, *The Sunflower: On the Possibilities and Limits of Forgiveness* (New York: Schocken 1997), p. 113.
3 *Ibid.*, pp. 186–7.
4 *Ibid.*, p. 185.
5 See Mishna *Baba Kamma* 92a, *Yoma* 87a.
6 *Ibid.*, p. 156.
7 Anne C. Minas, "God and Forgiveness," pp. 32–45 in *Contemporary Philosophy of Religion*, ed. Steven M. Cahn and David Shatz (New York: Oxford University Press, 1982).

10 Love and Justice

1 Reinhold Niebuhr, *Love and Justice: Selections from the Shorter Writings of Reinhold Niebuhr*, ed. D. B. Robertson (Philadelphia: Westminster Press, 1958), p. 28.
2 *Ibid.*, p. 26.

3   *Ibid.*, p. 27.
4   *Ibid.*, p. 28.
5   *Ibid.*, p. 29.
6   Stanley Hauerwas, *The Peaceable Kingdom: A Primer in Christian Ethics* (Notre Dame: University of Notre Dame Press, 1983), p. 145.
7   *Ibid.*, p. 142.
8   *Ibid.*, p. 147.
9   *Ibid.*, p. 148.

11   Duty, Law, Conscience

1   Christopher Browning, "One Day in Józefów: Initiation to Mass Murder," pp. 169–83 in his *The Path to Genocide* (New York: Cambridge University Press, 1992), p. 174.
2   Thomas Jefferson, letter of December 11, 1783.
3   In Christian thought, and especially Roman Catholic moral theology, this is formulated as the difference between *material* sin (when one's conscience is in error, but one follows it) and *formal* sin (when one does not obey the command of one's conscience). According to the tradition, he latter is far more morally and spiritually destructive.
4   This and the following quotations are taken from Hannah Arendt, *Eichmann in Jerusalem: A Report on the Banality of Evil* (New York: Harcourt Brace Jovanovich, 1965), here at p. 148.
5   *Ibid.*, p. 146.
6   *Ibid.*, p. 126.
7   The Posen speech by Himmler is available at www.en.wikipedia.org/wiki/Posen_Speech.
8   Arendt, *Eichmann in Jerusalem*, p. 148.
9   *Ibid.*, p. 150.

12   Capital Punishment

1   Ernest van den Haag and John P. Conrad, *The Death Penalty: A Debate* (New York: Basic Books, 1983), p. 225.
2   United States Catholic Conference, *US Catholic Bishops Statement on Capital Punishment* (Washington, DC: United States Catholic Conference, 1980), p. 11.
3   *Ibid.*, pp. 4–5.
4   *Ibid.*, p. 4.
5   Joseph Bottum, "Christians and the Death Penalty," pp. 17–21 in *First Things* 155 (August/September 2005).
6   J. Budziszewski, "Capital Punishment: The Case for Justice," pp. 39–45 in *First Things* 145 (August/September 2004), at p. 41, emphasis added.
7   *Ibid.*, p. 42.

13   War (I): Towards War

1   Humayun Saqib Muazzam Khan, Captain, US Army, died in Baqubah, Iraq, on June 8, 2004, attempting to stop a suicide car bombing. He was a captain in the First Infantry Division, and was posthumously awarded a Bronze Star and a Purple Heart.
2   For more on this see Reuven Firestone, "Holy War in Modern Judaism? 'Mitzvah War' and the Problem of the 'Three Vows,' " *Journal of the American Academy of Religion* 74, 4 (December 2006): 954–82.
3   Paul Ramsey, *The Just War: Force and Political Responsibility* (Lanham, MD: Rowman and Littlefield, 2002 [1968]), p. 143.
4   Reinhold Niebuhr, "Why the Christian Church is not Pacifist," pp. 28–46 in *War in the Twentieth Century: Sources in Theological Ethics* (Louisville, KY: Westminster/ John Knox Press, 1992), p. 31.
5   *Ibid.*, p. 39.
6   *Ibid.*, p. 28.
7   *Ibid.*, p. 29.
8   *Ibid.*, p. 30.
9   *Ibid.*, p. 39.
10 Stanley Hauerwas, *Vision and Virtue* (Notre Dame, IN: University of Notre Dame Press, 1981 [1974]), p. 201.
11 Quoted in Hauerwas, *Vision and Virtue*, p. 202.
12 See George Weigel, *Tranquillitatis Ordinis: The Present Failure and Future Promise of American Catholic Thought on War and Peace* (New York: Oxford University Press, 1987) and Rowan Williams, *The Truce of God* (London: Collins, 1983).

14   War (II): In War

1   For more on this episode, and the Kosovo war in general, see Ivo H. Daalder and Michael E. O'Hanlon, *Winning Ugly: Nato's Wars to Save Kosovo* (Washington, DC: Brookings Institution Press, 2000); and Gen. Wesley Clark, *Waging Modern War: Bosnia, Kosovo, and the Future of Combat* (Washington, DC: Public Affairs, 2001).
2   Frederic Manning, *The Middle Parts of Fortune: Somme and Ancre* (London: Filiquarian Publishing, 2007 [1929]), p. 5.
3   Mary Kaldor, *New and Old Wars*, 2nd edn. (Cambridge: Polity Press, 2006), p. 9.
4   Paul Fussell, "My War: How I Got Irony in the Infantry," pp. 40–8 in *Harper's*, January 1982, at p. 48.
5   Paul Ramsey, *The Just War*, p. 146.
6   Augustine, letter 189.6; see also 93.8.

15   Religion and the Environment

1   Lynn White, "The Historical Roots of Our Ecologic Crisis," *Science*, 155, 3767 (March 10, 1967), pp. 1203–7.

2   *Ibid.*, p. 1207.
3   *Ibid.*, p. 1205.
4   *Ibid.*, p. 1206.
5   Wendell Berry, "God and Country," pp. 95–102 in *What Are People For?* (London: Rider Press, 1991), p. 98.
6   *Ibid.*, p. 100.
7   Aquinas, *Summa Theologiae* II–IIae, q.66 a.7. (Translation modified from the Dominican Fathers translation.) Emphasis mine.
8   Karl Barth, *Church Dogmatics*, III/4,§ 55–6, ed. G. W. Bromiley and T. F. Torrance (New York: T. & T. Clark, 2009), pp. 27–8.
9   *Ibid.*, p. 28.
10 *Ibid.*, p. 30.
11 *Ibid.*, p. 30.
12 Quoted in Al-Hafiz B. A. Masri, "Islam and Ecology," pp. 1–23 in *Islam and Ecology*, ed. Fazlun Kahlid and Joanne O'Brien (London: Cassel, 1992), at pp. 6–7. In general a large number of *ahadith* relating to environmental concerns are found in the "Book of Agriculture," Book 39 of *Sahih Bukhari*, Bukhari's collection of *ahadith*.
13 A *hadith* recorded on the authority of Anas ibn Malik by Imama Ahmad in *Musnad* and al-Bukhari in *al-Adab al-Mufrad* by Abu Dawud al-Tayalisi in his *Musnud*. Interestingly, a very similar statement is attributed to Rabbi Yohanan ben Zakkai: "If there was a seedling in your hand and you were informed, 'King Messiah has arrived,' first go plant the seedling, afterwards go forth to greet him." *Avot de Rabbai Natan*, B.31; found in Ephraim E. Urbach, *The Sages: Their Concepts and Beliefs* (Cambridge, MA: Harvard University Press, 1987), p. 667.

16   Pursuits of Happiness: Labor, Leisure, and Life

1   Information and claims are drawn from two books here: Robert Wuthnow, *Poor Richard's Principle: Recovering the American Dream through the Moral Dimensions of Work, Business, and Money* (Princeton: Princeton University Press, 1996); Juliet B. Schor, *The Overworked American: The Unexpected Decline of Leisure* (New York: Basic Books, 1991).
2   Mark Aguiar and Erik Hurst, "A Summary of Trends in American Time Allocation: 1965–2005," pp. 57–64 in *Social Indicators Research* 93 (2009). See also J. P. Robinson and G. Godbey, *Time for life: The Surprising Ways Americans Use Their Time* (University Park: Pennsylvania State University Press, 1999); and D. Costa, "The Unequal Work Day: A Long Term View," *American Economic Review* 88, 2 (1998): 330–4.
3   Wuthnow, *Poor Richard's Principle*, p. 11.
4   Max Weber, *The Protestant Ethic and the Spirit of Capitalism*, trans. Talcott Parsons (New York: Charles Scribner's Sons, 1958 [1905]), pp. 181–2.
5   Josef Pieper, *Leisure, the Basis of Culture* (South Bend, IN: Saint Augustine's Press, 1998 [1948]), pp. 36–7.
6   *Ibid.*, p. 21.

7 Abraham Joshua Heschel, *The Sabbath: Its Meaning for Modern Man* (New York: Farrar Strauss Giroux, 2005 [1951]).
8 *Ibid.*, pp. 3, 8.
9 *Ibid.*, p. 6.
10 *Ibid.*, p. 24.
11 *Ibid.*, p. 10.
12 *Ibid.*, p. 6. Emphasis added.
13 *Ibid.*, p. 23.

17 Good and Evil

1 It is a point of some subtlety that Iblis is not quite an angel, but a djinn, another, lesser kind of spiritual creature; angels in Islam are understood not to have free will, while djinns do. For a nice discussion of the complications surrounding Iblis in Islamic thought, with special attention to Sufism, see Peter J. Awn, *Satan's Tragedy and Redemption: Iblis in Sufi Psychology* (Leiden: E. J. Brill, 1983).
2 Susan Wolf, "Moral Saints," *Journal of Philosophy* 79, 8 (August 1982): 419–39 at p. 435.
3 Robert Adams, "Saints," *Journal of Philosophy* 81, 7 (July 1984): 392–401 at p. 400.
4 *Ibid.*, p. 392.

Conclusion: What's So Funny 'bout Peace, Love, and Understanding?

1 Plotinus, *Enneads*, VI.9 [9].4 11–16.

Qur'an translations interspersed throughout the text are the author's own.

Index

274 *Index*